THE HISTORICAL OR
OF TERRORISM IN AMERICA

When we think of American terrorism, it is modern, individual terrorists such as Timothy McVeigh that typically spring to mind. But terrorism has existed in America since the colonial period, when small groups participated in organized and unlawful violence in the hope of creating a state of fear for their own political purposes.

Using case studies of groups such as the Green Mountain Boys, the Mollie Maguires, and the North Carolina Regulators, as well as the more widely known Sons of Liberty and the Ku Klux Klan, Robert Kumamoto introduces readers to the long history of terrorist activity in America. Sure to incite discussion and curiosity in anyone studying terrorism or early America, *The Historical Origins of Terrorism in America* brings together some of the most radical groups of the American past to show that a technique that we associate with modern atrocity actually has roots much farther back in the country's national psyche.

Robert Kumamoto is Professor Emeritus of History at San Jose State University.

THE HISTORICAL ORIGINS OF TERRORISM IN AMERICA

1644–1880

Robert Kumamoto

Routledge
Taylor & Francis Group

NEW YORK AND LONDON

First published 2014
by Routledge
711 Third Avenue, New York, NY 10017

and by Routledge
2 Park Square, Milton Park, Abingdon, Oxon OX14 4RN

Routledge is an imprint of the Taylor & Francis Group, an informa business

Library of Congress Cataloging-in-Publication Data
Kumamoto, Robert D., 1948–
The historical origins of terrorism in America : 1644–1880 / Robert
    Kumamoto.
    pages cm
    Includes index.
    1. Terrorism—United States—History.   2. Radicalism—United
States—History.   3. Extremists—United States—History.   I. Title.
    HV6432.K85   2013
    363.3250973′0903—dc23
    2013027360

ISBN: 978-0-415-53754-4 (hbk)
ISBN: 978-0-415-53755-1 (pbk)
ISBN: 978-1-3158499-6-6 (ebk)

Typeset in Bembo
by Apex CoVantage, LLC

Printed and bound in the United States of America by
Edwards Brothers Malloy, Inc.

Dedicated to my loving wife, Vernice, who continues to inspire me, and to the memory of Mom and Dad, the late Kazuko and Mitsuru Kumamoto. We all miss you still.

CONTENTS

ACKNOWLEDGMENTS

As with anyone who undertakes a project of this type, my debts are many. I am especially indebted to Kimberly Guinta and the folks at Routledge for their support and belief in this book. I am also grateful to the History Department and the College of Social Sciences at San Jose State University for providing the time and means to research and write. As most historians know, research can be challenging and tedious work, but I am constantly impressed with the cooperation and professionalism that I've encountered in various archives, libraries, museums, and private collections across the country. In particular, I'd like to express my appreciation to the staffs at the Vermont State Archives, the University of Vermont's Bailey/Howe Library and the Historical Society of Schuylkill County for providing valuable assistance beyond the normal call of duty. I must also acknowledge the many authors whose secondary works are referenced or cited herein. Their significant contributions established the foundation on which this work is built and I can only hope that I've given them appropriate credit. Lastly, I would like to extend special thanks to my wife, Vernice Shen, and to Colleen Hamilton, who both made significant contributions to the preparation of this manuscript.

INTRODUCTION

At no time in our nation's history have Americans heard as much discussion and speculation about the subject of terrorism as they did in the immediate aftermath of the terrorist attacks against the United States on September 11, 2001. Granted, Americans had confronted terrorism on a number of occasions throughout the 20th century, but the attacks on New York City and Washington, DC, created unprecedented death and destruction. The sheer magnitude of the 9/11 attacks—the audacity of the simultaneous skyjackings, the staggering death toll, the demolition of the World Trade Center, and the assault on the Pentagon—changed, perhaps forever, the lives of Americans, once thought to be insulated from the provocations of a violent and disordered outside world. A number of significant foreign policy changes would follow in their wake, including President George W. Bush's controversial PATRIOT Act and the Bush Doctrine, all of which contributed to the administration's self-proclaimed "War on Terror." In numerous speeches delivered in the aftermath of 9/11, President Bush would justify this military response, proclaiming that "freedom itself is under attack," and warning that although "the terrorists can kill the innocent, they cannot stop the advance of freedom." The president would further argue that terrorists represented an outside threat, suggesting that "there is only one course of action against them: to defeat them abroad before they attack us at home." President Bush, of course, was readying Americans for a long and protracted war that "will not end until every terrorist group of global reach has been found, stopped, and defeated."[1] Although these types of apocalyptic comments were meant to generate public support for the administration, create a consensus to rationalize its war on terror, and address the immediate threats to America's security, they also contributed mightily to public misperceptions about the nature and history of terrorism.

In essence, most Americans were left with the impression that terrorism is the antithesis of freedom, that terrorism is imported into this country from elsewhere, and that an aggressive military campaign is capable of eradicating terrorism. It is the intent of the present study to establish, through an analysis of American resistance groups of the 17th, 18th, and 19th centuries, that terrorism has a long and contentious legacy in America and, contrary to the president's post-9/11 comments, has at times been closely associated with popular democratic uprisings that were thought to advance the cause of freedom. This neglected legacy of domestic terrorism in America also undermines the notions that terror is necessarily a strategy imported from elsewhere and that terrorism can be eradicated through a strict military response.

While terrorist groups such as the Ku Klux Klan are widely recognized as especially unfortunate chapters in our sometimes-violent past, and Americans are familiar with names such as the Unabomber or Timothy McVeigh, most know very little about the early origins of domestic terrorism, since no comprehensive historical study yet exists—a void hopefully filled by this study. Virtually all historical and political studies of terrorism in America begin in the mid-19th century and trace the beginnings of terrorism to the Civil War and Reconstruction periods, without adequately explaining how terrorism evolved as a strategy of collective resistance. It is as if terrorism suddenly emerges spontaneously, with no historical precedents. In their purportedly comprehensive *Chronologies of Modern Terrorism,* authors Barry Rubin and Judith Colp Rubin suggest that radical abolitionist John Brown's attack on Harpers Ferry in 1859 was America's first terrorist act.[2] Joseph T. McCann, in *Terrorism on American Soil,* begins his narrative with the assassination of Abraham Lincoln in 1865.[3] Gus Martin, in his latest edition of *Understanding Terrorism,* suggests in a timeline entitled "Two Thousand Years of Terror" that the Ku Klux Klan was America's first terrorist organization.[4] Matthew Carr, in a recent study on the history of terrorism, argues that terrorism in America began a few years thereafter, beginning with the Haymarket anarchists of the 1880s.[5] Similarly, Jeffory A. Clymer begins his cultural study of American terrorism with the 1886 Chicago Haymarket bombing.[6] This perspective is perhaps understandable, given the dramatic increase in domestic violence beginning in the late 19th century. This viewpoint, however, completely overlooks premodern forms of terrorism. By contrast, the present study will contend that domestic terrorism began much earlier than generally acknowledged, predating the American Revolution. Although Brenda J. Lutz and James M. Lutz make this point in their brief study *Terrorism in America,* they, too, focus primarily on the post-1860 years and devote but 40 pages to pre-Civil War terrorism.[7] Consequently, the primary objective here is to provide a broad historical overview of collective violence in America before the 20th century, beginning with the colonial period, to ascertain how terrorism evolved as a violent form of political resistance. In order to do so, however, several logistical hurdles must be cleared. First, a definition of terms and some historical background are imperative.

Historians have long noted that the term *terrorism,* which was first popularized during the French Revolution, had, at first, a positive connotation. Terrorism was adopted by the French as a means of establishing order during a transitional period of upheaval and turmoil during the uprisings of 1789; thus, the so-called "reign of terror" was widely viewed as an instrument of governance used by the Jacobins in order to consolidate their power and, accordingly, terrorism became closely associated with ideals of virtue and democracy.[8] The revolutionary leader Robespierre believed that virtue had to be aligned with terrorism if democracy was to survive. As this study will suggest, many early American terrorist groups held similar views. However, the meaning of terrorism would evolve over the years and, by the beginning of the 20th century, terrorism became widely associated with destructive violence. Still, there exists no consensus as to how terrorism should be defined. The federal government once defined terrorism as "the threat or use of violence for political purposes by individuals or groups, whether acting for, or in opposition to, established governmental authority, when such actions are intended to shock, stun, or intimidate a target group wider than the immediate victims."[9] Cindy C. Combs, in her popular textbook on terrorism, recently defined terrorism as "a synthesis of war and theatre, a dramatization of the most proscribed kind of violence—that which is perpetrated on innocent victims—played before an audience in the hope of creating a mood of fear, for political purposes."[10] Whether or not one accepts these particular definitions, they do contain some instructive elements. First, they do not imply that deadly force need be employed, but rather that the mere *threat* of violence is sufficient to constitute a state of terror. As this study will affirm, America's first terrorists tried as much as possible, and usually with success, to avoid fatalities. This would change during the mid-19th century, but is essential in understanding the origins of domestic terrorism. Second, the definitions distinguish between the *immediate* victims of a terrorist attack and its *intended* target, since the act itself is aimed at a wider audience—a specific large-scale community. As the ancient Chinese proverb puts it, "kill one, frighten ten thousand."

In order to help determine what constitutes an act of terror, Alex P. Schmid closely examined 109 definitions of terrorism offered by various social scientists, and identified 20 of the most common characteristics suggested by these definitions. Of the 20 characteristics, the first 11 are most instructive for this study:

1. use of violence or force (common to 83% of the 109 definitions)
2. political nature (65%)
3. emphasis on fear, terror (51%)
4. implied threat (47%)
5. psychological effects and anticipated reactions (41%)
6. victim–target differentiation (37%)
7. purposeful, planned, systematic, organized action (32%)
8. method of combat, strategy, tactic (30%)

9. extranormality, breach of accepted rules, lack of humanitarian restraints (30%)
10. coercion, extortion, inducement to compliance (28%)
11. publicity aspect (21%)[11]

Schmid's study reveals quite starkly the problems associated with defining terrorism. Of the 20 most commonly cited characteristics, only three were identified in at least 51% of the 109 definitions, suggesting that the creation of a universal definition might be unrealistic. A United Nations subcommittee was once assigned the task of drafting a definition of *international terrorism,* but disbanded after two days of haggling, because it could not establish a consensus. Terminological controversy aside, because we are able to specify common characteristics of terrorism, it is possible to craft an operational definition for historical investigation using Schmid as a foundation and borrowing heavily from Combs: "A synthesis of conflict and theatre, a dramatization of the most proscribed kind of organized violence or threatened use of force, played before an audience in the hope of creating a state of fear for political purposes." An act of terror, as opposed to spontaneous rioting, must be the product of political discourse and systematic planning with specific, purposeful outcomes. As with the federal government's definition, our definition here does not require that an act of terror involve fatalities. The proper emphasis is on establishing a climate of fear through an implied threat of violence or force, which, in turn, effectuates a psychological reaction amongst the members of a wider, targeted community: thus, the significant differentiation between immediate victims of an act of terror and the broader intended audience. As both Combs and Brian Jenkins, decades earlier, have noted, terrorism is partly "theatre," as terrorists "perform" acts of violence in order to generate publicity and reach that larger audience.[12] Consequently, terrorism constitutes a form of violent propaganda, and the most effective terrorists are often those who are able to manipulate publicity and public opinion in their favor.

Aligned with Combs, our definition, through the word *proscribed,* also establishes a degree of extranormality or extralegality in terrorism; it is an unconscionable act outside acceptable social boundaries or in breach of accepted rules. As Jenkins has noted, terrorism constitutes violence against the "system," or organized society— from the terrorist's perspective, the rules or laws of the "system" are invalid.[13] Many pre-20th-century American terrorist groups established measures of extralegality, creating their own laws apart from governmental authority and administering justice as they saw fit, often through the establishment of mock courts. That such behavior is further *organized* suggests systematic planning and, for our purposes, a group identity, the product of an inclusive organization, usually evident through either a formal or informal hierarchy; thus, the emphasis here on group, rather than individual, behavior. Excluded here is terrorism conducted as a by-product of war. In general, terrorism is considered a "low level" violent act, as opposed to warfare, the ultimate "high level" state of hostility. One can argue, as many do, that war by nature is terroristic. Along these lines, the question, Was George Washington a terrorist? is often posed. Yet, social scientists tend to distinguish between warfare and terrorism, treating the latter as a distinctly different form of hostile confrontation. Consequently, the stories here of the Green Mountain Boys and the Sons of Liberty end with the outbreak of the Revolutionary War and their subsequent amalgamation into the Continental Army.

It is equally important to establish here that an act of terror need not be perpetrated by clandestine or covert agents. While many pre-20th-century American terrorists disguised themselves as Indians, acts of terror were also widely committed by persons unconcerned with anonymity, and, according to Schmid's study, only 9% of 109 definitions included a reference to the clandestine or covert nature of terrorism. Similarly, the immediate prey of terrorist acts need not be randomly victimized; Schmid discovered that only 21% of the definitions specified an element of arbitrariness or indiscrimination. Victims of the Sons of Liberty and the Reconstruction-era Ku Klux Klan, for example, were targeted by terrorists for specific reasons, and, in the modern era, the members of the 1972 Israeli Olympic team were deliberate targets. As this study will further maintain, prior to the late 19th century, most immediate victims of terrorist acts in America were, in fact, specifically selected.

Starting with the definition offered here and other stated criteria, the present study began with some basic questions: Given America's early legacy of collective violence, how did terrorism first evolve as a political strategy? Which resistance groups were most responsible for this early reliance on terrorist tactics, and how, exactly, did they effectuate their terror? Determining answers first necessitated a broad overview of group insurgency in early America, including discussions of civil insurrections and riots in order to determine how they differed from campaigns based primarily on terror, and how they contributed to the evolution of terrorism. It should also be noted that although no comprehensive historical studies about the early origins of terrorism in America yet exist, a number of studies about *rioting* have contributed significantly to our understanding of group violence, thereby shedding important light on the nature of home-grown terrorism. Inspired by the works of George Rudé, who studied extensively crowd behavior in Europe, historians of American history have similarly examined "popular uprisings," noting some differences from, but many striking similarities to, European riots.[14] Crowds in Europe, as in America, generally represented not lower-class rabble, but a cross section of classes representative of their communities at large. Crowds in both Europe and America also tended to be single-minded and discriminating in their behavior. Most notably, Pauline Maier argued that early crowd behavior in America was but one part of a broader Anglo-American political tradition that consequently bestowed a measure of "presumptive acceptability" on crowd or "mob" action.[15] Indeed, early American history is littered with examples of riotous behavior, and, as this study will establish, even group violence that rose to the standard of terrorism had its many supporters. However, as Rudé noted, riots tended to be spontaneous, void of leadership, and not necessarily violent, all of which, for our purposes, helps distinguish *riotous* behavior from *terroristic* behavior. Still, the reasons why riots were so common helps us understand how terrorism similarly managed to evolve in America. As Maier and others have suggested, there were no professional police forces in early America, leaving magistrates and other authorities helpless to combat group violence. Moreover, posses or volunteer militias, who were generally relied on to uphold the law, were likewise ineffective, because these units were often manned by the same persons who were guilty of perpetuating the riotous or terroristic behavior in question.[16]

Once terrorist groups were distinguished from rioters and insurrectionists, it became necessary to study the circumstances that led them to adopt terrorism as a political tactic. What do we know about the historical roots of their violent strategies? What were their objectives? What sort of demographic information exists about them? What have historians said about these groups? What measures were used to combat their terroristic ways? Ultimately, did these groups succeed or fail in their own particular pursuit of "justice"? The overriding presumption, of course, is that although the term *terrorism* was not popularized until the French Revolution, the tactic to which the appellation would be later attached, did, in fact, exist for many centuries beforehand. Many social scientists specializing in terrorism, including Walter Laqueur, Gus Martin, and Cindy C. Combs, trace the roots of terrorism back to the ancient Greeks and Romans, who regularly preached the virtues of tyrannicide, as evidenced by the assassination of Julius Caesar in 44 B.C. Moreover, the Jewish zealots (A.D. 6), the infamous *sicarii* (A.D. 66), the assassins of Persia (11th/12th century), and India's thugs (13th–19th century) are often identified by various social scientists as early terrorist organizations.[17] Accordingly, America's first terrorists were seldom, if at all, referred to by that term. Firsthand accounts usually described them as banditti, cutthroats, rioters, or as simply "the mob."

Using these historical parameters and the aforementioned questions, a close analysis of major American resistance groups beginning with the colonial period and ending with the late 19th century suggests that seven of these groups relied extensively and primarily on terrorist methods. Five are relatively unknown to most Americans: the North Carolina Regulators, the Green Mountain Boys, the White Indians of Maine, the Molly Maguires, and New York's Anti-Renters, sometimes known as the Calico Indians. Two are relatively better known: the Sons of Liberty and the Ku Klux Klan. Each will be dealt with individually and extensively in subsequent chapters. It should be noted that other radical dissidents profiled here, in particular the Whiskey Rebels and New Jersey land rioters, also incorporated some of the major elements of terrorism, but because they did so sporadically and secondarily, the aforementioned seven groups eclipse their stories. Some broad generalities about these seven are evident. Each campaign was waged for its own particular reasons, with virtually no overlap in membership. The Regulators were concerned about local political corruption, the Sons of Liberty were motivated by excessive Parliamentary authority, the Molly Maguires were driven by corporate abuse, and the Ku Klux Klan was incited by Radical Reconstruction. Only the Green Mountain Boys, the White Indians, and the

Calico Indians were propelled by a similar grievance: disputed property claims. Yet, some of the tactics employed by these groups were similar: "rescue riots" or jailbreaks were common, as was the use of intimidating "coffin notices" and the destruction, or "pulling down," of houses. Other than the Molly Maguires and the Klan, the other five groups, who operated during the revolutionary and early national eras, all justified their terroristic ways by associating their tactics with popular democracy, striking blows of freedom against the forces of repression.

The historical evidence also suggests that the very first American terrorists were part of long-established Anglo American legacy of popular protest that fostered a penchant for civil insurrections and riots. Terrorism did not evolve from this tradition until the mid-1760s, when the colonies were increasingly exposed to revolutionary rhetoric and behavior based, in large measure, on notions of republicanism and other elements of Real Whig ideology engendered by the European *philosophes* and the Age of Enlightenment. It is no mere coincidence that four of America's original terrorist groups had their genesis during the years immediately preceding the American Revolution. But, while these earlier groups focused primarily on local issues associated with popular democracy and freedom, the Molly Maguires and Ku Klux Klan, who appeared much later, tended to focus on broader, counterrevolutionary strategies meant to combat industrial/corporate abuse and the social transformation wrought by Radical Reconstruction.

Interestingly, an analysis of America's first terrorist associations also reveals the relative success of their political endeavors. Only the North Carolina Regulators and the Molly Maguires failed to attain any semblance of victory in pursuit of their objectives, although, admittedly, the specific goals of the Mollies were difficult to ascertain. Conversely, in Vermont, the Green Mountain Boys were able to establish their authority during the pre-Revolution years and, ultimately, their land claims, despite the active opposition of New York. The Sons of Liberty helped mobilize the patriot cause and undermined British authority on the eve of the Revolution by spurring the obstruction of Parliamentary legislation. Both the White Indians of Maine and the Calico Indians of New York were able to exact some change and reform, although the transformation in New York was far more drastic and protracted. And regrettably, the Ku Klux Klan, despite the passage of significant Congressional civil rights legislation, was able to preserve a racial caste system throughout much of the former Confederacy, in open defiance of federal and state authorities. With these varying instances of success, it is difficult to escape the notion that terrorism in pre-20th-century America could and did pay significant political dividends.

From another perspective, early efforts by authorities to combat terrorism rarely relied exclusively on strict military responses. North Carolina Governor William Tryon's triumph over the Regulators at the Battle of Alamance in 1771 was the only instance where military forces proved effective in ending a campaign of terrorism. Military intervention was used to put down an early anti-rent uprising in New York, but that was but a temporary solution, as the insurgency would reemerge decades later. Even the southern occupation by federal troops during Radical Reconstruction did very little to halt the vicious provocations conducted by the Ku Klux Klan. In the end, only aggressive legal prosecution or strict punishment afforded some measure of success in defeating campaigns based on terrorist methods. Both the White Indians and Molly Maguires, for example, met their ultimate demise before judges and juries. The Calico Indians of New York largely suspended their use of terror after rigorous prosecution, but also because the cumulative impact of both public sympathy and prolonged legislative land reform had rendered their violence counter-productive. Federal officials also sought to undermine the Klan through the court system, particularly in South Carolina, but the subsequent trials were limited, half-hearted, and mostly futile. The Green Mountain Boys and Sons of Liberty mostly managed to avoid any legal ramifications for their violent provocations. Just as insurgents in America were experimenting with the tactics of terror, authorities were also struggling to find effective responses to combat this new form of lawlessness.

The ending date of this study is also noteworthy and requires elaboration. Beginning roughly in the 1880s, terrorism would undergo a significant transformation as a direct result of the discovery and production of dynamite. This would have a profound impact on terrorism. Whereas earlier acts of terror required more personal, face-to-face types of confrontation between perpetrator and immediate victim, dynamite allowed terrorists greater opportunities for anonymity and detachment. Dynamite can also be employed to kill or maim indiscriminately, introducing an element of randomness to its depredations. These new developments would subsequently lead to a new modern phase or era in the evolution of domestic terrorism, incorporating the use of new technology and weapons of mass destruction. These new parameters, written about extensively elsewhere, exist beyond the scope of this study's limited intent to examine the unexplored, early origins of domestic terrorism.

Given the meaningfulness and contentiousness surrounding terrorism in today's world, any study that professes to trace its historical origins in America understandably leaves itself open to scrutiny. This is understandable, because other resistance groups certainly deserve some attention under the parameters established here, and questions may remain concerning those profiled. The primary intention here is to focus extensively on those groups who employed systematic and sustained terrorism as their primary weapon. Given the complete absence of other studies tracing its pre-20th-century origins, any subsequent historical and political discourse on American terrorism should begin with the seven groups that follow on these pages.

Notes

1. George W. Bush to Joint Session of Congress, September 20, 2001, and George W. Bush in address in Fort Bragg, North Carolina, June 28, 2005.
2. Barry Rubin and Judith Colp Rubin, *Chronologies of Modern Terrorism* (Armonk, NY: M.E. Sharpe, 2008), 11.

3. Joseph T. McCann, *Terrorism on American Soil* (Boulder, CO: Sentient Publications, 2006).

4. Gus Martin, *Understanding Terrorism,* 3rd ed. (Los Angeles: Sage, 2010).

5. Matthew Carr, *The Infernal Machine—A History of Terrorism* (New York: The New Press, 2006).

6. Jeffory A. Clymer, *America's Culture of Terrorism* (Chapel Hill: University of North Carolina Press, 2003).

7. Brenda J. Lutz and James M. Lutz, *Terrorism in America* (New York: Palgrave Macmillan, 2007).

8. Bruce Hoffman, *Inside Terrorism* (London: Indigo, 1998), 15.

9. *Patterns of International Terrorism,* a State Department research paper published by the Department of State, Washington, DC, July 1982. The report contained definitions for both "terrorism" and "international terrorism."

10. Cindy C. Combs, *Terrorism in the Twenty-First Century,* 4th ed. (Upper Saddle River, NJ: Pearson Prentice Hall, 2006), 11.

11. Alex P. Schmid, Albert J. Jongman, et al., *Political Terrorism: A New Guide to Actors, Authors, Concepts, Data Bases, Theories, and Literature* (New Brunswick, NJ: Transaction Books, 1988), 5–6.

12. Statements by Brian Jenkins of the Rand Corporation during hearings on international terrorism, House Committee on the Near East and South Asia of the Committee on Foreign Affairs, 93rd Congress, 2nd sess., June 24, 1974, 137.

13. Ibid.

14. George Rudé, *The Crowd in History: A Study of Popular Disturbances in France and England, 1730–1848* (New York: John Wiley & Sons, 1964); Pauline Maier, *From Resistance to Revolution* (New York: Vintage Books, 1974); Dirk Hoerder, *Crowd Action in Revolutionary Massachusetts, 1765–1780* (New York: Academic Press, 1977); Michael Feldberg, *The Turbulent Era—Riot and Disorder in Jacksonian America* (New York: Oxford University Press, 1980)

15. Maier, *From Resistance to Revolution,* 21.

16. Ibid, 16.

17. Walter Laqueur, *The Age of Terrorism* (Boston: Little, Brown and Company, 1987), 12–13; Combs, 22; James M. Lutz and Brenda J. Lutz, *Global Terrorism* (London: Routledge, 2004), 73.

1

THE ORIGINS OF POLITICAL VIOLENCE

I. Typologies of Political Violence in the Colonies

In February 1642, only a few years after its founding, Maryland, established by the second Lord Baltimore in large measure as a refuge for fellow Catholics, was teetering on the brink of open hostilities. The enmity created by the English Civil War between King Charles I and Parliament had made its way across the Atlantic to the sparsely populated colony, where Protestant Parliamentarians were about to make life miserable for the Catholic minority dependent upon the good graces of their protector and proprietor, Lord Baltimore, whose own family fortunes were tied to that of the monarchy. Describing conditions in Maryland, a County Court reported that "the tymes now doe seeme perilous."[1] Unfortunately, things would get worse for Maryland, for the colony would soon be in open rebellion, during an infamous period of lawless violence known as "the Plundering Time."

As dire as the situation in Maryland would become, in truth, the term "perilous tymes" could be used to describe virtually any period of the American colonial experience along the East Coast of North America. Almost from the moment British settlers arrived in Virginia in 1607, colonists in America would engage in violent encounters, first against native tribes, then eventually against competing European colonizers and runaway slaves, and sometimes even among themselves, for reasons both large and small. Maryland's Plundering Time was the first of many civil insurrections in the American colonies and offers a glimpse into the character of future incidents of civil disobedience and collective resistance, given its connection between political instability in England and emerging conflict in America. It also serves as a starting point from which to delineate the development of collective political violence in America, a tradition that would eventually culminate in the deployment of terrorist tactics by resistance groups during the mid-18th century.

Group violence during the colonial period can be organized into several types. First and most destructive was warfare, which can be further divided into two categories. The first consisted of wars between colonists and Indians, beginning with the first of three Powhatan Wars and including such violent conflicts as the Pequot War and King Phillip's War. Given the historical circumstances then enveloping the New World, perhaps these violent conflicts were inevitable. Second were the various wars between British, French, Dutch, and Spanish colonists for primacy in North America, usually extensions of wars fought primarily in Europe. These wars certainly contributed to the long-standing environment of conflict and violence, but remain outside of the focus of this study. There are, however, a couple of salient points that need to be made concerning the colonial military experience as it pertains to the evolution of terrorism in America. In his study of European and Native American warfare, Armstrong Starkey explained that the inability of Americans to adapt to Indian-style, or irregular, fighting led to the employment of regular or *grande guerre* tactics, a point questioned by John Grenier, who recently argued instead that Americans eventually did adapt *petite guerre* tactics and techniques.[2] An attendant philosophical issue that emerges from these opposing perspectives rests with the time-honored military ethics of the "Just War" doctrine. The notion of a "Just War" can be traced as far back as Cicero, but is most popularly associated with St. Augustine and medieval Christian theory. Just War theorists maintain that specific circumstances exist that legitimize war and codify how wars should be fought—with restraint and directed only against military objectives, while avoiding noncombatants and civilian property. But Americans, according to Grenier, "created a military tradition that accepted, legitimized, and encouraged attacks upon and the destruction of noncombatants, villages, and agricultural resources," activities that certainly stood in violation of some of the most sacred tenets of how a Just War should be properly waged.[3] Beyond this ethical consideration, Grenier's contention is important for our immediate purposes, for if Americans, fighting in large-scale military campaigns, did indeed embrace irregular war or Indian-style tactics, it is not unreasonable to assume that some soldiers might have brought this military mentality with them into their local posses and volunteer militias. Many of the terrorist groups under consideration here surreptitiously drew their numbers from these posses and volunteer militias that were primarily responsible for the defense of colonial settlements. We can never know to what extent wartime experiences with irregular or Indian-style tactics influenced a collective willingness to employ similar methods as part of an orchestrated campaign of terror, but the possibilities are worth consideration. At the very least, it is important to acknowledge that regardless of whether Americans adopted *grande* or *petite guerre* tactics, the eventual emergence of terrorism, a form of violence directed against the "system" and conducted outside the "rules" of civilized society, would alone subvert the ethical code of a Just War.

Slave rebellions or cases of racially motivated hostility, another type of colonial violence, could certainly prove to be bloody affairs, but are also excluded from the present discussion. In other countries, some slave rebellions did devolve into sustained campaigns dependent on terroristic methods to complement a wider guerrilla war, but in America, as with the Stono Rebellion of 1739, they occasionally erupted into short-lived but extreme forms of race-based violence, including mass murder by both blacks and whites. Many instances of mass murder were also perpetuated against Indians, including the infamous case of the Paxton Boys of Pennsylvania, who killed dozens of innocent Conestoga Indians during the winter of 1763–64. Such cases were founded on violence, but their objectives and methods differed from those employed by terrorists. The same can be said of vigilante movements, a third type. As Richard Maxwell Brown noted in his study of American vigilantism, only one movement of any significance operated during the colonial era, the South Carolina Regulators, who conducted a brutally violent yet successful campaign to combat lawlessness between 1767 and 1769.[4] In this episode, the widespread destruction of the Cherokee War (1760–61) had left the South Carolina frontier bereft of established law and order. Gangs of bandits freely roved the countryside until frustrated community leaders, with the tacit approval of the assembly and governor, finally organized vigilante forces that not only broke up the outlaw gangs but organized courts to prosecute and punish offenders. This type of usurpation of authority in cooperation with established government differs from the terrorist tactics under present consideration. Consequently, vigilante movements, as with race-based violence and warfare, remain separate subjects for other studies.

II. Civil Insurrections

The two remaining types of group violence—riots and civil insurrections—are of more immediate concern to a discussion of early terrorism in America. According to the terms established here, neither qualifies as terrorist activity, but extreme examples of both did constitute serious acts of violent resistance and together serve as an important foundation for the eventual emergence of terrorism. A basic understanding of both types begins with a recognition that when British colonists first arrived in North America, they brought with them not only aspirations for a better future and an English sense of how government should be structured, but also a healthy respect for the right of popular protest. For some time now, historians have acknowledged that early American radicalism had deep roots in Anglo American culture, which emerged from politically turbulent times in England.[5] Seventeenth-century British colonists were keenly aware of revolutionaries such as John Locke, John Milton, and Algernon Sidney, who preached that civil disobedience was acceptable, unavoidable, and healthy. Because Britain's Glorious Revolution of 1688–89 legitimized the right of the masses to replace tyrannical rulers through resistance or revolution, open attitudes toward civil uprisings merely constituted part of a broader Anglo American political tradition.[6] This tradition would persevere through England's Real Whigs or Commonwealthmen of the

18th century, who would then greatly shape the political thought of common folk in America, as well as revolutionaries such as Thomas Jefferson, who famously suggested that "a little rebellion now and then is a good thing," because "the tree of liberty must be refreshed from time to time with the blood of patriots and tyrants."[7] In his study of rioting in America, Paul A. Gilje similarly suggested that Americans early on accepted mob activity as "a quasi-legitimate part of the standing social and political order."[8] This position was founded on the commonwealth belief in the existence of two kinds of laws: laws of the land as enacted by government versus fundamental laws based on nature and reason. This dichotomy would inevitably lead to political differences or worse, government tyranny and the suppression of natural laws. But American society's saving grace was its notion of corporatism, the view of society as a single organic entity. Because members of society share a singular, identifiable interest, it was deemed perfectly acceptable for citizens to rise in unison to defend that interest through extralegal means.[9]

This penchant for popular protest in America did not, however, grant citizens license to engage in unlimited acts of violence. On the contrary, there was always an internal check on mob activity. American mobs shared characteristics with those in England, in particular, the cooperative relationship between plebians and patricians. Mob participants did not come exclusively from the lower classes. While the plebians may have dominated the action in the streets with an inclination toward violence, patricians usually operated covertly, providing leadership and resources as a conservative counterforce to these violent instincts. Consequently, while riots may have constituted legitimate means of political protest, the Real Whigs demanded that such displays of public resistance be conducted with order, restraint, and limited violence. Perhaps this explains why America's first terrorist groups, who were partly inspired by Whig ideology but had no compunctions about committing acts of injurious and destructive violence against persons and property, generally refrained from the taking of lives. As Pauline Maier suggested, this last paradox, the need to "reconcile the impulse toward resistance with the injunction to restraint," became "one of the central intellectual and practical problems of the American revolutionary movement."[10] Because crowd actions were legitimate, restrained and often represented the interests of the ruling classes, Maier also noted that civil uprisings in America were more likely to be *extra-institutional* in nature, as opposed to serving strictly *anti-authoritarian* forces. While limited violence in response to royal edicts was acceptable, direct threats to the king's authority were strictly prohibited. At its most radical, Anglo American political culture was not a revolutionary or proto-revolutionary culture, although levels of mob violence were seemingly higher in America than they were in England.[11] Only in rare and extreme cases could revolution ever be justified, and only after the exhaustion of all possible avenues of accommodation.

Other elements of violent radicalism in the colonies owe their roots to characteristics of political culture in Europe. One was the ceremonial and theatrical atmosphere surrounding public punishment, which included folk rituals such as *skimmington* and *charivari*. *Skimmington*, or "riding the stang," involved parading an offender on a wooden horse through avenues lined with jeering crowds, a form of punishment common in British military circles. Such processions, meant to ostracize lawbreakers and enforce social morality through public shame and humiliation, were often accompanied by *charivari,* or "rough music." The latter ritual, said to be of French origin, was a dissonant mock serenade of noisemaking, usually produced by tin horns and the banging of pots, pans, and other make-shift instruments.[12] *Charivari* would also eventually refer to other types of ritualistic public punishment, including tarring and feathering, a popular form of crowd action used by the Sons of Liberty as part of their campaign of terror just prior to the American Revolution. As noted earlier, terrorism is part theatre, a morality play before a rapt audience. This characteristic is consistent with the early radicalization of crowd activity. Perhaps no ritual in either England or America better exemplified this theatrical element of crowd action than the yearly celebration on November 5 known as "Pope's Day" to commemorate the failure of England's Guy Fawkes and his doomed "gunpowder plot" to destroy the king and House of Lords in 1605. Discovery of the conspiracy, which was meant to coronate a Catholic monarch following the murder of King James I, prompted a festive day of brawls, parades, bonfires, street theatre, and effigy burning, all the while exhibiting degrees of anti-Catholicism and class consciousness.[13]

In addition to the relatively benign practices of *skimmington* and *charivari,* there was another, far more hostile, English punishment imported to America: the pulling down or demolition of houses. Eighteenth-century Londoners, in particular, were infamous for pulling down Irish and Catholic houses, as well as pubs and chapels. In America, this popular form of collective retribution was usually accomplished by tying ropes to the frame of an offender's house and using horses or manpower to pull the entire structure to the ground. As shall be made clear, house pulling was usually associated with controversies over property ownership, when rioters or terrorists wished to dispossess families.

It is evident, then, that the earliest newcomers to America arrived with preconceived notions about their natural rights and the legitimacy of political protest. One must also consider, however, Alfred F. Young's admonition that, despite the connection between English plebian culture and American radicalism, there were some limitations to this particular form of transculturation. Certain conditions existed that often militated against the retention of English ways, and beyond retention there was also innovation, given the freedom of choice confronting American colonists.[14] Nonetheless, the philosophical and political connections to England were paramount, although other European sources provided motivation to radicals as well, including Masanielo, a fisherman, smuggler, and Italian folk hero from Naples, who was murdered and beheaded after leading a food-tax revolt in 1647. In America, civil insurrections led by Jacob Leisler (1689), John Coode (1689), and Nathanial Bacon (1676) were said to be "Masaniellian" in nature.[15] Consequently, civil insurrections, the fourth type of colonial violence, must be considered within the broader context of Anglo American political culture as well as the unfolding political events in both England and continental Europe.

In his study of violence in America, Richard Maxwell Brown identified 18 civil insurrections, or attempts to overthrow established government, between 1645 and 1760, ranging from the obscure to the infamous.[16] In terms of violence and destruction, Maryland's Plundering Time was one of the worst, and, although it and all other rebellions never developed into campaigns of terrorism, they are instructive in examining the ways that terrorism and insurrections differ. And any analysis of the origins of terrorism in America must consider the ways in which civil insurrections helped establish a foundation of popular resistance from which a legacy of terrorism would evolve. There were many reasons, on both sides of the Atlantic, that led to this constant political agitation. England's Civil War (1644–51) and Glorious Revolution (1688–89) would result in political instability throughout colonial America, leaving eager opportunists ready to seize control of their communities through violence or political manipulation. This state of upheaval was further exacerbated by the 18th-century wars for empire against France and Spain. In America, land disputes, religious differences, ethnic tensions, Indian policies, and personal grudges all further contributed to a volatile political environment that constantly undermined the public repose. Many of these rebellions were benign and relatively uneventful: even the most specialized studies of the colonies have little to say about the Davys-Pate uprising (Maryland, 1676), Josiah Fendell's two failed rebellions (Maryland, 1660 and 1680), or New Jersey's anti-quitrent revolt (1672), none of which turned violent or succeeded in toppling government authority. Some successful insurrections relied on a force of arms without resorting to bloodshed, as with the rebellions against governors Seth Sothel (North Carolina, 1689), Edmund Andros (Massachusetts, 1689), William Joseph (Maryland, 1689), and John Colleton (South Carolina, 1690), but armed force alone did not guarantee success, as with Edward Gove's failed attempt to overthrow the governor of New Hampshire (1682). Jacob Leisler briefly managed to assume gubernatorial powers in New York (1689–91), only to lose a power struggle with newly appointed governor Colonel Henry Sloughter, who tried, convicted, and executed Leisler for treason and murder. But of more immediate concern here are the two insurrections that resulted in the most violence, destruction, and political disruption: Maryland's Plundering Time and Bacon's Rebellion (Virginia, 1676).

No colony during the 17th century suffered from more political turmoil than did Maryland, which endured five insurrections in its first 55 years. Certainly the Catholicism of its ruler (Cecil Calvert, the second Lord Baltimore) and the colony's resultant mix of Protestants and Catholics contributed to this sensitive environment, but the troubles in Maryland were much more complex. Disparity in wealth and power between peasants and proprietors, long-standing personal grudges, fraught Indian relations, a contentious relationship with neighboring Virginia, and precarious connections to various political factions competing for power in England were all factors. When King Charles I and Parliament went to war, Protestant Parliamentarians in Maryland such as Richard Ingle and William Claiborne, who had chafed under the authority of Lord Baltimore and the Catholic ruling elite, saw an opportunity. In 1638, Governor Leonard Calvert, Lord Baltimore's younger brother, had seized Claiborne's trading post on Kent Island, an affront that Claiborne hoped to avenge by organizing an expedition in 1644 to retake the island as part of a wider conspiracy to persecute Catholics and seize political control from the governor. The leader of the larger insurgency was Ingle, a ship's captain and tobacco merchant, sometimes known as the "Mad Captain," befitting his reputation for violent outbursts. Ingle, originally from Middlesex County in England, had already established a contentious relationship with Giles Brent, who was appointed acting governor when Leonard Calvert departed for England in 1643. Brent ordered Ingle's detainment for treason in early 1644, but the Mad Captain managed to escape, and, using an alleged commission from Parliament to pillage Royalists and Catholics, began the infamous Plundering Time, also known as Ingle's Insurrection. Using his ship the *Reformation* and its crew, Ingle took control of St. Mary's, a small trading settlement, and, in the process, seized the *Looking Glass,* a Dutch vessel, for allegedly trading with Royalists, only to discover Giles Brent hiding in the ship's hold. By then, however, Brent had surrendered authority back to Leonard Calvert, who had returned from England to Virginia, where he began to plot a military expedition to retake Maryland. Ingle and his band of approximately 30 rebels then moved their base of operations outside of St. Mary's by seizing Cross Manor, the finest estate in Maryland, and making it a collection point for plundered goods and captured Catholics.[17]

For the next several weeks, Ingle and his rebels were joined by Protestant freemen as they plundered manors, stole tobacco, burned property, confiscated livestock, and captured several prisoners that Ingle hoped to try in England for crimes against Parliament. They were met with little or no resistance. The extent of the violence committed against the Catholic Royalists is difficult to assess. The only records from that period were documents of the proprietary government, which of course represented a decidedly one-sided perspective on the conflict, but even these records were either destroyed or ceased to exist once the rebellion broke out and government officials fled from Ingle's insurgents. Nonetheless, despite the widespread suffering inflicted by Ingle's insurgents, it is evident that the insurrection fell short of engaging in terrorist tactics. There was no differentiation between victims and target audience: in the case of government officials and Catholic Royalists, the victims and audience were one and the same. Consequently, there was no larger psychological manipulation facilitated by political propaganda. Plundering and destruction of Catholic or Royalist property were not means to an end but a primary objective of the insurrection. Above all, this was an insurgence against established government through force and destruction, not an effort to manipulate wider public behavior through the instigation of fear.

Whatever strategic advantages Ingle's insurrection might have gained were short-lived. The insurgents ultimately failed to capture Leonard Calvert and

William Claiborne failed to persuade the rebels on Kent Island to follow his lead. Furthermore, in April 1645, Ingle departed for London with his two ships laden with bounty and prisoners, hoping for laurels and a rich commission from Parliament. Upon his arrival eight weeks later, he would be severely disappointed: his prisoners were released, the *Looking Glass* was returned to its rightful owners, some of his victims filed suit against him, and a series of court decisions seemed to invalidate all he had done in Maryland. In the end, Ingle could not prove that Maryland had opposed Parliament's authority before his insurrection began, forcing the courts to disavow his actions. From that point forward, Richard Ingle seemingly disappears from the pages of history. Meanwhile, before invading Maryland and reclaiming the government, Leonard Calvert laid groundwork by offering advanced pardons to rebels and pursuing a policy of reconciliation with old enemies. His strategies worked to perfection. Calvert and his recruited forces arrived in Maryland in late 1646, met virtually no resistance, and by the following spring had retaken control of the entire colony. The Plundering Time was over.[18]

Other than the plundering of private property, Ingle's Insurrection proved to be relatively benign; no violence was seemingly directed against persons, although three Jesuits disappeared under mysterious circumstances while held captive by Ingle's forces. The same did not apply to the most significant and destructive insurrection of the colonial period: the 1676 rebellion against Virginia Governor William Berkeley at the hands of forces led by his cousin, Nathanial Bacon, Jr. For some time now, historians have disagreed about whether Bacon was a hotheaded, Indian-hating demagogue or a heroic torchbearer of democracy. Speculation about Bacon's motives and actions, however, are more properly and thoroughly discussed in the literature spawned by his rebellion.[19] Of immediate interest here is the violence behind the story. As one might imagine given its status as the first of 13 colonies and as very much an experiment, Virginia, like Maryland, was a colony in constant turmoil. Three bloody wars with the neighboring Powhatans left a lasting impression on long-time Governor William Berkeley, who sought accommodation with peaceful Indians still living in the Jamestown area. This passive policy did not sit well with newcomer Nathanial Bacon, an exiled scion, wealthy landowner, and Indian trader, or with a large group of frontiersmen who had long sought to decimate local Indians or at least banish them from treaty-protected land.

Tensions between the governor and frontiersmen were already building when, in 1675, a conflict over an unpaid debt led to a raiding party by Doeg Indians, who sought to confiscate hogs from Thomas Matthews, a local planter. A local volunteer militia was alerted, caught up to the raiding party and recovered the pilfered hogs, killing several Doegs in the process. Unfortunately, this set off retaliatory acts of violence between Indians and frontier militiamen, including the massacre of 14 friendly Susquehannocks in a tragic case of mistaken identity and the murder of 5 of their chiefs after they accepted an invitation to parley peacefully. The Susquehannocks responded with a vengeance: in January 1676, they killed nearly 60 settlers in Maryland, and, crossing into Virginia, massacred another 36 in a single attack near the Potomac River. The escalating violence led to further polarization between Berkeley, who denounced the depredations against peaceful Indians, and Bacon, who had become the unofficial "General of the Volunteers."[20] In an effort to provide greater security against attacks, Berkeley proposed the construction of nine nearby forts manned by local militia, forming a defensive perimeter around Jamestown. He also relied on the good graces of friendly tribes in the area, who acted as spies and intermediaries for the governor. Despite a crippling economy, Berkeley further proposed higher taxes to defray the costs and added a limitation on trade with all Indians, policies that did not satisfy Bacon and his own militiamen, who felt victimized by the trade prohibition and demanded a much more aggressive and invasive policy to root out the Indian menace. They were, no doubt, greatly influenced by King Phillip's War, then raging throughout New England, as well as by local rumors that warned of imminent Indian raids. They were further angered by the widespread suspicions that Berkeley was profiteering from his perceived guardianship of friendly Indians. However, as historian Alfred Cave recently suggested, Berkeley was primarily motivated not by profit nor by any benevolence toward Indians, but rather by a sense of vulnerability: he greatly feared that draconian policies toward the Virginia Indians might provoke a wider, pan-Indian alliance and uprising that would destroy the colony.[21] By May, Bacon had become openly defiant of the governor's authority, forging his own, independent anti-Indian agenda and subsequently forcing Berkeley to issue two proclamations, one relieving Bacon of his council seat and the other branding him a rebel.

In June, Bacon appeared in Jamestown to claim his seat in the Assembly as the recently elected burgess from Henrico County, but not before he and his militia slaughtered several Indians at an Occaneechee fort along the Roanoke River. Bacon was immediately detained and brought before the governor and House of Burgesses to face charges. After confessing his crimes and begging for forgiveness on bended knee, he was granted a pardon and allowed to take his seat. The governor and rebel then engaged in contentious discussions for two weeks about a possible commission officially charging Bacon with leading a government-sponsored expedition against hostile Indians. As Wilcomb Washburn acknowledged over half a century ago in his history of the rebellion, Bacon, now empowered by the addition of 600 armed men in Jamestown, was singularly concerned at this point not with reform legislation but with exacting this commission.[22] But he rejected from his orders any distinction between hostile and friendly Indians: in his view, they were all enemies and had to be exterminated or enslaved. Berkeley refused to accept these terms until finally, cowed by the threat of death, a vacillating House of Burgesses insisted that he surrender to Bacon's demands. It would be a decision that Berkeley and the burgesses would quickly regret. In preparation for his expedition, Bacon's small army began to confiscate arms, ammunition, and horses from local planters and threatened to destroy the homes of magistrates who dared doubt the legality of his commission and activities. Within weeks, he issued a "Declaration of the People" and a "Manifesto" outlining political positions he had staked out in an earlier "Humble Appeal," which condemned Berkeley for coddling hostile Indians and demanded more strident anti-Indian policies. Bacon then commenced hostilities that began as a racial war against local Indians but quickly transformed, after he heard rumors that Berkeley was attempting to recruit an army to challenge him, into a civil insurrection against the government that had granted his commission.

That fall, Bacon's army, frustrated in its failure to find Susquehannocks, attacked instead a camp of peaceful Pamunkeys who, in their eagerness to prove their friendliness, offered no resistance. Bacon and his men took 45 captives and killed at least eight. Meanwhile, other forces loyal to Bacon seized three ships moored along the James River to form a rebel navy. Bacon's next objective became the capture of William Berkeley, who had taken refuge among loyalists on Maryland's Eastern Shore. But when Bacon's navy, which had grown to four ships after another capture, arrived in August, a series of defections and surprise attacks amazingly allowed Berkeley to capture the entire fleet. Two of its captains were charged with treason and executed. Emboldened by this dramatic turn of events, Berkeley and a newly formed army and navy of recruits and defectors arrived at Jamestown in early September. Although 500 Baconists defended the capital, the governor's offers of pardon convinced most of them to abandon the cause, allowing Berkeley to reclaim Jamestown. Soon thereafter, Bacon arrived with an army of 600 and laid siege to the capital, at one point using captive female loyalists and Indians as human shields.[23] Subjected to artillery bombardment and a wave of defections, Berkeley was finally convinced to abandon the settlement and, after the governor fled to the safety of his ships, Bacon and his army marched into the capital, put it to the torch, and reduced it to ashes. According to Washburn, Bacon demonstrated "the psychology of terror" by waiting until nightfall to burn Jamestown "so that it might appear more dreadful in the dark."[24]

Washburn's interjection of terror as a psychological weapon into his 1957 account is particularly interesting given that terrorism wasn't the global phenomenon then that it is today. Regardless, he raised an interesting issue that requires further consideration here. Many elements of Bacon's Rebellion were similar to those characteristics that mark a campaign of terrorism. It was certainly violent, with widespread destruction and dozens of fatalities. Beyond that, there was a visible leadership and hierarchy in the rebel militia and Bacon's own public manifestos comprised a simple but effective effort at propaganda. Bacon's men also coerced all freemen in Westmoreland County to swear allegiance to the insurgents, under the threat of reprisal. Yet, in the end, Bacon's Rebellion did not exhibit the significant earmarks of terrorism. Bacon's violence was an end to itself, not a psychological ploy to sway a larger target audience, unless one considers his actions as a warning to Indians still living in the Jamestown environs. Unfortunately, we have no sense of what the Indians along the Virginia tidewater thought of Bacon's Army, and those colonial records that do survive seem to indicate that when Bacon attacked Indians he was more concerned with localized racial genocide than whatever broader messages he might be sending. Consequently, as far as the Jamestown Indians were concerned, there was no distinction made between victims and target audiences. The siege and subsequent torching of Jamestown was the ultimate act of a civil insurrection bent on overthrowing the legitimate government of Virginia through military might and the tactics of *grande guerre,* not an act of limited violence designed to entrain public behavior. The spectre of Jamestown in flames might have induced a sense of psychological terror as Washburn intimated, but the rebellion up to that point was founded on destruction by brute force rather than on violent psychological manipulation.

In the weeks that followed the Jamestown bonfire, Berkeley again retreated to the safety of the Eastern Shore, where he began to rebuild his forces. Meanwhile, Bacon's Army began to plunder the estates of those unwilling to sign loyalty oaths, revealing a ferocity that to some exposed strains of class warfare between plebian frontiersmen and loyalist gentry. Then, remarkably, Berkeley and his government benefited from another twist of fate: on October 26, Nathanial Bacon died of "flux" and an infestation of lice, leaving critics to lament that "lice and flux should take the hangman's part."[25] Joseph Ingram was selected to assume Bacon's position and, although the next few months would witness violent attacks and counterattacks between Baconites and loyalists resulting in dozens of fatalities and abductions, Berkeley began to reassert control as the rebel forces began to dissipate. Additional recruits, as well as defectors and deserters from the rebel army, allowed the governor to gain ground and summarily execute leading traitors along the way. Meanwhile, in February, much to his surprise, 1,000 of his majesty's troops arrived in Jamestown, headed by a three-man royal commission. Dispatched from London when news had first arrived of the rebellion, the troops were to suppress the rebel army, while the commission was charged with investigating and reporting on the rebellion. No one could have anticipated that, by the time the commissioners would arrive, Bacon would be dead, the rebellion suppressed, and Berkeley restored to power. Yet, much to the chagrin of Berkeley, the House of Burgesses, and the majority of settlers, the commission greatly exceeded its authority and began an immediate and extremely contentious power struggle with the governor over various issues related to the rebellion and its aftermath. By May, the commission finished its report, which criticized both Bacon and Berkeley, an affront that the beleaguered governor sought to challenge personally before the king. Unfortunately, shortly after arriving in London, William Berkeley died before securing an audience to clear his name. Neither the governor nor the rebel was destined to survive the bloodiest and most significant insurrection in the early history of the American colonies. In the end, in addition to the widespread devastation of property, 23 Baconites were executed for their part in the rebellion, and dozens of others, both Indians and whites, also lost their lives.

III. A Legacy of Riots

Bacon's Rebellion and Maryland's Plundering Time were the most violent civil insurrections of the colonial period, and, even though they did not evolve into campaigns of terrorism, they, along with the 16 other attempts to overthrow legitimate governments, certainly helped establish a foundation of collective resistance on this side of the Atlantic. Political instincts forged by a strong Anglo American political tradition based on corporatism and natural law included a willingness, if not an obligation, to question and even challenge authority. In the wilderness that was North America, transplanted English people living in smallish, relatively isolated communities had the unprecedented opportunity to put theory into practice, and they did so with alarming regularity. While these civil insurrections exposed and nurtured a strong anti-authoritarian tone in colonial America, riots, the fifth type of collective violence, tended to assume instead an extra-institutional nature. No subject concerning early political violence in America has received more recent scholarly attention than the subject of colonial riots. This scholarly trend was undoubtedly inspired by the pioneering studies of George Rudé, who analyzed European riots and offered surprising conclusions.[26] Rather than forming combustible, mindless mobs with no resources or direction, European rioters crossed class lines and composed single-minded and discriminating crowds whose actions were directly associated with specific grievances. Historians have found many of these traits among American rioters, too, particularly during the colonial and revolutionary eras. And because most Americans rioted not to overthrow governments but to reform them from within, riots often served a legitimate political and social function.

As with the subject of terrorism, the term *riot* conjures up any number of possible scenarios involving public disorder and, therefore, requires specification. In his history of rioting in America, Paul A. Gilje offered a well-reasoned definition based in legal precedent, while acknowledging that, because "one person's peaceful demonstration is another person's riot," any definition inevitably contains some "gray areas." "A riot is any group of twelve or more people attempting to assert their will immediately through the use of force outside the normal bounds of law," he wrote.[27] Based on this definition, rioting falls far short of terrorist activity. Similar to civil insurrections, the unlawful use of force here is an end to itself. There is no victim-target differentiation, no psychological manipulation, and no dissemination of political propaganda to justify force and generate favorable public opinion. But riots did tend to turn violent and were politically motivated, therefore contributing in their own way to establishing a foundation of violent, collective resistance that would facilitate the evolution of terrorism. In some ways, rioting served as a link between the devastation of civil insurrections and the outbreak of terrorism just prior to the American Revolution. Of the 18 civil insurrections identified during the colonial era, 15 occurred during the 17th century, whereas the vast majority of riots were conducted in the 18th century. Several forces played a role in that pattern, including the abdication in 1688 of James II, who was extremely unpopular in America. Population numbers were also significant. In 1690, following England's Glorious Revolution and the ascension of William and Mary to the throne, the total population in the American colonies was just over 210,000 and was generally confined to the eastern seaboard; by 1770, the population had swelled to more than 2.1 million persons, filling the coastal plain to the eastern slope of the Appalachian Mountains. If one assumes that smaller, sparsely populated colonies were more vulnerable to hostile takeovers, it stands to reason that once the colonies established a stable foundation in America and an unpopular monarch was deposed, anti-authoritarian insurrections generally fell into disfavor and extra-institutional, low-level rioting became the norm.

As popular as civil insurrections proved to be in colonial America, riots were by far the most common form of collective violence. Two sources estimated that between 1740 and 1775, 159 riots were recorded, most of which were related to food shortages.[28] Another study counted 44 riots between 1760 and 1775, most often in urban settings.[29] Demographic analyses reveal that riots usually consisted of 50 to 100 armed males, sometimes disguised, from a wide spectrum of economic and social backgrounds. Violence was generally directed against property, but assaults were common, and at least 19 persons lost their lives between 1700 and 1765.[30] Evidence also suggests that riots were viewed as forms of communal regulation, an extralegal method of enforcing behavioral standards by using hostile crowds to express displeasure with specific conditions and to exact punishment against certain offenders. But as the Real Whigs were quick to emphasize, riots could also serve as a check on government tyranny, a reminder that the restriction of government power was an important element of both liberty and natural law.[31]

As the evidence overwhelmingly suggests, Americans found any number of reasons to riot, creating several types. Each was a unique response to local social or political conditions that required public remonstrance through crowd action.

Tobacco Riots

In all likelihood, the first significant rioting in colonial America concerned tobacco, the backbone of the Virginia economy. In 1682, overabundant production caused a severe drop in prices, thereby debilitating the economy. Many Virginia planters wanted local measures to suspend all future planting that season but could not rally the necessary support, and their efforts were defeated. Undeterred, several planters, allegedly under the leadership of Robert Beverley, decided to effectuate what their Assembly would not. In a series of nighttime raids, planters-turned-rioters descended on farms and plantations and began to cut thousands of young tobacco plants. One estimate determined that rioters destroyed more than 10,000 hogsheads of tobacco.[32] With the bitter memories of Bacon's Rebellion still lingering, authorities executed at least three rioters for their tobacco cutting crimes and, although Robert Beverley was arrested and imprisoned, he was eventually released.

Four decades after the first riots, Virginia passed new tobacco legislation in 1730 in an effort to eliminate poor quality, raise prices, cut down on exports, and centralize marketing strategies. It further created a new currency by issuing tobacco receipts to planters in lieu of paper money. Tobacco that passed inspection under new and more stringent guidelines was placed in a public warehouse awaiting transport, while rejected tobacco was set afire. And in a move calculated to suppress any public backlash, the burning of public warehouses was made punishable by death. Predictably, these new laws set off a political firestorm of public protests and riots. The legislation, which demanded that approved tobacco be "good, well-conditioned and . . . free from trash," seemed especially arbitrary, bestowing broad powers on inspectors.[33] Poor planters who grew low quality tobacco on inferior soil felt particularly victimized. It was these lower-class growers who unleashed a wave of violence in 1732 that spread throughout several counties and accounted for the destruction of several tobacco warehouses. Some rioters in Prince William and King George counties were captured, but, due to sympathetic public pressure, were released without charges filed against them. While local militia units were called out to quell the violence that also spread to neighboring Maryland, the Virginia legislature responded by dismissing corrupt inspectors, offering rewards for the capture of rioters, and educating poor planters about the law. Eventually, tobacco prices began to rise and violent dissent began to dissipate, but the poorer planters would continue to suffer from an inspection system that worked against them. Accordingly, tobacco would continue to be a politically charged issue in eastern Virginia for many years to come.[34]

Food Riots

As in Europe, the prospect of food shortages motivated riots in America, especially in New England, where food riots broke out in Boston in 1710, 1713, and 1729. There were also violent episodes in Philadelphia, in 1741, and New York City, in 1754, over the availability and price of bread, but the riots in Boston were particularly destructive.[35] They also demonstrated how broader forces than the impulse to riot were at issue. In 1710, grain prices dropped precipitously in Boston, aggravated by a recent drought and fire. Hungry Bostonians demanded more grain for the common good, but Andrew Belcher, one of Boston's wealthiest merchants, preferred to export his grain elsewhere for higher profits. As Dirk Hoerder noted in his study of Bostonian crowd action, this division between Belcher and the Boston citizenry reflected nothing less than an ideological confrontation between free market or *laissez-faire* advocates and those who clung tenaciously to "the old concept of common weal in a corporate society."[36] In the face of Belcher's obstinacy, rioters destroyed the rudder of one of his grain-laden ships, rendering it incapable of setting sail. In response, a few rioters were prosecuted, but the

General Court did prohibit the exportation of grain, excluding that already stored on ships and ready to sail. Three years later, Belcher's refusal to stop the exportation of corn further inflamed over 200 rioters, who broke into his warehouse and distributed his stores. The General Court responded, not by prosecuting rioters, but by drafting new legislation restricting the exportation of food, establishing measures of price control, and ordering local distribution, all in the interest of the corporate public good. Thus, in this particular instance, a riot effectively served a semi-legitimate, extra-institutional function that ultimately benefited the wider community.

Pope's Day Riots

As described above, Pope's Day, known in England as Guy Fawkes Day, was traditionally held on November 5 to commemorate the failed gunpowder plot by English Catholics to murder Protestant King James I and replace him with a Catholic monarch. On November 5, 1605, Guy Fawkes was discovered with a cache of explosives beneath the House of Lords and, within days, English people began celebrating the survival of the Stuart monarch and their disdain for "popery" with bonfires, music, food, and military parades. This traditional celebration made its way across the Atlantic to America by the mid-17th century and, although it was generally recognized throughout the colonies, it was especially popular in New England. The festivities also included fireworks, bonfires, parades, street theatre, and other rituals. In Boston, the primary street revelers came from the plebian classes: sailors, apprentices, journeymen, mechanics, and others who demonstrated ill feelings toward not only the pope but also the patrician classes of Bostonian society.[37] Increasing ritualistic disorder eventually forced Boston to pass a Riot Act to suppress the violence, but authorities were unable to enforce the legislation. Beginning in the mid-1740s, Pope's Day regularly witnessed ceremonial melees between rival gangs of the North End and South End who held separate parades complete with effigies of the pope, the devil, and other assorted scapegoats. They both marched to Dock Square near the Old State House, where a riot would ensue as the rivals sought to capture each other's effigies. The winner had that year's honor of burning all the effigies in a festive and victorious bonfire. Americans eventually stopped celebrating Pope's Day by the early 1770s, as the target of popular enmity switched from the pope to the king, but, in an interesting historical footnote, over 400 years after Fawkes was executed, effigies related to his case are still being ceremoniously burned in parts of Great Britain on November 5.

Pine Tree Riots

Another significant wave of rioting was prompted by a series of acts passed by Parliament in 1691, 1711, 1722, and 1729 severely restricting the cutting of white pine trees. White pines were needed for royal and merchant ships because they produced superior, single-stick masts hewn from only one tree. With this valuable resource in mind, the last White Pine Act forbid the cutting of any white pine over one foot in diameter, saving them for masts. Deputy surveyors had to designate those trees reserved for the Crown and inspect sawmills for violations, punishable by fines or jail sentences. Opposition to the white pine legislation was concentrated in New Hampshire, where white pines were particularly abundant and where each town's charter declared that all white pines remain the exclusive property of the king, regardless of local property titles. Aside from the thorny issue of royal intrusion, the primary problem from the American perspective was that white pines were a major source of timber used for the construction of houses, especially floorboards. Fortunately, until the 1770s, the offending legislation was not enforced and conflict was mostly averted.

Despite the lax attitude toward enforcement of these acts, they did not go unchallenged. In 1734, their legality was contested, but the case languished in colonial and English courts for years before being dropped without resolution. During the next few decades, frustrated by their inability to void the acts, incensed landowners turned to vandalism and assault against royal surveyors as extralegal means of protesting the troublesome laws. When John Wentworth became governor of New Hampshire in 1767, he recognized the potential financial benefits from the acts and appointed surveyors to inspect sawmills and enforce the law. During the winter of 1771–72, Deputy Surveyor William Sherburn paid a surprise visit to six sawmills in Goffstown and Weare and discovered illegally felled white pines. The mill owners were fined and ordered to appear in court in February 1772. In preparation, the owners hired an attorney to represent them in court and challenge their fines, but when he met with Wentworth, the governor immediately offered him a position as Surveyor of the King's Woods. The turncoat lawyer quickly accepted the offer and subsequently informed his startled former employers that they were obligated to honor the law and pay their settlements. The Goffstown owners readily complied, but not those from Weare. On April 13, 1772, Sheriff Benjamin Whiting and his deputy John Quigly rode into South Weare in search of sawmill owner Ebenezer Mudgett, the leader of the resistance movement, hoping that his capitulation would set an example for fellow dissidents. The sheriff and deputy found Mudgett before dark and agreed that they would meet in the morning to settle his fine, but during the evening word quickly spread and scores of rioters gathered at Mudgett's house. At dawn, more than 20 disguised rioters, including Mudgett, burst into the local inn, grabbed Whiting and Quigly from their beds and beat them mercilessly with tree switches and split floorboards. Horses belonging to the sheriff and deputy were brought around to the inn's door where rioters immediately cropped off the horse's ears and sheared their manes and tails. The sheriff and deputy were then forcibly mounted on their horses, which were slapped by jeering townspeople as the steeds galloped out of town through a human gauntlet. Later that spring, after Whiting returned and arrested one of the rioters, others came forward to offer bail and face charges. Throwing themselves before the Superior Court and its four judges, the eight rioters were given modest fines that were quickly settled. The light punishment was widely viewed as a tacit acknowledgement by the judges that resistance to the White Pines Acts, while technically unlawful, was at the very least understandable.[38] The unjust laws would remain, but concerns in New Hampshire over ownership of white pines would be overtaken soon by the revolutionary fervor then spreading throughout the colonies.

Impressment Riots

Impressment, or the forcible conscription of men without notice into naval service, originated in the 13th century and was legalized by Parliament in 1563. Although renewed in England many times, impressment in British North America was of doubtful legality because of subsequent legislation and procedural ambiguities. Nonetheless, under British law, any able-bodied man could be drafted into the Royal Navy in emergency situations, especially during wartime; it was thus common for British ships to pull into British ports, where press gangs would be sent ashore to round up new "recruits" between the ages of 18 and 45. Exemptions to the law existed, but mostly for those occupations traditionally held by patricians. This left the plebian classes as primary impressment targets, which further exacerbated existing class tensions. Because of its popularity as America's leading port and its location in relation to Canada and Europe, Boston, above all other seaport towns, was a favorite target of British press gangs, which often loitered in the waters of New England. But it was also Boston that served as a sanctuary of sorts for deserters from the Royal Navy, who quickly found employment on outgoing American merchant vessels. Aside from the considerable individual hardships suffered under impressment, the impact on the local economy was debilitating. Merchant ships avoided Boston when press gangs were nearby. The kidnapping of local sailors left sea traders undermanned or without crews, preventing them from sailing and conducting business. Shortages of supplies and manpower caused wider economic disruptions, giving Bostonians plenty of reasons to resent impressment. It was no surprise, then, that violence often ensued when press gangs were discovered afoot in Boston.

In November 1745, while at war with France and in desperate need of sailors, the captain of H.M.S. *Wager* successfully obtained press warrants that specifically excluded residents of Boston and local veterans of the recent Louisbourg expedition. The *Wager*'s press gang, however, disobeyed the warrants, apprehended several men indiscriminately, including war veterans, and, after being notified that their actions were illegal, attacked and killed two of their captives with knives and axes. A few months later, in February, H.M.S. *Shirley,* responsible for the impressment of more than 90 men, dropped anchor in Boston and sent a press gang ashore. However, after securing the required warrants, the pressers were attacked by a mob of rioters, who beat their victims senseless and left them sprawled in the streets.[39]

Without a doubt, the most serious and infamous impressment riot was the Knowles Riot of 1747, precipitated in November when a naval squadron under the command of Commodore Charles Knowles sailed into Boston in search of supplies and men, only to suffer a number of desertions. On the evening of November 16, Knowles sent out press gangs without warrants but with orders to press men indiscriminately. No sooner had his gangs apprehended 46 men then angry Bostonians replied in kind, seizing several British officers and sailors as hostages. Confronted by a mob the next day, Governor William Shirley managed to secure the release of some of the mob's hostages, but he and the freed men were forced to retreat to safety in the governor's mansion. The crowd then produced one of the governor's sheriffs who had previously earned Boston's wrath by helping the Royal Navy press innocent men. He was taken to the courtyard of the mansion and, before the governor, beaten and placed in the stocks.[40]

The crowd eventually dispersed, but, sufficiently intimidated, Shirley called for backup from Castle William, ordered out the local militia, and sought relief from the General Court that evening. However, the court building was quickly surrounded by thousands of rioters who demanded the release of Knowles's captives in exchange for the remaining hostages held by the mob, as well as an end to the nefarious practice of impressment. From there, the rioters seized a barge that they mistakenly assumed was the king's property, hauled it to the common, and set it on fire. The next day, November 18, Shirley and the British seamen slipped out of town. The seamen made their way back to their fleet, while Shirley sought refuge at Castle William because the militia, other than its officers, failed to appear in support of the governor—the vast majority either were active rioters or supporters of their cause. Frustrated, and livid at this show of defiance of the king's navy, Knowles threatened to bombard Boston. At first, the provincial government tacitly sympathized with the rioters through its inaction but was finally prevailed upon to support the embattled governor two days later. The General Court then ordered out the militia to quell the riot and ordered the release of the mob's hostages, whereupon a distressed Shirley, after much effort, convinced Knowles to exchange his impressed captives for the mob's hostages. The crisis was over. On November 21, with no threats of future rioting, a newly cooperative militia appeared and escorted the governor back to his mansion without incident; a week and a half later, the much-despised Knowles set sail for the West Indies, full of malevolence and short of sailors.[41]

Despite the impact of the Knowles Riot, England refused to suspend impressment. A nighttime raid in New York in 1757 captured 800 men, the equivalent of one-quarter of the city's adult male population. Another 73 men were taken from New York City in 1758, and 31 were similarly captured from Virginia during a two-day period in 1771.[42] Other coastal communities were similarly victimized. In his groundbreaking study of Revolutionary-era seamen, Jesse Lemisch noted that, although there is a general perception that American riots during this period managed to avoid fatalities, this contention does not hold up when extended to seamen's resistance to impressment. Seamen were desperate to escape kidnapping and often fought their abductors with determined ferocity. Violent riots remained commonplace, and both sides committed murders. In June 1765, approximately 500 seamen, many of whom were African Americans, rioted after five weeks of impressment. Additional impressment riots also occurred in New York (1764 and 1765), Newport (1764), and Casco, Maine (1764). As with other American rioters, hostile seamen might have appeared irrational to many contemporary observers, but Lemisch also argued that seamen's riots were discriminating and purposeful. This became more evident when seamen extended their rioting to include protests against the Stamp Act, beginning in late 1765.[43] As England and her American colonies drifted toward war, impressment would take a backseat to other, far more pressing issues, but did not disappear completely. Few could have predicted then that continued impressment of Americans would prove to be one of many polarizing maritime issues that eventually provoked a second war with England 40 years later.

Doctors' Riots

While the majority of colonial riots focused on economic or political issues, scientific controversy, particularly the experimentation with smallpox inoculation, sparked the doctors' riots. *Variola major,* the virus that carries smallpox, preceded the British to North America by about a century, using Spanish soldiers and colonials as hosts, since the virus can only spread through human contact. Smallpox, known to have existed for approximately 3,000 years before its eradication in 1979, not only killed at an alarming rate, but also scarred, blinded, and maimed. In some areas of North America, the fatality rate often exceeded 50%. By the mid-18 century, only isolated pockets of the Pacific Northwest had escaped the smallpox plague. There were three epidemics in New England alone between 1677 and 1702.[44] At the time, there were only two possible responses to the spread of variola. One involved isolation, usually through a process of quarantine, which all colonies excepting Pennsylvania drafted laws to regulate. Isolation could also include flight, but quitting an infected area put other communities at risk should evacuees unknowingly carry the virus. The second option, inoculation, was based on the knowledge that the only persons truly immune from variola were those who had previously contracted the virus and survived. Consequently, inoculation, known for centuries in Asia and Africa but unknown in Europe until the early 1700s, involved deliberately planting live smallpox virus into an incision on the arm or hand. After a brief incubation period and for reasons still unexplained, the patient would then contract smallpox but, in most cases, a much more benign form: fewer pustules, less scarring, and a significantly reduced fatality rate. Inoculated patients could still die from the milder virus, but, despite this risk, people with means and intellect, such as Thomas Jefferson, George Washington, and John and Abigail Adams, willingly underwent the procedure.

The notion of deliberately harvesting variola in order to implant it into a willing victim living within a populated area horrified a large segment of colonial society, fearful of an accidental outbreak, and became a divisive issue whenever doctors opened inoculation clinics. People's worst fears materialized in 1767 when John Smith set up an inoculation center in Yorktown, Virginia, and prematurely released a small group of patients who ended up spreading the virus and starting an epidemic. Accused of "playing God," inoculation doctors and those who lent them support became common targets of mob activity. The Reverend Cotton Mather, who, along with Dr. Zabdiel Boylston, first introduced inoculation to the colonies in the midst of a smallpox epidemic in Boston in 1721, had his home firebombed. Riots became commonplace during the 1760s, as improvements in the inoculation process made the controversial treatment increasingly popular. There are at least two ways to break down the demographic profiles of those who did or did not approve of inoculation. On one hand, the treatment was expensive and generally affordable only by the well-to-do. This meant that unless there was an epidemic that spurred free inoculations, the poor had no choice but to stand exposed to variola, while the wealthy stood to benefit from the procedure; consequently, the rich, unlike the poor, tended to support inoculation.[45] In his study of smallpox riots in Norfolk, Virginia, Patrick Henderson argued that the anti-inoculationists were predominately debtors or "patriots," while the targets of their wrath were loyalists of the Crown or other symbols of royal authority, thus putting a different spin on the then-deteriorating relations between the colonies and mother country.[46]

The smallpox disturbances of Norfolk between 1768 and 1769 were the most noteworthy of the many colonial doctors' riots. The 1768 crisis was precipitated when Dr. John Dalgleish inoculated a group of families at the home of Dr. Archibald Campbell, a staunch loyalist. On June 27, in the midst of a thunderstorm, a mob of patriots drove the infected families from Campbell's property to the public pest house and then returned to vandalize the homes of the recently inoculated. The controversy flared up again a year later when Dalgleish inoculated three blacks and an infected seaman who had recently arrived on a ship owned by Norfolk's mayor, Cornelius Calvert, who had charges pending against the 1768 rioters. After Dalgleish was arrested and imprisoned for conspiracy to spread smallpox, a mob again formed, marched to Calvert's home, broke more than 50 pieces of glass, and coerced a promise from the mayor to drop all charges. The mob then moved on to the home of Dr. Campbell, who also had filed criminal complaints against rioters, and, despite his similar promises to drop all charges, broke his windows and consumed his liquor supply.

The crisis in Norfolk not only helped spur inoculation control laws in Virginia, South Carolina, and New York City, but it also coincided with public protests aimed at the recently legislated Townshend Revenue Acts, as Americans began to shift their attention to the burgeoning crisis with England. But such was the success of smallpox inoculation in America as opposed to Europe, many English parents sent their children to America for both their education and safety from the dreaded variola.[47] Riots against doctors and controversial medical procedures would continue after the American Revolution, but the focus would shift away from inoculation to the use of human cadavers. But, in the interim, there were still a number of reasons for Americans to riot during the colonial period.

Other Forms of Riots

Many other issues could motivate Americans to riot. As England set up imperial regulations to establish customs duties and to prohibit certain types of trade, anti-customs rioters often responded by seizing confiscated ships and surreptitiously unloading smuggled goods. During the 1750s and 1760s, when English military forces began to assume a more visible presence in America, mutual antagonism between civilians and soldiers often erupted into riots and drunken brawls completely unrelated to a specific grievance. When Jews began to populate New York City in greater numbers during the 1740s, anti-Semitic riots broke out. In one infamous episode in 1749, rioters pulled down the house of a Jewish immigrant and threatened to rape his wife.[48] Election improprieties, such as those surrounding a controversial Philadelphia election in 1742, could also induce riotous behavior. In this case, violence between German-born Quakers and Anglicans over voting procedures resulted in more than 50 arrests and subsequent steps toward election reform.

Americans also used riots to enforce community morals and standards. In "bawdy house" riots, prostitutes' dwellings were vandalized or pulled down, forcing the prostitutes to flee for their safety. Many communities employed riots to force male adulterers to mend their ways and return to their abandoned wives. In Elizabeth, New Jersey, groups of rioters, in an act full of ritualistic symbolism, painted their faces, dressed in women's clothing, and flogged men accused of beating their wives.[49]

Despite the diverse types and considerable prevalence of rioting, there was one sustained political issue that spawned far more violence and had far more significance than any other reason for rioting. Disputes over land ownership not only would plague most colonies and inspire impassioned riots up and down the eastern seaboard but would also, in some instances and in due time, degenerate into campaigns based on terroristic methods. Two colonies would find themselves particularly embroiled in this early contentiousness and hostility: New York and New Jersey. Because the controversies in New York would endure well into the 19th century (discussed in Chapter 7), the immediate attention here shifts to New Jersey.

IV. New Jersey Land Riots

As with many colonial disputes, the controversy over land ownership that would plague New Jersey for well over a century originated in England. In 1660, King Charles II was restored to the throne, and four years later the English captured

New Amsterdam (soon to be renamed New York), a prized New World possession; the king then promptly granted the nearby lands between the Hudson and Delaware rivers, which became the new colony of New Jersey, to his brother James, Duke of York. When James, in turn, ordered New York's acting governor, Richard Nicholls, to populate the area, Nicholls authorized two groups of Puritan yeomen to purchase Indian lands, which formed the basis of the Elizabeth Town Tract and the Monmouth Patent. The larger of the two grants, Elizabeth Town, contained about 400,000 acres, and within one year 80 associates would hold rights to town allotments. Unfortunately for the yeomen, and unbeknown to the governor, James had also granted all proprietary rights to New Jersey to two loyal courtiers, Sir George Carteret and Lord John Berkeley, who recruited Carteret's cousin, Philip Carteret, as governor. Included in the Carteret–Berkeley grants were lands still occupied by Indians and tracts previously purchased from Indians by other newly arriving yeomen, including a large contingent of Dutch-speaking exiles from New York. This overlapping authority, along with subsequent conflicting land claims, was the foundation of New Jersey's problems. When Governor Philip Carteret arrived in August 1665, he sent out mixed signals. On one hand, he announced that all of the Nicholls grants were "posterior" to the Carteret–Berkeley charters, a decision that seemingly invalidated the Elizabeth Town and Monmouth grant. But, on the other hand, the new governor also resided in Elizabeth Town and even acquired a share in the patent. No wonder, then, that the yeomen interpreted the governor's actions as evidence that their titles were clear of any legal association to the two proprietors, George Carteret and Berkeley. Matters became further complicated in 1674, when a bankrupt Lord Berkeley sold his western half of the colony to a group of Quakers, and, in 1682, when Sir Carteret died and his heirs sold their eastern share to new proprietors. Consequently, the troubled colony was now divided into two smaller colonies, West and East Jersey, with an additional controversy over the precise boundary line that separated the two. This also set up the enduring confrontation over conflicting land claims between the proprietors and the yeomen, including an active group of Elizabeth Town associates. None of these far-reaching events helped unravel the lingering land disputes, despite a 1697 court decision, *Fullerton vs. Jones,* that apparently established the validity of the original Nicholls grants.[50]

In the aftermath of *Fullerton vs. Jones,* issues became increasingly complex and controversial. Many yeomen sought to avoid further trouble by deferring to the proprietors, giving up their Nicholls claims and purchasing proprietary deeds, sometimes under duress. While the proprietors sought unsuccessfully to negotiate with the Elizabeth Town Associates, they began to file ejectment suits against yeomen in other areas. Meanwhile, Newark land claimants, who had purchased a patent from Governor Carteret, seemingly expanded their authority by defying the proprietors and purchasing additional Indian deeds adjacent to their original tract. This and other subsequent purchases by proprietary settlers resulted in overlapping land claims *among* the proprietors, which were further complicated by opposing lawsuits, inaccurate surveys, and poor recordkeeping. The unification of the two Jerseys in 1702 had no effect on the lingering controversies, and by 1745, possession of nearly a half-million acres was contested, affecting the lives of thousands of individuals. In his analysis of early American radicalism, historian Gary Nash described the connection between land and conflict: "Coming from Europe, where land was scarce and beyond the grasp of most people, immigrants made the acquisition of cheap land and secure title to it their most treasured goal. Land was the holy grail, and control of it became a cause of incessant conflict—both with native peoples and the Europeans who coveted it."[51] Most historical accounts of early New Jersey attribute much of the controversy to the proprietors' insistence on quitrents from their settlers, but in his study of the crisis, Thomas Purvis suggested that, in light of the expanding spectrum of contentious issues, the quitrent dispute was relatively minor.[52] There certainly were wider matters of substance at stake, including the vision of how New Jersey should be structured. The proprietors, most of whom were Scottish, considered their royal titles irrevocable and envisioned New Jersey as their personal fiefdom, where they would lord over deferential tenant farmers and indentured servants. The yeomen, a more diverse constituency, foresaw an egalitarian community of freehold titles based upon their Indian deeds and improvement of untamed lands. But as both Nash and Brendan McConville, who wrote the most comprehensive study of New Jersey's land riots, noted, religious differences also played their part. While the majority of the proprietors were Anglican, the yeomen were mostly Congregational, Baptist, Quaker, and Presbyterian. The yeomen were also greatly influenced by the Great Awakening that spread throughout New Jersey during the 1720s, preaching a new democratizing spirituality and "provid[ing] a potent language with which to contest the gentry's position in property disputes."[53] Given the severely polarized positions in New Jersey, perhaps it was inevitable that these volatile issues would eventually stoke the fires of hostility and violence.

Between 1735 and 1745, in response to the ejectment suits filed by the proprietors, crowds of yeomen began to either defend dispossessed yeomen, or rise against proprietary claimants and surveyors with increasing acts of violence. Surviving documents do not provide specific details of these generally non-lethal assaults on persons and property. McConville noted that 22 of 36 known incidents during this period were directed against proprietary tenants settled on property claimed by local yeomen with non-proprietary titles. He also suggested that at this stage, the yeomen rioters were led by a woman of Dutch extraction, Magdalena Valleau, and, because Dutch women were especially active in public life, her leadership can be understood as "an assertion of Dutch cultural, gender, and legal norms in a rapidly Anglicizing world."[54]

Typical of the yeomen riots was action taken during the spring of 1740 against Samuel Brower, a proprietary tenant who lived in the Ramapo Tract. Wishing to drive him away and force the abandonment of his claim, a crowd of rioters forcibly entered his home, threw out his family, and proceeded to pull down his house.[55]

By 1745, similar land riots had become commonplace, and disaffected yeomen everywhere sought to consolidate the anti-proprietor movement. Consequently, having previously relied on local committees to provide legal representation, the scattered yeomen established a coalition in late 1745 by creating an extralegal unicameral assembly to centralize and represent their interests.[56] From that point forward, rioting intensified and, as the proprietary board of East New Jersey lamented, rioters, "to the great damage and terror of the people," were akin to "a torrent bearing down all before them & trampling upon all law & authority."[57] In September 1745, Samuel Baldwin of Newark, a leader of the resistance movement, was arrested for trespassing on proprietary lands. Soon thereafter, a crowd of 150 appeared at the Newark jail, and, when the sheriff refused to free Baldwin, the crowd, armed with clubs, axes, crowbars, and cudgels, stormed the jail and freed Baldwin. As the jubilant yeomen rioters departed, they warned the sheriff not to seek warrants against them or they would return with 100 Indian allies in tow, despite the fact there were only two known Indians living within a 50-mile radius of Newark.[58] This type of jailbreak, or "rescue riot," introduced a new element to the anti-proprietary campaign, one that would be repeated over and over again, with similar results. Four months later, when three yeomen were arrested for their participation in Baldwin's rescue, rioters freed one prisoner in transit and another 300 advanced on the Newark jail. There, they confronted a cowed militia, most of whom deserted their ranks and, instead, stood alongside the rioters. The bolstered rioters then stormed the enfeebled militia, assaulted the sheriff, and freed the two remaining prisoners. Nearly two years later, some 200 rioters, accompanied by fiddlers and "armed with Clubs and Staves to the great Terrour of the Inhabitants . . . marched on Foot in a Warlike Manner" into Perth Amboy to rescue John Bainbridge, who had been arrested for rioting. After assaulting and seriously injuring the sheriff, mayor, and other officials, the rioters broke open the jail door, freed Bainbridge, and carried him off, to rousing cheers.[59]

From mid-1747 to 1752, there were at least another dozen rescue riots, forcing the New Jersey Assembly to pass a riot act that called for stiff punishment of offenders, but also contained provisions for pardons, should repentant yeomen admit their guilt and offer to make amends. Very few rioters accepted the terms. While the rescue riots were certainly violent and undermined proprietary authority, they were primarily aimed at liberating detained compatriots, as opposed to intimidating a wider public. There were, however, acts that precisely delivered this type of impact: crowd assaults on persons in order to eject them from contested lands. As early as 1735, families were routinely and violently evicted from their property and houses, which were often destroyed in the process. The infamous case of Joseph Dalrymple, a proprietary client living on lands claimed by yeomen with Indian titles, was fairly typical. Late one night in March 1747, Dalrymple and his pregnant wife were startled to hear knocks on their door. Although the stranger outside requested only a light for his pipe, Dalrymple, cognizant of recent eviction riots in the area, immediately realized that rioters had come to dispossess him. He denied the rioters entry, but they quickly pried the door open, entered the house, and ordered him out, grabbing his wife in the process, despite her delicate condition. Only then did a neutral party plead on behalf of the frightened woman, who, as was pointed out, could not possibly tolerate nights without shelter. After a short deliberation, the rioters gave Dalrymple 14 days to vacate the property. When, after two weeks, he still refused to budge, approximately 30 rioters broke down his door, carried Dalrymple and his wife outside, threw out all of their possessions, and turned the empty house and attendant property over to others.[60]

By 1746, rioters in Newark had dispossessed several families living on tracts claimed by John Burnett, a proprietary client. In Bergen County, a dozen rioters threatened a proprietary claimant, Edward Jeffers, with eviction, until he reluctantly negotiated a seven-year agreement. In 1747, threats of a similar riot against Justice Daniel Cooper forced local military officers to supply him with more than 100 armed men to protect his life and property; the rioters declined a confrontation. Abraham Phillips, a proprietary claimant, was not as fortunate. In 1749, six rioters besieged his property, tearing down fences, scattering livestock, uprooting crops, and pulling down the roof of his house.[61] These types of riots, as well as attacks on survey parties, had a much broader impact because of the many thousands of persons living on similarly contested lands. Depending on individual circumstances, people responded to the riots in different ways. Many elected to stand by their original claims, but some, like Jeffers, came to terms with the yeomen coalition; others sought protection by purchasing proprietary titles, even if they were already in possession of conflicting proprietary deeds. Still others chose to abandon their contested lands. In areas such as Somerset, the population dropped significantly as families fled to avoid further conflict, evidence that the rioters were indeed impacting a wider target audience.[62]

Aside from the psychological impact of the eviction riots, the antagonists in New Jersey also attacked each other in competing propaganda campaigns, extending the war of lands to a war of words. Because New Jersey had no newspapers, the deep-pocketed proprietors often used the pages of the *New York Weekly Post-Boy* to articulate their political positions, while the yeomen coalition tended to rely on pamphlets, many of which were published by Anna Catherine Zenger, wife of noted publisher John Peter Zenger. The yeomen also found support in the 1746 publication of *A Brief Vindication of the Purchasers Against the Proprietors in a Christian Manner*, a semi-religious tract by Griffen Jenkins that forcefully advocated the validity of Indian titles. Such was the impact of Jenkins's work that the proprietors thought it necessary to respond with their own four-part rebuttal in the *Post-Boy*.[63] By then, the opposing positions were known to all who cared. The proprietors continued to maintain that, despite some errors in recordkeeping, the original Nicholls/Indian titles were illegal under provincial law, and that the rioters were defying royal authority in very un-Christian-like ways. From the yeoman perspective, the proprietors were greedy and unscrupulous tyrants who sought to steal land that was legally purchased and improved by God-fearing people.

While propaganda helped publicize the differences in land policy between proprietors and yeomen, cast by historians as a morality play between villains and victims, both the diversity of the New Jersey settlers and the complexity of their situations defy such a simplistic explanation of their disaccord. As Thomas Purvis pointed out, the Board of East Jersey Proprietors actively sought to negotiate an amicable agreement with the ElizabethTown Associates and chose to exclude ElizabethTown lands from ejection actions filed elsewhere. Further, the gentry class in New Jersey was not necessarily allied at all times with the proprietary interests, as there was occasional covert collusion between yeomen rioters and members of the local gentry whose property was also jeopardized by proprietary lawsuits. As discussed above, this type of alliance between patricians and plebians was not unusual. Rudé found this element in European riots, and other historians have discovered this relationship in various forms of American collective violence, including, as this study maintains, campaigns of terrorism. These patrician leaders believed in their right to challenge unjust authority that threatened public welfare, as long as such protests were conducted with restraint. Thus, Purvis saw the New Jersey land riots as "civil disturbances . . . which were *extra-institutional* in character more often than they were anti-institutional." Indeed, Purvis downplayed these riots, defining them as defensive in character, limited in scope, reactive, well-disciplined, and conducted with a minimum of violence.[64]

While it is misleading to speak of the proprietary interests as if they represented a political monolith, the yeomen coalition also suffered from tenuous and often-shifting alliances that undermined its solidarity. Amos Roberts, who assumed a greater leadership role in 1747 following the early years of Magdalena Valleau, was eventually challenged by a more conservative element among the yeomen, forcing him to establish a new coalition only a year later. Still, this muddled political landscape does not negate the fact that, in hindsight, the violence perpetrated in New Jersey appears to have incorporated rudimentary elements of terrorism in both its intent and impact. Despite Purvis's attempt to downplay yeomen violence, emphasizing instead the restraint demonstrated by rioters, the repercussions of their hostile attacks should not be underestimated. If they were not significant, why would proprietary allies speak of New Jersey's "dangerous and terrible insurrection" and of the "ruin and destruction" perpetrated by rioters?[65] Beyond the violence, yeomen rioters also created a propaganda campaign to generate publicity and spread their political messages. As a group, they devised a hierarchical organization that enabled systematic and purposeful action. There were times when rioters demonstrated a sense of theatre, witness the rescue riot for John Bainbridge wherein rioters were accompanied by fiddlers and a pennant-bearer. Yet, despite all of these elements, one hesitates to categorize the New Jersey land rioters as a terrorist organization. The distinction is subtle but meaningful. The New Jersey rioters constituted an amorphous combination with no real group identity. As noted above, the yeomen coalition created a semblance of leadership but suffered from political fractures and in-fighting. And because the lands in question were spread throughout most of northern New Jersey, and the contention for them involved thousands of persons over several decades, the rioters never maintained a sustained, consistent form of group protest. Instead, there was an ebb and flow with up and down years of riotous activity. Further, Purvis's characterization of the riots as reactive, and thus defensive, in nature is certainly valid when strictly applied to the rescue riots that dominated the yeoman agenda from 1745 on. After that point, rioters were seemingly more determined to liberate their allies from jail than intimidate their communities. Even then, after the yeomen coalition weakened in 1748, rescue rioters became less numerous, less emboldened, and less theatrical in their actions. One Newark riot appeared more surreal than frightening when the liberated prisoners quickly turned themselves back in, "convinced of the illegality of their proceedings."[66] In the end, rioters in New Jersey employed some of the tactics that would eventually serve as the foundation for future campaigns of terrorism elsewhere, but would never combine these strategies in a persistent and calculated fashion. Moreover, these tactics were often directed at immediate victims rather than wider target audiences and therefore cannot be defined as violent propaganda. The New Jersey riots were more a hostile but sporadic response to a seemingly intractable stalemate that endured for more than 80 years and embraced half a colony.

V. Afterword

By the early-1750s, the violence had begun to wane in New Jersey. The land controversies remained, but external circumstances had changed. Rather than fight claimants in court, proprietors and New Jersey Governor Jonathan Belcher employed a more paternalistic approach toward the yeomen, hoping to induce cooperation. Meanwhile, more conservative elements seized control of the yeomen coalition, also seeking an end to the riots. A brief recurrence of the violence took place in 1769–70, but by then the anti-proprietary movement had become increasingly usurped by the emerging anti-authoritarian and Whig-like rhetoric that would fuel the American Revolution. When a majority of the proprietary gentry sided with England during the Revolution, they ultimately forfeited their titles in the wake of the war.

In retrospect, the New Jersey land controversies, far more impactful than other forms of rioting, can be viewed as a bridge connecting the early colonial traditions of insurrections and riots to the terrorism engendered by the approaching American Revolution. Americans, borrowing from European customs and the tenets of natural law, had embraced the right of popular protest and accepted the obligation of challenging unjust authority. With a sense of bravado and impunity, they had toppled recognized governments, plundered civilian property, battled officers of the king, abused local governors, dispossessed families, and torched a town. But, the psychological impact on the many engendered by violence against a few was only then beginning to be understood by resistance leaders. By the early 1760s, this willingness to employ fear as a weapon against an entire community was strengthened by the popular protests then circulating throughout the colonies, creating a political and social context in which terrorism would eventually emerge.

Notes

1. Timothy B. Riordan, *The Plundering Time—Maryland and the English Civil War, 1645–1646* (Baltimore: Maryland Historical Society, 2004), 94.
2. Armstrong Starkey, *European and Native American Warfare, 1675–1815* (Norman: University of Oklahoma Press, 1999); John Grenier, *The First Way of War* (Cambridge, UK: Cambridge University Press, 2005), 1–12.
3. Grenier, *The First Way of War,* 10.
4. Richard Maxwell Brown, *The South Carolina Regulators* (Cambridge, MA: The Belknap Press of Harvard University Press, 1963).
5. Pauline Maier, *From Resistance to Revolution* (New York: Vantage Books, 1974); Margaret C. Jacob and James R. Jacob, eds., *The Origins of Anglo-American Radicalism* (Atlantic Highlands, NJ: Humanities Press, Int. Inc., 1991); Richard Maxwell Brown and Don E. Fehrenbacher, eds., *Tradition, Conflict and Modernization—Perspectives on the American Revolution* (New York: Academic Press, 1977); Alfred F. Young, "English Plebian Culture and 18th-Century American Radicalism," in Jacob and Jacob, *The Origins of Anglo-American Radicalism,* 185–212.
6. Maier, *From Resistance to Revolution,* 27–29.
7. Nicholas N. Kittrie and Eldon D. Wedlock, Jr., *The Tree of Liberty—A Documentary History of Rebellion and Political Crime in the United States* (Baltimore: The Johns Hopkins University Press, 1988).
8. Paul A. Gilje, *Rioting in America* (Bloomington: Indiana University Press, 1996), 21.
9. Ibid., Dirk Hoerder, *Crowd Action in Revolutionary Massachusetts, 1765–1780* (New York: Academic Press, 1977), 22.
10. Maier, *From Resistance to Revolution,* 28.
11. Young, "English Plebian Culture and 18th-Century American Radicalism," 206.
12. Ibid., 189–194; Jack Tager, *Boston Riots—Three Centuries of Social Violence* (Boston: Northeastern University Press, 2001) 41–51; Paul A. Gilje, *The Road to Mobocracy—Popular Disorder in New York City, 1763–1834* (Chapel Hill, University of North Carolina Press, 1987) 23–30, 39–40.
13. George Rudé, review of Pauline Maier, *William and Mary Quarterly,* 3rd ser., 30 (1973): 153.
14. Young, "English Plebian Culture and 18th-Century American Radicalism," 186.
15. Gary B. Nash, *The Urban Crucible—Social Change, Political Consciousness, and the Origins of the American Revolution* (Cambridge: Harvard University Press, 1979) 49.
16. Richard Maxwell Brown, *Strain of Violence* (New York: Oxford University Press, 1975).
17. Riordan, *The Plundering Time,* 193.
18. Ibid., 207; J. Thomas Scharf, *History of Maryland—From the Earliest Period to the Present Day* (Hatboro, PA., Tradition Press, 1967), 144–152.
19. For a brief historiography on Bacon, see Michael Leroy Oberg, ed., *Samuel Wiseman's Book of Record—The Official Account of Bacon's Rebellion in Virginia, 1676–1677* (New York: Lexington Books, 2005), 22–25. Basic reading on Bacon includes Wilcomb

Washburn, *The Governor and the Rebel–A History of Bacon's Rebellion in Virginia* (Chapel Hill: University of North Carolina Press, 1957); Thomas Jefferson Wertenbaker, *Torchbearer of the Revolution—The Story of Bacon's Rebellion and Its Leader* (Princeton: Princeton University Press, 1940); Warren M. Billings, *Sir William Berkeley and the Forging of Virginia* (Baton Rouge: Louisiana State University Press, 2004); Charles Maclean Andrews, ed., *Narratives of the Insurrections, 1675–1690* (New York: Scribner, 1915)

20. Washburn, *The Governor and the Rebel,* 37.
21. Alfred A. Cave, *Lethal Encounters—Englishmen and Indians in Colonial Virginia* (Santa Barbara: Praeger, 2011), 171.
22. Washburn, *The Governor and the Rebel,* 57–60.
23. Cave, *Lethal Encounters,* 162; Oberg, *Samuel Wiseman's Book of Record,* 20.
24. Washburn, *The Governor and the Rebel,* 83.
25. Cave, *Lethal Encounters,* 163.
26. George Rudé, *The Crowd in History.*
27. Gilje, *Rioting in America,* 4.
28. Charles Tilly, "Collective Action in England and America, 1765–1775," in Brown and Fehrenbacher, 63.
29. Gilje, *Rioting in America,* 50.
30. Ibid., 25.
31. Maier, *From Resistance to Revolution,* 28–33.
32. John Fiske, *Old Virginia and Its Neighbors,* vol. 2 (Boston: Houghton, Mifflin and Co., 1897), 112.
33. Alan Kulikoff, *Tobacco and Slaves—The Development of Southern Cultures in the Chesapeake, 1680–1800* (Chapel Hill: University of North Carolina Press, 1986), 110–115.
34. Ibid.; John Andrew Doyle, *English Colonies in America: Virginia and Maryland* (New York: Henry Holt and Co., 1889), 261–262.
35. Gilje, *Rioting in America,* 28; Tager, *Boston Riots,* 14–15, 26–38.
36. Hoerder, *Crowd Action in Revolutionary Massachusetts,* 54–55.
37. Ibid.; Gilje, *Rioting in America,* 23; Tager, *Boston Riots,* 41–51.
38. Strother E. Roberts, "Pines, Profits, and Popular Politics: Responses to the White Pine Acts in the Colonial Connecticut River Valley," *New England Quarterly,* vol. 83, no. 1 (March, 2010): 73–101.
39. Tager, *Boston Riots,* 64.
40. Ibid., 73.
41. Ibid., 52–75; Maier, 10–13; Gilje, *Rioting in America,* 31; Gary B. Nash, *The Unknown American Revolution—The Unruly Birth of Democracy and the Struggle to Create America* (New York: Penguin Group, 2005), 18; John Lax and William Pencak, "The Knowles Riot and the Crisis of the 1740s in Massachusetts," *Perspectives in American History,* vol. 10 (1976): 163–214.
42. Jesse Lemisch, "Jack Tar in the Streets: Merchant Seamen in the Politics of the American Revolution," *William and Mary Quarterly,* Third Series, vol. 25, no. 3 (July, 1968): 383–384.
43. Ibid., 396.
44. Elizabeth A. Fenn, *Pox Americana—The Great Smallpox Epidemic of 1775–1782* (New York: Hill and Wang, 2001), 13–28.
45. Ibid., 42.
46. Patrick Henderson, "Smallpox and Patriotism—The Norfolk Riots, 1768–1769," *The Virginia Magazine of History and Biography,* vol. 73, no. 4 (October, 1965): 413–424.
47. Ibid., 424.

48. Gilje, *The Road to Mobocracy,* 16; Gilje, *Rioting in America,* 30.
49. Gilje, *Rioting in America,* 29.
50. Thomas L. Purvis, "Origins and Patterns of Agrarian Unrest in New Jersey, 1734–1754," *William and Mary Quarterly,* vol. 39 (1982): 603–604.
51. Nash, *The Unknown American Revolution,* 4.
52. Purvis, "Origins and Patterns of Agrarian Unrest in New Jersey," 610–614.
53. Nash, *The Unknown American Revolution,* 6; Brendan McConville, *These Daring Disturbers of the Public Peace—The Struggle for Property and Power in Early New Jersey* (Philadelphia: University of Pennsylvania Press, 1999).
54. McConville, *These Daring Disturbers,* 125.
55. The Minutes of the Board of Proprietors of the Eastern Division of New Jersey from 1735–1744, vol. 2, published by the General Board of Proprietors of the Eastern Division of New Jersey (Perth Amboy, 1960), 112. Hereafter referred to as "Board of Proprietors."
56. McConville, *These Daring Disturbers,* 144.
57. Board of Proprietors, vol. 3, 150; McConville, *These Daring Disturbers,* 156.
58. William Adee Whitehead, ed., *Documents Relating to the Colonial History of the State of New Jersey,* vol. VI, 1738–1747 (Newark: Daily Advertising Printing, 1882), 398–404, hereafter referred to as "New Jersey Archives"; Board of Proprietors, vol. 3, 90; Gary S. Horowitz, *New Jersey Land Riots,* (PhD Dissertation, The Ohio State University, 1966), 67–69.
59. New Jersey Archives, 456–470; McConville, *These Daring Disturbers,* 137; Horowitz, *New Jersey Land Riots,* 88.
60. New Jersey Archives, 427–432; McConville, *These Daring Disturbers,* 159–160; Horowitz, *New Jersey Land Riots,* 85–87.
61. Horowitz, *New Jersey Land Riots,* 83–84, 139; New Jersey Archives, 426.
62. McConville, *These Daring Disturbers,* 134.
63. Board of Proprietors, vol. 3, 61–62; Horowitz, *New Jersey Land Riots,* 69; McConville, *These Daring Disturbers,* 87–88.
64. Purvis, "Origins and Patterns of Agrarian Unrest in New Jersey," 624.
65. Horowitz, *New Jersey Land Riots,* 89.
66. McConville, *These Daring Disturbers,* 178.

2

THE NORTH CAROLINA REGULATORS

I. Background

By the early 1760s, population growth in the colonies, combined with the allure of the West, would create strains on British authority. A number of controversies were associated with westward migration into the colonial backcountry stretching from Maine to the Carolinas, where conflicting land claims, economic and social polarization, and challenges to governmental authority would not only severely test British officials determined to establish royal control, but would ultimately prove troublesome to American authorities as well, come independence. Many of these issues would eventually lead to the almost simultaneous formation during the 1760s and 1770s of four resistance movements that employed terrorist tactics: the North Carolina Regulators, the Green Mountain Boys of Vermont, the first wave of anti-rent insurgents in New York, and the Sons of Liberty. Because the Regulators were the first to meet their ultimate demise, the narrative concerning the historical origins of terrorism in America begins in the isolated backcountry of North Carolina.

White settlement of North Carolina did not begin in earnest until the second decade of the 18th century, when a series of wars devastated the Tuscarora Indians. Quickly, despite continued Cherokee threats to the west, North Carolina's three distinct natural regions began to fill with settlers: the coastal plain, the mountains along the western border, and the Piedmont in between. It was in the Piedmont where a number of insurgents known as the Regulators began a three-year campaign of terror against local authorities. Given the area's relative isolation, compounded by the lack of wide, navigable rivers, life in the Piedmont during the colonial era proved exceedingly difficult. As a result, Piedmont settlers were almost totally self-sufficient. Adding to their considerable problems, these settlers felt particularly exploited by local authorities, who collected exorbitant taxes and pocketed most of the public funds. Having failed to instigate change through legitimate political means, resisters began to call themselves *regulators*, signaling their intention to regulate or reform these grievous social conditions. The term *regulator* had been commonplace since first used in England in 1655 to refer to someone appointed to adjust government malfunctioning.[1] For three years, the Regulators refused to pay taxes, prevented the work of land surveyors, and obstructed the judicial system, all the while employing violent methods to intimidate the government of Royal Governor William Tryon and members of the broader community. The resistance movement eventually came to an abrupt and decisive end when government troops under Tryon's command defeated a combined force of Regulators near the Great Alamance Creek in May 1771.

The Regulators of the North Carolina Piedmont should not be confused with the similarly named South Carolina Regulators, a group that started out as a vigilante movement but eventually morphed into a backcountry combination of self-government and social control.[2] In fact, beyond the common name, there were few similarities between the causes, strategies, and outcomes of the two movements. And while the North Carolina Regulators apparently took their name and inspiration from their southern neighbors, there is no evidence of any cooperation between the two. An overview of historians' treatment of the Regulators of the Piedmont will help define a broad analytical context in which to appreciate fully their impact and legacy. The first scholarly accounts of the Regulator rebellion were produced by 19th-century Whig historians such as John Hill Wheeler (1851), George Bancroft (1855), and John Fiske (1891). These accounts, some very brief, others more detailed, tended to portray the Regulators in sympathetic terms, suggesting in particular that the War of the Regulation should be more broadly considered within the context of the American War for Independence.[3] It was Wheeler who argued that the Battle of Alamance represented "the first blood spilled in these United States, in resistance to exactions of English rulers, and oppressions by the English government."[4] Fiske maintained that, had the Battle of Alamance ended differently, it would have assumed significance equal to that of Lexington and Concord.[5] As George Adams pointed out, these Whig interpretations reflected the patriotic zeal that characterized most 19th-century historians.[6] Nonetheless, as late as 1949, William S. Powell continued to argue that the Regulators prompted the armed resistance that would later ignite the American Revolution.[7]

By the 20th century, two additional schools of thought began to emerge. Many historians, including progressives such as Frederick Jackson Turner (1920), saw the War of the Regulation as a manifestation of class conflict—a violent confrontation between the poor backcountry farmers and the colonial elite.[8] Elisha Douglas (1955) and Marvin L. Michael Kaye (1965) similarly traced the Regulator movement to the exploitation of the oppressed lower classes by wealthy property owners and government officials.[9] Others, however, viewed the War of the Regulation as part of an east-west sectional struggle between the isolated and politically underrepresented backcountry and the more populous and powerful coastal plain. John Spencer Bassett first broached the subject of sectionalism in his classic treatment of the Regulators, published in 1894.[10] Samuel Eliot Morrison and Henry Steele Commager later confirmed this point in their popular survey text published in 1950, as did Hugh Talmage Lefler and Albert Ray Newsome in their 1954 history of North Carolina.[11] At first glance, it is easy to see how these two more recent interpretations have gained adherents. At a very simplistic level, the War of the Regulation did contain sectional elements, as well as factors related to class conflict. However, the Regulator movement was anything but simple, and many elements are, in fact, difficult to understand. Not all anti-Regulators were rich, and the Regulators themselves drew strength from every rank of Piedmont society. Some were large landowners. Hermon Husband, said to be the leader of the Regulators, accumulated nearly 11,000 acres near the Deep River region of Orange County. The wealthiest Regulator, Thomas Person, owned 23 slaves and more than 20,000 acres.[12] There is much similar evidence that seems to contradict a strict class analysis. Moreover, what can we make of a sectional theory when many of the government's militia who opposed the Regulators at Alamance came from counties in the Piedmont? They were offered 40 schillings for their military service, but that alone does not explain their choice of battle lines. The evidence, or lack of it, is inconclusive on this point. Many westerners actually opposed the violent methods of the Regulators and, as James Whittenburg suggested in a 1977 article, given the many backcountry settlements and connecting roads, the isolation of the Piedmont from the coastal plain wasn't nearly as onerous as many believed, further undermining the theory of an east-west dichotomy.[13]

Still, the perception of class or sectional tensions persists. So does the belief that the War of the Regulation should be properly connected to the American Revolution, despite the fact that most historians acknowledge that the Regulators opposed not British authority but certain local officials who exploited their positions in the royal government. Time and time again, the Regulators swore their loyalty to the king, subverting the notion that their activities represented an open revolt against the Crown. There is also widespread speculation that many who led the anti-Regulator coalition at Alamance eventually became leading patriots during the War for Independence. Regardless, old notions die hard, particularly patriotic ones, and even modern-day visitors to the Alamance battleground site who absorb the information on old monument plaques are left with the impression that the Revolution did, indeed, start in the Piedmont, not New England. Nonetheless, recent historians tend to view the Regulator rebellion not as part of the Revolution, nor as a clash between sections or classes. Many see the Regulators purely as a local response to immediate and specific backcountry grievances that plagued the Piedmont. George Adams made this point in a historiographical essay in 1972.[14] Whittenburg suggested that the War of the Regulation was actually an old-fashioned power struggle *within* the Piedmont, pitting old planters against a newly arriving class of merchants, lawyers, and royal officials "in the perennial pursuit of gain."[15] From the historian's viewpoint, what has made this historiographical debate so much more contentious is that, prior to 1980, most previous research and writing on the Regulators had been presented in short monograph form; no book-length treatment of the Regulators had yet been produced. The standard works continued to be John Spencer Bassett's 70-page article published in 1894 and William S. Powell's 20-page account from 1949. Since 1980, however, three major books have appeared that tell the Regulator story from distinctly different approaches. One, by A. Roger Ekirch, detailed the larger context of North Carolina culture and politics, and another, by Wayne E. Lee, described the larger, evolving culture of violence. Only one, a study by Marjoleine Kars, devoted itself entirely to the Regulator rebellion.

The first of the major studies to appear was A. Roger Ekirch's *Poor Carolina: Politics and Society in Colonial North Carolina, 1729–1776,* which was published in 1981. Owing to the works of Bernard Bailyn and Pauline Maier, Ekirch focused on ideology, noting that the Regulators developed an ideology of resistance founded on Whig notions of liberty and legitimate protest. Discounting class antagonisms, Ekirch argued that the corruption of particular office holders ultimately undermined longstanding basic rights, thereby legitimizing violent resistance.[16] Two decades after Ekirch's study, Marjoleine Kars's *Breaking Loose Together: The Regulator Rebellion in Pre-Revolutionary North Carolina* (2002) became the only book-length treatment to focus exclusively on the War of the Regulation. Kars saw the Regulators as early populists, oppressed agrarians fighting for basic democratic rights such as secret ballots, taxation reform, and governmental accountability. Kars further argued that the Regulators should be understood as products of the Great Awakening and Protestant revivalism, which contributed to a "creative and subversive religious climate" that ultimately sustained the resistance movement. As far as the backcountry farmers were concerned, economic wealth, while not itself objectionable, did not absolve one from moral obligations to the community. The Protestant insistence on moral responsibility, combined with Whig ideologies of legitimate dissent, provided a justification for the Regulator rebellion.[17]

One year before Kars's exhaustive and seminal study, Wayne E. Lee's *Crowds and Soldiers in Revolutionary North Carolina* detailed the War of the Regulation as part of a larger analysis of North Carolina's culture of violence. Borrowing from George Rudé's influential studies of European riots, Lee saw the War of the Regulation as part of a wider effort to define the limits of justifiable resistance. Both the Regulators and their government adversaries recognized the importance of public perception and labored mightily to spin the details of their bloody confrontation in ways that would legitimize their particular methods and responses to the crisis. This point is particularly relevant, for, the terroristic methods of the Regulators notwithstanding, the repressive anti-Regulator tactics employed by Governor Tryon could be loosely construed as terroristic, as well. Lee's emphasis on the evolving culture of violence, quite understandably, connects with this particular study, yet he and all other historians, with the exception of John Spencer Bassett, have studiously avoided the term *terrorism* in their narratives and analyses of the Regulators.[18] This study places the Piedmont resisters within the paradigm of *terrorism* established above and argues that the Regulators should be considered among the very first American terrorists.

II. Early Origins of Backcountry Resistance

When North Carolina became a royal colony in 1729, its settlers were largely English and confined to the coastal plain in cities such as New Bern, Bath, Edenton, and Brunswick. By the late-1750s, the population had swelled with German, Scot Highlander, and Scot-Irish immigrants, most of whom settled west, in the Piedmont. Much of the northern half of the Piedmont belonged to Lord Earl Granville, an absentee landowner who never once set eyes on his domain in North Carolina. This absentee ownership represented the first of many problems for the local settlers, for it meant that all transactions had to be conducted with Granville's agents, most of whom proved alarmingly dishonest. In particular, Francis Corbin was an unmitigated disaster. Over time, Corbin and his close circle of co-conspirators held multiple positions of power, charged excessive legal fees, double-charged for quitrents, sold identical pieces of property to multiple buyers, conducted duplicitous surveys, and kept virtually no records of legal transactions. Moreover, he openly disregarded orders from Granville himself, prompting a reprimand in 1756. Yet, Corbin stayed on the job. Local petitions to the Assembly against Corbin prompted an investigation that uncovered widespread fraud and corruption; still, no legal action was taken against Corbin and his associates.[19] It was at this point, after means of legal redress had been exhausted, that British popular traditions that justified violent resistance took hold in the Piedmont.[20]

When Corbin's chief deputy, John Haywood, suddenly died, local residents exhumed his body to verify that Haywood had not feigned his own death in order to escape prosecution. Then, during the night of January 25, 1759, several rioters detained Corbin's co-agent Joshua Bodley in Enfield, while some two dozen others traveled to Corbin's home near Edenton, kidnapped the shocked agent, and forced him to travel the nearly 70 miles to his offices in Enfield. The four-day captivity of Corbin and Bodley became known as the Enfield Riot, although neither captive was harmed and no property was damaged. Corbin and Bodley were eventually released after signing, undoubtedly under much duress, articles promising to adjust economic affairs, to return misappropriated funds, and to establish guidelines for future disputes. Hardly a riot, the Corbin affair was remarkable for its restraint.[21] Nonetheless, the desecration of Haywood's grave and the subsequent seizure of Corbin and Bodley were clear signs that something was amiss in the Piedmont, and, accordingly, the Assembly offered a reward of 25 pounds sterling for any information leading to the arrest of those responsible for recent "riots, routs, combinations, and conspiracies."[22] Although Governor

Arthur Dobbs was convinced of Corbin's guilt, he succeeded in arresting a few of Corbin's abductors. They were quickly freed, however, during a rescue riot conducted by a group of sympathizers. Corbin was subsequently fired by Granville, and, in early 1760, Dobbs banned Corbin from positions of local power.

While the confrontation between insurgents and Frances Corbin brewed in the Granville District, settler grievances were arising elsewhere in the southern Piedmont. Newcomers from Virginia and Pennsylvania were flooding into Mecklenburg and Cumberland counties, and illegally squatting on land owned by Henry McCulloh, Sr., George Selwyn, and Governor Dobbs. These squatters had difficulty understanding how absentee landlords who did nothing to improve their holdings could possess wild lands. An early attempt by McCulloh to survey his property in Rowan County had been cancelled in 1755, when a survey party was confronted by a group of men armed with guns, swords, and clubs, who threatened to "break the bones" of the surveyors should they attempt to draw lines. About the same time, squatters along the Sugar and Sandy creeks in Mecklenburg County abused and insulted the local sheriff when he attempted to collect taxes. When the sheriff responded by raising a posse, a group of squatters beat and wounded several lawmen.[23] When, in 1762, this same group of settlers found their lands surveyed by Dobbs's agent, a half-dozen rioters confronted the survey team and threatened its members with bodily harm. For the next three years, the squatter community would continue to resist survey attempts and ejection orders. Marjoleine Kars noted that indictments issued against the rioters could not be executed, "by reason of the threats and frequent abuses committed upon the officers of justice."[24] The spirit of resistance was beginning to spread intimidation and fear.

Meanwhile, in 1764, Henry Eustace McCulloh became George Selwyn's agent in the Sugar Creek area. He immediately began to draw survey lines and issue notices of ejection to uncooperative settlers who refused to negotiate rents on his terms. A series of contentious negotiations with the Sugar Creek settlers failed to produce a mutually agreeable compromise on rent prices. In response to grievances filed by the disgruntled squatters, William Tryon, who succeeded the recently deceased Arthur Dobbs as governor, ordered McCulloh in early 1765 to cease his attempts to survey lands or dispossess settlers until the Assembly could investigate. On May 7, McCulloh, completely disregarding these orders, sent a seven-man survey team into the Sylwyn tract. There, they were confronted by a dozen men disguised with blackened faces, who proceeded to beat and whip the surveyors, leaving one victim with a cracked skull. McCulloh was convinced that had he accompanied the survey team, he would've been murdered. In a letter to his close friend Edmund Fanning two days later, McCulloh wrote of the "horror" created by the rioters' behavior and appearance, and confessed that, because he could not travel the woods "without the justest apprehensions of being murdered," he had become "mad enough to do anything." He drew up a will the very next day. Thus ended a local episode that McCulloh dubbed "the War of the Sugar Creek."[25]

The so-called Sugar Creek War may be inappropriately titled and largely forgotten, but Wayne E. Lee noted that this violent confrontation represented a distinct departure in the tactics of resistance. In particular, the use of whipping, while not unknown in England as a form of judicial punishment, began to assume new meaning in America, evolving into "a colonial innovation in the rituals of riot." In this instance, whipping became a communal form of justice, meted out at the local level. Moreover, whipping was the penalty of choice in naval and military contexts; consequently, whipping contributed "to a growing impression of military imagery in riotous behavior and its pretentions to legitimacy."[26] Another point here is also relevant. The Sugar Creek rioters intimidated not only land agents but also neighbors who agreed to McCulloh's terms, for any crack in the solidarity of the settlers undermined the impact of resistance. The Sugar Creek rioters were using violence and intimidation not only to resist one particular agent but also to spread a broader message across the community at large.

But what, exactly, was this message? Certainly, the settlers had made their grievances known through their petitions to the Assembly. One month after the Sugar Creek confrontation, these same grievances were articulated in the *Nutbush Paper,* written by George Sims, a schoolmaster who hailed from the Nutbush area of the Granville District. Sims railed against excessive legal fees, lamenting that "a poor man works more than twenty-seven days to pay for one minute's writing ... nineteen days more to cover attorney's fees, and another nineteen days to pay the local sheriff." On top of all that, he added, "you may go home to see your horses and cow sold and all your personal estate for one-tenth part of the value, to pay off your merchant." Sims warned, "these cursed hungry caterpillars will eat out the very bowels of our commonwealth if they are not pulled down from their nests." Change, according to Sims, would result only from communal resistance and solidarity.[27]

Although the Regulators would not appear for another three years, a backdrop of defiance in the Piedmont had set the stage for a major resistance movement, one that would ultimately rely on terrorist tactics. Violence was commonplace. Fear and intimidation were spreading. Political grievances had been articulated, and a justification for legitimate resistance was gaining wide acceptance. Within a year, spurred on by the exhortations of the *Nutbush Paper,* the settlers along Sugar Creek would further commit themselves to terrorism as a form of collective resistance.

III.   The Regulators Appear

Aside from its violent context, the Sugar Creek War was an important development because of the additional impact it had on Governor Tryon and the Assembly. Greatly offended by the boldness of the rioters, the colonial government turned against the settlers and refused to consider their original petition. Meanwhile, Henry Eustace McCulloh took the offensive. He filed lawsuits against suspected resisters and pressed rioting charges against 47 of them. Accordingly, despite the fear of retaliation from rioters, many settlers deserted the cause and agreed to McCulloh's terms. By early 1766, the Sugar Creek crisis, already on the wane, was eclipsed by the larger colonial protest against Parliament's recent Stamp Act, further strengthening the spirit of popular resistance. In response to the Stamp Act protests in North Carolina, local judges refused to hear civil cases, creating a backlog that placed McCulloh's ejection suits in judicial limbo. In March, the charges against the suspected rioters were dropped. That same month, Parliament repealed the Stamp Act.

The Sons of Liberty, who were instrumental in preventing enforcement of the vexatious legislation, spurred successful demonstrations against the Stamp Act. The North Carolina Sons, who operated out of the Cape Fear area, were a particular source of inspiration to many settlers and rioters in the Piedmont; motivated by the efficacy of the colony-wide Stamp Act protests, the Carolina Sons orchestrated public demonstrations of their own in New Bern, Wilmington, and Cross Creek.[28] One interested observer of these events was Hermon Husband, a farmer and landowner from the Sandy Creek region of Orange County. A Quaker and pacifist, Husband was born in Maryland in 1724 but settled in North Carolina in 1755.[29] In 1766, Husband helped organize the Sandy Creek Association, a group of reformers who sought redress for their grievances through legitimate political channels. Both Husband and the Association, like the North Carolina Sons of Liberty, were very much impressed by the Stamp Act protests and emboldened by the power of popular resistance.

By now, the grievances of the Piedmont settlers were many and well known. Taxes were excessive and Governor Tryon reluctantly acknowledged that, "the sheriffs have embezzled more than one-half of the public money ordered to be raised and collected by them."[30] The absence of banks and the scarcity of hard currency created a reliance on personal loans that left homesteads at great risk. Sheriffs, judges, lawyers, and clerks often conspired to double charge for services rendered or to dispossess farmers of their holdings for debts unpaid. Compounding these problems was a political system based on patronage that allowed a small coterie of men to control virtually all public offices. As far as the Sandy Creek Association was concerned, all of these injustices were manifested in one man: Edmund Fanning—local attorney, register of deeds, judge of the Superior Court, colonel of the militia, and the aforementioned associate of Henry Eustace McCulloh. It would be the infamous Fanning who would ultimately fill the role of antagonist in the Regulator saga.

The Sandy Creek Association published a series of petitions and requested a face-to-face meeting with county officials, including Fanning. However, on the day of a scheduled meeting in October, Fanning declined to appear, refusing to cooperate in what he termed an "insurrection."[31] Harassed by Fanning and rebuffed in yet another attempt to have their grievances heard by the government, the Sandy Creek Association quickly dissolved. But disillusionment and resistance remained intact. Sometime in early 1768, from the seeds sown by the Sandy Creek Association, rose the Regulators, devoted to "Regulating publick Grievances & abuses of power."[32]

Inspired by both the Sons of Liberty and the South Carolina Regulators, the Piedmont rioters would now assume a new identity and a more militant form of resistance as they gradually transformed themselves into terrorists. Moreover, the Regulator movement would extend beyond Orange County to nearby Anson, Rowan, and Mecklenburg counties. Hermon Husband denied any participation in directing the Regulator movement, and he notoriously abandoned the battlefield before the Battle of Alamance, but independent sources confirmed his position of leadership, even as he tried to disavow himself of responsibility. He might not have sought direct participation or leadership, but the insurgents in Orange County very much looked to him for guidance. Certainly, Governor Tryon and Colonel Fanning were convinced of Husband's leadership role, having arrested him twice for directing seditious activities. Some suggest that, given the Regulators had no one publicly acknowledged leader, his role was essentially reduced to one of agitator and propagandist.[33] There does seem to be little disagreement about Husband having spent considerable effort voicing the need for moderation and peaceful compromise, not violent confrontation. Yet, his detractors at the time depicted Husband as depraved, seditious, ignorant, vulgar, and cowardly. Historians today consider him in far more generous terms, at least during his time in North Carolina—sober, honest, intelligent, industrious, and devout—and there is still a tendency to think of him as the very embodiment of the Regulator cause or, as one put it, the "heart and soul" of the movement.[34] This regard was at least partly due to Husband's authorship of the 1770 document most often cited as the best representation of the Regulator viewpoint, *A Continuation of the Impartial Relation of the First Rise and Cause of the Recent Differences in Publick Affairs in the Province of North Carolina.*[35]

The small circle of Regulator leadership was also said to include James Hunter, known to many as the "General of the Regulators." A man of action, a forceful speaker, and a deliverer of petitions, he would survive the Battle of Alamance and become a Whig assemblyman during the American Revolution. On occasion, Hunter was asked to represent the Regulators, and he often traveled among Regulator communities, providing legal advice. Such was the respect accorded him that he was entrusted by the Regulators to collect their taxes and to arbitrate grievances between farmers and officeholders. But he was a general in name only. At Alamance, as the Regulators prepared to confront Tryon's troops, he was asked to assume battlefield command but declined, reasoning that "they were all free men and every one must command himself."[36] Another key voice for the Regulators came from Rednap Howell, formerly a New Jersey schoolteacher, who was known as the poet laureate of the resistance movement. He is primarily remembered for composing several satirical ditties, poking fun at Fanning and other adversaries. Yet, he was considered a "master spirit" of the Regulation, with a far-reaching vision of justice for the oppressed. It would be an intercepted letter in his name concerning the Regulator ability to raise forces against the government that ultimately prompted Governor Tryon's march into the backcountry, which culminated in the decisive showdown.[37] Also identified as resistance leaders were Thomas Person, the largest Regulator landowner, and the Gillespie brothers, Daniel and John, both of whom fought at Alamance. The point here is that, while the Regulators were first referred to as "the Mob," they were anything but mindless rioters in want of guidance and direction. They agreed to make decisions by majority vote, but they consistently selected representatives to act on their behalf from the same small circle of farmers, which included God-fearing men such as Hermon Husband. Although lacking strict formality, the Regulators had an organizational and hierarchical structure that, according to Marjoleine Kars, very much reflected "strains of backcountry Protestantism."[38]

In January and March 1768, the Regulators issued two of several "advertisements" that, over time, would help establish the Regulator frame of thought. Through these, the Regulators announced they would pay no taxes or excessive fees. The ire of the Regulators was further inflamed when rumors began to circulate that public monies would be used to finance the construction of an elaborate mansion for the benefit of Governor William Tryon. Then, on April 8, a seemingly minor event occurred that would escalate hostilities and ultimately help ignite the War of the Regulation. While en route to nearby Hillsborough to attend to private business, a Regulator had his mare seized by the sheriff, in lieu of unpaid taxes. Almost immediately, a group of nearly 100 armed insurgents mobilized, overtook the sheriff, tied him up, mounted him on a horse, and paraded him into Hillsborough, only to stop at the front porch of Edmund Fanning, the highest-ranking public official in Orange County and arguably the most despised man in the Piedmont. According to Regulator testimony, a man then emerged from Fanning's home, brandishing pistols and threatening to shoot into the crowd. It was then that "some heated unruly spirits" fired several shots into Fanning's house, shattering some second floor windows. The Regulators then secured the mare in question and withdrew.[39]

In his study of North Carolina's culture of violence, Wayne E. Lee suggested that, by demonstrating restraint in this particular instance, the Regulators should be remembered for what they did *not* do. They failed to harm the offending sheriff and inflicted relatively little damage on Fanning's home. By limiting the extent of their violence, the Regulators were playing to public sympathy and certifying that their actions were legitimate.[40] Applying a paradigm of terrorism, however, begs a reexamination of the "mare affair," that focuses instead on its broader effect of generating fear and intimidation. Assessing a collective psychological reaction is, of course, risky business, whatever the circumstances, but the surviving evidence suggests that the public backlash was significant. Sources do not reveal what impact the affair had on the sheriff in question, but Edmund Fanning documented his state of distress. In a report to Tryon, Fanning lamented the "traitorous and rebellious conduct" of the insurgents and warned that, unless they were stopped, "we may no longer expect our persons protected or our properties secured by the laws of the land, but to lye open and exposed to the attacks of lawless violence and brute force." Fanning also warned that these "traitorous Dogs" were "threatening death and immediate destruction to myself and others," at which point Fanning promised, "to bravely repulse them or nobly die."[41]

The impact on the larger community was made painfully evident to Fanning when he directed the Orange County militias to mobilize in order to suppress the Regulator rebellion. Instead, a total of seven companies managed to produce less than 120 volunteers, most of whom were reluctant to take up arms against their Piedmont neighbors.[42] In a report to Fanning, Francis Nash and Thomas Hart acknowledged that the local militiamen were intimidated by the Regulators and fearful of reprisals; they further conceded that "unless some measures can be fallen upon . . . no man will be safe among us in the possession of his life or property and it will end in ruin and destruction among ourselves." Such was the influence of the Regulators that Nash and Hart suggested accommodation with the insurgents and proposed "a kind of treaty with the leading and most reasonable men of the rioters . . . to keep them from making any violent attempt upon those who appeared openly against them, or upon the town to which they threaten destruction."[43]

Governor Tryon responded to the riot by issuing a proclamation ordering the Regulators to dissolve. Fanning, meanwhile, had other plans. On May 1, he and a posse of about 40 men rode to Sandy Creek in the dead of night, rousted Hermon Husband and William Butler out of their beds, and whisked them away to the Hillsborough jail, intending to charge them with instigating a riot. The response from the farming community was swift: by sunrise the next morning, hundreds had heard about the abductions and had gathered outside of Hillsborough. According to a Regulator advertisement, the incident "alarmed the Whole County, Regulators or Anteregulators, all were unanimous in the recovery of the prisoners, many who had till then opposed the prevailing measures . . . as judging none were now safe, whether active, passive, or neutral."[44] A rescue riot seemed inevitable. Fanning certainly thought so: he quickly allowed the prisoners to post bail and had them released. Fanning, accompanied by the governor's secretary, then rode to the outskirts of town and promised the assemblage that, if everyone dispersed peacefully, the governor would accept their petitions and attempt to redress their grievances. With that, the crowd quickly assented and dispersed. While a crisis had seemingly been averted, Fanning's problems had just begun.

Meanwhile, the spirit of discontent spread to Edgecombe, Johnston, and Anson counties, where Regulator disturbances also took place. Accordingly, Fanning warned Tryon that the insurgency was "by indefatigable pains and industry extending itself far and wide through this part of the province," and that people everywhere were "conspiring and confederating by solemn oath and open violence."[45] Wild rumors contributed to the existing tensions. Tryon was said to be recruiting Indians for a military campaign against the Regulators, who, according to the whispers, were planning an attack on Hillsborough. The political environment was so incendiary that, in August, a false rumor led to a short and nonviolent confrontation between 1,000 Regulators and about 250 militiamen mustered by Colonel Fanning. Another potential disaster was avoided in September, when the "mare affair" trials were held. Hermon Husband, William Butler, and others were accused of participating in the Hillsborough riot. Oddly, because of Tryon's promises to root out corruption, Edmund Fanning was also tried on charges of extortion. Anticipating trouble, Tryon had earlier toured the Piedmont, courting various militia leaders and their troops, hoping to recruit enough volunteers to protect the Hillsborough courthouse from a Regulator intrusion. Consequently, by the time court opened on September 22, he was able to muster more than 1,400 militiamen. The Regulators and various supporters who had gathered outside of Hillsborough, however, were said to possess superior numbers. Fortunately, both sides sought a peaceful resolution and, even though negotiations failed to produce an accord concerning the trials, the Regulators simply walked away and allowed the court to proceed. The Regulators had long expressed their loyalty to the king and royal government, focusing instead on specific cases of local corruption and the need for government responsiveness to their grievances. Overthrowing British authority was never a consideration. In the end, most charges against the Regulators were dropped. William Butler was found guilty of rioting and sentenced to a fine and prison time. Hermon Husband was found not guilty. Edmund Fanning was found guilty of extortion, but, because the court also ruled that his actions had been due to a "misconstruction," he was fined only a penny for each offense.[46]

For the next two years, from late 1768 to the fall of 1770, the Regulators and the royal government participated in a political power struggle involving dirty politics, broken promises, and violence. For their part, the Regulators again tried to compel change through legitimate political channels. They drafted petitions, took depositions, elected their own to political offices, and brought suits against corrupt officials. The Tryon government, meanwhile, assumed a harder position against the insurgents. The governor continued to recruit militiamen and made promises to the Regulators that he quickly rescinded. At the same time, the Assembly stonewalled Regulator petitions and the courts failed to convict corrupt officials. In Orange County, Edmund Fanning continued to obstruct Regulator efforts to seek legal redress. From the colonel's perspective, the insurgents were contemptible enemies of the English Constitution, and he would inflexibly resist any attempt on their part to usurp authority that officially belonged to him and his privileged associates. All the while, Tryon's new governor's mansion in New Bern, paid for with tax monies, began to take shape. The Regulators, rebuffed yet again in their search for justice, responded with renewed violence. In November 1768, a rescue riot took place in Edgecombe County. In March 1769, a planned ambush of Edmund Fanning failed. A month later, Sheriff John Lea was whipped while attempting to serve a process. Sometime during the next winter, Regulators flogged Samuel Spencer, a militia colonel and justice in Anson County.[47]

As the deadlock between the two sides tightened, the Regulator resolve hardened, although exact Regulator numbers are difficult to calculate. There are no existing membership lists, but there are names signed to various Regulator petitions. Hermon Husband's two historical accounts of the War of the Regulation contained names, as did other published contemporaneous accounts. It is likely that many who were called Regulators never actually participated in terrorist behavior but only sat in on meetings. Hermon Husband was one such person. There were also those who were largely motivated only when it came time to bear arms alongside their neighbors. Interestingly, no female names appear on any of the Regulator petitions or advertisements, leading one to believe that the Regulators were exclusively male. As Marjoleine Kars noted, this was largely a function of 18th-century life in colonial America, and she surely had a point. Kars speculated, however, that women did contribute to the Regulator cause in a supporting role, either by participating in crowd activity, helping nurse the wounded at Alamance, or managing family farms in the absence of their husbands. Kars cannot document any of this female activity, but given what historians know about the participation of women during the American Revolution, her presumptions appear entirely reasonable.[48] Wayne E. Lee also commented on this lack of female visibility and noted that, in Europe and parts of the northern colonies, women were active in public riots. Lee offered no specific explanation but suggested that, in North Carolina, female participation in politics had declined and that the military character of riots might have precluded the direct participation of women.[49]

Through their advertisements, depositions, and petitions, the Regulators were able to clarify and enumerate their political demands. Aside from their longstanding pleas for greater government accountability, the Regulators also sought:

- increased currency
- an end to exorbitant fees charged by clerks and lawyers
- secret ballots
- abolition of poll taxes
- payment of taxes with farm produce
- establishment of taxes "in proportion to profits"
- freedom to celebrate marriages according to denominational ceremony and custom.[50]

These political demands were well known, for the Regulators found other methods to propagandize their cause. Hermon Husband published two historical accounts of the Regulator uprising, both with long, tortuous titles: the aforementioned *A Continuation of the Impartial Relation of the First Rise and Cause of the Recent Differences in Publick Affairs in the Province of North Carolina* (1770) and *A Fan for Fanning and a Touchstone to Tryon, Containing An Impartial Account of the Rise and Progress of the So Much Talked of Regulation in North Carolina* (1771). Although Husband did not affix his name to either of these publications, there is little doubt that he was, indeed, their author. Most historians agree that *A Continuation of the Impartial Relation* is a much better historical resource, given that *A Fan for Fanning* is largely redundant.

Hardly an impartial observer, Husband railed against the royal government's "illegal attempts of Arbitrary Power," vowing that the insurgents would "stand like a Rock, firm and immovable against all the waves of Corruption."[51] Although the Regulators should not be thought of as a first wave of anti-British patriots devoted to independence, their way of thinking, very much reflected in Husband's writings and other advertisements, was duly influenced by the Real Whig notions of legitimate dissent and the democratizing aspects of the Great Awakening that were then helping to stir other extremists and the disaffected masses toward revolution.

Contributing to the Regulator attempt to win public support were the many poems, ballads, and ditties crafted by Rednap Howell and others. Howell wrote this stanza mocking Edmund Fanning and the colonel's close friend John Frohock, an alleged horse thief:

> Says Frohock to Fanning, to tell the plain truth,
> When I came to this country I was but a youth;
> My father sent for me; I wa'n't worth a cross:
> And then my first study was to steal for a horse.
> I quickly got credit, and then ran away,
> And hav'n't paid for him to this very day.[52]

Howell wrote more than 40 ballads and jingles. He wasn't alone. In the aftermath of the showdown outside Hillsborough in 1768, when a crowd of Regulators led by Ninian Bell Hamilton helped secure the release of imprisoned Hermon Husband, a Regulator song commemorated the triumphant moment:

> From Hillsborough town the first of May
> March'd those murdering traitors.
> They went on to oppose the honest men
> That were called the Regulators.
>
> Old Hamilton surrounded the Town,
> He guarded every quarter;
> The Regulators still marching on,
> Full fifteen hundred after.
>
> But old Hamilton, like an angry man,
> He still craved satisfaction
> For taking of Husbands away to the town.
> It was a most villainous action.[53]

By the fall of 1770 then, the Regulators had created a resistance movement with specific grievances, respected leaders, political objectives, an informal organizational structure, a propaganda mill, and a strategy of violence meant to instill a broader environment of fear and intimidation. Certainly, their support from the wider community helped sustain the Regulator spirit of defiance. They were also encouraged by the mass demonstrations and anti-authoritarian fervor then spreading throughout the colonies. As political stakes grew higher, forms of popular protest became more emotional and subsequently more destructive toward both persons and property. As long as Tryon, Fanning, and the Assembly continued their collective recalcitrance, a larger and more violent confrontation seemed inevitable.

IV. From Hillsborough to Alamance

While the Regulators grew increasingly frustrated with the unresponsiveness of the government, a number of them fell victim to various lawsuits, including Hermon Husband, who was sued for debt in March 1770. As a result, a number of cases were pending before the Hillsborough court as it opened its session on Monday, September 24, 1770. Presiding that day was Judge Richard Henderson, who, according to rumor, refused to try Regulator cases. By the time the courthouse doors opened that morning, a crowd of at least 200 Regulators had already surrounded the building and were, according to Henderson's retelling, "shouting, hallooing, and making a considerable tumult in the Streets."[54] The crowd then poured into Henderson's courtroom. Having received permission to speak, a spokesman announced that the Regulators wanted the court to proceed with its business with but one slight adjustment: the current jury members would be replaced with jurists selected from among the Regulators themselves. A rather chaotic 30 minutes followed, while various participants debated back and forth, trying to come to an understanding. Just then, as John Williams, an Attorney of the Court, approached the courthouse, the crowd suddenly overtook him. According to Henderson, the attackers fell upon Williams "in a most furious Manner with Clubs and sticks of enormous size."[55] A news account reported that Williams was dealt "violent blows with loaded whips on the head and different parts of his body."[56] The crowd then turned its wrath on Edmund Fanning, who, quite unfortunately for the colonel, was standing right before them in Henderson's courtroom. As the *Virginia Gazette* described it, "They seized him by the neck, dragged him down the steps, his head striking violently on every step, carried him out the door, and forcing him out, dragged him on the ground over stones and brickbats, struck him with their whips and clubs, kicked him, spit and spurned at him, and treated him with every possible mark of contempt and cruelty."[57] Henderson reported that the Regulators had rained their blows on Fanning "with such violence that I had no doubt his life would instantly become a sacrifice to their rage and madness." His concern was quite warranted: Fanning nearly lost an eye in the assault.[58] Williams and Fanning were able to save themselves by seeking refuge in a nearby building, but the Regulators continued to hold the town hostage. Sheriff Thomas Hart, Justice Alexander Martin, and Superior Court Clerk John Litterell were among the many who felt the sting of Regulator whips. Other clerks and justices managed to escape unscathed. Judge Henderson, who understandably feared for his own life, was assured by James Hunter and other Regulators that he faced no danger so long as he continued the day's court proceedings—under their terms.

At the end of the day, Henderson was escorted to his room and Fanning, after promising to return the next day presumably to stand trial before the Regulators, was allowed to return home. That night, according to one witness, the Regulators patrolled the streets "to the terror of the inhabitants."[59] Nonetheless, Henderson managed to sneak out of his room and quietly fled Hillsborough. The next morning, the Regulators, having discovered Henderson's escape, seized Fanning and sentenced him to death. Some of the more moderate Regulators intervened to save his life, and Fanning was allowed to flee Hillsborough. The Regulators then moved on and nearly demolished Fanning's home. They shattered walls, windows, glassware, and fine china; destroyed every piece of furniture; scattered his books and private papers; and littered the streets of Hillsborough with bits and pieces of Fanning's personal belongings. Money was also stolen, though the Regulators would deny culpability. Such was the destruction of Fanning's home that Henderson later suggested, "a small breeze of Wind will throw down the remains."[60] In a crowning gesture of contempt, the insurgents emptied Fanning's wine collection, imbibed the colonel's finest, donned his dandiest attire and, mocking his aristocratic air, paraded up and down the streets of Hillsborough. The crowd then approached the local church and debated whether to tear it down as well. Fearful that destroying the church would betray their religious convictions, they decided against it, but seized the handsome bell that Fanning had personally donated to the church and shattered it to pieces. Before the end of the day, the Regulator mob also damaged other houses, broke windows everywhere, and ran other merchants and inhabitants out of town. An account in the *Virginia Gazette* claimed that the Regulators placed a corpse of a recently executed black convict on a lawyer's seat and filled the judge's courtroom seat with human excrement, although no other first-hand accounts offered corroborating testimony, including that of Judge Henderson, who provided the most detailed account of the riot.[61] By that night, things began to settle down, and, by Wednesday, the Regulators had left town, leaving a shocked community in their wake.

In his assessment of the riot, Wayne E. Lee again maintained that the Regulators "displayed traditional characteristics of restraint and target selection." Because no one was killed and only one house was destroyed, the Regulators made their defiance "legitimate in a way that uncontrolled havoc was not."[62] Lee may have had a point, but other factors were certainly at work. The courthouse takeover and the treatment of Colonel Fanning and his personal property were made into public spectacles. Fanning was the Piedmont's highest-ranking public official, and the courthouse was the region's most visible government institution. The

Hillsborough riot might have targeted Henderson's courtroom and Fanning himself in an immediate sense, but the wider audience was the Tryon government and those in the Piedmont who opposed the Regulator methods, especially the volunteers who made up the various county militias that could potentially muster against the insurgents. And while the Regulators might not have killed Fanning, they came close to it: he nearly lost an eye in the assault and was initially sentenced to death. Aside from the attack on Fanning and his property, other homes and businesses were vandalized; government clerks and lawyers were whipped and beaten. Such was the larger impact of the riot that several prominent Hillsborough officials immediately complained to the governor, "we think ourselves hourly in the most imminent Danger not only of losing our Lives and Fortunes, but of every connection which we esteem valuable."[63]

Lee did acknowledge that the Hillsborough riot was a departure from previous protests, explaining that the Regulators thus moved from an "in-group" to an "out-group" which delegitimized their insurgency in the minds of the public. This demonization of the Regulators, aided by sensationalized newspaper accounts of the riot, contributed to the growing perception that the insurgents were "no longer subject to the same set of rules."[64] The takeover of Henderson's courtroom and the substitution of juries was an indication that the Regulators, for want of justice from the existing government bureaucracy, would create their own "system" and thereby establish themselves as an extralegal authority.

On the night of November 12, nearly three weeks after the Hillsborough riot, Judge Richard Henderson's barn and stable were set afire; two days later, his house was torched. Although no one claimed responsibility, there seemed no doubt that the Regulators were somehow culpable. Meanwhile, Tryon prepared to put closure to the Regulator rebellion. Earlier that summer, he had received word that he was to assume the governorship of New York, a post that he had long coveted, and he did not want to leave unfinished business in North Carolina before his departure in the spring. His Attorney General Thomas McGuire had written the governor informing him that, under existing laws, the Regulators could be tried, not for rebellion, but for a misdemeanor riot only. McGuire did suggest that the Assembly could pass laws designed for prosecuting the Regulators and added that he thought it prudent for the governor to muster the local militias in an attempt to gauge their loyalty to the Royal government.[65] The attorney general's letter did not sit well with the governor. The Regulators were traitorous extremists who subverted the English Constitution and needed to be punished accordingly. He insisted that the term "regulators" not be used because, as he saw it, the insurgents were devoted to overthrowing authority, not adjusting it.[66] And because he saw them as operating out of the bounds of law, he saw no alternative but to respond with a similar lack of civility. When the Assembly opened its session on December 3, Tryon provided the ugly details of the Hillsborough riot and condemned the Regulators as a "Seditious Mob, Men who . . . have torn down Justice from Her Tribunal, and renounced all Legislative Authority . . . These men have broken through all the Bounds of Human Society." In so doing, Tryon signaled the "outsider" status of the insurgents and crafted a context in which he, too, could violate established guidelines in order to defeat the terrorists.[67] If the Regulators would not play by the rules, neither would he. Consequently, as we shall see, the governor himself would ignore the law and military protocol in his heavy-handed response following the confrontation at Alamance.

On December 15, Assemblyman Samuel Johnston, a lawyer and merchant, proposed legislation that would come to be known as the Johnston Riot Act. Based on the English Riot Act of 1714, it provided a legal definition of riotous behavior, made participation a felony, and authorized the governor to call up militias at public expense. In some cases, it also equated riotous behavior with treason, and, if conditions so indicated, rioters could be shot on sight. Beyond that, the Assembly decided to apply the act retroactively, making all of the Hillsborough rioters subject to its provisions. While the proposal was moving its way through the bureaucracy, Hermon Husband was expelled from his seat in the House, accused of libel, and imprisoned in New Bern by Tryon, who then appeared before the Assembly and announced that the Regulators were plotting a rescue riot. Fear descended upon New Bern, and people wondered if the same fate was to befall them as had befallen the citizens of Hillsborough. One resident believed that terrorists intended to burn the town and "murder everyone who shall oppose them." He added that he could not sleep, knowing "when I lay down in my bed but my throat may be cut before the morning."[68] That the Regulators never committed such acts is, from the perspective here, irrelevant; what is important is that the Regulators had forged such an intimidating presence that people believed that they *could happen*. And therein lay the power of terror. It wasn't just Colonel Fanning and the others in Hillsborough who were victimized by the riot; its repercussions stretched from the Piedmont all the way to the coast, to the homes of sleepless residents in New Bern. On January 2, the Assembly quickly passed the Johnston Riot Act.

From January to February, Governor Tryon continued to sound the Regulator alarm, insisting that the insurgents were planning to rescue Hermon Husband. His foreboding was not unwarranted. Several hundred Regulators were, in fact, marching toward New Bern but finally dispersed and returned home in early February when they received word that the grand jury had dropped all charges against Husband. A crisis had been averted, but only temporarily, for the Regulators and their allies had been whipped into a frenzy by the passage of the Riot Act. The act further radicalized the insurgents, convincing even the moderate fence-sitters in the Piedmont that the government had forsaken them and given up on addressing their grievances, in favor of new forms of political repression. As the Regulators likened the terms of the Riot Act to the Spanish Inquisition, their power and influence began to grow. Spokesmen traveled throughout the Piedmont, urging local farmers to withhold taxes and to avoid the government's courts, promising justice instead through Regulator arbitration. Regulator crowds

continued to disrupt court proceedings and intimidate witnesses and government officials. The environment had become so volatile that many officials simply
refused to travel outside of their home communities. Reflecting their newfound
frustration, the Regulators spoke more openly about killing their enemies. One
Regulator boasted that "now we shall be forced to kill all the Clerks and Lawyers,
and we will kill them; I'll be damned if they are not put to Death."[69] Other Regulators further cultivated the climate of fear by covertly posting notices among the
Yadkin River settlements warning of impending Cherokee attacks throughout
the backcountry. The influence of the Regulators had spiked so significantly that
Rednap Howell boasted in a written report that the insurgency had spread into
Edgecombe, Bute, Halifax, and Northampton counties. It was this intercepted
report that ultimately fell into Tryon's hands and finally convinced the Assembly
to approve the governor's request to raise a militia against the Regulators.

V. The Battle of Alamance

For the next few weeks, Governor Tryon set about to recruit an army capable of
destroying the Regulators, no small task given the paltry number of volunteers
who had mustered previously against the terrorists. But Tryon was nothing if
not determined. In his appeal to the people of North Carolina, he emphasized
honor, duty, and loyalty to the king. He also offered the inducement of 40 shil-
lings to those who would join the governor's army. Through his sheer will and a
hint of coercion, Tryon was able to raise two armies, both much smaller than he
had anticipated. His own force consisted of about 1,100 troops and would march
to Hillsborough from the east; a smaller force, led by General Hugh Waddell,
would number about 280 and would approach Regulator country from the west
through Salisbury. There is no detailed socio-economic analysis of the Alamance
army, although it appears that the vast preponderance of the volunteers came from
the more prosperous east. Marjoleine Kars estimated that about 10% of the army
consisted of members of the East Coast gentry ("gentlemen volunteers"), a figure
perhaps higher than one might expect but certainly not sufficient to characterize
the War of the Regulation as a conflict between classes.[70]

Tryon and his forces began their march on May 4, 1771, and arrived in Hillsborough on May 11, taking several prisoners along the way. General Waddell was
not so fortunate. On May 2, nine insurgents, known as the "Black Boys of Cabar-
rus," disguised themselves as Indians, blackened their faces with soot, and attacked
one of Waddell's supply convoys, blowing up several powder wagons before disappearing into the woods. On May 9, about 2,000 Regulators surrounded Waddell's
camp. Finding his militia unwilling to engage the insurgents and facing mass
desertions among his troops, Waddell had no choice but to retreat to Salisbury
on May 10. Hearing the news, Tryon set out to join Waddell in Salisbury, and,
on Monday, May 13, he camped along the west bank of the Great Alamance
Creek. Not far away, between 2,000–3,000 Regulators also set up camp. These

opposing forces were on a collision course. What had begun three years earlier as a campaign based on terrorist methods had now escalated into a full-blown civil conflict about to be decided by a historic battle between two armies with a combined force of more than 3,000 combatants.

The two armies spent the next two days trying to reach a compromise, but Tryon refused to negotiate and the Regulators refused to disband. A last-minute attempt by Reverend David Caldwell to mediate a truce failed to check the unavoidable showdown. During the two days spent exchanging messages, the opposing troops managed to creep gradually forward until they were only 300 yards apart. Despite the tension in the air, many among the Regulators failed to grasp the seriousness of what was about to ensue. Several of them frolicked and wrestled playfully until they were scolded and warned of impending enemy fire. In reality, the entire Regulator militia was ill prepared and ill armed. There was no leadership or direction at this crucial moment. When the violent confrontation became inevitable and there was nothing he could do to prevent the bloodshed, Hermon Husband mounted his horse and rode away. When James Hunter was asked to assume military command, he refused. Many Regulators threatened to walk out when two of Tryon's scouts were captured and put to the whip.

By May 16, the opposing armies stood only 30 to 50 yards apart, separated only by a small, flat meadow on the road between Hillsborough and Salisbury (now State Route 62). An exchange of prisoners was held up while last-minute talks continued; just then, Tryon himself shot and killed one of his prisoners right in front of the Regulator lines, an act that has generated some historical debate. Wayne E. Lee argued that the prisoner, Robert Thompson, had broken away from the governor's guards, and, despite being warned, was approaching the Regulator formations. Marjoleine Kars referred to Thompson's shooting as an "execution" meant to shock the insurgents into surrendering.[71] Considering what we know about Tryon's behavior during the next few days, one might well imagine that he was, indeed, intending to send the message that Regulators should not expect mercy. What seems undeniable is that there was now no turning back. Shortly thereafter, Tryon gave his army orders to fire on the enemy. According to legend, his troops hesitated at first but commenced only after Tryon screamed, "Fire on them, or fire on me."[72] The Battle of Alamance had begun.

The Regulators had a decided advantage in numbers, but not all of them were armed, and many fled as soon as the shooting began. Moreover, the governor's troops had several artillery pieces that they quickly fired. Fortunately for the Regulators, the cannon balls fell far short of their lines, giving the insurgents an opportunity to dash behind trees, fences, and a small clump of rocks. From there, they began sniping at the artillery gunmen, even managing to capture one of the cannons for a brief moment. Tryon's troops eventually set fire to the woods, driving the snipers out from their cover while other Regulators in the field began to run short of ammunition. The Regulators, lacking any coordination between their various companies, held their ground for the better part of an hour but were ultimately no match for Tryon's army. Slowly, their numbers diminished until the final insurgents took to their heels. After two hours, the battle was over. There continues to be a wide discrepancy in estimates of the number of killed and wounded at Alamance. The most-often-cited statistics claim that from among the governor's troops between nine and 20 lives were lost, and about 60 men were wounded. The Regulators also lost anywhere from nine to 300 lives, and counted up to 300 wounded.[73] Tryon also took about 15 prisoners from the Regulator ranks. One of them was James Few, a 25-year-old carpenter by trade and the fiancé of a young woman who was allegedly debauched by none other than Edmund Fanning. A day after the battle, perhaps at Fanning's insistence, Tryon ordered that Few be summarily executed. Few was hanged from a tree after refusing to denounce his actions, a concession that would have spared his life.

For the next four weeks, Tryon and his army marched throughout the Piedmont, hunting down Regulators and spreading misery and destruction. They routinely destroyed the homes, barns, and crops of suspected terrorists and innocent farmers alike. They also tore down fences, cut down orchards, and seized supplies and provisions from a defenseless community. In the process, they laid waste to the homes and property of James Hunter and Hermon Husband. When Tryon finally arrived back at Hillsborough on June 13, his troops, despite the pleas of mercy from local residents, destroyed the home of William and Mary Few, the parents of James Few. Evidently, Tryon's response to terror was to spread terror of his own. He had, in fact, been establishing the context for this type of response ever since the Hillsborough riot. By consistently portraying the Regulators as outsiders with no regard for established authority, he was justifying the use of irregular tactics in his campaign against them. Meanwhile, the objects of Tryon's attention were scattering to the winds. Most Regulators simply returned home to await their fate, while others hid in the woods for as long as they could. Many who had run from the battlefield were caught, made prisoners, and subsequently punished. Some, like Hermon Husband, fled North Carolina, never to return. By 1772, about 1,500 ex-Regulators had moved out of the Piedmont, many migrating to Tennessee and Kentucky.[74] Tryon later offered pardons to all insurgents who agreed to come forward, surrender their arms, and take oaths of allegiance that included promises to pay taxes and obey all laws. Excluded from the offer were those already in custody or wanted by the government. All told, more than 6,400 men, or about 75% of all free males from the Piedmont, accepted Tryon's terms. Almost instantly, the War of the Regulation came to an end and the Regulators, as a collective body, ceased to exist.

William Tryon wasted no time administering his own brand of justice. The 14 remaining Regulator prisoners who had been captured at Alamance were brought to trial under the terms of the Johnston Riot Act on June 15, only two days after the governor's return to Hillsborough. Tryon summoned all of his gubernatorial powers to insure a speedy trial as well as the imposition of the death penalty. By May 18, the prisoners were found guilty, and, on May 19, six were hanged from a tree as a public spectacle after two were acquitted and others were pardoned. One of the condemned men was Benjamin Merrill, who had intended to join the Regulators at Alamance but retreated with 300 other insurgents once they received word of the disastrous battle. Another was James Pugh, who, like Merrill, stood on a barrel with a rope around his neck before the assembled crowd. When granted a last opportunity to speak, he began to rant against the sins of Edmund Fanning, until the offended colonel had the barrel on which Pugh was standing kicked out from under him in mid-sentence.[75] Pugh's last words, abbreviated as they may have been, were also the last words of the Regulator movement. The voices of resistance, once emanating from the Piedmont with resonance, had finally been silenced.

VI.   Conclusion

Eleven days after hanging six Regulators, William Tryon and Edmund Fanning boarded a ship bound for New York, with Tryon as the new governor and Fanning as his personal assistant. Little did Tryon know that he was about to confront a similar resistance movement in his new colony. He would be replaced in North Carolina by Josiah Martin, a well-connected man who was genuinely determined to heal the wounds that Tryon had left. Martin's justices were similarly disinclined to pursue further legal action against the remaining Regulators, and the Assembly eventually issued pardons to all, with the exception of Hermon Husband. Not that it mattered much to Husband. After Alamance, he fled to western Pennsylvania, where he was eventually reunited with his family. Although he once again became a prosperous landowner, the fires of resistance still burned in his belly, and Husband later found himself in the midst of the Whiskey Rebellion. For that, he was imprisoned and then eventually pardoned. He died shortly thereafter, in 1791. Rednap Howell eventually relocated to Maryland, but James Hunter returned to the Piedmont ten months after Alamance and remained a much-respected member of the community.

Despite sensationalized anti-Regulator newspaper accounts that appeared locally in the aftermath of Alamance, a noticeable pro-Regulator sympathy began to evolve as the spirit of resistance against British legislation began to spread throughout the colonies. The North Carolina Sons of Liberty, however, would disassociate themselves from the Regulators, for fear that the embattled farmers from the Piedmont represented a lower-class rabble that would undercut the influence of the upper-class revolutionaries who would later direct the movement toward independence.[76] The North Carolina Sons had no reason to worry. The War of the Regulation had left the Piedmont farmers in such a state of bitter resentfulness that, when the time came for independence, many chose to sit the Revolution out rather than run the risk of being twice burned. Ironically, many who led North Carolina's effort in support of independence were those who had fought the Regulators at Alamance.

The War of the Regulation was, of course, not a war. Neither was it a sectional confrontation, an example of class conflict as the Sons of Liberty believed, nor the opening salvos of the American Revolution. It was, above all else, a local conflict based on opposition to government impropriety that escalated into a campaign of terrorism and ended with a single military showdown. The Regulators had specific grievances, which led to well-defined political objectives made public through numerous advertisements, petitions, songs, and publications. Their use of violence inflicted both physical and psychological damage, and its impact radiated across North Carolina from the Piedmont to the coast, creating a climate of intimidation. And however ill defined it might have been, there was an informal organizational hierarchy within the Regulator movement. By selecting representatives to speak on their behalf or to run for office, the Regulators let it be known that men such as Hermon Husband, James Hunter, and William Butler were among those to whom they looked for direction and guidance. As Wayne E. Lee suggested, Regulator violence might have been an attempt to adapt English concepts of resistance to New World conditions, and, as Marjoleine Kars later argued, Regulator violence might also be considered within the context of a creative and subversive religious climate. None of this need detract from the reality that the Regulators conducted a campaign based on terrorist methods. However, other resistance groups of the 1760s and 1770s were similarly motivated by the increasing revolutionary rhetoric and popular participation of the times and soon began to promulgate terrorist strategies of their own. Anti-rent insurgents along the Hudson Valley were already challenging the monopolization of land, while the Sons of Liberty were instigating resistance to British authority. And in the New Hampshire Grants, the Green Mountain Boys were about to complicate life for none other than William Tryon, newly arrived in New York and fresh from his triumph at Alamance.

Notes

1. Marjoleine Kars, *Breaking Loose Together—The Regulator Rebellion in Pre-Revolutionary North Carolina* (Chapel Hill: University of North Carolina Press, 2002), 138.
2. Roger Maxwell Brown, *The South Carolina Regulators* (Cambridge, MA: The Belknap Press of Harvard University, 1963).
3. John Hill Wheeler, *Historical Sketches of North Carolina from 1584 to 1851* (Baltimore: Regional Publishing Co., 2 volumes, 1964) I, 59; George Bancroft, *History of the United States of America* (Boston: Little, Brown, and Co., 6 volumes, 1855), VI, 381–384; John Fiske, *The American Revolution* (Boston: Houghton Mifflin Co., 2 volumes, 1891), I, 74–76.
4. Wheeler, *Historical Sketches,* 59.
5. Fiske, *The American Revolution,* 74–76.
6. Adams, "The Carolina Regulators," 347.
7. William S. Powell, *The War of the Regulation and the Battle of Alamance, May 16, 1771* (Raleigh, NC: State Department of Archives and History, 1949).
8. Frederick Jackson Turner, *The Frontier in American History* (New York: Henry Holt and Co., 1920), 248.

9. Elisha Douglas, *Rebels and Democrats: The Struggle for Equal Political Rights and Majority Rule During the American Revolution* (Chapel Hill: University of North Carolina Press, 1955), 71–72; Marvin L. Michael Kay, "The North Carolina Regulation, 1766–1776: A Class Conflict," in Alfred F. Young, ed., *The American Revolution—Explorations in the History of American Radicalism* (DaeKalb: Northern University Press, 1976), 71–123.

10. John S. Bassett, "The Regulators of North Carolina, 1765–1771," *Annual Report of the American Historical Association for the Year 1894* (1894): 141–212.

11. Samuel Eliot Morrison and Henry Steel Commager, *The Growth of the American Republic* (New York: Oxford University Press, 2 volumes, 4th ed., 1950); Hugh Talmadge Lefler and Albert Ray Newsome, *North Carolina: The History of a Southern State* (Chapel Hill: University of North Carolina Press, 1954).

12. A. Roger Ekirch, "*Poor Carolina*": *Politics and Society in Colonial North Carolina, 1729–1776* (Chapel Hill: University of North Carolina Press, 1981), 166.

13. James P. Whittenburg, "Planters, Merchants, and Lawyers: Social Change and the Origins of the North Carolina Regulation," *William and Mary Quarterly* 34, no. 2 (1977): 218.

14. Adams, "The Carolina Regulators," 345–352.

15. Whittenburg, "Planters, Merchants, and Lawyers," 221.

16. Ekirch, *Poor Carolina.*

17. Kars, *Breaking Loose.*

18. Wayne E. Lee, *Crowds and Soldiers in Revolutionary North Carolina* (Gainesville: University of Florida Press, 2001).

19. Ibid., 24–27; Ekirch, *Poor Carolina,* 133–142.

20. Lee, *Crowds and Soldiers,* 25.

21. Ibid., 25.

22. Ibid., 26.

23. Petition of John Campbell and Alexander McCulloh, October 13, 1755, CRNC, 5: 494.

24. Kars, *Breaking Loose,* 41.

25. Henry E. McCulloh to Edmund Fanning, May 9, 1765, CRNC, 7: 32–33. McCulloh referred to the attackers as "a pack of ungrateful brutal Sons of Bitches." Concerning his personal safety, he also confessed to Fanning that given he was a predestinarian, "whatever will be will be."

26. Lee, *Crowds and Soldiers,* 33.

27. Ibid., 160; Ekirch, *Poor Carolina,* 185.

28. Kars, *Breaking Loose,* 112.

29. RNCD, 584. Powell contains mini-biographies of all the significant persons associated with the War of the Regulation.

30. Bassett, "The Regulators of North Carolina," 152.

31. Lee, *Crowds and Soldiers,* 50.

32. Kars, *Breaking Loose,* 138.

33. Prefatory Notes, CRNC, 8: xxiv.

34. Bassett, "The Regulators of North Carolina," 136.

35. Hermon Husband, *A Continuation of the Impartial Relation of the First Rise and Cause of the Recent Differences in Publick Affairs in the Province of North Carolina &c.,* Second Part, Printed for the Author, 1770. Edited by Archibald Henderson, *North Carolina Historical Review,* 18, no. 1 (1941): 48–81.

36. Prefatory Notes, CRNC, 8: xxx; RNCD, 584.

37. Prefatory Notes, CRNC, 8: xxvi–xxvii; Lee, 76.

38. Kars, *Breaking Loose,* 139.

39. Regulators' Advertisement No. 11, May 21, 1768, RNCD, 119. For other details of this confrontation, see John Gray to Edmund Fanning, April 9, 1768, RNCD, 80 and Edmund Fanning to John Gray, April 13, 1768, RNCD, 81.

40. Lee, *Crowds and Soldiers*, 51–52.

41. Edmund Fanning to William Tryon, April 23, 1768, CRNC, 7: 716; document also available in RNCD, 86. Fanning might have been a bit delusional when he further claimed that, "if I can rally force to withstand one attack I then shall plume myself as being the commanding Officer in this County & then shall expect to be joined immediately by numbers who now think it desperately dangerous and almost inevitable death to oppose them."

42. Francis Nash and Thomas Hart to Edmund Fanning, April 17, 1768, RNCD, 82.

43. Ibid.

44. Regulators' Advertisement No. 11, May 21, 1768, RNCD, 120.

45. Edmund Fanning to William Tryon, April 23, 1768, RNCD, 84.

46. Lee, *Crowds and Soldiers*, 63–64.

47. Ibid., 66.

48. Kars, *Breaking Loose*, 143–144.

49. Lee, *Crowds and Soldiers*, 43–44.

50. Prefatory Notes, CRNC, 8: xv–xvi.

51. Husband, *A Continuation of the Impartial Relation*, 63; Hermon Husband, *A Fan for Fanning and a Touchstone to Tryon, Containing an Impartial Account of the Rise and Progress of the So Much Talked of Regulation in North Carolina*, Edited by William K. Boyd (Raleigh: Edwards & Broughton Company, 1927).

52. Husband, *A Continuation of the Impartial Relation*, Introduction by Archibald Henderson, 54–55.

53. Arthur Palmer Hudson, "Songs of the North Carolina Regulators," *William and Mary Quarterly*, 4, no. 4, (1947): 480; quoted also in Kars, *Breaking Loose*, 146.

54. Richard Henderson to William Tryon, September 29, 1770, RNCD, 244–248.

55. Ibid.

56. *Virginia Gazette,* October 25, 1770; see also RNCD, 250.

57. Ibid.

58. Richard Henderson to William Tryon, September 29, 1770, RNCD, 246.

59. Deposition of Ralph McNair, October 9, 1770, RNCD, 261.

60. Richard Henderson to William Tryon, September 29, 1770, RNCD, 248.

61. *Virginia Gazette,* October 25, 1770; Richard Henderson to William Tryon, September 29, 1770, RNCD, 244–248.

62. Lee, *Crowds and Soldiers*, 68.

63. James Watson and Others to William Tryon, September 30, 1770, RNCD, 249. Aside from Watson, the letter was signed by Robert Lytle, Thos. Hart, Francis Nash, William Johnston, James Thackston, and James Monro.

64. Lee, *Crowds and Soldiers*, 69.

65. Thomas McGuire to William Tryon and the Council, October 18, 1770, *The Correspondence of William Tryon and Other Selected Papers,* vol. 2, edited by William S. Powell (Raleigh: Division of Archives and History, Department of Cultural Resources, 1981), 515.

66. Kars, *Breaking Loose*, 149.

67. William Tryon to the Assembly, December 5, 1770, CRNC, 8: 283–284.

68. Unsigned and undated letter sent to Thomas Barker, Military Collection, War of the Regulation, Box 2, North Carolina Department of Archives and History, Raleigh. The letter writer described the Regulator-plagued Piedmont as "this land of folly and

wickedness" and seemed unsure how to respond. On one hand, he confessed, "I am determined to fly into our neighboring colony Virginia, for if success should attend these rascals in any one instance, the mischief will become universal," yet also suggested, "I am now preparing to sell my house, plantations and every species of property I own in America that I may be enabled to turn my money in person to advantage in England . . . here, positively, I neither can nor will stay."

69. Kars, *Breaking Loose,* 194–195.
70. Ibid., 197–198.
71. Lee, *Crowds and Soldiers,* 87; Kars, *Breaking Loose,* 201.
72. Powell, *The War of the Regulation,* 23.
73. *Virginia Gazette,* June 6, 1771; Bassett, "The Regulators of North Carolina," 205; Kars, *Breaking Loose,* 201; Lee, *Crowds and Soldiers,* 87.
74. Powell, *The War of the Regulation,* 26.
75. Prefatory Notes, CRNC, 8: xxxi.
76. Kars, *Breaking Loose,* 208–210.

3

THE GREEN MOUNTAIN BOYS

I. Background

When William Tryon, former Governor of North Carolina, arrived in New York in July 1771 to assume new gubernatorial duties, he must have experienced feelings of both accomplishment and trepidation. His heavy-handed methods had purged the North Carolina Piedmont of the Regulator menace, but New York was experiencing its own problems with a violent group of dissident farmers in its northern areas bordering New Hampshire. There, a group of rebels known as the Green Mountain Boys, led by their fearless leader Ethan Allen, dominated an area then known as the New Hampshire Grants, now part of Vermont, in complete defiance of Yorker authority. The legal issues in the "Grants" were far more convoluted than those that had plagued the Piedmont, based in large measure on conflicting land claims issued by both New Hampshire and New York. It remained to be seen how Tryon would respond to the threat represented by the Green Mountain Boys. Yet, as he would discover, the insurgents in the Grants were driven by circumstances similar to those experienced by the Piedmont Regulators. The Green Mountain Boys, too, would see themselves oppressed by injustice and corruption, with, in their case, Yorkers attempting to evict them from their homesteads. They, too, would attempt to redress their grievances through legitimate political processes, only to be denied the opportunity to establish clear title to their farms. And they, too, out of desperation, with seemingly no viable alternatives, would rely on terrorist tactics to confront their enemies. Tryon had long coveted the New York post, but little could he have known that the problems wrought by Allen and the Green Mountain Boys would be every bit as vexatious as those associated with the War of the Regulation.

Because the story of Ethan Allen and the Green Mountain Boys has been so inextricably linked to the American Revolutionary War and the subsequent establishment of the state of Vermont, it is difficult to sift through the early portrayals, which tended to lionize Allen, in order to understand exactly who he was and what motivated him throughout his storied life. Further, the outlaw period of Allen and the Green Mountain Boys was but one chapter of both Allen's legacy and Vermont's struggle for statehood, routinely overshadowed by the capture of Ticonderoga, the war against Britain, Allen's detention as a prisoner of war, and the postwar machinations between Congress and the New Hampshire grantees. Thus, the years 1769–1775 have become but a footnote to the legends of both Vermont and the Green Mountain Boys, who were often referred to as the "Bennington Mob." Yet, the period is a significant one, for it reveals the depths of frustration, desperation, and hostility felt by the grantees as they struggled to make meaning of their lives, long before independence became a viable objective.

Given the tight links among the Green Mountain Boys, the American Revolution and the establishment of Vermont, perhaps it is inevitable that all three would be cast as heroic struggles against great odds. Subsequently, the first histories of the Green Mountain Boys and the making of Vermont, published during the early 19th century, were consistent with the romanticism of this era's American historians. Zadock Thompson's *History of the State of Vermont* (1833) and Jared Sparks's *The Life of Colonel Ethan Allen* (1858) were similarly celebratory and respectful of Allen and the Boys.[1] Sparks, for example, suggested that when it came to the Green Mountain Boys, "to drive one of them from his house, or deprive him of his hard-earned substance was to threaten the whole community with an issue fatal alike to their dearest interests . . . it was no wonder, therefore, that they should unite in common cause." Sparks, who had penned an earlier study of Allen in 1834, made it clear in his latter biography that "if riots existed, they were caused by those who came among (the grantees) for molestation and injury," the very same New York authorities who "exhibited attitudes of menace and contempt, armed with the mandates and terror of the law."[2] Similar themes were reinforced by two fictional accounts written by Judge D. P. Thompson, which helped fix the popular image of the Green Mountain Boys for the remainder of the 19th century. *The Green Mountain Boys* (1839) and *The Rangers* (1857), which together went through more than 50 editions, also portrayed the insurgents in the Grants as simple, innocent farmers battling the evil forces of Yorker corruption. If there was any doubt, Thompson's sentiments were made clear in his dedication to the 1839 edition, which suggested that because the Allen clan had been so "intelligent, enterprising, and fearless," Vermont was "deeply indebted for her existence . . . and for her present prosperity."[3] Throughout Thompson's pages, the Green Mountain Boys come across as "plain and hardy sons of liberty, unflinchingly engaged face to face, and often arm to arm, in deadly strife."[4] During the same time period, two books by Henry De Puy, *Ethan Allen and the Green Mountain Heroes of '76* (1853) and *The Mountain Hero and His Associates* (1855), repeated the by-then-familiar themes. Allen and the Boys were noble and staunch patriots, defenders of liberty and early symbols of liberal democracy.[5]

By the end of the 19th century, the popular image of Ethan Allen and the Green Mountain Boys was so firmly entrenched into our historical consciousness that with but one exception, Henry Hall's reverential biography *Ethan Allen: The Robin Hood of Vermont* (1892), no major works on the subject appeared for the next 70 years.[6] In 1928, James B. Wilbur's *Ira Allen: Founder of Vermont, 1751–1814* generated renewed interest in the Allen clan, and a year later John Pell's *Ethan Allen* provided the first modern scholarly treatment of the mountain rebel. In the words of one reviewer, because previous accounts of Allen had been "highly fanciful . . . to the point of being unworthy of scholarly notice," Pell's account helped "rescue Ethan Allen from the limbo of folklore" by making sound and judicious use of primary sources.[7] Pell acknowledged Allen's shortcomings, including the disastrous Montreal campaign and Allen's brief flirtation with the British during the final stages of the Revolution, but still delivered a largely sympathetic account. Pell also cast Allen and the Boys as "outlaws" during the controversy in the Grants but managed to downplay their reliance on violent tactics, suggesting instead that Allen maintained a sense of proportion and often treated his victims with unexpected leniency. Unfortunately, Pell focused his attention almost entirely on Allen, depicting the Green Mountain Boys as bit players. Yet, Pell never developed a real sense of who Allen was, leaving it to the reader to discern Allen's motivations, attitudes, and beliefs. In the end, as with all previous portrayals, Allen's outlaw period was but a small chapter in his larger-than-life story.[8]

In 1939, Matt Bushnell Jones's *Vermont in the Making* provided the best account yet of the legal entanglements surrounding the controversy in the Grants and thus passed no particular moral judgment on Allen. Jones, however, also minimized the violence instigated in the Grants by the Green Mountain Boys, maintaining that Allen's enemies "were frightened from the field of battle by lurid threats and bold invective instead of bloodshed and death."[9] A year later, Allen received another full biography treatment, more than half a century since the last. Stewart A. Holbrook's *Ethan Allen* was a throwback to the romantic histories of the 19th century, a portrayal that shed some light on Allen's darker side, earning Holbrook a measure of hostility from some folks in New England but ultimately serving as yet another example of Allen idolatry. Partly because of this and partly because it does not cite sources, Holbrook's work largely escaped the notice of academics, despite seven printings. In it, Allen could be profane and violent but was just as likely to appear kind and compassionate. Holbrook canonized Allen for his brilliant leadership and, as America was moving toward global war in 1940, argued that what America needed most was "Green Mountain seasoning." Holbrook joined the chorus of those who deemphasized Green Mountain violence during the Grants controversy, noting that the Bennington Mob "would rather frighten recalcitrants into submission than use actual violence."[10]

Holbrook's treatment set off a modest wave of Allen biographies spread over the next 50 years. In 1969, Charles A. Jellison's *Ethan Allen—Frontier Rebel* provided a balanced perspective of the Allen legacy, promising in the introduction to pick up where John Pell had left off. Indeed, Jellison referred to the Green Mountain Boys as a "rowdy bunch of bullies and outlaws" and described Allen as "a demigod to some and to others an unconscionable thug."[11] Yet, Jellison, like those before him, downplayed the violence in the Grants, reminding readers that Allen and his allies never took a life during the Grants controversy, relying instead on "friendly persuasion, threats and, all else failing, violent coercion."[12] Despite Jellison's objectivity, in the end, the Green Mountain Boys still emerged as "rough but kindly and honest backwoods yeomen," and, while Allen was motivated in large measure by "carefully reasoned self-interest," his actions also "stemmed from a deep seated ideological commitment to the rights and dignity of man."[13] And James Duane, one of Allen's chief New York adversaries, was described as a "money grubbing, shifty-eyed . . . bona-fide, flesh and blood villain."[14]

In 1976, Edwin P. Hoyt's *Damndest Yankees—Ethan Allen and His Clan* was both an interesting and disappointing contribution to the literature. Its primary problem was that Hoyt, a freelance journalist, failed to provide either footnote citations or a bibliography. It was unique, however, in that approximately one-third of the book was devoted to the outlaw period in the Grants. And Hoyt did not underplay Allen's use of violence. Acknowledging that "Allen and his gang kept the land in constant terror," Hoyt detailed a scene where, in order to make a point to a Yorker official, Allen and some Green Mountain Boys sliced a pet dog to pieces with their swords, held up the bloody carcass, and promised to do the same to the governor. Hoyt referred to the attack on the hapless animal as "a miserable performance."[15] And where other writers minimized the effect of whipping, suggesting instead that 200 lashes were preferable to death, Hoyt pointed out that, elsewhere, many men had died from less.

The next Allen biography appeared in 1993: Michael A. Bellesiles's *Revolutionary Outlaws—Ethan Allen and the Struggle for Independence on the Early American Frontier.* Bellesiles cast Allen as a charismatic and magnetic leader of legendary proportions, a man who gave voice and structure to the concerns of the poor and powerless settlers in the Grants holding New Hampshire titles. Bellesiles argued that the outlaw era was a defining period in Allen's life and helped lay the foundation of Vermont's statehood by bringing together disparate communities into a single political unit. Despite these admirable qualities, Bellesiles's Allen was also "a thug, a bully, a loudmouth terrorist" who deserved his reputation "as a scoundrel, a charismatic charlatan of enormous strength and character, and a braggart of almost mythical proportions," a "Davy Crockett in a tricorne."[16] Ultimately, the campaign in the Grants possessed a larger meaning beyond the lush ridges of the Green Mountains, according to Bellesiles. The conflict was part of the general revolutionary and democratic movement then sweeping the colonies. It was representative of a resistance movement among agricultural frontier communities north and south against the machinations of distant governments under the control of wealthy, urban speculators. It thus had elements of class warfare, pitting the rich and powerful against the poor.

Yet, somewhat paradoxically, Bellesiles also managed to downplay the violence in the Grants, which he rendered as "essentially a nonviolent conflict." Nevertheless, he confirmed the use of some terrorist tactics by acknowledging that Allen's resistance movement was "based on political theatre and psychological warfare to win battles without the loss of life." Allen sought not to hurt or kill his opponents, because he and the Bennington Mob had discovered that "humiliation and terror proved more effective" in "neutralizing" their adversaries.[17] Thus, Bellesiles saw elements of a terrorist campaign but characterized them as benign, nonviolent forms of conflict. To suggest that Allen could routinely dole out 200 lashes as punishment without intending to do harm is, of course, preposterous.

Shifting the focus from Allen to his surrounding community, Robert E. Shalhope's *Bennington and the Green Mountain Boys* (1996) provided a penetrating portrait of the diverse political, economic, and cultural forces that converged in the Grants and helped spawn liberal democracy. Expanding on the sophistication of analysis introduced by Bellesiles, Shalhope posited the notion that these forces consisted of three different elements: the egalitarian communalism of strict Congregationalists, the hierarchical elitism of federalist "gentlemen," and the democratic individualism of the Green Mountain Boys. Together, these forces helped create a formidable alliance of resisters devoted to confronting the depredations of the vile Yorkers. Within this context, the Green Mountain Boys, who received relatively benign treatment from Shalhope, are but one element in the complex issues that coalesced in the Grants. Yet, Shalhope did not ignore the provocations committed by the mob from Bennington, detailing their worst offenses and acknowledging the broad impact of Green Mountain violence.[18]

Just when it appeared that the Ethan Allen literature had run its course, a new treatment, by Willard Sterne Randall, appeared in 2011, *Ethan Allen—His Life and Times.* Randall, who had penned earlier biographies from the Revolutionary era, sought to strip away the mythical veneer enveloping Allen by humanizing a man often compared to Robin Hood, Davey Crockett, and Paul Bunyan. Placing a heavy emphasis on Allen's childhood development and early adult years, Randall demonstrated how Allen was very much a product not only of his time and place but also of the many influential people in his life, particularly his father, Joseph, his schoolmaster the Rev. Jonathan Lee, and his mentor Dr. Thomas Young. The Allen that emerges from Randall's study is a multi-dimensional, paradoxical egotist who seemed to be motivated as much by greed as by philosophy or politics. But anyone familiar with the Allen literature most likely already recognized these characteristics that comprised this complex man. Consequently, while Randall provided the freshest and most detailed take on Allen, he didn't offer anything revelatory about the many well-known vignettes that make up Allen's storied life. However, Randall did raise one especially interesting point of immediate concern here. While lamenting the violence perpetuated by the Green Mountain Boys, as well as by the Sons of Liberty, Randall posed the question "Was America founded, at least in part, on terrorism?"[19] While he never bothered to answer his own question, the perspectives offered here and in the next chapter provide an emphatic response.

II.   Controversy in the Grants

The area referred to as the New Hampshire Grants was a vast bloc of land located just north of western Massachusetts and extending westward from the Connecticut River to the southeastern environs of Lake Champlain. Now the southern half of Vermont, the area is dominated by the rolling hills and river valleys of the Green Mountains. When, in 1664, Charles II granted his brother, the Duke of York, a generous tract of land in North America, the eastern border of New York, which then abutted New Hampshire, was thus established at the Connecticut River, though the actual course of the river was unknown at the time. During the 1740s, Benning Wentworth, the governor of New Hampshire, began to issue grants cheaply to areas west of the Connecticut, despite the troublesome fact that the areas in question were apparently located within New York's jurisdiction. Wentworth argued that he had orders to settle the area since New York had not yet established a presence in these remote lands, and he may, in fact, have believed that he had legitimate claims to these grants, given a judgment in 1747 by Britain's Royal Council that placed the New York border only 20 miles east of the Hudson River. Yet, there can be little doubt that he also recognized an opportunity to aggrandize himself and close acquaintances by controlling the sale of these huge tracts of unsettled land. Wentworth eventually issued grants totaling nearly 3 million acres, including 65,000 acres for his personal enrichment and grants for 129 townships, one of which he immodestly named Bennington.[20]

New York belatedly challenged Wentworth's actions and exacerbated the problem further by issuing grants of its own, many in the same areas that New Hampshire had already granted; however, in 1764, the king and the Board of Trade reaffirmed the Connecticut River as the boundary separating New York from New Hampshire, presumably putting an end to the dispute. They did not, however, invalidate the Wentworth titles nor resolve the problem of uncertain legal ownership of double-granted tracts of land. Consequently, in 1767, the Crown also forbade any further issuance of grants in the disputed area until it could investigate the matter further. This seemingly left the door open for the Wentworth grantees to maintain their defiance of New York's jurisdiction. Compounding the situation, over the next several years, in complete defiance of the king's orders, New York would issue additional grants covering more than 2 million acres. Many of these patents, most of which were sold to absentee proprietors and New York's political elite, overlapped with the Wentworth titles. William Tryon, soon-to-be governor, would hold title to 32,000 acres.[21] In a dilemma similar to New Jersey's, the groundwork had, thus, been established for an impassioned and protracted struggle to determine jurisdiction and ultimately ownership of vast expanses of land.

The people who held title to these lands, be they Yorkers or New Hampshire grantees, can be excused for their constant state of frustration and uneasiness. The Privy Council in England ordered them to acknowledge New York law, but John Wentworth, who had succeeded his uncle Benning as governor in 1764, advised them to "regulate themselves according to their Grants from New Hampshire."[22] Adding to the legal complexity of life in the Grants, great social and religious diversity contributed to the political instability. Most of the settlers in the Grants had come from New England in general and Connecticut in particular, having followed the Connecticut River northward. The Green Mountains, which run north-south, divided the Grants into a western sector, which strongly opposed New York jurisdiction from the start, and an eastern, which demonstrated some support for New York claims. Robert Shalhope noted that the folks of Bennington, which sat in the western sector, represented a cross section of individualists, communalists, and hierarchical elites.[23] Many were New Lights, adherents of the Great Awakening, who had come to the Grants in search of religious liberalism, but there were also Old Lights, resulting in a bitter sectarian rivalry which undermined any common identity in the Grants beyond the sharing of New Hampshire titles.

It was with good reason that these New Hampshire grantees evaded New York authority. New York's northeastern courts were not just tools of the rich but notoriously corrupt and inept, a condition that contributed significantly to New York's inability to establish unquestionable jurisdiction.[24] The New Hampshire grantees knew that they stood little chance of getting New York to honor their titles, yet they continued to persist in seeking legal redress, both in England and through the colonial courts. Their arguments were founded on a number of premises: that the New York–New Hampshire border ran only 20 miles east of the Hudson River, that the Wentworth titles superseded any granted by New York's governors, that the lands in question had already been occupied and improved by the Wentworth grantees, and that the king had not yet delivered a final determination on the controversy. However, by 1769, New York was ready to act more forcefully. Cadwallader Colden had become acting governor for a second time and began an aggressive campaign to establish his authority. In an effort to encourage greater Yorker settlement in the Grants, he issued further patents and sent in New York surveyors to run lines and partition tracts of land.

On October 19, 1769, one such survey team was sent to the Walloomsac Patent, to survey and subdivide land occupied by James Breakenridge, who held a Wentworth title. Breakenridge had gathered some men to help harvest corn, but, aware that a survey team was in the area, recruited several armed neighbors to provide protection. This assemblage was far more than a simple gathering of farmers. Since 1764, nearby Bennington had had a local militia, and Breakenridge was its lieutenant. Some of the armed neighbors who had answered Breakenridge's call were members of this militia.[25] John Munro, a New York justice of the peace, then approached Breakenridge, informing him that a team of Yorker surveyors was about to approach and that neither Breakenridge nor his allies should challenge their authority. Once the surveyors arrived on the scene, Breakenridge began to parley with the Yorkers, while his armed neighbors looked on menacingly from a distance. Each side presented its case to the other, and Breakenridge, eager to avoid a violent confrontation, consented to having his land surveyed, under the conditions that the survey be witnessed by some of his neighbors and that his farm be designated as "Disputed Land." The Yorkers refused to abide by these conditions and, unwilling to confront an armed and hostile crowd, wisely decided to withdraw from the patent and returned to New York.[26] Violence had been averted, but the Breakenridge affair was only the beginning of a series of increasingly hostile confrontations between Yorker commissioners and Wentworth grantees. In December, New York Governor Colden issued a proclamation calling for the arrest of several rioters for their participation in the Breakenridge affair.

While the fallout from the Breakenridge standoff continued to send political ripples throughout the Grants, a court case, *John Small v. Josiah Carpenter,* began to wend its way through New York's judicial bureaucracy. Major John Small, who held a New York title, had discovered New Hampshire grantees living on his patent and, in 1769, filed an ejectment suit against the squatters.[27] It quickly became evident that this test case, along with eight other ejectment suits scheduled to be heard in Albany in June 1770, would constitute one last chance for the New Hampshire grantees to convince New York authorities of the validity of their legal titles. As with most cases heard by Yorker courts regarding New Hampshire titles, the odds were stacked significantly in New York's favor. In an obvious conflict of interests, the presiding judges, Robert Livingston and George Ludlow, held titles in the disputed Grants, as did Attorney General John Tabor Kempe and James Duane, attorney for the plaintiffs. The New Hampshire defendants, fully aware of these significant obstacles, met in Canaan, Connecticut, to raise funds and devise a collective legal strategy. Ultimately, they would be represented in court by two appointees: Jared Ingersoll, Sr., a prominent attorney from Connecticut, and a newcomer to the Grants, Ethan Allen. At the time, few people could have appreciated that the appointment of Allen, a man with a checkered and colorful past, would greatly intensify the showdown in the Grants and take the resistance movement to a whole new level of violent confrontation, culminating in a campaign based on terrorist methods.

III. Ethan Allen and the Green Mountain Boys

America has seen few characters the likes of Ethan Allen. He was, at various times in his life, a land speculator, entrepreneur, propagandist, survivalist, conspirator, patriarch, military hero, prisoner of war, Congressional lobbyist, terrorist, and, above all else, an opportunist of grand proportions. Born in Connecticut in 1737 as the eldest of eight children, Allen assumed patriarchal duties as a teenager when his father, Joseph, passed away. At 19, he volunteered for duty during the French and Indian War but never saw combat. Soon thereafter, he invested in a blast furnace, the first of many short-lived money-making schemes involving family members, and in 1762 he took a wife, Mary Brownson. Allen also developed a close relationship with Dr. Thomas Young, who, as his tutor, nurtured Allen's thirst for knowledge and lively discussion. Young, a rebel of sorts, encouraged similar thinking by Allen, as the good doctor attacked entrenched wealth and privilege, the Great Awakening preachers, supernatural religion, and the vagaries of science. Young went so far as to inoculate Allen for smallpox, an act that not only violated the law but also the admonitions of the vast majority of physicians and theologians.[28]

Beginning in 1765, Allen's fortunes began to wane. A series of bad investments, lawsuits, physical assaults, and a propensity for profane language and drunken behavior offended enough people that Allen was evicted from two communities: Salisbury, Connecticut, and Northampton, Massachusetts. By 1770, Allen and his family seemingly had nowhere to go. Allen, however, had a vision. Two years earlier, on an exploratory trek during the thick of winter into the wilderness of the Green Mountains, Allen had seen the lush river valleys, the endless panorama of rolling hills, and the boundless opportunities to own vast tracts of land. He had returned frequently to hunt, to visit with old friends from Connecticut, to make new acquaintances, but mainly to visit with his cousins Remember Baker and Seth Warner, who had settled in the Grants a few years earlier. Allen and his extended family would eventually head to Bennington, and the history of what would become Vermont was forever altered.

When the defendants in the Albany ejectment suits met in early 1770 to plot their legal defense, Ethan Allen was a newcomer to the Grants, but hardly unknown. By then, he, too, was a New Hampshire proprietor, having purchased three lots of land in the Grants—two in Poultry and one in Castleton—accumulating about 100,000 acres in the process.[29] Already, he commanded a measure of respect, as his selection as lead representative of the defendants would indicate. Having secured the legal services of Jared Ingersoll, who agreed to defend Allen's clients, the two arrived in Albany on June 28, 1770, to begin trial. When during the proceedings for *Small v. Carpenter,* the presiding judge refused to accept into evidence Josiah Carpenter's Wentworth title on the basis of its invalidation, Ingersoll's defense immediately collapsed. The ejectment trials were over before they had a chance to begin, a development that many could have predicted. Before Allen returned to Bennington, however, he was approached by James Duane, attorney for the plaintiffs, and Attorney General John Tabor Kempe, who offered Allen a bribe of cash and land to switch sides in the Grants controversy. True to form, Allen took their money but refused to turn against his friends and family. When Duane warned that the Yorkers "had might on our side," Allen famously responded, "the gods of the hills are not the gods of the valley." When the attorney general inquired as to his meaning, Allen ominously suggested that, should Kempe accompany him "to the hill in Bennington, the sense will be made clear."[30] Most historical accounts seize on this exchange as mutually threatening and portentous of violent times to come. Yet, there is greater meaning to Allen's words when one considers that he also signaled the status of the New Hampshire grantees as outsiders, separate and apart from the jurisdiction of New York. Later, Allen and the Green Mountain Boys would reinforce their separateness by conducting their own courts of law and meting out their own forms of punishment.

Allen returned to Bennington and called together his neighbors to deliver the bad news. Assembling in the Catamount Tavern, which would soon become their primary meeting place, attendees of the convention heard Allen's report, vowed to defend their homes against the Yorkers, and quickly reestablished their local militia, appointing Ethan Allen as commander. Thus was born the company that was to become known as the Green Mountain Boys. On several counts, the historical records agree. The Boys identified themselves by sticking fir twigs onto their hats. Most were typical farmers in the Grants, having found their way from Connecticut, and many had served in Bennington's military company since 1764. Although their ages ranged from 14 to 70, the most-active conspirators tended to be in their late twenties and early thirties.[31] There is some minor disagreement, however, about when they attained their famous moniker. Charles Jellison and John Pell claimed that the name was adopted in 1770, shortly after the Albany trials, to mock Governor Cadwallader Colden and his boast that he would drive the Bennington rioters into the Green Mountains.[32] Robert Shalhope suggested instead that it was Colden's successor, William Tryon, who made the boast, and, because Tryon didn't assume gubernatorial duties in New York until July 1771, this would place the naming sometime later.[33] The most reliable source concerning this issue, indeed the source cited by Pell and most likely used by Jellison, is a history of Vermont published in 1798 by Ira Allen, Ethan's brother. Ira Allen pinpointed precisely neither when the name was adopted nor which governor it was meant to mock, but did imply that it occurred in the immediate aftermath of the Albany trials.[34]

Whether known primarily as the Green Mountain Boys or the Bennington Mob, the resistors in the Grants were variously referred to as rioters, levelers, and banditti. They were also terrorists. Precise numbers of the Boys can be difficult to ascertain, for inclusion in the company was fluid. In 1996, however, in an article published in *Vermont History,* Donald A. Smith, using methodologies based on earlier research by Edward P. Hoyt, put the precise number of Green Mountain Boys at 436. Hoyt had conducted research on Ethan Allen's expeditionary force during the Ticonderoga campaign, and Smith's estimate is partly based on the assumption that Allen would recruit Green Mountain Boys to fill his military ranks. This is, perhaps, a logical conclusion, yet a bit presumptuous, given the distinct difference between defending one's family and home against legal obstructions versus invading hostile territory as an act of war against a sovereign state. Nonetheless, in perhaps the most penetrating analysis of the social origins of the Green Mountain Boys, Smith also suggested that the Boys were hardly Ethan Allen clones.

While Allen, as Smith described him, was a "profane, hard-drinking, irreligious adventurer," he "neither epitomized nor originated the spirit and character of the Green Mountain Boys." Allen was largely a land speculator; the Boys were mostly middle-class yeomen farmers and small-scale proprietors. Moreover, Smith argued, "the Boys derived their radical politics from religious dissent, not Ethan's deistic, liberal, Enlightenment thought." Based on his extensive demographic research, Smith further maintained that more than half of the Green Mountain Boys had formed their attitudes from earlier religious and political conflicts in eastern Connecticut, southern Massachusetts, and the infamous New York anti-rent riots of the early 1760s. These were the refugees who ultimately settled in the Grants, bringing with them "the contagion of rebellion."[35] Allen, then, did not ignite the resistance movement but, rather, effectively tapped into an existing groundswell of radical dissenters with a history of confrontational politics.

Whatever their precise numbers, as with the original Bennington militia, whenever an emergency in the Grants developed, whoever among the Boys was ready and willing answered the call. Typically, this meant that anywhere from a dozen to several dozen men might appear at any given time. And like the militia, the Green Mountain Boys had a hierarchical structure. In addition to Ethan Allen's selection as colonel commander, two of his cousins, Remember Baker and Seth Warner, along with Robert Cochran and Gideon Warren, were appointed captains. Soon, various other companies of Green Mountain Boys appeared in other communities spread across the New Hampshire Grants. They often conducted their activities in blackened faces, Indian garb, or various other disguises to protect their identities, but they didn't always feel the need. Ethan Allen, for example, reveled in his outlaw status and took few precautions to mask his complicity in the resistance movement.

The convention that appointed Allen as commander and subsequent conventions passed additional resolutions expressing defiance of the Albany courts. Yorker officials could not abduct persons from the Grants without permission; New York surveyors were forbidden from running lines anywhere in the Grants; and transgressors of these resolves were to be punished according to local courts established either by community elders or commanders of the Green Mountain militias.[36] This punishment could be extremely brutal. Ira Allen, in *The Natural and Political History of the State of Vermont,* described the treatment administered to one New Yorker: "Mr. Hugh Monroe, an old offender, was taken, tried, and ordered to be whipped on his naked back; he was tied to a tree and flogged until he fainted; on recovering, he was whipped again until he fainted; he recovered and underwent a third lashing until he fainted; his wounds were then dressed, and he was banished [from] the district of the New Hampshire Grants."[37] Ira Allen acknowledged that this type of punishment was employed to undermine local support for New York claimants; he further suggested that, because these violent reprisals were so successful, "the Green Mountain Boys soon became the terror of their adversaries."[38] From mid-1770 to April 1775, when the hostilities at Lexington and Concord ignited the American Revolution, Ethan Allen and the Bennington Mob did, indeed, terrorize Yorkers. While it is true that they never took a life, their vicious assaults on persons and property, the psychological impact of their violent tactics of intimidation, their use of propaganda to publicize their political motivations, their sustained campaign, which extended over five years, and their hierarchical structure qualify the Green Mountain Boys as one of America's first terrorist organizations. Moreover, they were terrorists who, in the end, escaped capture and punishment for their provocations in the Grants.

IV. Terror in the Grants

Following the Albany trials, New York decided to press its New Hampshire claims more forcefully, and in September 1770 attempted yet again to run lines through the farm of James Breakenridge. Once more, an armed company of rioters thwarted the Yorker surveyors. New York then issued a proclamation ordering the arrest of 16 persons, including Silas Robinson, "as the principle authors and actors in the riot and breach of peace."[39] Consequently, on November 29, Henry Ten Eyck, sheriff of Albany County, accompanied by John Munro, set out to arrest Robinson. Entering the Walloomsac Patent carefully so as to escape detection, the two were sheltered for a night at the home of Ebenezer Cole, a Yorker sympathizer, who warned them that, in anticipation of their visit, the Bennington Mob was armed and ready to mobilize. Undeterred, Ten Eyck and Munro set out the next day, apprehended Robinson, and quickly retreated with their prisoner to the home of Cornelius Van Ness, who resided in nearby Sanchoick. During the late evening, the Van Ness house was surrounded by about 40 armed Green Mountain Boys, who demanded that Robinson be released. Munro helped a young boy from the household escape through a back window to seek assistance and then warned the crowd that help was on the way. At sunrise, the rioters fired off a volley of gunshots and then dispersed into the woods. Silas Robinson was then accompanied to Albany without further incident, where he remained jailed for several months.[40] From this point forward, no other New Hampshire grantee would be jailed for his participation in the resistance movement.

In the aftermath of this failed rescue riot of Silas Robinson, New York was further emboldened, and in December a New York constable and his deputies arrested Moses Robinson (relationship unknown) for his part in obstructing the attempts to survey Breakenridge's farm. This time, however, a large company of disguised terrorists assaulted the constable and successfully retrieved Robinson. When the constable gave chase, he was assaulted a second time. When he warned the insurgents that they were acting in violation of the law, the Boys responded by damning the laws of New York and declaring that they had laws of their own.[41] James Breakenridge, meanwhile, eager to resolve his situation peacefully, continued to petition the king, requesting timely adjudication of the Grants controversy, but his Walloomsac farm would remain at the heart of New

York's attempt at establishing its authority in the Bennington area. In early January 1771, an Albany sheriff and two officers attempted to deliver writs of possession to Breakenridge and his neighbor Josiah Fuller but, on arrival at the two properties, found them occupied by Green Mountain Boys, who threatened to blow out the sheriff's brains if he proceeded further. The sheriff retreated, but two days later he returned, this time reinforced with a dozen men. They proceeded to the home of Isaiah Carpenter, who also threatened to blow out the brains of anyone who threatened him with dispossession. This time, the sheriff and his men broke through Carpenter's front door and seized the enraged farmer before he could fire off a shot. Inside, the Yorkers discovered a whole cache of arms but left peacefully after Carpenter agreed to either settle with his rival New York claimant or surrender his land.[42]

The defiance of the Green Mountain Boys began to escalate throughout 1771. In May, William Cockburn, a New York surveyor, attempted to run lines through a Socialborough tract also claimed by the New Hampshire grants of Rutland and Pittsford. Three local settlers confronted Cockburn, proclaimed him in violation of the king's edict of 1767, and warned him that, because "Nathan [Ethan] Allen was in the woods with another party blacked and dressed like Indians," Cockburn would likely be killed. Cockburn did not tarry; he promised never to return to the Grants and quickly took his leave.[43]

On July 28, Sheriff Ten Eyck, determined not be intimidated by the Bennington Mob, took command of a 200-man Yorker posse and set out to evict James Breakenridge from his Bennington farm. This small army consisted of volunteers, many unarmed, from a variety of backgrounds, including poor farmers, gentry, aldermen, attorneys, and even Abraham Cuyler, the mayor of Albany. A body that large advancing on the Grants could hardly evade detection; consequently, the Green Mountain Boys had plenty of time to prepare an appropriate reception. About 150 men positioned themselves near Breakenridge's farm, with nearly 100 of them stationed on a ridge above his house. They were armed with firearms, swords, and clubs. Eighteen men barricaded themselves inside Breakenridge's cabin, holding a red flag that was to be flown should they need immediate assistance. Breakenridge's family had safely abandoned the scene sometime earlier. When the sheriff and his posse reached a bridge half a mile from Breakenridge's farm, they encountered half a dozen armed guards who had orders to obstruct their passage. After a short parley, the guards agreed that a small party would be allowed to pass, as long as no one else crossed until their return. Mayor Cuyler and a small company then proceeded to the farm, where they hoped to convince Breakenridge to surrender his property. There, they found him in the immediate company of about two-dozen neighbors with well over a 100 more stationed within 100 yards. When Cuyler demanded that Breakenbridge surrender his possession, the farmer responded that the town of Bennington had taken the farm under its protection and that the community would never give it up. Cuyler, ever aware of the armed company around him, then returned to the bridge and apprised Sheriff Ten Eyck of the seemingly hopeless situation. The sheriff would have none of it. He ordered his posse to advance, whereupon no more than 20 of his company dared cross the bridge. Despite their greater numbers, Ten Eyck's recruits, most of whom had no direct interests at stake, were simply unwilling to exchange hostilities with the Green Mountain Boys. Many were poor farmers from the Hudson Valley who understood the hardships suffered by the New Hampshire grantees. Undeterred by this pronounced lack of support, the sheriff advanced to the Breakenridge property with his token posse and engaged the farmer in a spirited debate over the whole slew of issues associated with the Grants controversy. Sheriff Ten Eyck then approached the barricaded cabin and, finding the door locked, demanded that those inside abandon the property. When his demands were met with continued resistance, he read aloud the writ of possession and ordered one of his deputies to provide him with an axe. Just as Ten Eyck was about to smash open the front door, several of the Green Mountain Boys moved forward, cocked their firearms, and aimed them directly at the startled sheriff. The situation had grown so intense that, according to eyewitness accounts, had Ten Eyck not immediately stopped his assault on Breakenridge's home, many lives would have been lost that summer day, including that of the sheriff.[44] Still, Ten Eyck persisted. After wisely retreating back to the bridge, he requested that the posse now accompany him to the farm of Josiah Fuller for the same eviction purposes. His company, however, had seen enough. Half his militia quickly began to disperse "with all commendable speed" to their homes, leaving the sheriff with no recourse but to cancel the rest of his operation.[45]

Ethan Allen does not appear to have been directly involved in the extended Breakenridge affair, but it didn't take long for him to take the offensive against New York claimants. Thus far, the resistance movement had been largely defensive, maintaining a long-established policy of seeking accommodation by petitioning the Crown and keeping a reasonable lid on the violence against the Yorkers by sustaining a rigorous defense of Wentworth titles. This was all about to change. On October 29, Charles Hutcheson, a former corporal in the British army, was working on a 200-acre tract of land near Rupert granted to him by New York which happened to overlap with the New Hampshire claims of Robert Cochran. Cochran, Ethan Allen, Remember Baker, and six others surrounded the cabin Hutcheson had built and began to demolish it. When Hutcheson approached, he was informed that his house would be set afire as "a burnt sacrifice to the Gods of the world." Allen and company then threw burning logs onto Hutcheson's cabin, threatened to smash his head with two clubs, and demanded that he leave Rupert without further word and without further delay. They then cut loose with a barrage of insults and obscenities and promised to kill any constables sent to arrest them. Abandoning his home, now engulfed in flames, Hutcheson quickly fled to New Perth. The Green Mountain Boys moved on that day and also set ablaze the home of John Reid, another New York grantee. During the next few weeks, at least eight other families with New York claims also fled the Grants for New

Perth, adding to a small community of exiles with similar stories of being driven from their homes by the Bennington Mob.[46]

By now, William Tryon had arrived from North Carolina to become governor of New York. No doubt mindful of his experiences during the War of the Regulation, he released a proclamation which reinforced New York jurisdiction in the Grants and ordered warrants for the arrests of Ethan Allen, Robert Cochran, and the others involved in the assault upon Charles Hutcheson. A reward of 20 pounds sterling was added for each of the offenders. The warrants were issued by Alex McNaughton, justice of the peace in New Perth, but he was convinced of their ineffectiveness, writing to Tryon's secretary Edmund Fanning that because of the sheer numbers of "New Hampshire rioters and traitors . . . I am of Opinion no Sheriff or constable will apprehend them." Familiar with the hardships encountered by the exiled families in New Perth, McNaughton lamented that "on the very Eve of a long hard winter it is very Schocking to see so many poor familys reduced to so great Distress."[47] In a written response to Governor Tryon's proclamation, which also took New Hampshire to task for tacitly encouraging riotous behavior in the Grants, Governor John Wentworth denied the existence of disturbances in the environs of the Connecticut River, suggesting instead that the troubles were more directly related to areas of the Hudson River inhabited by transgressors from Massachusetts and Connecticut.[48]

Despite McNaughton's dire analysis of the state of lawlessness in the Grants, Yorker authorities persisted in executing the arrest of Allen and his fellow Green Mountain conspirators. In March 1772, John Munro, justice of the peace from Albany, still smarting from his failed attempt to evict James Breakenridge the previous summer, recruited a dozen men and set out to capture Remember Baker. Munro, despite repeated threats from the Green Mountain Boys, had continued to issue ejectments from his court and was now determined to strike first. Before sunrise on the March 21, Munro and his posse broke into Baker's home and, after a fierce struggle, abducted the captain of the Green Mountain Boys and whisked him away, but only after nearly severing Baker's thumb in the process and leaving behind Baker's shocked and battered family. Baker's wife, whose arm was broken during the melee, made her way to her neighbors, who assembled a rescue team that quickly overtook Munro. Surrounded by Green Mountain Boys, ten of Munro's posse immediately ran into the woods and disappeared. The Boys secured Baker's release and then took Munro and his two remaining deputies as captives themselves. Munro would be eventually released, but his torments had not yet come to an end. For the next few weeks, the Green Mountain Boys paid regular nighttime visits to Munro's home, firing their guns into the air and terrorizing Munro's family. In some instances, they entered his house brandishing their firearms, and, on at least one occasion, a shot was fired at the constable. Munro petitioned New York for immediate relief, given that "the rioters in that part of the Country are listing men daily . . . and thus Strike Terror into the whole Country."[49]

Remember Baker's rescue riot became a *cause celebre* in the Grants, partly due to the sensationalized reporting in the *Connecticut Courant,* the largest newspaper in the area. The *Courant* published Ethan Allen's narrative of the assault on Baker and his family, which he described as a "wicked, inhuman, most barbarous, infamous, cruel, villainous, and thieving act" wherein Munro and posse entered Baker's abode "and with weapons of death, spread destruction round the room, cutting with swords and brusing with firearms and clubs." In order "to procure a full draught of human blood to quench [his] thirst," he added, a posse member "instantly thrust his sword at Mrs. Baker with an intention to have ended, in that instant, her life."[50] In many regards, the *Connecticut Courant* became a mouthpiece of the Green Mountain resistance movement, publishing anonymous letters by Allen under pen names like "Lover of Truth and Reason" or "Friend of Liberty and Property." During the spring, two such letters appeared in the *Courant* summarizing all of the familiar legal positions maintained by the New Hampshire claimants. Allen described the impact of New York's draconian methods of ejectment, which had left "women sobbing and children crying, and men pierced to the heart with sorrow and indignation." Allen reminded his readers of Tryon's brutal treatment of the North Carolina Regulators, rehashing the story of Tryon's infamous killing of an unarmed prisoner just before the hostilities at Alamance. Regarding his fellow resisters in the Grants, Allen boldly predicted that Tryon would "find them of a different mettle from the southern province" and that "it looks highly probable his northern expedition will be attended with different consequences."[51] Allen had now begun his new role as chief propagandist for the Bennington Mob.

Tryon, however, appeared determined to avoid a repeat of Alamance and, in May, sent a letter to Reverend William Dewey of Bennington, offering to negotiate a peaceful resolution with representatives of the New Hampshire grantees. Tryon tempered his offer by warning the grantees that they should not deceive themselves into assuming that their homes would ever be annexed to the government of New Hampshire, and further declaring that he would not accept Ethan Allen and several others as representatives, due to their outlaw status. Tryon suggested the appointment of Dewey, James Breakenridge, and Stephen Fay, owner of the Catamount Inn, instead.[52] After several towns in the Grants sent representatives to Bennington to consider Tryon's overture, Stephen Fay and his son Jonas were selected instead to parley with the governor in New York. When the Fays arrived in Albany, they brought with them two letters, one from the Grants representatives and another signed by Ethan Allen, Seth Warner, Remember Baker, and Robert Cochran, but authorized by the Bennington convention.

These two letters are particularly instructive, for they succinctly summarize the legal positions long held by the New Hampshire grantees and provide a unique glimpse into Allen's philosophical convictions at this stage in his life. In the first, the Green Mountain Boys assured Tryon that they assented to his authority and that they acknowledged the king's 1764 decision establishing the Connecticut

River as the easternmost boundary of New York. However, they further argued, because a change in jurisdiction did not alter ownership of land, the king's decision did not invalidate the Wentworth titles. They maintained that, moreover, because New York had openly violated the king's edict of 1767, the Yorker authorities were the real lawbreakers, engaging in illegal and unconstitutional attempts to evict the Wentworth grantees. If only New York recognized the validity of their claims, the grantees promised to abide peacefully by Yorker laws. Allen's letter took the argument much further, elaborating on themes he had first broached in his letters to the *Connecticut Courant*. The controversy in the Grants was much more than a dispute over land titles, he asserted; it was nothing less than a struggle between classes, the speculative interests of elite absentee proprietors against the concerns of simple, industrious yeomen. Allen pointed out that the speculators from New York made money from a distance and without labor, while the New Hampshire farmers struggled to work and improve the lands on which they lived, "bringing their farms out of a wilderness state, into that of fruitful fields, gardens, and orchards." Citing a popularized version of John Locke's social contract, Allen argued that the laws of nature, which allow the defense of one's property, was not only eternal but "can never be abrogated by the Law of men."[53] As with the Sons of Liberty and other radicals of this period, his rhetoric was greatly influenced by notions of natural law and liberal democracy, partly owing to his earlier relationship with his tutor, Dr. Thomas Young. Allen was also spurred to action by the tactics of terror employed earlier by the Stamp Act resisters and the anti-rent insurgents along the Hudson River, who were also locked in controversy with wealthy and powerful landlords.[54]

What the Fays sought in Bennington was a truce: a temporary suspension of all litigation and ejectments in the Grants until the king made known his pleasure. Tryon and his council were inclined to cooperate. Tryon was, no doubt, personally motivated to avoid the type of bloodshed that marked the War of the Regulation, for he was keenly aware that his heavy-handed methods there had sullied his reputation. The council, for its part, acknowledged that the grantees had legitimate grievances. If the Yorker exiles who had fled the Grants were allowed to return unmolested, and if the New Hampshire grantees promised to abide by New York laws and cease their hostile behavior, a truce was indeed possible. The Fays returned to Bennington, whereupon, on July 15, 1772, a large meeting of settlers voted unanimously to accept the provisions of the proposed truce. Having vindicated their campaign of resistance, they then celebrated with drink and discharge of musket and canon fire.[55]

Unfortunately for all involved, the truce was terribly short-lived. During the negotiations in New York, word had reached Bennington that William Cockburn had returned to the Grants to run survey lines near the Onion River to the north. Cockburn, who had fled the Grants a year earlier fearing for his life, became the object of a manhunt as a party led by Remember Baker and Seth Warner set out to capture the bold but unwitting surveyor. On their way northward, the party happened upon a small settlement of Yorkers near the lower falls of Otter Creek in what is now Panton. Several families had moved into the area as tenants of Colonel John Reid, an earlier victim of Green Mountain violence. The Boys drove Reid's tenants away from Otter Creek and eventually caught up to Cockburn near the Onion River. They then spirited him away to Castleton to stand trial before the court of Ethan Allen. By then, Allen had learned of the truce brokered by the Fays in New York and saw to Cockburn's release. These provocations led to an angry exchange of letters between Governor Tryon and Allen, each accusing the other of having broken the truce. Allen's actions here were at least partly motivated by his own interests in the northern lands along the eastern bank of Lake Champlain. Ethan had purchased 500 acres near Otter Creek in 1770, and his brother Ira was then examining lands near the Onion River as a possible base of financial operations for the Allen family.[56] Indeed, that winter, the Allen brothers, along with Remember Baker, would form the Onion River Company.

While Ethan Allen might have argued that the Green Mountain Boys were genuinely unaware of the truce at the time of the provocations, it is equally true that the Boys did nothing from that point forward to give any indication that they sincerely sought to enforce its provisions. Two months after the July accord, a party of Green Mountain Boys led by Remember Baker and Ira Allen accosted Benjamin Stevens, another Yorker surveyor, near the Onion River. Members of the survey team were stripped of their possessions, and one of them, John Dunbar, was beaten, bound, and tossed onto a bonfire. Dunbar survived and a reward of 100 pounds sterling each was offered for the apprehension of either Baker or Ira Allen.[57] The truce, if ever there was one, had quickly evaporated.

The next summer, Ethan Allen received word that Colonel John Reid had once again settled tenants on disputed land near Otter Creek. In early August 1773, about 100 Green Mountain Boys, led by Ethan and Ira Allen, Seth Warner, and Remember Baker, gathered near the Reid settlement outside of Panton after a four-day march. There, about a dozen Scot families had been abandoned by Reid, who, after supervising their settlement, quickly left for New York, leaving the unsuspecting immigrant tenants to fend for themselves. On August 11, the Green Mountain Boys crossed Otter Creek and laid the settlement to waste. For two days, the Boys terrorized the Scot settlement as well as the families of nearby Yorker claimants, burning homes to the ground, destroying a grist mill, stampeding horses through corn fields, completely destroying precious crops, and threatening to tie victims to trees before skinning them alive. They also promised to chop off Reid's head, should he be captured. When one of the victims inquired by what authority the Boys would wreak such violence, Remember Baker replied that they lived out of the bounds of any law, save that represented by their guns. Baker also boasted that the ability of the Green Mountain Boys to engage in "bush fighting" would neutralize any attempt by New York to raise large armies against them. Before driving off the dispossessed tenants, Allen offered them plots of free land from his own Onion River properties. Approximately half took up the offer; the others returned to the safe confines of New York.[58] The wanton destruction sent shock waves throughout the Grants. John Munro, the notorious Yorker justice of the peace, wrote a passionate appeal to Governor Tryon, seeking help from the "rage and indignation of such a Riotous Mob, before the remains of my Property is destroyed, myself to Death and my helpless family to ruin and want."[59] In Bennington, Benjamin Hough, another Yorker official, requested from Tryon an armed force to provide protection against "the violence of a riotous set of men distinguished by the name of the Bennington Mob, and who in defiance of the dictates of Justice and Compassion, daily perpetuate the most flagrant acts of cruelty, outrage and oppression."[60]

While terror began to spread throughout the Grants, the Green Mountain Boys set their sights on Benjamin Spencer, the justice of the peace in Charlotte County, a new jurisdiction created by New York deep in the Grants. The justice was well known to the Green Mountain Boys. Spencer, as did many Yorkers, held title to lands in Durham and was among the most outspoken critics of the New Hampshire claimants. Late Saturday night, November 20, 1773, Ethan Allen, Remember Baker, and a party of Green Mountain Boys smashed open the front door of Spencer's Durham home with hatchets and rousted him out of bed. When he failed to dress quickly enough, Allen gave him a pistol whip to the head, while other gun barrels were directed at Spencer's family. Spencer was abducted and taken to nearby Kelso, where he was held captive by armed guards for two days. On Monday, Spencer was taken back to his home to stand trial before a Green Mountain court and about 130 armed Boys. Remember Baker then erected a "Judgment Seat" and he, Ethan Allen, Seth Warner, and Robert Cochran assumed their seats as both prosecutors and judges. Spencer was found guilty of conspiring with New York to invalidate the Wentworth titles and promoting Yorker authority, thereby undermining the resistance movement. Although Remember Baker insisted that Spencer be whipped as punishment, the justice was not subjected to this indignity. His house, however, was not spared. Because Spencer had not bothered to purchase a New Hampshire title, his house was deemed a public nuisance and the roof was set afire. Before the whole house was destroyed, the burning roof was detached, leaving the outside frame intact. Before withdrawing from Durham, the Boys set several other houses ablaze, threatened to burn several more, and promised to whip their owners in the process.[61]

Five days later, Jacob Marsh, another Yorker justice, was given similar treatment to that meted out to Spencer. While traveling outside Socialborough, Marsh was detained at gunpoint by Philip Perry, who held the justice captive until about 30 Green Mountain Boys emerged from a nearby home. In yet another expression of their self-proclaimed extralegal authority, the Boys hauled Marsh into a cabin under armed guard, and, before a panel of judges appointed by Remember Baker and Seth Warner, he was accused of crimes against the New Hampshire claimants. Marsh was found guilty. Although Remember Baker again recommended a public whipping, the justice was released unharmed but bearing a written order to cease his activities on behalf of New York or face "the pain of having his house burned and reduced to ashes and his person punished at pleasure." When Marsh finally returned home, he found that the roof of his house had been destroyed and other property vandalized. In a deposition to New York authorities, Marsh warned that, should he continue in his capacity as justice, "his Effects and property would be destroyed by the said Mob . . . and that his Life would be in danger."[62]

V.   The Green Mountain Boys as Terrorists

By the fall of 1773, the acts of terror committed by the Green Mountain Boys had taken on a familiar pattern. By establishing their own courts to dispense justice, they further confirmed their extralegal status as outsiders unbound by the laws of New York. By elevating himself and others as judges and jurors, Ethan Allen was very much playing a role as if on stage, for the benefit of the New Hampshire and Yorker claimants alike. This was typical of Allen's bravado and his love of attention. But it was also very much consistent with the notion that terrorism is part "theatre," conducted outside the accepted rules and procedures established by "the system," in this case, the authority of New York. At no time was this more evident than in the "trial" of Dr. Samuel Adams of Arlington, not to be confused with Samuel Adams of Boston. Dr. Adams had spoken harshly of the Green Mountain Boys and had advised residents to purchase lands under New York titles. He had also been warned to discontinue his activities under threat of punishment. Yet, Adams not only persisted in his pro-Yorker activism, but he also armed himself with two pistols and publicly declared that he would silence any man who dared molest him. To the surprise of almost no one but the good doctor himself, Adams was seized by the Green Mountain Boys and taken to Stephen Fay's Catamount Tavern in Bennington. There, he was tried and found guilty of crimes against the New Hampshire claimants. He was then tied to an armchair, taken outside, and hoisted 25 feet high alongside the front of the tavern, where he spent the next two humiliating hours. Adams was eventually released and dismissed by the Green Mountain court. He never again defended New York titles nor spoke harshly in public about the Green Mountain Boys.[63]

The Green Mountain Boys further confirmed their extralegal status by holding several conventions, which passed at least 18 local laws applicable to the Grants, establishing the Bennington Mob as a legislative, as well as judicial, body. As Donald A. Smith has noted, this form of mob law was divided into four categories: 1) those laws applicable to local governance of the Grants, 2) regulations directing Green Mountain military operations, 3) directives for the conduct of the Green Mountain courts, and 4) laws against the New York government. These Green Mountain laws were primarily concerned with terminating Yorker authority in the Grants, ordering the dispossession of all settlers holding New York titles, and prohibiting all inhabitants of the Grants from holding or executing New York commissions, but they also underscored the extent to which the Boys had established their own independent jurisdiction, upheld by military force. In essence, these laws further empowered the Green Mountain Boys to indict, try, and punish all those who dared violate their undisputed authority.[64]

Extralegal status was but one element of Green Mountain terrorism. The selective use of violence to defy Yorker authority and to induce fear and cooperation from both New York and New Hampshire claimants was, of course, an essential element of the insurgency. This tactic of intimidation was further enhanced by the military operations of the Bennington Mob. They constructed fortifications, gathered supplies of weapons, and drilled regularly in "bush fighting" tactics. As noted earlier, because the Green Mountain Boys took no lives, most historians of the Grants controversy tend to downplay the use of violent tactics by the Bennington Mob. This misses the point. Yorkers were beaten, pistol-whipped, and tossed onto bonfires. Their lives were constantly threatened until they surrendered their New York connections. Many had their homes burned to the ground or otherwise partially destroyed. Fences were torn down and crops destroyed. Confronted by armed companies, surveyors and sheriffs alike were driven from the Grants. But beyond these substantial elements of violence, the physical abuse of Green Mountain prisoners was soon to escalate. Public whippings, which Remember Baker had consistently recommended, and mass destruction of property would become particularly harsh and violent components of terrorism in the Grants.

Benjamin Hough was one such victim of the most extreme form of Green Mountain justice. Like Benjamin Spencer, Hough was a Yorker justice of the peace in Durham. For some time, he had been petitioning the New York authorities, defaming the Bennington Mob, identifying the perpetrators by name, and asking for help. On January 26, 1775, about 30 Green Mountain Boys surrounded Hough as he stood outside his cabin. They were armed with firearms, swords, and hatchets. Led by Peleg Sunderland, the Boys then whisked Hough 50 miles away to a settlement, where he was held captive for four days. On January 30, Hough stood before a court of seven judges, including Ethan Allen, Robert Cochran, and Seth Warner. Hough was charged with three crimes: complaining to Yorker authorities about the Green Mountain crime wave; discouraging residents from "joining the Mob"; and taking a New York commission in Charlotte County, in complete defiance of the Green Mountain laws. Allowed to plead for himself, Hough made a compelling defense. He had never personally molested anyone, had never attempted to evict settlers, and had never, as a magistrate, committed an act of injustice. Allen and the court had to agree that Hough was correct on all counts, just as Hough had to consent to having committed the offenses for which he was being charged. After further testimony, the judges withdrew for three hours before rendering a guilty verdict. Given the foregone conclusion to this case, one wonders why the deliberations took as long as they did. Perhaps the judges wanted to create the impression of objective and prudent consideration of Hough's defense, given the harshness of his sentence. Hough was taken outside the tavern, tied to a tree, stripped naked, and given 200 lashes on his back with whips of cord. He was told to abandon the Grants, never to return, under threat of 500 additional lashes. Badly wounded, faint, and bleeding profusely, Hough was then handed over to a doctor, who took him to a nearby house for treatment. Having sufficiently recovered by the next day, Hough set out for New York City. Along the way, he paid visits to two fellow New York magistrates who lived near Bennington. What he found were two families and a community living in fear. Both Bliss Willoughby and Ebenezer Cole had packed their homes with armed neighbors and friends in anticipation of an immediate attack by the Green Mountain Boys. Hough later described the people of Pownal as in "great commotion and uneasiness," so much so that a great number of them surrendered their New York leases.[65]

In light of the public fallout from the Hough affair, as well as other infamous aggressions by the Green Mountain Boys, there is no doubt that their violent tactics effectively created a climate of fear and intimidation, a psychological impact reaching beyond the immediate victims of the Bennington Mob. Many New York claimants, for instance, who managed to escape the wrath of the Green Mountain Boys, nonetheless fled the Grants, creating small exiled communities in cities such as New Perth and Albany. Other Yorkers stayed, surrendered their New York claims, and bought New Hampshire titles in order to stave off the Bennington Mob. Most of the people of Durham, a community known for its Yorker sympathies, ultimately purchased New Hampshire titles. Benjamin Hough was one who did not.[66] Volunteer militias in the Grants had already proven ineffective against the Mob, because most of their citizen-soldiers had heard about the Green Mountain Boys, and, if they did not openly support the resistance movement, it is certainly understandable that they would choose not to oppose it. Such was the environment of intimidation that John Munro had complained earlier to Yorker authorities that the Green Mountain Boys "strike Terror into the whole Country."[67] One Yorker from Brattleboro spoke for many when he proclaimed, "Ethan Allen is more dreaded than death with all its Terrors."[68] Benjamin Hough warned in a petition that the Mob, having erected two forts in Charlotte County, "encourages them in their Confidence and presumption [and] gives additional Terror to your Petitioners." Hough's petition added that Yorker claimants "are daily exposed to the most imminent Danger in their Persons and Properties, as while their magistrates are treated with so much Inhumanity, they can have no reason to look for the least mercy."[69] In another petition requesting an armed force to protect the settlers of Durham, Hough acknowledged that "the Civil authority in that part of the Country terrified and obstructed by the most insolent outrages, is altogether Silenced, neither Magistrates nor inferior Officers being able to Officiate in their respective Stations either in the protection of the persons or for the recovery of the debts of the injured."[70] There can be no doubt that Green Mountain violence was so exceedingly successful in creating an environment of intimidation that many normal, law-abiding settlers either lived in fear or accommodated the Boys by abandoning their homes and

Yorker titles. These claimants, far and wide, understood that the only law and order that existed in the Grants was that established and upheld by the Green Mountain Boys.

As with other terrorist groups, the Green Mountain Boys had a definite organizational chain of command. Ethan Allen was, of course, the undisputed leader of the Boys, a man with a reputation larger than life. Fables of Allen's superhuman strength and courage circulated throughout the Grants, making it difficult to separate man from myth. What is undeniable, however, is the respect accorded him by those who constituted the resistance movement, as evidenced by his selection as colonel commander of the Bennington Mob in 1770, after having only recently arrived in the Grants. As noted above, Allen's chief captains were his cousins Remember Baker and Seth Warner, while two other captains, Robert Cochran and Gideon Warren, were seemingly one notch below. None of the Green Mountain trials occurred without either Allen or one of his captains present as judges. Benjamin Hough, for example, was held captive for four days before his trial in order to allow Allen and his fellow judges sufficient time to reach Durham. It was this hierarchical structure that would allow the Green Mountain Boys to make the relatively easy transition during the American Revolution from a band of terrorists to a military unit.

Ethan Allen not only provided military leadership but was also the primary spokesperson for the resistance movement, carefully and sometimes clumsily articulating political perspectives and demands. His anonymous letters to the *Connecticut Courant* in 1772 had provided valuable propaganda for the insurgents, arguing the validity of New Hampshire titles and castigating the Yorker authorities for atrocities committed during their capture of Remember Baker. He also demonstrated keen propaganda skills in 1772 when New York offered rewards for the capture of several Green Mountain Boys. In response, Allen printed and widely distributed similar posters offering rewards for the capture of John Tabor Kempe, attorney general of New York, and James Duane, the infamous Yorker. Both had been instrumental in New York's successful prosecution in the *Small vs. Carpenter* case in 1769. The wanted posters were a humorous yet pointed attempt to portray the resistance movement as having its own independent system of justice. As Michael Bellesiles noted in his treatment of Allen, the fake posters "went beyond mockery, denying the validity and efficacy of New York's authority and placing the legitimacy of the Grants claimants on an equal footing with the royal province."[71] New York and James Duane responded to Allen with a propaganda campaign of their own. In 1773, Duane published two pamphlets, offering a strict legal defense of Yorker claims.[72] Unable to resist a retort, Allen further refined his political perspectives a year later with the publication of *A Brief Narrative of the Proceedings of the Government of New York Relative to Their Obtaining the Jurisdiction of That Large District of Land, to the Westward from the Connecticut River.* More than 200 pages long, Allen's account was hardly brief. It was also a disjointed compilation of short prose, documents, petitions, testimony, and various letters, all pertaining to the Grants controversy. As J. Kevin Graffagnino has noted, whereas Duane's accounts tended to dwell on "dusty" legal precedents and the letter of the law, Allen's publication countered that the laws of nature and self-preservation gave the New Hampshire claimants an inalienable right to the lands on which they toiled and survived.[73] Even if New York truly held authority in the Grants, Allen argued, it was only through annexation from New Hampshire, which, by itself, did not invalidate preexisting titles originally granted by the Wentworths. Allen portrayed the Grants controversy as class warfare, pitting the powerful, wealthy, and aristocratic elites of New York, who "fared sumptuously every day," against poor and destitute yeoman farmers, who endured "extreme Fatigue, Hunger, and infinite Hardships . . . in the Settlement and Cultivation of a Wilderness Country."[74] Ethan and his brother Ira would eventually become fairly prodigious writers, expounding on other issues of their time, particularly the establishment of Vermont, the ill-advised Franco-American conspiracy against British Canada during the 1790s, the state of religion, and, of course, Ethan's captivity as a British prisoner during the American Revolution. But it was during the Grants controversy that Ethan first honed his propaganda skills, gradually recognizing the power of the written word to complement violence and intimidation.

VI. From Terrorists to Patriots

By early 1775, the controversy in the Grants had become overshadowed by a much larger and pertinent resistance movement. Ever since the ill-fated Stamp Act of 1765, various chapters of the Sons of Liberty had been fanning the flames of resistance against British authority, most notably in Boston. Anglo–American relations had deteriorated sufficiently that the Coercive Acts of 1774 helped motivate unprecedented inter-colonial cooperation, as evidenced by the First Continental Congress, which met later that year in Philadelphia. Ethan Allen, ever sensitive to the direction of the prevailing political winds, began to equate the Green Mountain insurgency with the emerging resistance against British rule that would culminate in the American Revolution. Allen found much in common between his Green Mountain Boys and the Sons of Liberty. His rhetoric, for example, as well as that of other Green Mountain spokespersons, was greatly impacted by the prevailing radical viewpoints from the Age of Enlightenment, and his campaign of terror against the Yorkers was equally inspired by the politicized violence provoked by the rebellious Sons. This particular approach had a broader impact beyond generating sympathy for the resistance movement. Allen had always found his greatest support from the settlers on the west side of the Green Mountains. Eastsiders, most of whom had migrated from the conservative and affluent areas of eastern Connecticut and Massachusetts, tended to be more moderate, and Cumberland County, in particular, was decidedly pro-Yorker. But by portraying his resistance against Yorker authority as part of the broader defiance against Parliament and king, Allen was able to undermine Yorker support throughout the troublesome east side and create greater solidarity among the settlers throughout the Grants.[75]

Ethan Allen would receive additional support from the east side in the aftermath of the most violent and deadly episode of the entire Grants controversy, an episode that took place in Cumberland County and did not initially involve the Green Mountain Boys. In early March 1775, about 80 farmers from the eastside, desperate to forestall legal foreclosures of their properties, gathered in Westminster and attempted to postpone the opening of court until after the harvest season. At least one chief justice, Thomas Chandler, agreed that a stay was reasonable, but Yorker judges, backed by Sheriff William Patterson, were determined to begin the spring session and hear a full docket. This led to an inevitable confrontation, and, on March 13, Patterson's pro-Yorker posse opened fire on a group of partially armed resisters who had forcefully seized the courthouse. What became known as the "Westminster Massacre" left two dead and ten wounded; dozens of resisters were arrested.[76]

There is no evidence to suggest that the Green Mountain Boys were complicit in the deadly showdown, but anyone familiar with the goings on in the Grants certainly knew what next to expect. Cadwallader Colden, the ex-governer of New York, now William Tryon's acting-governor, wrote to the Crown that he "had no doubt that [the Westminister resisters] will be joined by the Bennington Rioters who will endeavour to make one common cause of it, tho they have no connection but in their violence to government."[77] As if on cue, two days after the massacre, Robert Cochran and a company of Green Mountain Boys arrived in Westminster, seeking "blood for blood."[78] By then, however, the dirty work had already been done. The day before Cochran's arrival, a mob of 400 had freed the prisoners and incarcerated their Yorker jailers. Nonetheless, as Colden had predicted, Allen, ever the skillful propagandist, knew how to exploit the massacre. An immediate Green Mountain inquest found the Yorker jailers guilty of murder and ordered their expulsion from the Grants. Further establishing his extralegal authority, Allen subsequently arrested and banished several New York judges from the west side and encouraged the creation of committees to oversee the expulsion of additional Yorker officials. He also called for a convention of New Hampshire representatives to discuss a collective response to the events at Westminster. In the end, many of the moderates in Cumberland County, horrified over the bloodshed at Westminster and, thus, vulnerable to Allen's entreaties, turned their allegiances to the Green Mountain insurgents.

On April 11, the convention called for by Allen met in Westminster, with the venerable leader in attendance. To his utter delight, the Eastsiders passed a series of resolutions that called on settlers of both sides of the Green Mountains to unite in opposition to the government of New York. But the convention went one step further and demanded that the citizens of the Grants be removed from "so oppressive a jurisdiction" and be permitted to be "either annexed to some other government or erected and incorporated into a new one."[79] There it was: the first collective suggestion of separatism in the Grants. Allen himself had been moving in this direction but feared that the notion lacked popular support. Following the convention, on April 16, Allen and several other Green Mountain Boys, including Seth Warner, Remember Baker, and Robert Cochran, signed an open letter to the inhabitants of the Grants. In it, they declared New York laws "null and void" and resolved to inflict immediate death upon anyone who attempted to apprehend them or their friends. They further boasted that, because their "martial Spirits glow with bitter Indignation and consummate Fury," they "were ready for a Game of Scalping."[80] Two days after issuing this defiant challenge, events in Massachusetts rendered the controversy in the Grants relatively meaningless for the next several years. On the night of April 18–19, 1775, American colonists in Lexington and Concord exchanged bloody gunfire with British regulars, igniting the war for American independence.

The beginning of the American Revolution represented a new chapter in the saga of Ethan Allen and the Green Mountain Boys. They are, in fact, best known to most Americans for their contributions both to the Revolution and to the subsequent statehood of Vermont. These later storylines are more appropriately covered in broader secondary sources, for the present concern, that of terrorist activity, essentially ends when the Green Mountain Boys, motivated by many of the same forces that inspired the patriot cause, transformed themselves from terrorists into soldiers of the Continental Army. Some of these story strands, however, are worth summarizing here for the sake of closure. The Green Mountain Boys were crucial to early military victories in the north, helping Allen and Benedict Arnold capture Ticonderoga and assisting Seth Warner in the capture of Crown Point. Under Warner's command, they fought throughout the Revolution with great distinction. Allen, in the aftermath of the disastrous Montreal campaign in which he was captured, spent two and a half years as a British prisoner. Upon his exchange in 1778 for a British official held by Americans, he was awarded a commission in the Continental Army but never again assumed active duty. He would spend the next several years, during the Revolution and beyond, continuing to write and working tirelessly on behalf of the Grants, seeking separation from New York by playing the British against the Continental Congress, a risky game that earned him widespread enmity and accusations of treason. He died of natural causes on February 17, 1789, and was interred in Colchester, two years before Vermont was granted statehood and admitted to the Union. Only then did New York and Vermont negotiate an end to the long-standing controversy over land titles, much to the satisfaction of the original Wentworth grantees. Vermont paid New York $30,000, which was distributed to those who had held, and were then forced to concede, their Yorker titles.

In the end, Ethan Allen and the Green Mountain Boys were as responsible as anyone for the emergence of Vermont's statehood, and, considering the significant role that terrorism played in that process, perhaps the time has come for historians to reevaluate this "outlaw period." Rather than benign and trivial, it was violent and consequential. And it demonstrated that terrorism could be effectively employed by simple folks who profess to struggle for justice and equality against the perceived provocations of the corrupt and powerful.

Notes

1. Zadock Thompson, *History of the State of Vermont from its Earliest Settlement to the Close of the Year 1832* (Burlington, 1833); Jared Sparks, *The Life of Colonel Ethan Allen* (Burlington: C. Goodrich and Co., 1858).
2. Sparks, *The Life of Colonel Ethan Allen,* 105–106.
3. D. P. Thompson, *The Green Mountain Boys* (New York: Grosset & Dunlap, 1839), dedication; D. P. Thompson, *The Rangers or The Tory's Daughter: A Tale Illustrative of the Revolutionary History of Vermont and the Northern Campaign of 1777,* 10th ed. (Boston, 1890).
4. D. P. Thompson, *The Green Mountain Boys,* 323.
5. Henry De Puy, *Ethan Allen and the Green Mountain Heroes of '76,* (Boston: 1853); De Puy, *The Mountain Hero and His Associates* (Boston: 1855).
6. Henry Hall, *Ethan Allen: The Robin Hood of Vermont* (New York: 1892).
7. James B. Wilbur, *Ira Allen: Founder of Vermont, 1751–1814,* 2 volumes (Boston: Houghton Mifflin, 1928); John Pell, *Ethan Allen* (Lake George, NY: Adirondack Resorts Press, 1929). Quote from Charles A. Jellison, *Ethan Allen: Frontier Rebel* (Syracuse: Syracuse University Press, 1969), viii.
8. Pell, *Ethan Allen.*
9. Matt Bushnell Jones, *Vermont in the Making, 1750–1777* (Cambridge: Harvard University Press, 1939), 282.
10. Stewart H. Holbrook, *Ethan Allen* (Portland, ME: Binford & Mort Publishing), 273, 711.
11. Jellison, *Frontier Rebel,* 39, vii.
12. Ibid., 45–46.
13. Ibid., 103.
14. Ibid., 35.
15. Edwin P. Hoyt, *The Damndest Yankees: Ethan Allen & His Clan* (Brattleboro, VT: The Stephen Greene Press, 1976), 45.
16. Michael A. Bellesiles, *Revolutionary Outlaws—Ethan Allen and the Struggle for Independence on the Early American Frontier* (Charlottesville: University Press of Virginia, 1993), 1, 4.
17. Ibid., 89, 93.
18. Robert E. Shalhope, *Bennington and the Green Mountain Boys* (Baltimore: The Johns Hopkins University Press, 1996).
19. Willard Sterne Randall, *Ethan Allen—His Life and Times* (New York: W. W. Norton and Co., 2011), 255.
20. Bellesiles, *Revolutionary Outlaws,* 42; Jellison, *Frontier Rebel,* 20.
21. Bellesiles, *Revolutionary Outlaw,* 71.
22. Ibid.
23. Shalhope, *Bennington and the Green Mountain Boys,* 52–58.
24. Bellesiles, *Revolutionary Outlaws,* 72.
25. Abby M. Hemenway, *Vermont Historical Gazetteer,* 5 Volumes (also known as *Vermont Historical Magazine*), Volume 1 (Burlington, 1868–1791), 143.

26. Affidavits of James Breakenridge and Samuel Robinson, February 14, 1770, DHSNY, vol. 4, 380–381.
27. Bellesiles, *Revolutionary Outlaws,* 81; Jellison, *Frontier Rebel,* 36; Holbrook, *Ethan Allen,* 43.
28. Bellesiles, *Revolutionary Outlaws,* 21; Shalhope, *Bennington and the Green Mountain Boys,* 34; Pell, *Ethan Allen,* 19.
29. Jellison, *Frontier Rebel,* 33; Bellesiles, *Revolutionary Outlaws,* 33.
30. Ira Allen, *The Natural and Political History of Vermont, One of the United States of America* (London: J. W. Myers, 1798), republished in J. Kevin Graffagnino, ed., *Ethan and Ira Allen: Collected Works,* Volume 3 (Benson, VT: Chalidze Publications, 1992), 16. This storied exchange also appears in most Allen biographies: see Shalhope, *Bennington and the Green Mountain Boys,* 75; Hall, *Ethan Allen,* 119; Jellison, *Frontier Rebel,* 38; Pell, *Ethan Allen,* 32; Holbrook, *Ethan Allen,* 44.
31. Bellesiles, *Revolutionary Outlaws,* 32.
32. Jellison, *Frontier Rebel,* 39; Pell, *Ethan Allen,* 33.
33. Shalhope, *Bennington and the Green Mountain Boys,* 356, no. 50.
34. Ira Allen, *Natural and Political History,* 17.
35. Donald A. Smith, "Green Mountain Insurgency: Transformation of New York's Forty-Year Land War," *Vermont History,* 64 (1996): 198–224.
36. Ira Allen, *Natural and Political History,* 17.
37. Ibid.
38. Ibid.
39. "Proclamation of the Government of New York, for Seizing James Brakenridge, and Others, for Riotously Obstructing the Partition Of Wallumschack Patent," December 12, 1769, DHSNY, vol. 4, 379–380.
40. "Public Disorders Fomented by New Hampshire," February 27, 1771, DHSNY, vol. 4, 420. See also Munro to Duane, December 5, 1770, Folder 72, Allen Family Papers, Wilbur Collection, UVB.
41. "Public Disorders," 420.
42. Ibid., 422.
43. William Cockburn to James Duane, September 9, 1771, Ethan Allen Papers, VA.
44. Affidavits of Volkert P. Douw, October 12, 1771; Jno R. Bleecker, October 12, 1771; Christopher P. Yates, October 22, 1771; Gysbert G. Marselis, October 12, 1771; DHSNY, vol. 4, 450–452. See also deposition by Robert Yates to John Toberkough and James Duane, July 20, 1771, Folder 91, Allen Family Papers, Wilbur Collection, UVB; Robert Yates to John Kempe and James Duane, July 20, 1771, Ethan Allen Papers, VA; Hemenway, 148.
45. Hemenway, *Vermont Historical Gazetteer,* 150.
46. ESQr Munro to Governor Tryon, November 6, 1771, DHSNY, vol. 4, 454–455.
47. Ibid.
48. "Proclamation Reiterating the Right of New York To The Territory In Dispute," December 11, 1771, DHSNY, vol. 4, 458.
49. "Account Of The Temper Of The Rioters In the Eastern Parts of the Province," April 15, 1772, DHSNY, vol. 4, 472. See also Ira Allen, *Natural and Political History,* 19; John Munro to James Duane, March 28, 1772, Ethan Allen Papers, VA.
50. *Connecticut Courant,* June 2–9, 1772.
51. Ibid., April 21–28, 1772; March 24–31, 1772.
52. Governor Tryon to the Inhabitants of Bennington, May 19, 1772, DHSNY, vol. 4, 473–474.

53. Ethan Allen, Seth Warner, Remember Baker, and Robert Cochran to William Tryon, June 5, 1774, William Slade, ed., *Vermont State Papers* (Middlebury: J.W. Copeland, Printer, 1823), 25.

54. Randall, *Ethan Allen,* 227–229.

55. Ibid., 481–482.

56. Jones, *Vermont in the Making,* 303–304.

57. "Order of Council on Petition of Benjamin Stevens," October 21, 1772, DHSNY, vol. 4, 485–486. See also Benjamin Stevens Deposition, September 29, 1772, Folder 76, Allen Family Papers, Wilbur Collection, UVB.

58. Esq. Munro to Governor Tryon, August 22, 1773, DHSNY, vol. 4, 510–511; "Minute In Council Calling For A Military Force," August 31, 1773, DHSNY, vol. 4, 511; Genl Haldimand to Governor Tryon, September 1, 1773, DHSNY, vol. 4, 511; "Order In Council On Gen. Haldimand's Letter," September 8, 1773, DHSNY, vol. 4, 512; Affidavits Relating to the Destruction by the Bennington Mob of Colonel Reid's Settlement on Otter Creek, September 25, 1773, DHSNY, vol. 4, 512–514.

59. Munro to Tryon, August 22, 1773, 510–511.

60. "Application for an Armed Force to Protect the Settlers of Durham From the Bennington Mob," February 2, 1774, DHSNY, vol. 4, 518–519.

61. "The Bennington Mob Erect Their Judgment Seat," December 6, 1773, DHSNY, vol. 4, 520. For other provocations regarding Benjamin Spencer, see Benjamin Spencer to James Duane, April 11, 1772, Ethan Allen Papers, VA.

62. "The Bennington Mob Erect Their Judgment Seat," December 6, 1773, DHSNY, vol. 4, 521–522.

63. Ethan Allen, *A Brief Narrative of the Proceedings of the Government of New York, Relative to Their Obtaining the Jurisdiction of That Large District of Land, to the Westward from Connecticut River* (Hartford: Eben and Watson, 1774), republished in J. Kevin Graffagnino, ed., *Ethan and Ira Allen: Collected Works,* Volume 1 (Benson, VT: Chalidze Publications, 1992), 26–27.

64. Smith, "Green Mountain Insurgency," 221–222; Donald A. Smith, *Legacy of Dissent: Religion and Politics in Revolutionary Vermont, 1749–1784* (unpublished doctoral dissertation, Clark University, 1981), 6.

65. "Affidavit In Support of the Preceding Petition," March 7, 1775, DHSNY, vol. 4, 541. For Hough affair, see also Notes for Benjamin Hough's Deposition, January, 1775, and Hough Deposition, March 23, 1775, Ethan Allen Papers, VA.

66. Shalhope, *Bennington and the Green Mountain Boys,* 91.

67. "Account of the Temper of the Rioters In the Eastern Parts of the Province," May 26, 1772, DHSNY, vol. 4, 472.

68. John McWilliams, "The Faces of Ethan Allen: 1760–1860," *The New England Quarterly,* 49 (1976): 265.

69. "Fortifications Erected on Onion River and Otter Creek by the Bennington Mob," September 1, 1774, DHSNY, vol. 4, 529.

70. "Application for an Armed Force to Protect the Settlers of Durham From the Bennington Mob," February 2, 1774, DHSNY, vol. 4, 519.

71. Bellesiles, *Revolutionary Outlaws,* 98.

72. J. Kevin Graffagnino, "Introduction," *Ethan and Ira Allen: Collected Works,* Volume 1, ix.

73. Ibid., x.

74. Ethan Allen, *A Brief Narrative,* 4.

75. Bellesiles, *Revolutionary Outlaws,* 106.

76. E. P. Watson, ed., *Records of the Governor and Council of New York,* Volume 1 (Montpelier, VT, 1873), 330–331; "Riot and Bloodshed in Cumberland County," March 22, 1775, DHSNY, vol. 4, 545–548; Affidavit of John Griffin, March 27 & 28, 1775, DHSNY, vol. 4, 548–550.

77. Lt. Gov. Colden to Lord Dartmouth, April 5, 1775, DHSNY, vol. 4, 551.

78. "Riot and Bloodshed in Cumberland County," March 22, 1775, DHSNY, vol. 4, 546.

79. Jellison, *Frontier Rebel,* 99.

80. Ethan Allen, *A Brief Narrative,* 24.

4

THE SONS OF LIBERTY

I. Background

The year 1764 was a significant time post for the burgeoning terrorist movements in colonial America. That May, a violent confrontation in North Carolina between squatters and the agents of absentee landlords resulted in the so-called Sugar Creek War, a significant episode in the making of the War of the Regulation. Across the Atlantic, England's King George III and its Board of Trade reaffirmed the Connecticut River as the boundary separating New York from New Hampshire, presumably ending a long controversy over the validity of grants issued by New Hampshire governor Benning Wentworth, but resulting instead in the campaign of terror waged by the Green Mountain Boys. In April, Parliament passed the Sugar Act, the first of many British reforms meant to provide greater oversight of the increasingly lucrative trade with the American colonies. The Sugar Act also placed import duties on a number of items, with the unabashed purpose of raising much-needed revenue for the mother country. This type of revenue taxation, reinforced through subsequent legislation in the same vein, would ultimately inspire a resistance movement that would incorporate elements of terrorism and culminate in the war for American independence.

The Sugar Act was but one of many significant changes in British North America since the conclusion of the French and Indian War in 1763. England's victory resulted in the acquisition of a vast stretch of the continent that would require both an extensive overhaul in colonial administration and, for the first time, a peacetime standing army in America. Because the accompanying expenses would greatly depress an already troubled home economy saddled with a huge war debt, Parliament decided to generate new sources of revenue in America. Taxation and standing armies, however, weren't the only issues.

Parliament's Proclamation Line of 1763, the expanding jurisdiction of England's vice-admiralty courts, and the restriction of printed paper money in America all provoked rage and indignation among colonists, who viewed such encroachments as an infringement on their liberties. Several colonial assemblies issued official protests that varied greatly in tone, and some merchant groups tried with little success to generate a boycott of goods subject to the new taxes. The American perspective was perhaps best summarized in James Otis's stirring pamphlet *The Rights of the British Colonies Asserted and Proved,* which denied Parliament's right to tax its American colonies and seriously questioned England's contention that Americans were "virtually" represented in that legislative body. Nonetheless, George Grenville, who had become British prime minister in 1763, was determined to stay the course. The result was the Stamp Act, passed in March 1765 and set to take effect that November.

The Stamp Act placed excise duties on a broad range of printed documents that could only be circulated with government stamps purchased from designated distributors appointed by the Crown. Whereas the Sugar Act could be broadly interpreted as within Parliament's right to regulate trade, the Stamp Act, for the first time, applied a direct tax on British subjects in North America, a distinction not lost on most Americans. The reaction was swift, decisive, and ultimately revolutionary. Few on either side of the Atlantic could have predicted that the Stamp Act, so close on the heels of the Sugar Act, would inflame resentment and resistance in America that would terminate only with the acquisition of independence. As if to add insult to injury, several weeks after passage of the Stamp Act, the Grenville ministry passed one additional piece of legislation before falling from power during the summer of 1765, the Quartering Act, which required the American colonies to provide housing for the much-despised British regulars.

Resistance in America to the Stamp Act ran along two parallel tracks. One was a movement to lodge protestations and grievances through recognized legal channels. In late May, the Virginia House of Burgesses, inspired in no small measure by the oratorical skills of Patrick Henry, passed a series of resolutions that denied Parliament's right to tax the colonies. Massachusetts governor Francis Bernard would refer to these Virginia Resolves as "an alarm bell to the disaffected."[1] In early June, the Massachusetts Assembly proposed an inter-colonial convention to develop a collective response to England's recent provocations. During the next few years, Americans would continue to pursue redress through legitimate dissent and nonviolent protest. However, England's steadfast refusal to consider seriously American grievances and entreaties would leave disgruntled Americans but one other means by which to roll back the troublesome British legislation. Throughout the colonies, small irregular or extralegal groups began to mobilize and communicate. By early 1766, these resistance groups would come to be known collectively as the Sons of Liberty.

II.   Who Were the Sons of Liberty?

Many of these groups had existed under different names prior to the Stamp Act, providing both a social setting and political forum for local activists. In Boston, a small group called the Loyal Nine would eventually provide the nucleus of that city's chapter of the Sons of Liberty. Virginia's Westmoreland County Association and Christopher Gadsden's Artillery Company in South Carolina fulfilled the same purposes in those southern colonies. There seems to be little doubt about the origins of the common name that these groups would quickly adopt. During the Parliamentary debates over the Stamp Act, Isaac Barré, a veteran of the French and Indian War and a forceful defender of Americans as a member of Parliament, admonished his colleagues for the offending legislation that "caused the blood of those sons of liberty to recoil within them."[2] Historian Pauline Maier later noted that prior to the Stamp Act, the prefix "sons of" was then commonly used by members of clubs and lodges and that the title "sons of liberty" was very much a generic term, interchangeable with "sons of freedom." Its patriotic connotation fit perfectly with Barré's pointed reference.[3] Other than agreement about the source of their name, so much of what we know about the Sons of Liberty is clouded by interpretation, decentralization, disjointedness, and contradiction. Consequently, there exists no single, scholarly, book-length source on the Sons of Liberty, despite their prominent role in the struggle for independence.

One recent attempt to fill this void, Les Standiford's *Desperate Sons* (2012), promoted itself as a "groundbreaking narrative" and "political thriller," but disappointingly proved to be neither. Standiford, who built an early reputation as a crime novelist, offered a strict narrative of familiar historical events associated with the American Revolution, but made no attempt to examine who the Sons of Liberty were, what they believed, or how they operated. The radicals serve only as an occasional backdrop in his account, which offers no interpretive analysis, no scholarly attribution, nor anything particularly revelatory about the Sons. In his preface notes, Standiford did suggest that the Sons might be considered terrorists, but failed to elaborate further on that contention.[4] Thus, one who seeks to learn more about the Sons of Liberty must examine the literary intersection where four separate streams of historical topics cross paths:

1.   accounts of major events of the American Revolution, particularly the Stamp Act (1765) and the Boston Tea Party (1773)
2.   biographies of key players such as Samuel Adams, James Otis, and Thomas Hutchinson as well as studies of lesser players such as Francis Bernard, John Lamb, Ebenezer Mackintosh, and Charles Gadsden
3.   studies of crowd action and mob activity in pre-revolutionary America
4.   local and regional histories of colonies such as Massachusetts Bay, New York, and South Carolina

There are, fortunately, a few shorter studies that specifically examine the Sons of Liberty, albeit in an extremely limited manner. In 1959, Richard Walsh published *Charleston's Sons of Liberty,* and, in 1969, Henry B. Dawson weighed in with *The Sons of Liberty in New York;* neither work exceeded 140 pages of text.[5] Two book chapters have actually produced the most detailed treatment of the Sons. Edmund S. Morgan and Helen M. Morgan's *The Stamp Act Crisis* (1953) and Pauline Maier's *From Resistance to Revolution* (1972) supplied key chapters that together have provided the most comprehensive information available on the radicals.[6] Beyond that, scattered articles about Sons-related issues have filled in some of the huge gaps in the literature.[7]

There are a number of reasons for the dearth of scholarship on the Sons of Liberty. The Sons of Liberty never represented a monolithic resistance movement. Most colonies had their own regional chapters, very much influenced by local political, personal, social, and economic issues, which often left them vulnerable to dissension and inaction. There was no centralization of authority or direction, which, for the scholar, leaves a legacy of disjointedness and a diversity of research materials stretching from South Carolina to Massachusetts. Compounding the problem is the inescapable but seldom understood fact that the Sons of Liberty were a contradiction. On the one hand, they often sought secrecy, frequently disguised themselves to protect their identities, and sometimes manipulated events from behind the scenes, away from the public eye. On the other hand, they openly attended public meetings of the Sons, signed petitions, and had their names frequently published in local documents. The Sons of Liberty were noted for their violent tactics, yet did what they could to suppress this type of terrorism. The Sons were very much part of the broader colonial resistance movement against British authority, yet remained very much responsive to local considerations. The Sons would consistently swear allegiance to the king and the English Constitution, but specialized primarily in extralegal tactics. And, as many have acknowledged, the internal composition of various chapters of the Sons was also somewhat contradictory, a combination of "mobbish" elements alongside aristocratic elites. Added to these contradictions is the fact that membership in the Sons of Liberty was extremely fluid, and virtually anyone who happened to oppose British policies could claim to be a Son, creating what Pauline Maier described as "terminological confusion."[8] For a group as notable as the Sons of Liberty, this type of amorphous structure is difficult to reconcile. Most scholarly analyses of the Sons, such as that conducted by Maier and Dirk Hoerder, tended to fit the groups' activities into paradigms defining "crowd" or "mob" action, but the Sons of Liberty have also been described as terrorists without any attempt to explain the basis of that emotionally charged appellation.[9] The present study, however, will firmly and systematically establish the Sons as terrorists, much like the North Carolina Regulators, New York's anti-rent insurgents, and the Green Mountain Boys of the same pre-Revolution years.

Not surprisingly, then, there is no consensus as to where the Sons of Liberty first appeared. In 1939, Herbert Morais suggested that the Sons originated in eastern Connecticut, and Merrill Jensen, in his extensive 1968 study of the

Revolution's early years, agreed. However, Henry B. Dawson suggested a year later that the true birthplace was New York, and Pauline Maier tended to side with Dawson in her 1972 study.[10] Then there is the case for Boston, which was made by Edmund and Helen Morgan.[11] The Sons of Liberty might have appeared first elsewhere, but there is no denying that the Boston Sons were at the forefront of the resistance movement and set the standard for activism, militancy, and violence. In Boston, organized resistance to the Stamp Act coalesced around a small group of businessmen, artisans, and shopkeepers known as the Loyal Nine. Although there is disagreement as to who constituted the Nine, there is consensus over seven of these "middling gentlemen": John Avery and Thomas Chase, distillers; John Smith and Stephen Cleverly, braziers; Thomas Crafts, a painter; Benjamin Edes, a printer/newspaper editor; and Henry Bass, a merchant. Contemporary accounts confirm these seven, but at least three other names appear in some, but not all, of these accounts, leaving the identity of the remaining two members very much subject to conjecture: Henry Welles, occupation unknown; George Trott, a jeweler; and Joseph Field, "master of a vessel."[12] The relationship between the Loyal Nine and that indomitable and nonpareil agitator Samuel Adams is difficult to define. If he wasn't officially a member, he was, without doubt, an extremely close associate, as was James Otis. It is most probable that Adams and many of his closest confidants plotted in conjunction with the Loyal Nine and met with them frequently to coordinate the resistance movement, perhaps in "Liberty Hall," a room in Chase and Speakman's southend distillery in Hanover Square, which served as the Nine's primary meeting place. Adams and other high-ranking Boston Whigs such as James Otis, John Hancock, Joseph Warren, and Thomas Young would supply elite leadership and direction for the Sons by pulling the strings of resistance but very much from behind the curtain of secrecy.

If the Loyal Nine were to succeed in fomenting mass resistance, they would also need the cooperation of street protesters and toughs, oftentimes described by both contemporary and latter-day historical accounts as the "mob" or "crowd." This meant that the Loyal Nine would need to unify and harness the violent dynamics associated with the rough-and-tumble competition between Boston's two most notorious gangs: the Southend mob, led by Henry Swift, and the Northend mob, led by Ebenezer Mackintosh. These two gangs met regularly each Pope's Day to hold competing parades, burn effigies, and assault each other in a culminating melee that left bodies bloody and broken. For the most part, these gangs consisted of mechanics, sailors, journeymen, or what observers called "the lower class of people."[13] By openly courting Swift and Mackintosh, the Loyal Nine were able to cement an alliance with the two gangs, who willingly agreed to redirect their united hostilities toward British authority. Consequently, by the end of the year, three levels of Bostonian Stamp Act resisters, galvanized by the Loyal Nine, had merged. They became known thereafter as the Sons of Liberty. With approximately 300 to 400 members, the Boston Sons had, therefore, a hierarchical structure with the popular masses guided by the elite leadership of the Loyal Nine, which functioned as a "clearinghouse" or "steering committee."[14]

Once word of the impending Stamp Act reached America during the spring of 1765, the Loyal Nine not only reached out to Mackintosh and Swift but, by the ensuing summer, began to develop a resistance strategy based on symbolic but intimidating action against the crown-appointed stamp masters. On August 14, 1765, Bostonians walking along Orange Street, a busy thoroughfare leading into the center of town, discovered hanging from what would become known as the "Liberty Tree" an effigy of Andrew Oliver, the local stamp master, alongside a boot with the head of the devil protruding from it, a visual pun meant to disparage the Earl of Bute, an ally of George III. Thomas Hutchinson, the American-born chief justice of Boston, ordered the sheriff to take down the offending effigies, but by then the surrounding crowd had grown so large the sheriff refused, for fear of reprisal. While the town council met immediately to consider appropriate action, the crowd seized the Oliver effigy, placed it on a bier, and paraded outside of the Town House, where the council was then deliberating. By now, the crowd consisted of not only Mackintosh and rioters from the Southend and Northend mobs, but also a considerable number of "higher ups" and men of reputation, including members of the Loyal Nine, disguised as working men. The crowd, jeering and chanting, then moved on to Kilby Street, where it completely destroyed a new building financed by Oliver and rumored to be his future Stamp Office. From there, the crowd then proceeded to Oliver's home, just a short distance away, where they beheaded the effigy and showered his abode with rocks and stones. Finally, the crowd moved on to nearby Fort Hill, where the remnants of the effigy were burned in a ceremonial bonfire. Believing that the evening's activities had thus concluded, the Loyal Nine and other "respectable" crowd members retreated to their homes, unaware of what was to ensue. Still thirsty for action, the crowd reassembled, with Mackintosh in the lead, and returned to Oliver's home. Oliver had already taken his family and fled to Castle William for protection, but had entrusted his home to the care of some close friends, who barricaded themselves inside in a noble, but ill-advised, attempt to defend the property. They were simply overcome by the crowd, who tore down fences, smashed open the front doors and windows, entered the house, and damaged furniture. Nothing was stolen, but the crowd did imbibe much of Oliver's wine collection before agreeing to disperse— but only after stoning Hutchinson and the sheriff, who appeared on the premises to break up the riot, only to flee for their safety.[15]

Even though Bostonians agreed that the riots of August 14 were the most destructive the city had ever witnessed, the crowd action was met with widespread approval. The impact was immediate. Ministers from the pulpit praised the crowd's activities. Andrew Oliver made it clear that he would not execute the Stamp Act. One seemingly brave townsman boasted publicly that if appointed stamp master, he would not allow mobs to intimidate him. When he was subsequently informed by associates of the Loyal Nine that a date had been set for the destruction of his home, he quickly recanted.[16] Because of Thomas Hutchinson's actions on August 14, and because he was also widely (and mistakenly) regarded as one of the primary architects of the Stamp Act, the Loyal Nine turned their attention his way. On the night of August 26, a large mob formed and split into two smaller crowds. One crowd viciously vandalized the home of William Story, deputy registrar of the Admiralty Court, and the other did the same to the home of Benjamin Hallowell, comptroller of Customs. The crowd then reunited under the direction of Ebenezer Mackintosh and proceeded toward the home of Hutchinson. There, the mob destroyed doors, shutters, windows, furniture, and part of the roof. They also stole cash, silverware, and important documents.[17]

The riot of August 26 was unlike that of August 14 in that the higher ups in Boston were appalled by the viciousness of this attack and very few were willing to condone it. Even a town meeting disavowed the attack, despite the fact that many of the rioters were in attendance. Yet, a pattern of violence and intimidation was beginning to develop, one that would continue not only in Boston, but also throughout many of the colonies as the resistance to the Stamp Act grew exponentially. While the crowd action on August 26 may have been widely panned by Boston's upper-crust, there is evidence that the Loyal Nine and their elite leaders were very much complicit in the attack on Hutchinson's home. Governor Francis Bernard believed this to be the case, and William Gordon, who arrived in Boston in 1768 and would come to know many of the rioters, would later write that "a secret influence" was behind the attack, for the express purpose of destroying documents related to the Kennebec River controversy in Maine.[18] Aside from the hidden hand of the elite leadership, law enforcement would experience constant frustration in establishing order and bringing rioters to justice. Governor Bernard attempted to call out the local militia but was informed by his leading officers that for all intents and purposes the militia and the mob were one and the same. Ebenezer Mackintosh was the first to be arrested, but threats and behind-the-scenes maneuvering, most likely by the Loyal Nine, led to his release.[19] Others who were arrested and waiting indictment were either freed as a result of a rescue riot or were discharged because the grand jurors refused to prosecute the rioters. Such was the climate of intimidation created by the mob, as well as the spirit of cooperation with the mob. Ever mindful of his delicate situation in Boston, Governor Bernard complained to his superiors, "all civil power ceased in an instant and I had not the least authority to oppose or quiet the mob."[20]

The events in Boston were widely publicized throughout the colonies, a clarion call to other Stamp Act resisters. On October 31, a group of disgruntled merchants met at Burns's Coffee House in New York City to consider a non-importation pact, to appoint a committee to maintain correspondence with other like-minded groups, and to coordinate their resistance with other colonial militias. In attendance were leading New York radicals such as Isaac Sears, John Lamb, Gershon Mott, William Wiley, and Thomas Robinson, all of whom would together serve as the backbone of the newly born New York Sons of Liberty. In his monograph about the New York Sons, Henry B. Dawson noted that there was a precedent in New York for this type of resistance: in 1744, the "Liberty Boys" attempted to lessen the impact of British authority by enlarging the powers of the local assembly.[21] Historian Herbert Morais (1939) would later detect similarities to the Boston Sons. Collecting biographical information on as many of New York's Sons as he could, Morais noted that the New York Sons were essentially a lower-class organization of mechanics, artisans, and workingmen, with the city's leading merchants and lawyers providing direction from above.[22] A study by Beverly McAneer (1947) similarly concluded that the Albany Sons of Liberty consisted largely of young men who were directed by an "older, conservative, property holding dominant class."[23] The Connecticut Sons of Liberty were also led by men of standing, who first mobilized to force the resignation of Jared Ingersoll, Sr., former attorney for the Green Mountain Boys but then a newly appointed stamp master.

This same type of elite leadership was also evident in Rhode Island. Ezra Stiles, an active participant in the Revolution, provided the most extensive background information of any of the Sons' chapters and maintained that the Rhode Island Sons were "as respectable as could have been chosen in Newport, and the most respectable Committee of the Sons of Liberty on this Continent."[24] Similarly, the Sons of Liberty in South Carolina were described elsewhere as men of "easy circumstances," and the Sons in Virginia and North Carolina as "gentlemen and planters."[25] By early 1766, then, various chapters of the Sons of Liberty could be found up and down the urban East Coast, but they had varying degrees of activism and organization. Yet, a familiar pattern of leadership in key colonies had evolved: direction was largely provided by reputable, middle- to upper-class men of standing, often including merchants, lawyers, printers, and shopkeepers.[26] But it was the incorporation of the lower, rowdier elements of society that gave the Sons impact—an impact that often exceeded respectable resistance, creating a climate of terror directed at those who would uphold the right of Parliament to tax its colonies.

III.   The Tactics of Resistance

While the Sons of Liberty primarily focused their energies on resistance to the Stamp Act, there were certainly other issues involved. The shocking attack on Thomas Hutchinson's home and, in particular, his personal objects of vanity and prosperity suggested to many that the mob's wrath was directed more toward Hutchinson's social standing as a man of wealth and privilege as opposed to his government title. Governor Francis Bernard saw it that way, maintaining the purpose of the mob was to take "away the Distinction of rich and poor."[27] Aside from signs of class conflict, personal grudges were also brought to bear. Virtually every biographer of Samuel Adams concedes that his attacks on British authority emanated, in no small measure, from his personal resentment surrounding the

Massachusetts land bank controversy, which had plagued him and his father for more than 25 years. Many of the Connecticut Sons held vendettas against Jared Ingersoll, for a variety of social and religious reasons dating back to the Great Awakening. Local issues were especially influential in determining the degree of activism engaged in by the various chapters of the Sons. The Philadelphia Sons of Liberty professed that its numbers were meager because "unfortunate Dissensions in Provincial Politics keep us rather a divided people."[28] The New York Sons were likewise manipulated by internal divisions and political rivalries.[29]

Yet, despite these varied experiences with British authority and local politics, opposition to the Stamp Act subsumed all other issues and managed to bring together disparate elements of colonial society. Almost from the time when Americans first received word of the impending tax on stamps, a resistance strategy began to evolve, the direction of which would soon be commanded by the emerging chapters of the Sons of Liberty. To a certain extent, radicals sought to make their grievances and legal arguments public by registering their opposition through government bodies, a strategy similar to the Virginia Resolves. Boston's proposal for an inter-colonial congress of American legislatures was an extension of such an effort. However, as long as colonial legislatures were subject to British administration, governors routinely refused to summon their assemblies, as a way to obstruct resistance to the Stamp Act. For the determined Sons of Liberty, this left other, less-traditional forms of protest by which to make their case against Parliament's violations of American liberty. A concerted effort, for example, was made to educate the masses about the Stamp Act through an ambitious propaganda campaign partly waged through the press. Fortuitously, the Sons of Liberty included in their ranks some of the most influential printers and publishers in the colonies. Benjamin Edes, publisher of the *Boston Gazette,* was a member of the Loyal Nine, and his co-publisher, John Gill, was an avid Son. William Goddard, publisher of the *Providence Gazette,* and William Bradford, publisher of the *Pennsylvania Journal,* were also acknowledged Sons. John Holt, publisher of the *New York Gazette,* while not a Son, certainly was a close associate. Through their control of certain newspapers, the Sons of Liberty were able to articulate their politics, sensationalize British provocations, slur local officials, and rally the masses. Mindful of the value of propaganda, the Sons skillfully employed other creative means of promoting the cause of resistance. Rallies, sumptuous dinners, parades, and bonfires were all used to attract public attention, generate popular support, and intimidate those who supported British policies. Designated "liberty trees" or "liberty poles" were part of this endeavor. Even celebratory songs, poems, and essays constituted what Merrill Jensen characterized as "literary violence," which "stirred the populace to action against the day when the stamps would arrive, and pointed the way to independence."[30]

The Sons of Liberty also did what they could to develop cooperation and coordination among their various chapters. A colony-wide network never materialized, but many colonies developed individual or group associations with one another. In December 1765, the Sons of Liberty in New York and Connecticut forged an unprecedented political and military alliance. In most other colonies, Committees of Correspondence were thus formed for the express purpose of uniting the Sons into a more cohesive whole. Of the colonies most actively engaged in resistance to the Stamp Act, only the Sons in South Carolina, North Carolina, and Virginia chose not to integrate into the correspondence union.[31] By far the most potent and contentious tactic of the Sons involved obstructing the execution of the Stamp Act by using terror to coerce the resignation of stamp masters. Terrorist tactics would also be used to enforce the non-importation of British goods and to force open ports and courts without the despised stamps, a direct violation of Parliament's will. From their inception to the outbreak of the Revolutionary War, the Sons of Liberty never took a life. Yet, they generated an environment of fear that extended far beyond immediate victims such as Thomas Hutchinson and Andrew Oliver. Francis Bernard lamented to the Board of Trade that "the violence of this Town and the madness of the country make good people afraid to speak their sentiments."[32] One letter writer to New York's lieutenant governor, Cadwallader Colden, complained that mob violence was "equally dangerous to the sober and well-disposed part of the people, The ease and Quiet of the City, and Subversive of all order and Authority."[33]

The attacks in Boston on August 14 and 26 seemingly established the parameters for direct resistance. In Newport on August 29, a painted-faced crowd armed with axes destroyed the houses of two local supporters of British policies, Dr. Thomas Moffat and Howard Martin, Jr., two days after their effigies, along with that of Augustus Johnson, had been paraded about town. The mob, said to be directed by Newport's gentlemen of standing, also approached the home of Johnson, Newport's stamp master. His house was spared, but many of his personal belongings were seized. Johnson resigned his position the next day, while Moffat and Howard, who had sought refuge aboard a British man-of-war moored in the harbor, never returned to shore and sailed away to England at their first opportunity. Rhode Island's governor, Samuel Ward, wasn't around to witness the destruction; he had fled in fear, only to return after the riots had ceased. Even then, he refused to bring indictments or enforce the Stamp Act and failed to support Newport's customs collector, John Robinson, who, in turn, refused to keep the customs house open without the use of stamps. Faced, however, with an uncooperative and clearly intimidated governor, as well as an increasingly hostile community, Robinson finally relented, and, by the end of November, Newport was conducting business as usual without stamps.[34]

Throughout the colonies, stamp masters feared for their safety. On September 2, Maryland's stamp agent, Zacharias Hood, despite having had his house pulled down, refused to resign and fled to New York to escape the mob. He was eventually apprehended on Long Island, by nearly 100 of the New York Sons of Liberty, where, under threat of being shipped back to Maryland to face his antagonists, he resigned.[35] In New Jersey, William Coxe resigned as stamp master on September 2, despite the fact that, according to his own account, "no spirit of undutifulness or disrespect has yet appeared."[36] New Hampshire's stamp master, George Meserve, had not yet arrived from England, but, while en route in mid-September, he resigned before setting foot in America. He thus managed to escape harm but, ever mindful of his circumstance, always slept with a firearm nearby.[37] In Connecticut, the Sons of Liberty apprehended Jared Ingersoll, held him captive, and threatened him with imprisonment or death until he reluctantly resigned on September 19, confessing that "the cause is not worth dying for."[38] On October 7, John Hughes of Philadelphia promised not to execute the Stamp Act in Pennsylvania. In South Carolina, Caleb Carr fled to Fort Johnson when the stamps arrived in Charleston in mid-October, there to be joined by another stamp agent, George Saxby, who had his home vandalized by the Sons of Liberty. On October 28, both traveled into Charleston and, before a crowd of 7,000 witnesses, announced that they would not execute the Stamp Act. Two days later, George Mercer arrived in Virginia as its new agent; confronted immediately by a "gentlemanly mob," he resigned the next day.[39] In New York, James McEvers resigned in early December after the Sons of Liberty directed the demolition of a house belonging to Major Thomas James, who had infamously boasted that he would cram British stamps down American throats with his sword.[40] Major James fled to England six days after the attack. By November 1, the day that the Stamp Act was to take effect, North Carolina and Georgia had not yet received identification of their new stamp masters. In North Carolina, once Dr. William Houston received his commission on November 16, he promptly resigned. George Angus, Georgia's agent, didn't arrive until the following January, and, after two weeks on the job, he simply vanished.[41] Yet Georgia would remain the only colony that managed to execute the Stamp Act. Elsewhere, violent resistance had successfully nullified the onerous legislation.

It is, of course, impossible to determine with any precision how much of this climate of terror was directly attributable to the Sons of Liberty, as opposed to the actions of spontaneous and mindless mobs bent on destruction, whatever their motivation (Pauline Maier's "terminological confusion"). Yet given the known connections between mobs and the Sons, as well as other accounts of the riots as noted, it is difficult to deny that the Sons of Liberty either directed much of this activity from behind the scenes or, at the very least, motivated mobbish behavior through its aggressive propaganda campaign. Governor William Bull of South Carolina complained to the Lords of Trade that, "although these very numerous Assemblies of the People bore the appearance of common populace; Yet, there is great reason to apprehend they were animated and encouraged by some considerable Men, who stood behind the curtain."[42] Of the crowd that had forced Virginia's George Mercer to resign his stamp commission, Governor Francis Fauquier wrote, "This Concourse of People, I shall call a Mob, did I not know that it was chiefly if not altogether Composed of gentlemen of Property in the Colony."[43] The Connecticut Sons who had abused Jared Ingersoll included ministers, merchants, and magistrates. And as William Gordon, the contemporary observer and latter-day historian, noted, the Stamp Act riots were not "chargeable solely on the dregs of the colonies. Merchants, assemblymen, magistrates, etc., united directly or indirectly in the riots, and without their influence and instigation, the lower class inhabitants would have been quiet; but great pains were taken to rouse them into action."[44]

The coerced resignations of stamp masters constituted but one element in the battle against the Stamp Act. In early October 1765, the proposed inter-colonial convention, dubbed the Stamp Act Congress, met in New York with 27 delegates from nine colonies in attendance. There, the Congress adopted a declaration of rights, statements of grievances, and petitions to the king and Parliament. Three weeks later, merchants in New York signed an agreement to boycott British imports. Similar non-importation agreements were soon adopted by Philadelphia in November and Boston in December. Yet, resignations and non-importation did not resolve a vexing question that faced the Sons of Liberty. If stamps could not be distributed, what effect would that have on customs collection and court proceedings, especially at the county level? Many in the colonies, including Massachusetts governor Francis Bernard, assumed that the Sons would forcefully cease all activities that required stamps. Indeed, many ports and courts began to close once the stamps arrived but could not be distributed. Virginia and Rhode Island had other ideas. Virginia went about its business without stamps, and, in early November, customs officials in Newport were warned that, if they didn't clear ships without stamps, they would be driven out of town. Thus, the Sons made clear their position. They would completely ignore the presence of stamps, force open ports and courts, and conduct business as usual, as if the Stamp Act were non-existent. The decision in some colonies to keep ports closed actually created a volatile situation that worked in favor of the Sons, because out-of-work sailors, growing increasingly restless and hostile, were simply added to the large, disaffected mobs which had already tested the limits of law and order. This was certainly the case in Boston, where the Sons of Liberty, faced with a government that was unsure how to proceed, seized the initiative. On December 17, the Sons demanded that Andrew Oliver resign his stamp commission a second time, before 2,000 witnesses in a pouring rain. He readily complied, and that afternoon, evidently intimidated by the day's proceedings and a recent series of riots against British officials, customs agents opened the port. New York and Philadelphia opened their ports in November, and, by the following March, all colonial ports, except in Georgia, were open for business, many under threat from the Sons of Liberty. Fortunately for Americans, their ships were able to land in England without stamps, because the Royal Navy did little to enforce the Stamp Act.

Just as stamp masters and customs agents were compelled to disavow their parts in the execution of the Stamp Act, lawyers and judges would need to be similarly convinced to ignore the Act and do their part to reopen all colonial courts. As before, some would balk and others would comply, either willingly or grudgingly.

Inferior courts proved easier to manipulate than superior courts. Again, in many instances, the fear of the mob would play an essential role. Maryland's inferior courts opened quickly in November, but its superior courts did not open until the following April and only after the Sons of Liberty made clear their demands. In January, a chief justice in North Carolina promised to open his court after the Sons of Liberty roused him out of bed in the middle of the night. In February, pressure applied by the Sons forced the opening of courts in New Jersey. Yet the attempt to force open colonial courts met with mixed success. By the time that the Stamp Act had been repealed in late March 1766, only Rhode Island, New Hampshire, Maryland, and Delaware had opened all of their courts.

While many lawyers and judges were coerced into opening their courts, the fact that many did so without being directly victimized by the Sons of Liberty was partly attributable to the restraint encouraged by many of the mob leaders, who feared that destructive violence could prove counterproductive. But it also is an effect of the environment of terror that the Sons had already carefully cultivated. In many counties, the mere demand by the Sons that certain courts open without stamps was enough to get the deed done. As for those local officials who were lucky enough to escape unmolested by the Sons, they were impacted nonetheless by the general spirit of popular discontent and hostility, which, as they knew, remained volatile and vulnerable to the exhortations of the Sons. Connecticut's Jared Ingersoll lamented that, "all the springs of Government are broken and nothing but Anarchy and Confusion appear." Even though New York's lieutenant governor Cadwallader Colden sought refuge in Fort George, he went to bed "expecting every Evening to be attacked by the Mob."[45] It's no wonder. On the day the Stamp Act took effect, a broadside was printed and distributed by the New York Sons which warned Colden, "If you dare to perpetrate any such murderous act, you'll bring your grey hairs with sorrow to the grave, you'll die a martyr to your own villainy, and be hanged, like Porteis upon a sign-post, as a memento to all wicked governors, and that every man, that assists you, shall be, surely put to death."[46] In Boston, Thomas Hutchinson conceded that "the authority of every colony is in the hands of the sons of liberty," and Francis Bernard complained that he was but "a Prisoner at large, being wholly in the power of the people."[47] Thus, with equal parts of pride and spite, Samuel Adams could boast that "our presses have groaned, our pulpits have thundered, our legislatures have resolved, our towns have voted; the crown officers have everywhere trembled, and all their little tools and creatures have been afraid to speak and to be seen."[48]

The climate of terror that the Sons had created was not entirely founded on the threat of harm to selected persons or property. It was based, in large measure, on the fear that the Sons could raise an armed militia large enough to challenge the British regulars. The early alliance between the New York and Connecticut Sons was established for that very purpose. Ezra Stiles wrote that three-quarters of the men in Connecticut were ready to take up arms. Major Thomas James, who left for England shortly after his house was demolished by the Sons, warned his superiors upon arrival that "There can be assembled in New York and the Jerseys 50,000 fighting men."[49] The Boston Sons were said to be capable of assembling 3,000 armed men within two hours notice and had the ability to muster 40,000 volunteers from both Massachusetts and New Hampshire. Another report put the number of potential recruits in Massachusetts at 30,000.[50] Rumors also circulated that the Sons of Liberty had enlisted the cooperation of the Six Nations, who, in exchange for wampum belts, were ready to attack British regulars who ventured too far into the western frontier.[51] The military threat posed by the Sons, real or most likely imagined, provided a dilemma for many of the radical elite. They had helped to politicize the masses—an important objective from the start—yet the spirit of resistance had seemingly given way to mass destruction and the potential for militant insurgency. Terrorism not only gave the Sons their power but also caused many gentlemen of standing to ponder whether they had conspired to create good or evil.

When word first reached America in April 1766 that the Stamp Act had been repealed less than five months after taking effect, the timing could not have been more fortuitous. In many colonies, mounting pressures were on the verge of exploding into increasingly destructive behavior by the mobs. Many courts remained closed. While some stamp supplies had been destroyed, others remained under British guard. Communities were divided over the efficacy of non-importation. Debates continued over the exact extent of Parliament's authority. Newspapers continued to rail against British provocations. All this was seemingly swept away by the repeal, and a return to normality was much anticipated. For colonial elites, the respite offered a chance to reestablish control over the mob, for their primary objective was to uphold, not overturn, the British Constitution. As Pauline Maier noted, these gentlemen leaders sought to use the Sons of Liberty as a peace-keeping force, working closely with local magistrates to restrain mob violence.[52] The contradictory roles of the Sons revealed the extent to which the relationship between the radical leaders and the mob had grown somewhat tenuous, but it also showed the continued commitment among many to observe the parameters of what they perceived as legitimate dissent. Meanwhile, despite the contradiction, the rank and file Sons of Liberty celebrated the repeal, even though plans for their proposed inter-colonial union now collapsed. Life in America, however, would never be the same. Rather than earn America's affection with the repeal of the Stamp Act, Parliament's passage of the Declaratory Act in 1766 was a less than subtle reminder that it reserved exclusive rights to govern America, provoking ingratitude and continued resentment. Americans bickered over the Quartering Act, which remained intact, and compensation lawsuits filed on behalf of the victims of mob destruction created recrimination and dissension in many communities. And while the Sons of Liberty in many colonies retreated and lay dormant for the next year, some remained active and continued to harass British officials and soldiers. The Sons of Liberty were keenly aware that terror had helped nullify the Stamp Act, and, as long as there were pressing issues surrounding British authority, they would continue to foster the spirit of resistance whenever and wherever they could.

IV. The Townshend Revenue Acts

The glee with which Americans celebrated the repeal of the Stamp Act seemed to obscure the intent behind the accompanying Declaratory Act. Christopher Gadsden, however, leader of the Charleston Sons of Liberty, was skeptical. At a gathering under Charleston's Liberty Tree, Gadsden cautioned that the Declaratory Act contained the seeds of oppression and that the Sons needed to stay vigilant.[53] Meanwhile, more so than in any other colony, tensions in New York continued unabated. Compliance with the Quartering Act became an increasingly pressing issue as England withdrew troops from the frontier and redeployed them in coastal cities. As the number of British regulars grew in New York, tensions between citizens and soldiers escalated, resulting in a number of hostile skirmishes, particularly over the local liberty pole, which soldiers pulled down on several occasions, only to be resurrected by the townspeople.

Across the Atlantic, the king was adrift. The vehemence with which Americans had opposed the Stamp Act caught many by surprise. Grenville's government had fallen, the result of personal conflicts unrelated to events in America. It was the Rockingham Whigs who disavowed Grenville's policies, managed to seize control of the weakened ministry, and oversaw the dismantling of the Stamp Act. Shortly thereafter, George III resurrected the political career of William Pitt, who formed a new ministry but quickly fell victim to mental illness. Exploiting the situation, Charles Townshend, chancellor of the Exchequer, took control of the cabinet and rammed through new legislation, again designed to generate revenue in America. The Townshend Revenue Acts were approved in June and July 1767, some 15 months after the repeal of the Stamp Act. As opposed to direct, internal taxes, they called for external duties on glass, lead, paper, paints, and tea. They tightened collection of duties in America by creating an American Board of Customs to be housed in Boston and created a new American Department, to be headed by Lord Hillsborough. Worse still, the monies raised by the new duties would be used to defray the costs of maintaining British soldiers in America and to cover the salaries of royal officials in the colonies, a move that would make these officials independent from the local assemblies who coveted this power of the purse. Further, the New York assembly was suspended for non-compliance with the Quartering Act.

As with Grenville before him, Townshend badly underestimated America's distaste for any form of taxation. Still, the violent reaction to the Stamp Act certainly should have given Townshend pause. In view of the lingering impact of the Declaratory Act and his known disregard for insolent Americans, whom he considered mere disobedient children, one wonders how big a part simple spite played in his fateful decision. In late August, shortly after the word of the new duties reached America, writers in the *Boston Gazette* proposed that, in response, a policy of non-importation of British goods be revived. For the next several months, Boston merchants and popular leaders would wrestle over the effectiveness of non-importation versus an alternative strategy of non-consumption. Similar discussions were held in other major ports.

For the most part, the Sons of Liberty were able to suppress mob activity early on, although there remained scattered pockets of active resistance. The apparent slackening of violence was counterbalanced by the volatile words of pamphleteers and newspaper writers, whose stirring opposition to the Townshend duties helped undermine the public temperance. The *Boston Gazette* again took the lead, printing a number of inflammatory articles, including many by Samuel Adams. The attacks from the press were so vicious that General Thomas Gage, commander of all British forces in America, complained to Governor Colden that, "It must give every well-wisher to his Country the greatest Pain and Anxiety to see the Publick papers crammed with Treason, the Minds of the People disturbed, excited and encouraged to revolt against the government . . . Every Lye that malice can invent is propagated as truths by these Enemys of their Country to sow Dissention and create Animositys between Great Britain and the Colonys."[54] In December, the first of John Dickinson's *Letters from a Farmer in Pennsylvania* began to appear in serial form in the *Pennsylvania Chronicle*. Plain speaking and well reasoned, *Letters* conceded Parliament's right to regulate trade but denied its right to tax for revenue purposes. Taxation without actual representation was illegal and violated the rights of not only Americans, but also of English people everywhere. In the end, Dickinson added his voice to the call for the revival of non-importation. Dickinson's *Letters* helped forge colonial unity, but it also significantly augmented the growing body of literature that helped define and propagandize the legal viewpoints propounded by the Sons of Liberty and other radical elements of society that were then beginning to shape American notions of republicanism and would later justify the movement toward independence. These legal and ideological arguments were, of course, grounded in the Age of Enlightenment and the aforementioned Real Whig ideas regarding resistance, revolution, and restraint. The Sons of Liberty remained committed to the English Constitution, but any attempt, by Parliament or the Crown, to undermine the people's liberties had to be met with stern opposition.

In February 1768, the Massachusetts House of Representatives issued to other colonies a "circular letter" that repeated many of these positions and, by its very nature, implied an informal union of the colonies. The circular letter, in essence a petition to the king and Parliament, was the work of Samuel Adams, who articulated constitutional issues, offered a litany of grievances, and proposed that each colony consider its contents and offer input. When Lord Hillsborough, the new secretary of state, ordered the House to revoke its circular letter, the House refused by a vote of 92–17, thereby prompting Governor Bernard to dissolve the Massachusetts Assembly. Now denied their only means of legal redress, radicals once again turned increasingly toward extralegal means of protest.[55] Over the next several months, various chapters of the Sons of Liberty would be revived. By the end of the year, all colonies except New Hampshire had responded to the circular letter and added their support to the constitutional protests against the Townshend duties.

With heightened awareness now spreading throughout the colonies, events in Boston assumed greater significance. When Boston's grand jury refused to bring libel charges against Samuel Adams, James Otis, and the publishers of the *Gazette,* the Sons of Liberty were emboldened and the *Gazette,* whose articles were routinely published in other colonial newspapers, churned out even more incendiary articles. In March 1768, one month after the circular letter appeared, a number of merchants in Boston finally approved a conditional non-importation agreement. In 1918, Arthur M. Schlesinger, Sr., provided the first scholarly analysis of Boston's merchants. He suggested that their primary motive was an opportunity for commercial reform.[56] Other recent works have since emphasized other ideological or constitutional issues.[57] Merrill Jensen and Pauline Maier contended that popular pressure and coercion, backed by threats of violence, were the forces that compelled merchants to comply with non-importation.[58] Governor Bernard maintained that the merchants complied because "they would be obnoxious to the lower sort of people; others were threatened with resentment of the higher. Some were afraid for their persons and houses, others for their trade and credit." He estimated that more than half of the merchants reluctantly signed the agreement out of fear of the mob.[59] The same was apparently the case in Charleston. Goaded by Christopher Gadsden and capitalizing on a planter-mechanic alliance, a committee was assigned to enforce non-importation. Adopting a "sign or die" motto, the committee threatened violence against non-subscribers, who also faced ostracism and boycotts of their own businesses.[60] In Boston, the five new customs commissioners faced similar social isolation. Those recently arrived from England could not find lodging, because no one would dare rent them rooms. Charles Paxton was the primary object of the mob's discontent because he was a native and, therefore, considered a traitor among his own people. Concerted attempts by members of the Loyal Nine to restrain hostilities only partially succeeded. One effigy of Paxton was taken down, but at least one other was ceremoniously burned. On other occasions, his house, along with that of Commissioner William Burch, was surrounded by menacing mobs. Threats were also directed against Commissioner John Williams and Inspector General William Wooten, but in the end there would be no direct attacks upon people or property. Yet, even Thomas Hutchinson would admit on at least one occasion that a mob, which had inflicted no "actual mischief," was guilty of producing "terror."[61] By now, Hutchinson seemed to acknowledge that terror emanated not necessarily from direct attacks but also from the mere hint of an attack, for the people of Boston had come to understand that the wrath of the mob could be unleashed at any moment. Despite the popular uprisings in Boston and Charleston, non-importation failed to generate significant support anywhere else. New York and Philadelphia came close to adopting agreements but eventually abandoned their plans in June. There is reason to believe that non-importation would have died an honorable or ignominious death, depending on one's loyalties, had the British not graciously provided another catalyst for mob action.

During the spring riots, Governor Bernard and the customs commissioners had written letters to British officials complaining of their impotence in the face of Boston's mobs. In response, the 50-gun *Romney,* two other armed schooners, and a regiment of regulars were dispatched to Boston. The *Romney* arrived in May 1768, and on June 5, as if to incite a riot deliberately, its captain sent a press gang ashore to kidnap crewmen for service in the Royal Navy. When the press gang entered a tavern and attempted to abduct a young American, a melee ensued and the gang was forced to retreat to the *Romney* empty handed. Nonetheless, the *Romney*'s captain continued his efforts to impress crewmen for his undermanned vessel, agitating Bostonians no end. In a case of stunning mistiming, monumental naiveté, and sheer arrogance, five days later Joseph Harrison, chief customs collector, seized the ship *Liberty* for violating trade laws. The *Liberty*'s owner was none other than John Hancock, perhaps the wealthiest man in Boston and, along with Samuel Adams and James Otis, a figure at the forefront of Boston's Sons. Popular with the people and a tireless critic of British policies, Hancock was anything but a random victim. An earlier attempt in May to hold Hancock accountable had been rebuffed by Hancock's crew. After customs officials towed the *Liberty* out to the *Romney* in Boston harbor, they were viciously attacked by a mob when they returned to shore. Harrison and Benjamin Hallowell, another customs commissioner, barely survived after being savagely beaten with clubs and stones. Harrison's son was dragged through the streets by his hair. The mob, said to number more than 300, then proceeded to vandalize the homes of Harrison, Hallowell, and John Williams. Rioters also seized a pleasure boat owned by Harrison, dragged it ashore, and, under the Liberty Tree, held a mock trial that condemned the boat to a public bonfire. Stricken with fear, other customs officials fled with their families, first to the *Romney* and eventually to Castle William, for protection.[62] Four days later, on June 14, the Sons of Liberty held a meeting under the Liberty Tree. It was so well attended that it had to be relocated to Faneuil Hall, and by the end of the day, it had transformed into a town-wide meeting of thousands. A subsequent flurry of activity eventually culminated in a unique document that was part propaganda denouncing British provocations surrounding the *Liberty,* and part directive instructing Boston's representatives to the Massachusetts House. Unfortunately for the Boston radicals, the House was soon dissolved for its failure to rescind the circular letter. For the next several months, in an effort to resolve the customs issues, Hancock and British officials would posture before each other until the British finally decided to drop all charges in March 1769. One month after the *Liberty* riots, Lord Hillsborough ordered Governor Bernard to seek evidence against Boston's chief insurrectionists for the express purpose of bringing them to England to stand trial on charges of treason.

The British handling of the *Liberty* affair helped accomplish what Boston and Charleston could not: unify the colonies behind a policy of non-importation of British goods. On August 1, a Boston town meeting ratified a non-importation agreement prepared by a committee chaired by John Hancock. Merchants in New York, a colony consumed with its own royal concerns, approved a similar agreement four weeks later. Philadelphia's merchants, after much agonizing, joined the boycott in early 1769. By that summer, Virginia, Maryland, and South Carolina also agreed to participate, largely motivated by Parliament's intent to extradite resistance leaders to England for trial. The mere suggestion that Americans might be tried by British courts 3,000 miles away was enough to set off yet another maelstrom, and such a policy would obviously target the Sons of Liberty. In response, legislatures, first in Virginia and then in New Jersey, Delaware, New York, North Carolina, and Maryland, approved resolutions of protest, denying Parliament this right. In the end, Bernard never brought charges against any of Boston's leading Sons of Liberty, for he was well aware that to do so would endanger his own life and property. He had already conceded to Lord Halifax, "I am so utterly unable to oppose or correct an insurrection of this kind, that it would be the highest folly to attempt it."[63]

While the radical leadership in most colonies was able to restrain excessive mob action against the Townshend duties, the Sons of Liberty kept the resistance movement alive in ways that, even with limited violence, helped propagandize their cause and helped sustain a climate of intimidation. Ever since the Stamp Act riots, not only the *Boston Gazette* but also the *Providence Gazette,* the *Newport Mercury,* the *Pennsylvania Journal,* and the *New York Gazette,* all published by active Sons of Liberty, regularly printed inflammatory articles challenging Parliament's right to rule America and promising harsh treatment to those who conspired with the British. The first and only issue of the *Constitutional Courant,* which appeared during the Stamp Act crisis and was published secretly, was typical in its invective. Referring to the stamp masters as "vipers," the *Courant* had warned them that their names "shall be blasted with infamy, the public execration shall pursue you while living, and your memories shall rot, when death has disabled you." To Americans who dared plot with the British, the *Courant* had ranted "murder your fathers, rip up the bowels of your mothers, dash the infants you have begotten against the stones and be blameless; but enslave your country! . . . this is guilt, this calls for heaven's fiercest judgment."[64] British authorities considered the *Boston Gazette* so seditious that its publishers, Benjamin Edes and Jonathan Gill, along with fellow Sons Samuel Adams, James Otis, and Thomas Cushing, were among the radicals most closely watched by the British for possible extradition to England.

Of equal propaganda value to the Sons of Liberty was the way in which they publicized their cause, a shrewd public relations campaign that had all the elements of grand theater. And nothing they did was as theatrical as their mock trials, an attempt to establish the Sons as an extralegal authority while manipulating public perceptions with political satire. The trial of John Harrison's pleasure boat was typical. During the turmoil over the Stamp Act, the Boston Sons held a two-hour mock trial before 2,000 to 3,000 spectators. Before effigies of George Grenville and Lord Bute chained to a gallows, the Sons set up a courtroom, seated a judge and jury, brought criminal evidence against the accused (a British stamp), found the defendant guilty, and passed sentence. After a raucous parade, the effigies were burned under the gallows.[65]

Most of the mock trials, parades, and effigy hangings began near the local Liberty Tree or Liberty Pole, equally important symbols in the propaganda battle against British authority. Boston had the first Liberty Tree, a huge elm at the corner of Essex Street and Orange Street near Hanover Square known to locals as the "Great Elm" and said to have been planted in 1646.[66] This was the infamous elm that held the effigies of Grenville and Bute the morning of the August 14, 1765, riots. From that day forward, the elm became known as the "Liberty Tree," the public meeting place where the Sons held court. Often decorated with broadsides, public announcements, banners, and lanterns, it also held a staff upon which a flag would be raised whenever the Sons of Liberty wished to call a meeting. The tree was officially christened a month after the August riots when word reached America that the Grenville ministry had fallen and that William Pitt would succeed him. To honor the occasion, a copper plate bearing in gold the words "The Tree of Liberty" was affixed to the trunk. Ironically, given the terrorist tactics employed by the Sons of Liberty, a British flag inscribed "Pitt the Supporter of Liberty and the Terror of Tyrants" was hung from an upper limb.[67] News of Boston's ceremonial tree spread, and before long, local chapters of the Sons had their own symbolic tree or pole. New York's Liberty Pole, located near the army barracks, was a particular subject of contention, as British soldiers of the Sixteenth Regiment routinely pulled it down and New York Sons routinely rebuilt it, sometimes after bloody melees pitting regulars against townspeople.

These violent confrontations came to a head in January 1770. On the night of January 17, British regulars cut down the pole, sawed it to pieces, and deposited the splinters in front of De La Montagnie's tavern, the local meeting place of the New York Sons. The enraged Sons of Liberty held a public meeting the next day before 3,000 people, which resulted in a plea to New Yorkers to refrain from hiring off-duty soldiers, a practice that was undermining day laborers. A crowd began to form when someone suggested that the public boarding house used by the regulars be pulled down immediately, but a confrontation with soldiers armed with drawn bayonets was barely averted when city magistrates and army officers interceded. The next day, British soldiers were spotted posting broadsides that condemned the Sons of Liberty as enemies of the people because of their seditious activities and referred to the British regulars as the real defenders of British liberty. The broadside mocked the Sons, who "thought their freedom depended on a piece of wood."[68] Isaac Sears, a leading Son, helped to capture two of the soldiers while the rest ran off. Sears escorted the two to the mayor's house to be arrested on charges of libel, but about 20 regulars with drawn swords and bayonets soon arrived to rescue the prisoners. The soldiers withdrew at the mayor's command, but a bloody melee ensued on Golden Hill and the neighboring environs as rampaging soldiers ran through the streets brandishing their weapons and clashed with civilians armed with clubs and brickbats. Both sides suffered serious injuries and one person was killed. Fighting continued the next day before the "Battle of Golden Hill" came to an end. Two weeks later, Sears and some fellow Sons purchased a lot near the commons and, in an elaborate ceremony and parade, raised another Liberty Pole, this one as indestructible as possible; the new pole, 46 feet high, was surrounded by iron bars and hoops and topped with a gilded weathervane inscribed with the word "liberty." By now, it was evident that New York's Liberty Pole was more than mere wood, as the British would have it. It, along with all the other Liberty Trees and Poles, had become both symbols of freedom and hallowed grounds to the resistance movement.

While most of the parades and bonfires began under the Liberty Tree or Pole, many often ended with the Sons retreating to their favorite restaurants and taverns for sumptuous celebratory dinners. Some were regular social events. The Boston Sons yearly celebrated the riots of August 14, 1765, in either Roxbury or Dorchester, and their dinner in 1768 was a huge affair with close to 400 guests, many of whom arrived in chaises and carriages. The New York Sons regularly celebrated the March 18, 1766, repeal of the Stamp Act at De La Montagnie's tavern. Charleston's Sons dined at Dillon's tavern. Regarding the political value of such dinners, John Adams remarked, "This is cultivating the sensations of Freedom . . . they tinge the Minds of the People, they impregnate them with the sentiments of Liberty." These lavish dinners certainly served a political purpose, but, because they often excluded the mobbish sort, Dirk Hoerder understandably referred to the Boston Sons as "a middle class dining club."[69]

Songs and poems were other significant elements of the propaganda effort on behalf of the Sons of Liberty. Typically, many such songs were British tunes with new lyrics adapted to political conditions in America. Most were attributed to pen names in order to provide anonymity, although the identities of some authors were later revealed. At least two songs extolling the virtue of the Sons were based on a popular British song "Hearts of Oak Are We Still," a tribute to the Royal Navy written in 1759. A "Song for the Sons of Liberty in the Several American Provinces" first appeared in April 1766 in the *Boston Post-Boy and Advertiser*. Its lyrics professed allegiance to King George III but, as this excerpt demonstrates, also threatened bloody action:

> On our brows while we laurel crown'd Liberty wear,
> What Englishman ought, we AMERICANS dare;
> Tho' tempests, and terrors around us we see,
> Bribes nor fears can prevail on the hearts that are free.

With Loyalty, LIBERTY, let us entwine;
Our blood shall for both, flow as free as our wine.
Let us set an example, what all men should be,
And a toast to the world, Here's to those who dare be free.[70]

Two years later, John Dickinson, author of *Letters from a Pennsylvania Farmer,* teamed with Arthur Lee to co-write "The Liberty Song," sung to the same melody. Its most famous phrase was "By uniting we stand, by dividing we fall." The song became the most popular protest song of the era and was adopted by the Sons of Liberty as a rallying song at meetings.[71] In 1774, Dr. Joseph Warren, the renowned Boston Son of Liberty, penned a song to the melody of "The British Grenadiers" entitled "A Song on Liberty," which partially read:

Lift up your Hearts my Heroes and swear with proud Disdain,
The wretch that would ensnare you shall spread his net in vain;
Should Europe empty all her Force we'd meet in Arrays
And shout huzza! huzza! huzza for Brave America.

Torn from a World of Tyrants, beneath the western Sky
We form'd a new Dominion, a Land of Liberty:
The World shall own we're Masters here, then hasten on the day;
Huzza, Huzza, Huzza for Love and Liberty.[72]

Other songs celebrating the Sons included "An Excellent New Song for the Sons of Liberty in America" by Dr. Benjamin Y. Prime, written under the name "A Gentleman from New York," and "A New Song, Addressed to the Sons of Liberty on the Continent of America" by "a son of liberty." Arthur M. Schlesinger, in a short study of patriotic songs during the revolutionary era, noted the significance of "musical propaganda," and classified such tunes into one of three categories: narrative, hortatory, and martial. He noted that during the early crises over the Stamp Act and Townshend duties, songs largely fell into the first two categories, but, as the political situation grew increasingly tense, the songs also became more militant.[73]

Aside from songs and newspaper essays, Sons of Liberty poems were another form of "literary violence," to borrow Merrill Jensen's term. Thomas Paine contributed such an homage with "Liberty Tree," which appeared in *Pennsylvania Magazine* in 1775 and partially read:

But hear, O ye swains, 't is a tale most profane
How all the tyrannical powers,
Kings, Commons, and Lords, are uniting amain
To cut Down this guardian of ours
From the east to the west blow the trumpet to arms

Through the land let the sound of it flee,
Let the far and the near, all unite with a cheer
In defence of our liberty.[74]

In February, 1770, "The Liberty Pole" appeared. It contained the following stanza:

Come Listen, good neighbors of every degree,
Whose hearts, like your purses, are open and free,
Let this pole a monument ever remain,
Of the folly and arts of the time-serving train.[75]

In time, other Sons of Liberty poems would celebrate Dr. Joseph Warren, the notable Boston Son who would perish at Bunker Hill; the Boston Tea Party; the burning of the *Gaspee;* and, most famously, Paul Revere's historic ride to Concord. Together, these songs and poems, combined with the public spectacles of effigies, bonfires, dinners, trees, and poles, constituted a skilled propaganda campaign that mythologized the Sons of Liberty, while politicizing the masses and stirring them into action. They were an important element in creating a politically explosive environment that the Sons would exploit through terrorist tactics.

The most significant elements of this climate of terror were, of course, violence or the threat of violence and the attendant psychological impact on the community. The Sons of Liberty had already proven that they could stir the mobs into acts of destructive violence, although how much control they actually had was always subject to question. The massive resignations of stamp masters preceding the repeal of the Stamp Act clearly established the impact of this violence. The threat of bodily harm or property destruction at the hands of the mob was reinforced through the use of handbills or broadsides that were either widely posted or delivered in person. Most were directed at stamp masters and trade commissioners, demanding their resignations, or at violators of non-importation, demanding their compliance. As noted earlier, Lieutenant Governor Colden was also a recipient. Severe punishment, even death in Colden's case, was promised to those who dared defy these orders. These handbills and letters not only fulfilled both psychological and political purposes by terrifying the recipients into actions they might not have taken otherwise, but also served as a type of extralegal summons. In reality, everything the Sons did was founded on their position as an extralegal authority: demanding the resignations of public officials, refusing to acknowledge Parliamentary legislation and local enforcement, insisting on cooperation from colonial businessmen, and punishing offenders in very public ways. The Sons did not necessarily view matters from this perspective, however. They continued to swear allegiance to the king, and many of their policies were approved through ad hoc town meetings, giving their resistance movement an air of popular legitimacy, despite the fact that British authorities refused to acknowledge the legality of these public gatherings. In the end, however, it was always the perpetration or the prospect of violence that established the Sons as an authority, extralegal or otherwise.

Resistance to the Townshend duties has been generally portrayed as more restrained than the resistance to stamps, but the Sons of Liberty, in many areas, continued to carry out an aggressive campaign of violence and intimidation to enforce non-importation, while keeping the constant threat of mob activity alive in the minds of the people. In fact, a new tactic by the Sons, based on Old World traditions, would begin to appear with increasing frequency: tarring and feathering. Dating as far back as the 12th century in England, tarring and feathering was brought to America by British sailors and evidently made its first appearance as a folk ritual around the time of the Stamp Act. Although tar and feathers were not always readily available and this form of public punishment often incorporated syrup and cattails instead, the treatment was never considered benign. Hot pine tar caused blisters; cleaning with chemical solvents further irritated the skin; body hair was lost; and, oftentimes, victims had their feathers set on fire. Thomas Hutchinson referred to the practice as "American torture."[76] In 1766, a ship's captain, William Smith, was tarred and feathered in Norfolk, Virginia, for conspiring with customs agents. From then until the outbreak of the Revolution in 1775, dozens of persons were punished in this highly public manner. As Benjamin H. Irvin argued in a 2003 study, tar and feathers were used most significantly to uphold the non-importation agreements in protest of the Townshend duties. Yet, in Boston, primary targets were informers and customs officials, and, surprisingly, no one was actually tarred and feathered there for violating non-importation. Instead, personal property such as homes and stores were tarred and feathered and, in one case, the horse of merchant Henry Barnes. Alfred Young argued in 1985 that the colony-wide tar and feather assaults were committed largely by spontaneous, lower-class crowds, but Irvin, citing contemporary newspaper accounts, convincingly maintained that the Sons of Liberty and other gentlemen of standing were equally involved, thus making the crowds socially diverse, as they had been during the Stamp Act furor.[77]

With non-importation now a reality, the Sons of Liberty, particularly in Massachusetts and New York, refocused their energies on enforcing the boycott of British goods by intimidating British officials, informers, and uncooperative merchants. Governor Bernard despaired, "Boston has been left under the uninterrupted dominion of a faction supported by a trained mob," evidence that the leading Sons were still in control of Boston's crowds.[78] Quite understandably then, on August 1, 1769, weary of battling Boston's radicals, Bernard abandoned Massachusetts and departed permanently for England, leaving Thomas Hutchinson to govern in his stead.

Shortly after Bernard's departure, Boston's radicals compiled a blacklist of merchants guilty of violating the non-importation pact. On the list was John Mein, a supporter of British policies and the publisher of the *Boston Chronicle,* a competitor of, and political counterpoint to, the *Boston Gazette.* In response, Mein and the *Chronicle* printed documents supplied by the Customs Board revealing that many of Boston's most avid non-importers, including John Hancock himself, were secretly bringing British goods into America. The *Chronicle* also viciously lampooned Boston's other leading Sons, including Samuel Adams, James Otis, and Dr. Joseph Warren. In October, Mein was attacked by a group of merchants and suffered a large gash from an iron shovel but, brandishing a pistol, managed to escape to a nearby guardhouse.[79] George Gailor, a seaman, was not so fortunate. Accused of being a customs informant, Gailor was seized from Hancock's *Liberty* by "a large crowd of those who call themselves gentlemen" and promptly tarred and feathered. He was then loaded onto a cart and taken to the Liberty Tree, where he was forced to admit his misdeeds.[80] Meanwhile, Mein took refuge on a British warship and, unable to secure any guarantee from Thomas Hutchinson to provide protection from Boston's mob, quickly departed for England. Writing under a pen name in the *Gazette,* Samuel Adams vigorously denied all of Mein's charges, but the explosive revelations, confirming what many had long suspected, were a damaging blow to the reputation of Boston's leading merchants, many of whom were influential Sons.[81]

Feeling particularly betrayed by Boston were the New York Sons of Liberty, who were in the midst of their own political problems. Almost from their inception, the New York Sons had been divided into two factions surrounding two influential families, the De Lanceys, who attracted workingmen such as mechanics and sailors, and the Livingstons, who represented merchants and the landed gentry. During the Stamp Act riots, the more moderate Livingston clan, dismayed by the violence, split from the militant De Lancey faction, which included New York's leading Sons such as Isaac Sears, John Lamb, and Joseph Allicocke. Of the other prominent Sons, only John Morin Scott and Alexander McDougall remained loyal to the Livingstons. However, after the dissolution of the Assembly for its non-compliance with the Quartering Act, new elections were held in 1769, and the De Lancey faction emerged triumphant. Determined to consolidate their position, the De Lanceys did everything within their power to avoid another dissolution and another subsequent election.

As Roger Champagne noted in an extensive study of the New York Sons, concerns over the Quartering Act and the desperate need for more paper money dominated local politics, not necessarily constitutional issues related to British authority. Thus, the De Lanceys, courting favor with the government, soon approved provisions for the British Army, bringing New York into closer compliance with the Quartering Act. As a result, a remarkable reversal of roles transpired in New York. The ruling De Lanceys now became known as collaborators while the Livingstons became the party of resistance, especially after Sears and Lamb deserted the De Lanceys and reunited with the Livingston fold. The reunion of Sears and Lamb with Scott and McDougall had profound ramifications for New York's "United Sons of Liberty." While the De Lanceys continued to promote themselves as Sons, it was the Livingston Sons who vowed to enforce non-importation in

New York. John Holt proclaimed that the offending merchants who dared violate non-importation were "so odious and contemptible, that they are generally shunned as if infected with the plague, so that they live most unhappy and miserable lives, and most of them apprehend that they shall be obliged to leave the colony."[82] In his study, Champagne further argued that New York's merchants were unfazed by threats of this nature and, by mid-1769, were determined to put an end to non-importation, but, by his own admission, there remained significant violence, herein defined as terrorist activity. Isaac Sears was heard threatening violators of non-importation with death. One Boston merchant, Nathanial Rogers, who dared enter New York to undermine non-importation, was greeted with an effigy hanging from a gallows, which was paraded through the streets by the Sons of Liberty, who warned him to leave the city within 24 hours or face "disagreeable circumstances." Rogers departed immediately.[83] In order to enforce New York's non-importation agreement, a committee of inspection was formed that had the authority to search ships and store any goods "illegally" brought into the colony. In July, Simon Cooley was caught importing prohibited items and compounded his situation by refusing to allow the committee to store his goods. He was immediately denounced as "a pest to society, and a vile disturber of the peace, police, and the good order of this city."[84] On July 21, a crowd gathered and approached Cooley's house to force a confession, but he fled first to Fort George. When the commanding officer refused to provide personal protection, Cooley had no alternative but to face the mob and confess his sins next to the Liberty Pole. Within two months, Cooley left New York for England. In September, another offending merchant, Thomas Richardson confessed his guilt from a mock scaffold erected near the Liberty Pole and promised to store his goods with the inspection committee.[85] New York's merchants would ultimately win their battle against non-importation, but, until the repeal of the Townshend duties in 1770, the New York Sons maintained constant pressure, despite their factionalism.

In mid-December 1769, a broadside was posted throughout New York entitled "To the Betrayed Inhabitants of the City and Colony of New York" and was signed "A Son of Liberty." A direct attack on new governor Cadwallader Colden and the ruling De Lanceys, it condemned the provisions bill and called on the townspeople to obstruct the transfer of any funds to the British Army. A subsequent investigation by Colden to discover the broadside's author eventually exposed Alexander McDougall, who was promptly jailed for libel. Had this occurred during the Stamp Act crisis, a rescue riot most likely would've ensued, but the Livingston Sons of Liberty had now come to appreciate that there was far more to be gained by having McDougall sit in jail, as opposed to breaking him out. For the next three months, McDougall was the reigning folk hero, toasted and celebrated everywhere as "America's Wilkes," a reference to England's John Wilkes, the notorious radical rabble-rouser and author of *North Briton, Number 45* who was sitting in a London prison for sedition. The Sons had, for some time, recognized the similarities between their struggle against arbitrary power and the attempt by Wilkes and his followers to stem corruption within the king's government. Both Wilkes and the Sons had great faith in constitutional principles, particularly those concerning property rights, freedom of the press, and the illegality of writs of assistance. Beginning as early as June 1768, the Boston Sons maintained an ongoing exchange of letters with Wilkes, as did other chapters of the Sons of Liberty.[86] McDougall's imprisonment was a public relations bonanza for the Livingston Sons and helped pave the way for their reunification with Sears and Lamb. Refusing bail, McDougall sat in jail for 81 days before charges were eventually dropped, during which time he entertained dinner guests, welcomed crowds of admirers, and received numerous gestures of affection from the public. At one point, in both his and Wilkes's honor, McDougall was serenaded with the 45th Psalm, sung by 45 virgins, all 45 years old (or so it was claimed!).[87]

McDougall was still in jail when he heard the news of the Battle of Golden Hill, a sign that despite New York's maddening transferal of political allegiances, the air of hostility against the regulars remained constant. Non-importation might not have been terribly popular everywhere in America, and it certainly was difficult to enforce, yet evidence indicates that it had a tremendous economic impact, especially in New York. While imports to Boston and Philadelphia dropped by about 50%, imports into New York dropped about 85%.[88] And while, on the surface, the violence against the Townshend duties failed to approach the destructiveness of the Stamp Act riots, in reality, the hostilities were sufficient enough, especially in Boston and New York, to maintain a constant fear of mob reprisal and public ostracism, creating a climate of terror that was crucial in enforcing the non-importation agreements.

V. From Townshend to Tea

Despite the best efforts of the Sons of Liberty, by early 1770, non-importation was in serious trouble. For some time, word had been circulating that the Townshend duties would be soon repealed, and there were many who wished that non-importation would simply disappear. In January, Lord North headed a new ministry in England, giving further credence to the rumors. Merchants, mechanics, and shopkeepers in America had begun to feel the economic pinch and were campaigning hard for the dissolution of the boycott agreements. Moreover, the exposure of Boston's violators undermined the tenuous solidarity that existed among the radicals in the large port cities. Simply put, the violent tactics employed by the Sons, while effective early on in select areas, could not overcome the momentum toward dissolution, with one notable exception: Boston. Two of the original non-subscribers of non-importation there were Thomas Hutchinson's sons, Elisha and Thomas, Jr., who continued to hold out. In January, under threat from the Sons of Liberty, they finally gave in and complied. Everywhere, importers and customs agents were terrorized: homes were vandalized, persons were assaulted, effigies were burned, friends were threatened, and property was splattered with "Hillsborough treat," a combination of mud and feces. Owen Richards, a customs official and informer, was tarred and feathered and paraded about town for two hours.[89] Thomas Hutchinson, Sr., complained that Boston was "under the government of the mob ... we are sinking into perfect barbarism." The wife of one of Boston's blacklisted violators confessed that, "those daring Sons of Liberty are now at the tip top of their power and to transact anything contrary to their sentiments, or even to speak disrespectfully of the Well Disposed, is a crime equal to high treason."[90]

On February 5, a mob began to attack the home of Ebenezer Richardson, a customs informer. He drew his pistol and fired into the crowd, fatally wounding a 12-year-old boy and injuring two others. Only through the intervention of leading townspeople did Richardson escape severe punishment at the hands of the mob. He was later convicted of murder by a Boston court, but was eventually pardoned by the king. One month later, a group of British soldiers guarding the customs house on King Street also fired into a menacing crowd, killing five and wounding many others in what would forever be known as the Boston Massacre. A series of subsequent trials would acquit a British captain and eight regulars of murder; two others were found guilty of manslaughter and had their hands branded. The massacre was, of course, a milestone on the road to revolution, an event that would be mythologized in prose, poem, and song, almost from the moment the bodies of the victims were interred. Paul Revere, a Boston Son of Liberty, produced the most famous artistic depiction of the event, an engraving that put an inflammatory, anti-British spin on the tragedy. The Sons, innocent of any complicity in the riot but eager to capitalize on a tragic yet historic event, now had martyrs to the cause of freedom and would commemorate the massacre with anniversary dinners.

That same month, Parliament repealed all of the Townshend duties, with the exception of the one on tea. Non-importation began to die a slow death, and some chapters of the Sons of Liberty once again either dissolved or remained dormant. By mid-1772, all colonial ports had suspended non-importation. The radicals still had causes—the duty on tea and the payment of salaries to government officials—but would remain in disarray for the next two years. In Boston, the Sons of Liberty were shaken by the temporary defection of John Hancock to the Hutchinson faction. James Otis, the victim of an assault at the hands of a customs agent, had grown mentally incompetent and could no longer be counted on by the Sons. In New York, the Sons remained paralyzed by the ongoing political struggle between the Livingstons and De Lanceys. In June 1772, however, one brief but contentious affair promised to unify the radicals, just as the *Liberty* riots had done four years earlier. On June 9, in pursuit of smugglers, the *Gaspee,* a Royal Navy schooner, ran aground off the shore of Rhode Island. That evening, some of the leading citizens of Providence boarded the *Gaspee,* removed its crew, shot its captain, and set the ship aflame. The *Gaspee* affair was not a Sons of Liberty operation, although the alleged ringleader of the raid, John Brown, had been identified as a leading Son during the Stamp Act riots. Nonetheless, news of the *Gaspee* action electrified the colonies, and, even today, the event is much celebrated in Rhode Island. Each year, in formal ceremonies held in front of the State House, descendants of the *Gaspee* raiders are eligible to be indicted for their ancestor's crimes against King George III. Despite the local fascination and attention elsewhere, the *Gaspee* failed to galvanize the Sons, who had seemingly run out of causes around which to rally.

The decision in England to send a commission to America to investigate the *Gaspee* affair and bring back defendants for trial seemed to confirm that Parliament was determined to violate recognized legal channels in order to punish miscreants. Meanwhile, two attempts to develop a colony-wide network of communication began to materialize. During the fall of 1772, in a Boston town meeting, Samuel Adams proposed the establishment of a committee of correspondence to draft and distribute a declaration of rights. The subsequent declaration, inspired by the "law of natural reason and equity," featured a list of British provocations, including taxing without consent, threatening to establish Anglican courts, extending the powers of the vice-admiralty courts, and introducing standing armies in peacetime.[91] The resounding approval from towns and cities everywhere helped resuscitate the ailing resistance movement, and the following March, the Virginia legislature, following Boston's lead, called for the creation of intercolonial committees of correspondence. Then on May 10, 1773, Parliament, seemingly lulled into a false sense of security, approved the Tea Act, which actually reduced some duties on tea but gave the financially strapped East India Company the exclusive rights to sell tea directly to America. The Tea Act not only revisited the long-standing constitutional issues surrounding the remaining duty on tea but now introduced a new element into the discussion: contrived monopolization. Tea was no small matter: it was estimated that one-third of the 3 million American people drank tea at least twice a day, and Massachusetts alone imported 800,000 pounds of tea per year.[92] Of the Tea Act, Samuel Adams would later write, "the ministry could not have devised a more effectual measure to unite the colonies."[93]

The English tea trade in America had fallen victim to the non-importation agreements, leading to a lucrative black market in Dutch tea, which was less expensive anyway. Yet, the exclusive right granted the East India Company was widely interpreted as another attempt to enslave Americans. Tea traders, in particular, did not relish having to compete with a monopoly established and protected by the Crown. Somewhat surprisingly, given their previous lack of determination, the radicals in Philadelphia were first to respond, protesting Parliament's right to tax without consent and establishing a committee to demand the resignation of tea agents. Thus, the strategy that emerged for radicals in the major ports soon resembled that employed during the Stamp Act crisis: force the resignation of agents and oppose the landing of the vile objects of British repression, in this case, English tea. William Bradford and other Philadelphia Sons of Liberty vowed to oppose the landing of any such tea, and threatened to tar and feather any captain who dared steer a tea ship into the city.[94] In Charleston, tea agents quickly resigned, but a division between mechanics and merchants stalled any agreement about what to do with a shipment of English tea that had arrived on December 2. Eventually, the tea was unloaded and stored without incident, much to the shame of the Charleston Sons.

In New York, the Tea Act provided an opportunity for Isaac Sears, John Lamb, Alexander McDougall, and the Livingston Sons of Liberty to seize the initiative and regain political momentum. In October and November, the *New York Journal* recommended that non-importation be revived yet again and warned tea agents of "sudden and sure destruction."[95] In Late November, the Livingston Sons, back in action, drew up "Articles of Association" and appointed a committee that visited three tea agents, demanding that no transactions involving English tea be made. The agents agreed to the demands. Two days later in *Rivington's Gazetteer,* "Mohawks" threatened violence to anyone who helped unload English tea. Ultimately, the fate of tea headed to New York fell upon William Tryon, who had become governor two years earlier. For Tryon, it was yet another confrontation with an organization associated with terrorist methods. He had vacated North Carolina shortly after dispensing with the Regulators at Alamance. He had come to New York, only to encounter the problems posed by the Green Mountain Boys in the faraway Grants. Now he had the Sons of Liberty to contend with, who were apparently willing to accept Tryon's promise to unload and store tea shipments without the use of force. New York's resolve, however, was hardened after receiving a letter from the Boston and Philadelphia Sons stating their intent to send back to England any offending tea. The New York Sons then reversed course and informed the governor's agents that they intended to use violence, if necessary, to prevent the landing of any English tea.[96]

In Boston, quite surprisingly, there was no immediate outrage at word of the Tea Act. As usual, the *Boston Gazette* helped set the tone when eventually, in October, it compared the Tea Act to the "yoke of slavery," urged that English tea be sent back across the Atlantic, and began to publish the names of local tea agents. On October 23, after a meeting of the North End Caucus, handbills appeared which ordered the tea agents to resign their commissions before the Liberty Tree on November 3. The caucus, which included some of Boston's leading Sons of Liberty, such as Dr. Joseph Warren, Thomas Young, and Benjamin Church, demanded that offending tea be shipped back to England, and drafted a resolution that threatened "the weight of their just resentment" should the agents not appear.[97] The agents, backed by Thomas Hutchinson, whose own sons had been commissioned to distribute tea, refused to appear, despite a confrontation with a mob led by caucus leaders and William Molineux, another leading Son. The agents also defied resignation demands issued by Boston's town meeting, headed by Samuel Adams and John Hancock. At that point, the use of acknowledged institutions having failed, Adams began to single-handedly direct the resistance movement. Meeting with representatives from other nearby towns and cities, an Adams-led convention agreed to prevent the landing of tea and called for larger mass meetings of activists in what became known as the "whole body of the people," or simply "the Body."

On November 27, the *Dartmouth,* laded with English tea, arrived in Boston. Two other tea ships, the *Eleanor* and the *Beaver,* would arrive a few days thereafter. On November 28, fearful for their safety, five tea consignees and four customs agents fled to Castle William for protection. Once the three ships landed in Boston, a confrontation was inevitable. The Body wanted the ships to depart without unloading its tea. But the ships could not depart without permits from Governor Hutchinson, who refused to issue clearance papers without proper payment of import duties. Non-payment of duties raised the possibility of having the tea confiscated and unloaded by customs commissioners, which the mobs would certainly oppose. Armed guards had already been assigned by the radicals to watch the tea ships around the clock. British warships strategically placed in Boston Harbor could easily destroy any ships attempting to flee without payment of duties. No wonder then, on the night of December 16, after one last desperate attempt to convince Hutchinson to clear the ships had failed, Samuel Adams broke up a mass meeting at Boston's Old South Church with the words, "this meeting can do no more to save the country." Almost immediately, as if on cue, the crowd whooped and hollered, let out shrill Indian war cries, and departed into the night. That evening, about 50 men, many crudely disguised as Mohawks with soot-covered faces and Indian blankets, emerged in two separate groups from a variety of houses, taverns, and street corners—one from the Northend and the other from the Southend. Adding numbers as they marched through the streets, the crowd, now numbering about 150 persons, boarded the three ships docked at Griffin's Wharf and, in a meticulously coordinated three-hour operation, unloaded 342 chests of tea into Boston Harbor before thousands of silent spectators.

As Alfred F. Young has demonstrated, the riot at Griffin's Wharf did not become popularly known as the Boston Tea Party until a half-century later. Apparently, the tea riot, now considered the most defining and exalted moment of the Pre-Revolutionary Era, was an event that Bostonians immediately disowned. Parliament would respond in draconian fashion, making Bostonians pay dearly, and, as Young explained, the riot just didn't fit into the well-publicized image of an innocent and repressed people enslaved by an unjust government.[98] At the time, the tea party never assumed the mythological status of the Boston Massacre or the repeal of the Stamp Act and, accordingly, was never similarly commemorated. Another reason for its relatively low profile was the need for strict secrecy. Crimes had been committed and identities had to be protected, thus everyone associated with the riot would feign ignorance when queried. Yet, over the years, historians have identified more than 100 persons said to have been active that night at Griffin's Wharf, a great number of whom were Sons of Liberty. However, because most lists of participants used by historians were recalled many decades after the fact, reliability is an unavoidable issue. One deponent gave testimony 75 years later, when he was 113 years old.[99] Thomas Young and John Hancock, for example, appeared on some lists, but did not directly participate in the riot.[100] The Tea Party is, of course, considered the most historically significant event associated with the Sons, even if it was not exclusively a Sons operation once it began. The planning for the destruction of the tea, for example, took place at two hotbeds of sedition, known for their association with the Sons of Liberty: the "Long Room" over Edes and Gill's printing office and the Green Dragon tavern, home of the Masonic Lodge of St. Andrew.[101]

If Alfred F. Young has provided the best analytical study of the Tea Party (1999), Benjamin Woods Labaree wrote the best and most-detailed narrative, which, although written in 1964, remains the standard work on the subject, despite the recent publication of two additional Tea Party studies. Benjamin L. Carp's *Defiance of the Patriots* (2010) examined the broader, global context of the tea riot, while Harlow Giles Unger's *American Tempest* (2011) concentrated less on the actual Tea Party and more on the riot's impact upon the coalescing revolutionary movement.[102] Young divided the tea raiders into three categories: the *invited* participants who had been assigned to specific boarding parties; the *semi-invited,* volunteers who had been forewarned of direct action; and the *self-invited,* young spectators who got swept up by the events. According to information provided by the Boston Tea Party Historical Society, of the rioters who can be identified, two-thirds were 20 years old or younger and only nine were 40 or older. Most were from Boston, but some had come from as far away as Worcester and Maine. The vast majority was of English descent, but there were those of Irish, Scot, French, African, and Portuguese origins as well. All socio-economic levels of society were represented; doctors, merchants and other elites took an active part, and of the 34 known rioters who were listed on local tax lists, two-thirds owned little or no property, most of whom were carpenters, masons, skilled artisans, and mechanics.[103] Notable leaders of the Sons of Liberty such as Samuel Adams, Dr. Joseph Warren, and John Hancock, who had returned to the radical ranks, could not risk being seen at the riot. At least two of the Loyal Nine, Henry Bass and Thomas Crafts, took part, as did prominent Sons Paul Revere and William Molineux, the designated leader of crowds. Young also emphasized two other elements of the tea riot. One, it was a quasi-military operation, the boldest and most dangerous in Boston up to that time. Many of the rioters were armed with hatchets, pistols, and other weapons. The destruction of 90,000 pounds of private property was an act of wanton violence. No one knew for sure if the British regulars would respond with force; thus, every participant was risking life and limb. Fortunately, the British Army wisely refused to intercede, avoiding what surely would have been a bloody confrontation. Two, Young also noted that the tea party was the most "carnivalesque" event of the era, which is consistent with the theatrical elements of terrorism. The rioters played to an audience, by taking on Indian personas and by mocking genteel tea rituals of the haughty British. Ostensibly, the overriding purpose of the tea riot was to destroy the tea before Hutchinson seized an opportunity to unload it, but William Gordon would later attest that one other motive

was likely at work: the need for Boston's Sons of Liberty to reestablish their reputation as the leaders of the resistance movement, a status severely undermined by
John Mein's embarrassing expose.[104]

In England, as one would imagine, word of the tea riot was not well received.
Writing to Samuel Adams from London, Arthur Lee described the impact as
"an electric shock."[105] Both the ministry and Parliament were determined to
bring the offending parties to justice—which meant bringing defendants to England to stand trial. In the end, England's Privy Council was unable to uncover
enough evidence to implicate the leaders of the tea party. After all, they had wisely
avoided the scene of the crime. Thus denied the opportunity to punish individuals
for their role in the riot, Parliament turned, instead, to collective punishment and,
in March, began deliberations for what would become known as the Intolerable
(or Coercive) Acts. The Acts consisted of four separate pieces of legislation passed
between March 31 and June 2. The Port Bill, which closed the port of Boston,
was first. On May 20, the Massachusetts Government Act and the Administration of Justice Act together restructured the Massachusetts government, restricted
town meetings, and mandated that British officials accused of crimes be sent to
Canada or England for trial. Lastly, an amendment to the Quartering Act empowered British commanders to quarter troops wherever needed. Thus did Parliament
mete out punishment to Boston, long the hotbed of sedition and treachery, but, in
the process, once again inadvertently laid the groundwork for colonial solidarity
in the face of British authority.

The day after the tea riots, Paul Revere, an acknowledged Son, set off for
New York and Philadelphia by horse with a letter from Samuel Adams detailing recent events in Boston. Popular leaders in Philadelphia gave their stamp of
approval but determined that, in their particular case, sending the tea back to
England was the wisest course. When a tea ship, the *Polly*, arrived at Chester, the
tea agent who accompanied the shipment, Gilbert Barkly, quickly resigned his
commission on hearing the news from Boston. After landing in Philadelphia, the
Polly's captain encountered a mass meeting that demanded the ship turn back
for England without unloading its tea; after picking up additional stores, it did
just that. The Philadelphia Sons of Liberty patted themselves on the back and
quickly retreated into obscurity once again.[106] Meanwhile, the continued lack
of resolve in Charleston, where tea had been unloaded without incident, did
not go unnoticed by the Boston radicals. Samuel Adams sharply rebuked the
Charleston Sons of Liberty, asking, "how great then was our chagrin to hear that
through some internal division the grand cause was neglected . . . must then the
liberties of the present and future ages be sacrificed to some unhappy feud in
Carolina . . . ?"[107] Finally, in late January, Charleston radicals set up an executive
committee to enforce the non-importation of tea. In July, a tea ship arrived and,
despite promises made by its captain, quickly unloaded and stored its cargo of tea.
A mob boarded his vessel, but the captain managed to escape and took refuge in a
neighboring ship. When another tea shipment arrived soon thereafter, the crowds

were taking no chances and the merchants, for whom the tea was intended, were forced to toss the tea overboard.[108]

In New York, news from Boston undermined any chance that tea could be unloaded without incident. A secret agreement to send back tea shipments to England was struck between the New York Sons of Liberty and Henry White, a tea agent. The accord evidently had the blessing of William Tryon, who, in the aftermath of Alamance, was concerned about his reputation and chose to avoid the use of military force to unload tea.[109] Fortunately for all involved, the first tea shipments would not arrive until the following spring, providing a short but much-needed cooling-off period. In April 1774, two tea ships finally arrived and anchored at Sandy Hook; the *Nancy*, piloted by Benjamin Lockyer, arrived on April 18 and the *London*, captained by James Chambers, arrived four days later. The day after his arrival, Lockyer was presented with a letter from a group of "gentlemen," informing the captain that his tea could not be unloaded. He was then taken to the house of Henry White, who advised Lockyer about the agreement with the Sons and warned him not to approach the customs house, suggesting instead that Lockyer gather whatever stores he might need and depart without unloading his tea. Lockyer consented, but, as a precaution, the Sons of Liberty organized a group of watchmen to provide constant surveillance of the *Nancy*. Upon arrival of the *London*, Captain Chambers denied that he had tea aboard, despite documentary evidence to the contrary, and was taken by a crowd to Fraunces Tavern to be interrogated. Warned that his ship would be exhaustively searched, Chambers finally confessed not only to the presence of tea on board but also to being the sole owner of said cargo. Later that day, rioters, described as Mohawks, quickly boarded the *London* and dumped its tea overboard. Fearful for his life, Chambers soon retreated and sought refuge on the *Nancy*, and, when Lockyer's ship departed the next day, Chambers was still on board, having abandoned his ship and tea. Although New York's tea party is not generally credited to the Sons of Liberty, there seems to be little doubt that the Sons were complicit in the affair. It was the Sons who negotiated the original agreement with White to turn tea ships back, and Chambers's interrogation took place at Fraunces Tavern, a known meeting place of the New York Sons. Further, according to eyewitnesses, "persons of reputation" were present at the tea riot, keeping some sort of tally, perhaps an indication that certain leaders of the Sons were directly involved in the operation. And as the *Nancy* sailed beyond Sandy Hook back to England, it was accompanied for three leagues by a sloop commandeered by the Sons of Liberty. Moreover, to celebrate the dumping of New York's tea, a celebration followed, with bands, church bells, and a commemorative flag flown from the Liberty Pole.[110]

Back in Boston, events continued to unravel. The day following the tea riot, Thomas Hutchinson wanted to meet with Boston's town council but wasn't able to muster a majority until December 21. While the Sons of Liberty felt as though Hutchinson had given them no alternative to the dumping of Boston's tea, there were plenty of locals who condemned the riot, wanted guilty parties punished, and endorsed compensation payments to those financially injured by the riot. The governor was also anxious to punish those responsible but soon discovered that the council was not eager to cooperate, suggesting instead an investigation by the attorney general and subsequent report to the grand jury. In early January, a mob tarred and feathered John Malcolm, a minor customs official who had been given the treatment once before, in 1773, for being an informer. Malcolm, who fought against the Regulators at Alamance Creek, further earning him the enmity of the people, had been involved in a personal confrontation with George Robert Twelves Hewes, one of the many tea party rioters.[111] Hewes, a shoemaker by trade, would later become the focal point of Alfred F. Young's insightful study of the tea party. On March 6, the *Fortune* arrived from London with 28 chests of tea aboard and docked at Hubbard's Wharf, despite threats from Boston's Committee of Correspondence to punish users of tea. The ship's owners, apparently unaware that their vessel contained the offending tea, offered to send the cargo back, but the customs collector, Richard Harrison, refused to clear the *Fortune* without payment of the Townshend duty. Harrison was the son of Joseph Harrison, the collector who had seized John Hancock's *Liberty* back in 1768, the night a mob beat Richard and dragged him through the streets by his hair. The next evening, about 60 "Indians" boarded the *Fortune* and dumped its tea into the harbor. Less than three months after the original, Boston had its second tea party.[112]

VI.   The Road to Revolution

News of the Port Bill reached Boston on May 10, 1774. Three days later, a town meeting passed resolutions calling for a complete suspension of all trade with England and the West Indies, and asking for other colonial support. That same day, General Thomas Gage arrived in Boston to assume duties from Governor Hutchinson, who would depart for England on June 1, never to return to his native land. If Hutchinson felt any sense of melancholy upon abandoning his homeland, where he had become a much-despised outsider, his 17-year-old daughter, Peggy, who accompanied him, felt relief. In a letter to her sister-in-law, Peggy confessed that she had tired of "running from a mob since sixty-five" and relished the day when "I do hope to be out of their reach."[113] By the time that word of the last of the Intolerable Acts reached America, Bostonians and radicals in surrounding counties had begun a hostile campaign to obstruct Parliament's latest provocations. Town meetings were held everywhere, in direct defiance of the Massachusetts Government Act. Crowds threatened judges, lawyers, and other court officials in order to shut down the judicial system, thus undermining the Administration of Justice Act. But the most aggressive obstructionism was the coercion of the new councilors of the colonial council, once an elective office but made appointive via the Government Act. Faced with social ostracism, night raids, the destruction of their homes, and bodily harm, most of the new royal appointees resigned their commissions. As Dirk Hoerder noted in his study of mob activity in Massachusetts, of the 36 newly appointed councilors, 20 chose to resign rather than continue to live in fear.[114] Although individual Sons of Liberty were undoubtedly involved in many of these crowd actions against the Intolerable Acts, this campaign of resistance and intimidation in Massachusetts was so widespread, and at times so spontaneous, that it must stand apart from crowd actions more directly associated with the Sons of Liberty. Nonetheless, if the number of councilor resignations is any indication, the climate of terror generated by this campaign was every bit as effective as any directly involving the Sons.

By now, the Sons of Liberty had established a pattern of terrorism similar to that created by the North Carolina Regulators and the Green Mountain Boys. In the case of the Sons, resistance was primarily aimed at obstructing the Stamp Act and the Townshend duties, which meant that orchestrated acts of violence against persons or property were designed to intimidate a wider audience of customs agents, stamp masters, tea traders, importers, merchants, lawyers, judges, British officials, and other Americans. The Sons created a sophisticated propaganda campaign that was extensive and effective. The songs, poems, parades, handbills, and Liberty poles and trees were supplemented by a combination of sympathetic newspapers and editors who provided more traditional avenues of political expression. The use of tar and feathers and other forms of *charivari* as punitive methods of upholding community solidarity added to the theatrical elements of terrorism. The Sons also established a degree of extralegal authority, consistently operating out of the bounds of English law and flaunting their defiance of British officials. And although the Sons lacked centralized control, each chapter had its own established hierarchy, some from preexisting organizations. Following a familiar pattern, the more respectable elements of society provided direction, pulling strings from behind the curtain, while plebians controlled the action in the streets. In essence, the Sons of Liberty had constructed a campaign of terror that was crucial in establishing an environment of resistance that would eventually culminate in revolutionary warfare against Great Britain.

Boston's call on May 13 for a renewed boycott of British goods reopened relatively fresh wounds and generated significant opposition, particularly from conservatives and merchants. American radicals could not risk another flawed campaign of non-importation, and solidarity seemed beyond reach, especially in New York, where political dissension continued to rule the day. On May 16, one day before news of the Boston resolutions reached New York, a meeting of merchants revealed the opposing positions. Maintaining that Boston had an obligation to pay for the destroyed tea and that such compensation would quickly resolve the current crisis, the ruling De Lanceys would not commit to any campaign of non-importation until cooperation was pledged by other colonies. Conversely, the Livingstons, the faction most closely identified with the Sons of Liberty, wanted an immediate agreement of non-importation and non-exportation, with a colonial congress to provide oversight. In the end, a committee of correspondence was assigned to maintain constant communication with fellow colonies, but the De Lanceys were able to stack the so-called "Committee of 51" with like-minded supporters. Even after Paul Revere brought news of the Boston resolutions the very next day, the De Lanceys continued to stonewall the Livingstons. On May 23, the Committee of 51 officially responded to Boston's appeal for support by suggesting nothing could be done by New Yorkers without colony-wide cooperation. But in that spirit, the committee also offered support for a colonial congress that could potentially create some type of unanimity, an idea first approved by Rhode Island one week earlier. In reality, the De Lanceys held out hope that such a congress would never meet and that support for non-importation and non-exportation would hastily dissolve. Surprisingly, however, Philadelphia's own "Committee of 19" also consented to a colonial congress, thus forcing New York, much to the consternation of the De Lanceys, to comply as promised. With Providence, Boston, New York, and Philadelphia tenuously in agreement, the groundwork for the first Continental Congress was laid.

By the time the Continental Congress met in Philadelphia in early September 1774, the use of terrorism by the Sons of Liberty had begun to wane. The resistance movement had grown to such an extent that the tactics of terror had become somewhat superfluous. In response to the Coercive Acts, everywhere throughout the colonies, newly created popular governments had begun to displace royal institutions by regulating society, manipulating voters, and organizing local militias. The Sons would remain politically active, but mob action was no longer paramount in manipulating political behavior and public opinion. The Coercive Acts had inadvertently accomplished what the Sons of Liberty were never able to do: create unity and cooperation amongst the colonies. In effect, the Sons would now work through the Continental Congress to pursue their political ends. Many of the Sons had been selected to represent their colonies, and, of the key players in Philadelphia, certainly Samuel Adams and Christopher Gadsden stood out.

After two months of heated discussion, Congress managed to overcome a diversity of interests and accordingly approved policies of non-importation from England and Ireland beginning December 1, 1774; non-exportation to England, Ireland, and the West Indies beginning September 1775; and non-consumption beginning March 1, 1775. Congress also established the Continental Association to administer its newly created policies and voiced its approval of the fiery Suffolk Resolves, which called for outright resistance to the Coercive Acts. Along with other specified grievances and resolutions, Congress further endorsed a Massachusetts proposal suggesting that people take up arms as a matter of self-defense. The Continental Congress stopped short of recommending complete independence, but, for many delegates, some sort of future separatism appeared inevitable. This seemed especially likely given the consideration granted to a rejected proposal submitted by Joseph Galloway, one of the conservative leaders, which had called for significant American autonomy by establishing an American legislature to stand alongside Parliament in jointly governing the colonies. Events were now rapidly proceeding toward a violent, military confrontation. While many Americans took Congress's advice and began to stockpile weapons, England began a military buildup, enlarging its army and naval forces in preparation for duty in America. Speaking of the insolent Americans one month after Congress had adjourned, King George III told Lord North, "blows must decide whether they are to be subject to the Country or Independent."[115] As if on cue, those blows would come in mid-April when British regulars, in search of stockpiled arms, clashed with local militias at Lexington and Concord, thereby igniting the war for American independence.

Once the Revolutionary War began, the various chapters of the Sons of Liberty, whose campaign of terror had helped provoke the confrontation, generally drifted apart and became part of a larger effort that would ultimately overthrow British authority in America. Some Sons, such as Samuel Adams and John Hancock, supported the patriot cause by serving in the Continental Congress. Most, such as Joseph Warren, who died at Breed's Hill, Paul Revere, who became a lieutenant colonel, and New York's Alexander McDougall, who rose to the rank of major general, served in the ranks of the Continental Army. Others, such as Christopher Gadsden, did both: Gadsden represented South Carolina in Congress but later assumed command of the First South Carolina Regiment. Contrarily, Isaac Sears spent the bulk of the war accumulating wealth as a privateer. Their divergent paths notwithstanding, from 1765 to 1775, the Sons of Liberty had together conducted a resistance movement founded on terror that significantly altered America's transformation from colonies to sovereign state. This alone should not discredit the origins of the American Revolution. As John F. Kennedy once said in defense of native terrorists victimizing French Algeria in 1957, "The fever chart of every successful revolution . . . reveals a rising temperature of terrorism and counter-terrorism: but this itself does not of itself invalidate the legitimate goals that fired the original revolution. Most political revolutions—including our own—have been buoyed by outside aid in men, weapons, and ideas."[116] Little could the early Sons have known that their concerted effort to protest the imposition of stamp taxes would not only help ignite a resistance movement that would ultimately transform the western world but also seemingly validate, in the eyes of at least one future American president, the use of terror as a revolutionary tactic.

Notes

1. Francis Bernard to Lord Halifax, August 15, 1765, Bernard Papers, MS Sparks, IV, Volume 4, HLH, 137.
2. Merrill Jensen, *The Founding of a Nation* (New York: Oxford University Press, 1968), 63–64.
3. Pauline Maier, *From Resistance to Revolution* (New York: Vintage Books, 1974), 81.
4. Les Standiford, *Desperate Sons* (New York: HarperCollins, 2012).
5. Richard Walsh, *Charleston's Sons of Liberty* (Columbia: University of South Carolina Press, 1959); Henry B. Dawson, *The Sons of Liberty in New York* (New York: Arno Press & The New York Times, 1969).

6. Edmund S. Morgan and Helen M. Morgan, *The Stamp Act Crisis* (Chapel Hill: University of North Carolina Press, 1953); Maier, *From Resistance to Revolution.*

7. See for example, Arthur M. Schlesinger, "Liberty Tree: A Genealogy," *New England Quarterly* (December, 1952): 435–458; Roger J. Champagne, "Liberty Boys and Mechanics of New York City, 1764–1774," *Labor History* 8, (1967): 115–135; Pauline Maier, "John Wilkes and American Disillusionment with Britain," *William and Mary Quarterly,* 3rd ser., 20, (1963): 371–395.

8. Maier, *From Resistance to Revolution,* 83.

9. Dirk Hoerder, *Crowd Action in Revolutionary Massachusetts, 1760–1780* (New York: Academic Press, 1977).

10. Herbert M. Morais, "The Sons of Liberty in New York," in Richard B. Morris, ed., *The Era of the American Revolution* (New York: Harper Torchbook, 1939), 269; Dawson, 40–41; Maier, *From Resistance to Revolution,* 78.

11. Morgan and Morgan, *The Stamp Act Crisis,* 187–190.

12. John C. Miller, *Sam Adams: Pioneer in Propaganda* (Stanford: Stanford University Press, 1936), 53; Maier, *From Resistance to Revolution,* 307; Hoerder, *Crowd Action in Revolutionary Massachusetts,* 93.

13. Morgan and Morgan, *The Stamp Act Crisis,* 128; Hoerder, *Crowd Action in Revolutionary Massachusetts,* 96.

14. Estimates of numbers, see Francis S. Drake, *Tea Leaves: Being a Collection of Letters and Documents Relating to the Shipment of Tea to the American Colonies in 1773 by the East India Company* (Boston: A. O. Crane, 1884) xxiv; "clearinghouse" depiction in Hoerder, *Crowd Action in Revolutionary Massachusetts,* 94; "steering committee" depiction in Jensen, *The Founding of a Nation,* 148.

15. Bernard to Halifax, August 15, 1765, 137–141; William V. Wells, *The Life and Public Services of Samuel Adams,* Volume 1 (Boston: Little, Brown, and Company, 1865), 61; BEP, August 19, 1765; BG, August 19, 1765; BN, August 22, 1765.

16. Hoerder, *Crowd Action in Revolutionary Massachusetts,* 103; Morgan and Morgan, *The Stamp Act Crisis,* 131.

17. Peter Orlando Hutchinson, *The Diary and Letters of His Excellency Thomas Hutchinson, Esq.,* Volume 1 (London: William Clowes and Sons, undated), 67–72; Peter Orlando Hutchinson was the Great Grandson of Thomas Hutchinson; Francis Bernard to Lord Halifax, August 31, 1765, Bernard Papers, MS Sparks, IV, Volume 4, HLH, 148–156; BEP, September 2, 1765.

18. William Gordon, *The History of the Rise, Progress, and Establishment of the Independence of the United States of America* (London, 1788), I, 175.

19. Morgan and Morgan, *Stamp Act Crisis,* 134–135; Hoerder, *Crowd Action in Revolutionary Massachusetts,* 112–113.

20. Ezra Stiles, "Stamp Act Notebook," Stiles Miscellaneous Papers, folder 372, BLY, 56.

21. Dawson, *Sons of Liberty in New York,* 40–41.

22. Morais, "Sons of Liberty," 272–273.

23. Beverly McAnear, "The Albany Stamp Act Riots," *William and Mary Quarterly,* IV, (1947): 486–498.

24. Stiles, "Stamp Act Notebook," 72.

25. Maier, *From Resistance to Revolution,* 298–300.

26. Stiles, "Stamp Act Notebook," 58–65.

27. Francis Bernard to Lord Halifax, August 31, 1765, Bernard Papers, MS Sparks, IV, Volume 4, HLH, 153.

28. Philadelphia Sons of Liberty to New York Sons of Liberty, February 15, 1766, Lamb Papers, NYHS.

29. Roger James Champagne, *The Sons of Liberty and the Aristocracy in New York Politics, 1765–1790* (PhD Dissertation, University of Wisconsin, 1960).

30. Jensen, *The Founding of a Nation,* 130.

31. Maier, *From Resistance to Revolution,* 298.

32. Francis Bernard to the Board of Trade, January 10, 1766, Bernard Papers, MS Sparks, IV, Volume 4, HLH.

33. H. S. Conway to Cadwallader Colden, December 15, 1765, Letters and Papers of Cadwallader Colden, Volume 7, 1765–1775 (Collections of the New York Historical Society, 1923) NYHS, 97.

34. Stiles, "Stamp Act Notebook," 10, 48.

35. Isaac Leake, *Memoir of the Life and Times of General John Lamb* (Albany, Joel Munsell, 1850), 21; Journals of Capt. John Montresor, v, n.7 (1881) NYHS, 340.

36. Morgan and Morgan, *Stamp Act Crisis,* 159.

37. BG, September 16, 1765; BN, September 12, 1765; BEP, September 16, 1765.

38. The Connecticut Society of the Sons of the American Revolution website, connecticutsar. org/articles/scarlet_no6.htm.

39. Jensen, *The Founding of a Nation,* 121.

40. Thomas James to Cadwallader Colden, December, 1765, Letters and Papers of Cadwallader Colden, Volume 7, 1765–1775, NYHS, 99; Journals of Capt. John Montresor, 336–337.

41. Champagne, *The Sons of Liberty and the Aristocracy,* 69.

42. Morgan and Morgan, *Stamp Act Crisis,* 188.

43. Ibid, 189.

44. Gordon, *History,* 199.

45. Maier, *From Resistance to Revolution,* 92.

46. "Notice Served on Governor Colden Concerning the Stamp Act" (undated but delivered to Fort Gate on November 1, 1765), Letters and Papers of Cadwallader Colden, Volume 7, 1765–1775, NYHS, 85.

47. Francis Bernard to Lord Halifax, August 22, 1765, Bernard Papers, MS Sparks, IV, Volume 4, HLH, 148.

48. Jensen, *The Founding of a Nation,* 154.

49. Maier, *From Resistance to Revolution,* 95–96.

50. Extract of a letter from Providence, February 17, 1766, John Lamb Papers, NYHS; MS Sparks, X, Volume 3, Papers Relating to New England, George Chalmers Manuscripts, February, 1769, HLH, 19.

51. Journals of Capt. John Montresor, 367.

52. Maier, *From Resistance to Revolution,* 96–97.

53. Walsh, *Charlestown's Sons,* 40.

54. Thomas Gage to Cadwallader Colden, August 31, 1765, Letters and Papers of Cadwallader Colden, Volume 7, 1765–1775, NYHS, 58.

55. Gordon S. Wood, *The American Revolution* (New York: A Modern Library Chronicles Book, 2003), 33.

56. Arthur M. Schlesinger, *The Colonial Merchants and the American Revolution, 1763–1776* (New York: Longmans, Green & Co., 1918).

57. Hoerder, *Crowd Action in Revolutionary Massachusetts,* 195.

58. Jensen, *The Founding of a Nation,* 265; Maier, *From Resistance to Revolution,* 121.

59. Jensen, *The Founding of a Nation,* 270.

60. Walsh, *Charlestown's Sons,* 50.

61. Francis Bernard to Lord Shelburne, March 19, 1768, MS Sparks, X, Volume 2, Papers Relating to New England, George Chalmers Manuscripts, HLH, 75; Commissioners of the Customs to the Lords of the Treasury, March–1768, Massachusetts Historical Society "Proceedings," 55, MHS, 268–271.

62. Letter from William de Grey, July 25, 1768, Massachusetts Historical Society "Proceedings," 55, MHS, 275; Thomas Hutchinson, June 18, 1768 and August, 1768, *The Letters of Gov. Hutchinson and Lt. Gov. Oliver* (London: printed for J. Wilkie, 1774), MHS. For secondary accounts of the riot, see Jensen, 282 and Hoerder, 168.

63. Francis Bernard to Lord Halifax, August 16, 1765, MS Sparks, IV, Volume 4, Bernard Papers, HLH, 143.

64. Jensen, *The Founding of a Nation,* 130.

65. Hoerder, *Crowd Action in Revolutionary Massachusetts,* 130.

66. Stiles, "Stamp Act Notebook," 21.

67. Arthur M. Schlesinger, "Liberty Tree: A Genealogy," *The New England Quarterly* (December, 1952): 438.

68. Champagne, *The Sons of Liberty and the Aristocracy,* 227.

69. Hoerder, *Crowd Action in Revolutionary Massachusetts,* 138–139.

70. "Song for Sons of Liberty in the Several American Provinces," *The New Hampshire Gazette* (April, 1766).

71. "Military Songs," American Revolution and Before—The Liberty Song, www .sanftleben.com/Military%20Music/military%Music.

72. Arthur M. Schlesinger, "A Note on Songs as Patriot Propaganda," *William and Mary Quarterly,* 3rd ser., Vol. 11, no. 1 (January, 1954): 78–88.

73. Ibid.

74. Burton Egbert Stevenson, *Poems of American History* (Boston: Houghton Mifflin Company, 1908), 141.

75. Ibid., 131.

76. Drake, *Tea Leaves,* xliv.

77. Alfred F. Young, "English Plebian Culture and Eighteenth-Century American Radicalism," in Margaret Jacob and James Jacob, ed., *The Origins of American Radicalism* (London: Allen and Unwin, 1984), 185–212; Benjamin H. Irvin, "Tar, Feathers, and the Enemies of American Liberties, 1768–1776," *The New England Quarterly,* 76, 2 (June, 2003): 197–238.

78. Jensen, *The Founding of a Nation,* 290.

79. George Mason letter, October 28, 1769, MS Sparks X, Volume 3, Papers Relating to New England, George Chalmers Manuscripts, HLH, 47–51; BEP, October 30, 1769.

80. Irvin, "Tar, Feathers," 202.

81. Samuel Adams Papers, August 28, 1769, NYPL.

82. Champagne, *The Sons of Liberty and the Aristocracy,* 263.

83. Nathanial Rogers letter, undated, MS Sparks, X, Volume 3, Papers Relating to New England, George Chalmers Manuscripts, HLH, 44; BEP, May 21, 1770.

84. Champagne, *The Sons of Liberty and the Aristocracy,* 252.

85. Ibid.

86. John Wilkes to Boston Sons of Liberty, March 30, 1769, Samuel Adams Papers, NYPL; Pauline Maier, "John Wilkes and American Disillusionment with Britain," 371–395. See also John Gorham Pelfrey, *History of New England,* Volume 5 (Boston: Little, Brown and Co., 1890), 388.

87. Maier, *William and Mary Quarterly,* 386.

88. Champagne, *The Sons of Liberty and the Aristocracy,* 249.

89. John Woart to William Sheaffe, undated letter on the Richards affair, MS Sparks, X, Volume 4, Papers Relating to New England, George Chalmers Manuscripts, HLH, 1–2.

90. Jensen, *The Founding of a Nation,* 362–363.

91. Wood, *The American Revolution,* 36.

92. Drake, *Tea Leaves,* x.

93. Samuel Adams to Joseph Warren, December 28, 1773, Samuel Adams Papers, NYPL.

94 Jensen, *Founding of a Nation,* 442.

95. Champagne, *The Sons of Liberty and the Aristocracy,* 297.

96. Ibid., 310.

97. Drake, *Tea Leaves,* 26; Jensen, *The Founding of a Nation,* 449.

98. Alfred F. Young, *The Shoemaker and the Tea Party* (Boston: Beacon Press, 1999), 87–91.

99. Benjamin Woods Labaree, *The Boston Tea Party* (Boston: Northeastern University Press, 1979), 142.

100. Hoerder, *Crowd Action in Revolutionary Massachusetts,* 263, fn.

101. Drake, *Tea Leaves,* lxvi.

102. Benjamin L. Carp, *Defiance of the Patriots—The Boston Tea Party and the Making of America* (New Haven: Yale University Press, 2010); Harlow Giles Unger, *American Tempest— How the Boston Tea Party Sparked a Revolution* (Cambridge, MA: Da Capo Press), 2011.

103. Hoerder, *Crowd Action in Revolutionary Massachusetts,* 263.

104. Drake, *Tea Leaves,* 33; Jensen, *The Founding of a Nation,* 452.

105. Arthur Lee to Samuel Adams, January 31, 1774, Samuel Adams Papers, NYPL.

106. Drake, 363; BG, January 17, 1774; BEP, December 20, 1773.

107. Jensen, *The Founding of a Nation,* 442.

108. Walsh, *Charlestown's Sons,* 60–61.

109. Jensen, *The Founding of a Nation,* 447.

110. Drake, *Tea Leaves,* lxxxiv, 358; *New York Gazette,* April 28, 1774.

111. Jensen, *The Founding of a Nation,* 462; Hoerder, *Crowd Action,* 268.

112. Labaree, *Boston Tea Party,* 165.

113. Peter Orlando Hutchinson, *Diary and Letters,* 108.2

114. Hoerder, *Crowd Action in Revolutionary Massachusetts,* 292.

115. Wood, *The American Revolution,* 53.

116. John F. Kennedy, *The Strategy of Peace* (New York: Harper and Brothers, 1960), 71.

5

POPULAR PROTESTS IN THE NEW REPUBLIC

I. Post-War Polarization

More than a political upheaval, the American Revolution was the most violent and destructive military episode in North America up to that point in time. Precise numbers are elusive, but, due to various causes, at least 40,000 to 50,000 persons either were injured or lost their lives during the prolonged conflict.[1] Further, although the war involved both *grand guerre* and *petite guerre* tactics, it was the American reliance on irregular militia and the inability of the British to adapt accordingly that contributed to the American victory. Among the patriots who fought the war were citizen-soldiers who once called themselves Sons of Liberty, Green Mountain Boys, or Regulators. The eventual triumph of George Washington and the Continental Army highlighted one of many ironies that would emerge from the Revolution. Washington's Army was widely perceived as the savior of the republic, the lifeblood of liberty, and the protector of virtue. Such was its importance that the concept of a peacetime, standing army became increasingly palatable to those who feared subversive forces, be they foreign or domestic. The episodes of terrorism and rioting that preceded the Revolution certainly gave credence to these concerns, demonstrating that military strength was vital to the survival of the republic. Yet, many still considered a standing army a liability, a potentially repressive tool of government that could be employed against the citizenry, and, therefore, a direct threat to liberty.[2] That there was no consensus over this crucial issue should come as no surprise, as the newly created republic had many similar polarizing issues to resolve.

The Revolution was fought not only over independence but also on behalf of concepts that Americans dearly cherished: liberty, equality, natural law, and popular sovereignty—all crucial elements of a republican form of government as they defined it. But because there was no national consensus on what, precisely, these concepts meant in practical terms, severe differences would immediately emerge over the meaning of the Revolution itself. What form and structure should the American polity assume? Traditionalists have described this political polarization as a contest between nationalists, who demanded a powerful federal government, and states-rights advocates, who aspired to more local control, but the contentiousness was far more complex. The American experiment in republicanism often exposed an east-west or north-south sectional dynamic, as well as class distinctions, pitting patricians vs. plebians, which often manifested itself in the long-standing competition between eastern land speculators/proprietors vs. western squatters/farmers. Consequently, the issues at stake included not only the viability of a standing army but also land ownership, the role of centralized power, taxation, tariff policies, banking, ill-defined borders, and the problems of debt, be they national, state, or personal.

The Articles of Confederation, which governed the United States for eight years beginning in 1781, represented a triumph of sorts for those who favored decentralized federal power. The one-branch national government consisted only of a legislature that had great responsibilities but virtually no powers to fulfill those responsibilities, given its severe limitations. It would remain to be seen how effectively a weak federal government would bind 13 semi-autonomous states together into a corporate whole. Of particular interest to those who had urged a more powerful federal government was the ability of authorities (such as they were) to maintain law and order and to protect the citizenry against violent provocations. This was no small matter. There were Indian battles to be fought out west, and contentious border issues with England and Spain to be resolved. Moreover, the Revolution may have resolved the issue of home rule, but the elimination of British authority did not cleanse America of radical domestic violence, which continued unabated following the conclusion of the war. The responses of both state and federal government to this renewed domestic violence would test the limits of popular sovereignty as well as the powers of the newly installed government.

II. Shays's Rebellion

The end of the Revolutionary War would bring significant changes to the economy, already burdened by battlefield destruction and loss of life. In particular, farmers in central and western Massachusetts, who already suffered from higher taxes, falling prices, and escalating debt, became further victimized after the war when European traders refused to extend credit lines to Massachusetts merchants, insisting instead that debts be covered with hard currency. Despite the lack of such currency in many areas, East Coast merchants passed on these demands down the business chain until they ultimately reached many inland farmers who, unable to meet their financial obligations, ultimately ended up in debtor's courts, forfeiting their farms and possessions. The flames of rebellion still burned in parts of Massachusetts, for on January 5, 1782, only months after Yorktown, the Reverend Samuel Ely, a Yale-educated war veteran, stood before a convention in Sunderland and suggested that the Massachusetts state constitution be replaced with one he had written and tucked away in his pocket. He also argued that the infamous "chain of debt" that had plagued yeomen could only be severed by a closure of the state courts, which had become tools of eastern merchants and creditors. By April, he was exhorting a crowd of yeomen to attack the county debtor court in Northampton, clashing with militia during what became known as "Ely's Rebellion." Ely was eventually arrested and found guilty of treason, but he managed to escape during a rescue riot and eluded capture, fleeing north to Vermont. He was, however, banished from Vermont for seditious behavior and handed back to authorities in Massachusetts, who eventually released him in 1783 after his brother posted bond.[3] He finally settled in Maine, where other personal adventures would await. Meanwhile, resistance movements also appeared in Groton and Worcester County.

The chain of debt was not the only source of concern for the yeomen of Massachusetts, for other issues were at stake, undermining their chances for financial solvency. In the most recent scholarly analysis of these conditions, Leonard Roberts contended that the real issue was the decidedly undemocratic 1780 state constitution that placed power in the hands of the eastern elite and called for discriminatory taxation that benefited speculators holding war bonds. He noted that poor farmers were threatened more by tax collectors than by private creditors, and that many rioters were gentlemen of standing from wealthy backgrounds, united not only in opposition to Massachusetts but also by blood and marriage ties.[4] Whatever their primary motivation, conditions continued to deteriorate in central and western Massachusetts. In 1783, after the signing of the Treaty of Paris had acknowledged American independence, England cut off American trade with the British West Indies, creating additional hardships for East Coast merchants that were also passed down the business chain. In 1785, James Bowdoin was elected governor and immediately prodded the legislature to collect new and unpaid taxes. All the while, the state legislature continued to ignore the mounting collection of petitions and proposals submitted by various communities seeking the abolishment of the Senate and Court of Common Pleas, lowering of taxes, reduction of state officials' salaries, and the introduction of paper money and new tender laws. Poor farmers, increasingly frustrated by the failures of the state and the mercantile elite to address these grievances, grew angry and desperate.

In late August and early September 1786, crowds of rioters, many of whom were armed with muskets, swords, and clubs, forcibly closed the courts in Northampton and Worcester. When Governor Bowdoin ordered the local militia to be called out in Worcester to protect the court, soldiers ignored the call and mustered instead with the rioters. Within a week, a resistance movement had begun. On September 26, Daniel Shays and Luke Day, carrying the torch of rebellion first lit by Samuel

Ely, helped lead a force of over 1,000 rioters, now calling themselves *regulators,* in an attempt to shut down the Supreme Judicial Court in Springfield. A bloody showdown against 800 militia troops was barely averted, but the Shaysites, as they were also called, had made their case. Both forces withdrew after the judges agreed to adjourn without hearing any cases. By early October, crowd disturbances in Concord, Taunton, and Great Barrington also prevented courts from conducting business. Although the evolving rebellion would soon bear his name and he did command the largest group of rebels, Daniel Shays was hardly the sole instigator and *generalissimo* of the resistance movement, as the authorities would insist. Certainly Luke Day, Eli Parsons, Job Shattuck and others held key positions within the resistance movement. For their part, the Shaysites very much mirrored the male social makeup of rural New England: most were farmers, Congregationalists, war veterans, and descendants of English or Scot-Irish immigrants united through blood lines and neighborhood friendships.[5] They did not constitute an exclusive army of debtors and were not, as contemporary critics would maintain, a tool of British conspirators out to reinstitute a monarchical regime in America.[6]

Staggered by the resistance movement, Governor Bowdoin and the state government responded by, on the one hand, granting modest concessions on the payment of back taxes but, on the other, also taking repressive measures to quell Shaysite violence. In October, Bowdoin secretly procured the approval to employ federal troops against the insurgency, and the General Court approved both a Militia Act and Riot Act that together greatly prohibited public protests and seditious behavior. In an odd twist, Samuel Adams, the former radical patriot, helped draft the Riot Act provisions. The next month, the Assembly suspended the writ of habeus corpus and added an Act of Indemnity that offered pardons to Shaysites who signed an oath of allegiance to the state of Massachusetts. None of the Shays rebels, save one, signed the oath.[7] Instead, the armed disruption of courts continued throughout November and December, boosted by the inability of the Confederation Congress to raise enough money to provide Bowdoin with the promised federal troops. After a nighttime government raid captured three suspected insurgents, two Shaysites angrily proclaimed, "the seeds of war are now sown."[8] The rebel response was quick and decisive: on December 26, more than 300 Shaysites marched on Springfield and forced another court closure. With little or no help forthcoming from the federal government, neighboring states, or local militias, the governor had but one other viable option: the creation of a privately funded army. In January, with Bowdoin's endorsement, former Continental Army General Benjamin Lincoln began to solicit funds from merchants and other businessmen from Boston to finance an expedition to the west that he would personally command. He eventually raised enough money to recruit 3,000 troops, far short of his goal of 4,400. On January 19, 1787, Lincoln's army, consisting primarily of easterners, including many prominent merchants and speculators, began to march west. Many observers noted the irony of eastern elites such as Samuel Adams, who had encouraged anti-government crowd uprisings only a decade earlier, now having to assume desperate measures to curb similar types of protests. It was another manifestation of the growing political polarization that marked the post-Revolution era, this time pitting, to a large extent, the law and order impulses of the eastern, aristocratic elite against the egalitarian social principles of western commoners.[9]

News of Lincoln's army convinced most rebels that reform was no longer possible, and many now pushed for an invasion of Boston and the violent overthrow of the "tyrannical" state government. Toward this end, insurgents targeted the federal arsenal in Springfield and, in late January, began a three-pronged movement to seize the armory and its vast military stores. Because Lincoln's army was still on the move, standing in the rebels' way were 1,200 militia loyal to the state under the command of Hampshire Major General William Shepard, a veteran of the Continental Army, who had taken possession of the arsenal without authorization from the federal government. By January 24, the three separate rebel regiments led by Daniel Shays, Luke Day, and Eli Parsons had arrived in the Springfield environs and begun to plan their assault on Shepard and the armory. On January 25, Shays, Parsons, and their combined 1,500 troops began to move toward the arsenal, but a breakdown in communication left Day and his forces sidelined, unaware of the impending attack, which never materialized. Not a single rebel musket was fired against the government. As the Shaysites advanced on the arsenal, Shepard ordered two warning shots fired over their heads, which went unheeded. He then ordered cannon fire and at least a dozen rounds of grapeshot, which cut down a column of rebels, killing four and wounding 20. The assault immediately collapsed as Shays's army panicked and retreated, scattering in all directions throughout the countryside. The main force of rebels, under Shays's command, eventually made its way to Petersham, seizing several shopkeepers as hostages along the way. After marching his troops all night through a raging snowstorm, Benjamin Lincoln and his forces finally caught up to the rebel army and, on the morning of February 4, attacked the unsuspecting and shocked Shaysites, once again scattering the rebels. That same day, the Massachusetts legislature declared a state of rebellion, authorized the governor to declare martial law, and ordered an additional 1,500 troops to crush what remained of Shays's army. Although pockets of resistance to state authority would persist, including one last major confrontation in Stockbridge, most of the insurgents and their former leaders fled to neighboring states, seeking to avoid prosecution. Shays banded together with other fugitive rebels and eventually settled near Sandgate, Vermont.[10] The resistance movement was then permanently crippled and very few rebels spoke of attacking Boston. It was at this point, however, that the rebellion transformed itself from a civil insurrection to a decentralized movement of retributive violence.

Following the debacle at Petersham, many insurgents with strong local connections chose to stay behind and continue the beleaguered cause. Some took drastic measures and attempted to recruit Ethan Allen and Canadian governor Lord Dorchester to the faltering resistance movement. Allen declined, and, although Dorchester promised to provide weapons through an Indian intermediary, the British Foreign Office later overruled the governor's plans. Boosted by Dorchester's promises, however, remaining rebels decided to wreak vengeance on merchants, lawyers, and various state military and political leaders. Roving bands of rebels set fire to stores, small factories, barns, fences, and other property, including wheat supplies. They assaulted politicians who had opposed reform and set out to attack, kidnap, or assassinate various officers associated with the state military, including Benjamin Lincoln and William Shepard. But despite these hit-and-run tactics, the rebellion was no longer sustainable, and by June the raids finally began to dissipate.[11] By then, new governor John Hancock, another hero of the Revolution, had pushed for further anti-insurgent measures, bolstered the state's army with additional troops, and convinced most neighboring states to discourage Shaysite activity within their borders. Meanwhile, the state had also begun to prosecute hundreds of rebels, issuing several hundred indictments for treason. Hancock, with some exceptions, issued pardons to all. After a series of trials that stretched to October, the courts also handed down 18 death penalties, although only two persons would eventually hang for their crimes. In the end, 4,000 Shaysites eventually accepted offers from the state to disarm, confess, and sign loyalty oaths, the first steps of public atonement.

Although Shays's Rebellion was the most serious and violent challenge to government authority during the Confederation Era, it never relied on the tactics of terror. In a pattern similar to that established by many of the 17th-century civil insurrections, the Shaysites were singularly devoted to attacking their perceived enemy rather than psychologically manipulating the political behavior of wider target audiences through selective or symbolic violence. Aside from the lack of a victim-target differentiation, there were no attempts to propagandize the cause, or any attempt to establish a sense of extralegal authority, given the rebel propensity to dispense with state courts. Regardless, the rebellion had a huge political impact, forcing many citizens to question the effectiveness of government under the Articles of Confederation. Although plans for what would become known as the Constitutional Convention held that May in Philadelphia were already in motion, Shays's Rebellion is traditionally cited as one of the primary events that confirmed the absolute need to establish a stronger federal government. The Articles of Confederation certainly had its weaknesses and presented myriad problems, but the stark inability of either the state of Massachusetts or the federal government to quell a popular uprising without an investment of private funds exposed to all the vulnerability of a federation composed of semi-autonomous states. Certainly, a standing federal army would discourage and counteract such unlawful impulses. Consequently, those who favored greater centralization of power at the expense of states would win the day in Philadelphia, as the newly adopted Constitution added executive and judicial branches to the greatly empowered legislature. In 1789, George Washington assumed the Office of the Presidency as the nation entered into a new era after an abbreviated false start. The future was uncertain, and many wondered how the new national government would respond to a crisis on the order of Shays's Rebellion. Unfortunately, they would not wait long for an answer, for a test of the Washington administration's resolve would come far too quickly.

III.   The Whiskey Rebellion

One of many problems wrought by the Confederation Era that needed the immediate attention of the Washington administration was the problem of debt at both the national and state levels, which stood at $54 million and $25 million, respectively. The man primarily responsible for pulling the country out of its deep economic hole was, for better or worse depending upon one's perspective, Alexander Hamilton, former boy wonder, aide-de-camp to General Washington, and now the president's trusted advisor and treasury secretary. An aristocrat and centralist by nature, he sought to exploit the debt crisis to help create a financial system that would spur national unity, prosperity, and power and, as critics note, benefit a close coterie of northeastern creditors and speculators. After convincing Congress to assume the state debts, itself a controversial move, Hamilton needed additional revenue, hence the passage of an excise tax on distilled spirits in 1791, the first such tax levied by the federal government. This so-called whiskey tax did not sit well with many Americans, given their distaste for taxes in general, but a luxury or sin tax on distilled spirits was particularly hard on cash-strapped westerners who often relied on whiskey as a medium of exchange and needed to distill their grain into whiskey for transportation purposes. It was bad enough that fines for tax violations could exceed most people's yearly earnings, but the provisions of Hamilton's whiskey tax also appeared discriminatory against western distillers, one of many existing sectional grievances that frontiersmen had with a seemingly indifferent East Coast establishment.

Small farmers, already distressed from debt foreclosures, began a petition movement to repeal the offending legislation, but, when their grievances were overlooked, Pennsylvania westerners held two extralegal conventions to discuss a collective response. That a resistance movement would be spawned in the four counties of western Pennsylvania—Washington, Westmoreland, Fayette, and Allegheny—was no particular surprise. Folks who lived near the headwaters of the Ohio River in an area called the Forks loved their whiskey; one-quarter of all stills in America were located in this area.[12] Moreover, disgruntled citizens of western Pennsylvania had already established a legacy of hostile resistance that went as far back as 1765, as ritualized violence, rescue riots, court disruptions, and extralegal associations became common tactics in their efforts to stop traders in Philadelphia from trafficking in arms with western Indians.[13] In this particular case, the two conventions—held in Brownsville in late July 1791 and Pittsburgh in early September—again articulated grievances against the whiskey tax, and, in the end, protesters forwarded petitions to both the Pennsylvania Assembly and the U.S. House of Representatives. The meetings also revealed an early division among the protesters, as a group of moderates led by Hugh Henry Bracken-ridge and future congressman William Findley urged non-violence and sought a continued dialogue with the government through appropriate channels. The appeal for non-violent resistance was warranted. On the eve of the Pittsburgh convention, about 20 men disguised in blackface had attacked Robert Johnson, a tax collector traveling near Pigeon Creek in Washington County. They stripped him naked, cut off his hair, and covered him with hot tar and feathers. Despite the rough treatment, Johnson was able to identify some of his assailants, and in October, Joseph Fox, a federal marshal, arrived to serve warrants on Johnson's attackers. Concerned for the marshal's safety, General John Neville, the federally appointed tax inspector in western Pennsylvania, advised the apprehensive and endangered Fox to deliver the warrants by proxy. John Connor, a cattle driver and community simpleton, foolishly agreed to serve the warrants. After Connor was predictably tarred and feathered, Fox immediately fled the Forks and no further warrants were served until the following summer.[14] Later that month, in an odd case of mistaken identity, Robert Wilson, a suspicious newcomer and possible government spy, was similarly attacked, despite his complete innocence of any connection to either the state or federal government.[15]

By the spring of 1792, the political positions in western Pennsylvania had hardened. The tax agents appointed by the Washington administration, espe-cially General Neville, were determined to do their jobs and curry favor with the new government. Neville, a war hero and owner of a 10,000-acre plantation on Bower Hill, had initially opposed the whiskey tax but changed his mind once he accepted the position as federal tax collector. This sudden change of heart did not sit well with his neighbors, who now held the general in contempt. He not only stood to reap significant commissions from his new position, but, since he was a large distiller, the tax also worked to his financial advantage. At the same time, the resistance movement continued to splinter. Moderates tried to intercede with authorities, urging reconsideration of the tax and working hard to tread a delicate middle ground between the government and their more hostile allies. The radicals, demanding more aggressive resistance to the government, were gain-ing momentum, largely through the influence of the Mingo Creek Association, a group of 500 militant radicals with a long history of defiance to authority. Before long, the association would establish its own courts of law to adjudicate its own forms of justice. Meanwhile, in Philadelphia, the nation's capitol city, Alexander Hamilton's ambitious economic program, which included protective tariffs and centralized federal banking, had earned the wrath of critics, further exacerbating the emerging political polarization between the centralist-minded Hamiltonian-Federalists and the opposing Jeffersonian-Antifederalists. Regardless, the treasury secretary stood firm behind his financial vision for America and largely ignored the protestations from western Pennsylvania, defiantly arguing that his contro-versial excise actually taxed consumption, not production, as the smaller distillers had complained. Thus, as far as Hamilton was concerned, the western grievances could be easily addressed: drink less whiskey. Yet, sensitive to the resistance movement, which was now spreading rapidly to neighboring areas, Congress managed to modify the excise that May, lowering the tax with a one-cent reduction but including more stringent methods of enforcement and additional advantages for larger distillers.

One month later, responding to portions of the revised excise law demanding that all stills be registered, General Neville sought to rent space for registration offices near Pittsburgh. Only one person, tavern owner Captain William Faulkner, was willing to risk the wrath of his neighbors and offer Neville office space. Ignoring repeated and often hostile warnings from friends and neighbors not to associate with the federal tax agent, Faulkner refused to withdraw his offer to Neville. Faulkner's defiance enraged the radicals who had now co-opted the resistance movement, which held a second Pittsburgh convention on August 21 and 22. Moderates such as Brackenridge and Findley chose not to attend, as their association with insurrectionists could be interpreted by the federal government as treasonous activity. Without voices of moderation, the convention, dominated by the Mingo Creek Association, issued a stronger resolution that was more insistent, desperate, and radical than those previously submitted. The rebels demanded that General Neville resign and that the whiskey tax be repealed and replaced with a progressive tax on wealth. With Faulkner clearly on their minds, the radicals also threatened social ostracism and other retaliatory action against any resident who conspired with federal officials to enforce the current excise laws. In addition to selected acts of terror against offending tax agents, an environment of fear and intimidation directed against the larger community was beginning to take shape throughout the Forks. Two days later, about two dozen rioters adorned with war paint rode up to William Faulkner's home looking to tar and feather the tavern keeper. Finding him absent, the crowd proceeded to vandalize the house and adjacent tavern, destroying furniture and firing pistol shots into the ceilings. Later, after narrowly escaping the wrath of another crowd, Faulkner promised to retract his offer to Neville, and, on August 25, the *Pittsburgh Gazette* published Faulkner's retraction. A frustrated Neville confessed to an associate that he was now "obliged to desist from further attempts to fulfill the law."[16]

President Washington and Secretary Hamilton did not take news of the second Pittsburgh convention lightly, for both were convinced that the resistance movement was dangerous and subversive and needed to be crushed by the weight of federal authority. Their concerns appeared legitimate, for the anti-tax rebellion had now spread far beyond the Forks to the western sections of Kentucky, the Carolinas, Virginia, and Maryland. Moreover, after the Mingo Creek Association issued warnings to citizens not to bring suits against each other without first seeking mediation through its own extralegal courts, lawsuits for debt collection dropped off significantly. As the association's warning and the treatment accorded Faulkner made clear, not just federal tax collectors but all citizens of the Forks were now alerted that their behavior was being closely scrutinized by the whiskey rebels. Hamilton responded to these recent developments in two ways. On his own initiative, he drafted a presidential proclamation condemning the resistance movement and threatening retaliatory measures if the rebels did not desist from their criminal activities. Washington signed the proclamation on September 15, and it promptly appeared in newspapers as a broadside. The treasury secretary also dispatched George Clymer, a Pennsylvania tax official, out to the Forks to investigate personally and report on the political climate. After a clumsy and frightened quest into rebel country where he donned foolish disguises and conducted hurried depositions, Clymer submitted to Hamilton a grossly exaggerated portrayal of a barbaric and lawless community enabled by complicit magistrates and clergymen. Unfortunately, the misguided and distorted report would greatly influence how Hamilton and Washington would respond to the growing crisis out west.[17]

Although most citizens in the Forks complied with the rebel demands to disassociate themselves from tax officials and lawsuits for debt collection, there were many committed to local enforcement of the excise laws, especially county tax collectors such as Benjamin Wells. Wells not only benefited from tax commissions but also reaped rewards for reporting unregistered stills and providing testimony against whiskey rebels in court, the very type of behavior that the Mingo Creek Association was trying to discourage. Throughout 1793, Wells went about his work, seemingly unfazed by repeated physical assaults against him and constant threats to him and his family. Finally, during a late November evening, six armed men with blackened faces stormed into his home and pointing cocked pistols in his face, demanded that he resign from office and surrender all official papers and documents. After an early show of defiance, Wells relented and promptly announced his resignation in the *Gazette*.[18] Not long thereafter, Wells would travel to Philadelphia on three separate occasions to give depositions before federal officials. While the Wells episode was unfolding, hostile notes and letters warning others not to cooperate with tax officials were beginning to appear in local newspapers mysteriously signed by "Tom the Tinker," a pseudonym adopted by the whiskey rebels.[19] It was during this period, beginning with the second Pittsburgh convention, that the Whiskey Rebellion began to broaden its tactics. Moving beyond the violent victimization of selected tax officials, Tom the Tinker and his fellow rebels had made it clear to the wider community of the Forks that any compliance with the excise laws, including a willingness to register stills, was unacceptable, traitorous behavior worthy of extremely punitive countermeasures. William Findley later acknowledged that by this point the insurgents had become "more outrageous, proceeded to fresh acts of violence, and expressed as great a degree of resentment against those who complied with the law as they did against the officers who acted under it."[20] Consequently, those who chose to cooperate with federal officials put themselves at great risk as rebels destroyed barns, crops, animals, stills, gristmills, and other property. Such was the air of intimidation created by Tom the Tinker's men that John Webster, a tavern owner and tax collector, admitted that, "I expect every night I lay down that I shall have to arise with fire about my head. Not a traveler that comes down the road but brings the newse I am to be burnt out next." Webster's concerns were justified: after rebels set fire to his stable and haystacks, he reluctantly resigned from his post.[21] By 1794, effigies of General Neville had been torched and liberty poles began to appear more frequently in the Forks as the spirit of insurrection continued to disquiet the Washington administration, already predisposed to think unkindly of the Forks, particularly in the aftermath of George Clymer's critical commentary.

Of particular interest to government authorities was the composition of the whiskey insurgents' group. Contemporaries mostly provided unflattering descriptions, referring to the rebels as ignorant, deluded, and miserably poor. Even William Findley described his radical neighbors as "the meanest rabble."[22] In the most detailed demographic analysis of the insurgents, Dorothy Fennell found that the contemporary accounts were not far from the truth and that, for the most part, the radicals were indeed poor and owned no property. But they were also representative of their community at large in that both prominent and ordinary people were actively involved. Only a minority of the insurgents actually owned stills; most rebels were customers of distillers or relied on whiskey or grain as mediums of exchange. Moreover, the vast majority of the rebels were not merely followers acting out of blind deference to their leaders. As a collective whole, the rebels acted more like principal actors bound together not only by their dislike of the whiskey excise but also by ties to family, neighborhood, and local militia units.[23] Already frustrated by economic inequality, federal Indian policies, and the government's inability to secure navigation of the Mississippi River, these insurgents were now expanding their operations and beginning to incorporate terrorist methods.

During the spring, a frustrated Alexander Hamilton, in conjunction with the Attorney General's Office, began to formulate a more ambitious response to events in the Forks. Using evidence submitted by Benjamin Wells, a list of whiskey tax violators was compiled, and, accordingly, arrest warrants were issued on May 31, 1794, thus setting the stage for prosecution and trial in Philadelphia, which would necessitate an arduous and costly journey from the west. Interestingly, and perhaps not coincidentally, only days later, a new law was signed allowing new federal tax cases to be heard in local, frontier courts and thus eliminating the costs and inconvenience of appearing personally in Philadelphia, but the terms of all previous warrants remained in effect. Whether or not Hamilton's initiative was deliberately designed to incite further rebel activity and, therefore, justify a military response from the federal government is subject to debate.[24] Less uncertain was the predictable response to a requirement published in the *Gazette* by General Neville that all stills be registered before the end of June. When tax agent John Wells, son of Benjamin, opened a tax office in the home of Philip Reagan, another tax official, rebels burned down Wells's barn and for several days exchanged gunfire with the two agents as they defended Reagan's home. John Lynn, who rented office space to General Neville in Washington County, was attacked in his home at night and tarred and feathered by a dozen men in black face. William Cochran, a distiller, received threatening letters from Tom the Tinker, had his millhouse vandalized, and had gunshots fired at his still until he agreed to stop cooperating with excise officials.[25] But the terrorist tactics briefly employed by the whiskey rebels quickly dissipated as the resistance movement, on account of its split personality, began to waver between an outright insurgence against federal authority and utter submission. The catalyst for this chaotic transformation of tactics in the Forks was the appearance of U.S. Marshal David Lenox, who, with no small measure of apprehension, arrived in July to deliver the federal warrants issued that May.

Early on, Lenox went about his rounds in Cumberland, Bedford, and Fayette counties without trouble. However, on July 15, Lenox made a fateful decision to invite the much-despised General Neville to accompany him as he began to serve writs in Allegheny County, not far from Mingo Creek. As the two officials rode from farm to farm encountering hostile citizens, a growing crowd of 20 or 30 men began to shadow their movements. Finally, an angry exchange of words resulted in gunshots fired in the direction of the officials as Neville quickly rode off to his now-fortified mansion on Bower Hill and Lenox fled to Pittsburgh. More than 30 armed whiskey rebels under the command of John Holcroft began to mobilize that evening, and, by the next morning, they had surrounded Bower Hill. At daybreak, Holcroft, a veteran of Shays's Rebellion and widely believed to be the anonymous author behind the Tom the Tinker *nom de plume*, demanded that the absent Lenox surrender himself. Neville, who was barricaded inside with his family and defiant as ever, responded by firing a weapon that mortally wounded Oliver Miller, one of the rebels. This set off a 25-minute exchange of gunfire. From their quarters, Neville's slaves also opened fire on the rebel militia, and, while none in Neville's home was injured, several additional rebels were wounded. Frustrated by the bloody standoff, Holcroft finally ordered a retreat, and the rebels withdrew to nearby Couch's Fort. Enraged by the death of Miller and eager to avenge his "murder," the rebels considered financing the assassination of Neville, until the plot was narrowly averted by a close vote.[26] Nonetheless, plans called for another assault of Bower Hill, and, despite the best mediation attempts by Hugh Henry Brackenridge and other moderates, some 600 rebels had now gathered at Couch's Fort ready to do battle. They were further motivated by false rumors that debtors were being hauled off by federal officials to stand trial in Philadelphia. General Neville knew another attack was imminent and sent out distress calls to officials that went unheeded until Major Abraham Kirkpatrick and ten soldiers from Fort Pitt agreed to defend the besieged general. Kirkpatrick might have been genuinely obligated by a sense of duty, but it is worth noting that he was also a brother-in-law of Neville's wife.[27]

During the early evening of July 17, the rebel militia paraded from Couch's Fort to Bower Hill and, marching to the beat of drums, assumed positions surrounding Neville's mansion. James McFarlane, commander of the rebel militia, sent a summons to the house demanding that the general surrender and resign as tax collector. The note was received not by Neville but by Kirkpatrick, who had arrived earlier with his soldiers and ushered the general away to safety in a nearby ravine. Kirkpatrick informed the messenger that the general was absent, and, after discussions regarding a search of the house failed to produce a compromise, the rebels allowed the women to evacuate the home while the soldiers inside readied their weapons. A gun battle that lasted for more than an hour quickly ensued. At one point, McFarlane, thinking that Kirkpatrick wished to parlay, stepped out in the open to halt the rebel volleys and was promptly shot and killed by someone in the house. Enraged, the rebels resumed their gunfire and put a torch to surrounding buildings and the main mansion. With flames and intense heat now enveloping them, Kirkpatrick and his men had no alternative but to surrender. By nightfall, Kirkpatrick was a prisoner of the rebels and the evening sky above Bower Hill was glowing, lit by the entire plantation as it burned throughout the night.[28] Not only McFarlane but also at least one other rebel had died in the battle, but the precise number of killed and wounded was never determined. David Lenox, who had started this whole climactic episode while serving writs, was also captured that night and treated roughly, but both he and Kirkpatrick managed to escape their captors and flee to Pittsburgh, where the Neville family had also taken shelter.

The day after the Battle of Bower Hill, an enraged community buried James McFarlane, widely perceived in the Forks as having been murdered by Major Kirkpatrick. Many among the mourners spoke of invading, looting, and destroying Pittsburgh, which the whiskey rebels now dubbed "Sodom." With all moderates now viewed with suspicion, David Bradford emerged as the rebel leader, and it was his decision to intercept the U.S. mail from Pittsburgh, which, two days later, revealed that many of that city's leading citizens were complaining to federal authorities and offering written testimony about the treasonous activities in the Forks. An angry Bradford, in consultation with his closest confidants, immediately distributed a circular letter that called for a muster of all local militias on August 1 at Braddock's Field, located just miles east of Pittsburgh. Their objectives represented outright secession: attack Pittsburgh and arrest those sympathetic to federal authority. As soon as this assembly was called, its meaning and magnitude understandably began to weigh heavily on everyone in the Forks. Not only moderates but also many radicals now flinched at the notion of waging war against the government of George Washington. At this point, the rebellion resumed its tactics of intimidation. When Bradford and James Marshall, another rebel leader, appeared to weaken and second guess the fateful decision, angry whiskey rebels made it clear that there was no turning back: insurgents tarred and feathered the door to Marshall's home, effectively declaring that all those who did not muster with the rebel army would be accorded the same treatment as federal tax agents.[29] Little wonder then that come August 1, nearly 7,000 men had answered the call and gathered at Braddock's Field.

The assembly at Braddock's Field represented more than mere opposition to the whiskey tax. Years of unheeded grievances from destitute westerners frustrated with a seemingly indifferent federal government had led to this defiant showdown that revealed distinct secessionist leanings. Speaking loudly of independence, radicals carried the colors of a newly designed flag with six stripes, each representing a western county in rebellion (five in Pennsylvania and one in Virginia). Fortunately for all involved, reason and common sense would prevail, and there would be no bloodshed. The night before the muster, a committee dispatched by the citizens of Pittsburgh had met with David Bradford and other rebel leaders in a last-ditch attempt to avoid destruction of the city and undermanned Fort Fayette. The committee, which included the Forks moderate Hugh Henry Brackenridge, had no choice but to express its support for the rebel cause, submit its will to the rebel army, and agree to banish from Pittsburgh all federal tax officials and those citizens who had written the offending intercepted letters. Included among the banished was Major Abraham Kirkpatrick, defender of Bower Hill and alleged murderer of James McFarlane. General Neville and David Lenox, the other primary targets of the rebel army's wrath, had wisely and discreetly slipped away from Pittsburgh days earlier and were no longer party to the unfolding events. Consequently, on the day of the scheduled muster, the rebel army was limited to a peaceful and symbolic march through Pittsburgh, where frightened but relieved citizens ingratiated themselves by providing complimentary food and whiskey. By the end of the day, the only casualties were the farm buildings of Kirkpatrick, which were set afire and burned to the ground.

In the aftermath of the aborted demolition of Pittsburgh, the rebel army began to demobilize as the majority of the insurgents dispersed and returned to their homes. Several hundred rebels, however, continued to wreak vengeance on their federal enemies. Tax officials Philip Reagan, Benjamin Wells, and his son John, who had all endured earlier rebel abuse, were apprehended, tried, and court-martialed after extralegal trials. Reagan managed to escape after surrendering his official papers, but rebels sacked the Wells home and set it ablaze. Two weeks later on August 14, 226 delegates from the six rebellious western counties held a convention at Parkinson's Ferry to determine a future course of action. Among the outspoken delegates was none other than Hermon Husband, the former Regulator who had fled North Carolina as a fugitive following the ill-fated battle at the Great Alamance Creek back in 1771. Husband's role in the Whiskey Rebellion is a matter of contention. Thomas P. Slaughter, who wrote what many consider the standard history of the rebellion, paid little heed to Husband, suggesting his impact was minor.[30] However, William Hogeland, who authored the most recent interpretation of these events, argued instead that Husband's itinerant preaching, seditious writing, and vision of a "New Jerusalem" in the Forks had provided a rationale and impetus for violent resistance to unjust government tyranny.[31] Whatever historians may think of Husband and his years in North Carolina, he was viewed by many contemporaries in Pennsylvania as a delusional eccentric, and there is no denying that he was high on the government's list of subversive radicals. However, Husband, as he had done at Alamance, was now urging peace, but, despite his best efforts, the convention assumed a defiant tone, until it surprisingly received notice that a presidential commission had just arrived in the Forks hoping to negotiate a resolution to the anti-government disturbances.

President Washington and Secretary Hamilton were, of course, far from disinterested observers of events in the Forks. Especially galling to the administration was the embarrassing reality that the whiskey rebels were defiantly operating in the same state that housed the federal government in Philadelphia. If the new government empowered by the Constitution could not control its home state, how could it possibly succeed where the Confederation government had failed? In many ways, the rebellion had become a test case of how the newly structured federal government would respond to challenges to its authority, conducted either by its own citizens or by foreign states. Accordingly, while Washington dispatched his three-man peace commission to the Forks, Secretary of War Henry Knox also sent orders to the governors of four states to call out a federal militia. On August 7, the president issued a proclamation announcing that unless insurgents in the Forks abandoned their cause and dispersed by September 1, a federal army would march to western Pennsylvania to suppress the rebellion. Back in Pittsburgh, the peace commission began to meet with a rebel committee comprised of both radicals and moderates. Thomas P. Slaughter referred to the peace negotiations as a "sham," suggesting, as do most historians, that the president and treasury secretary had already decided to go to war.[32] From the administration's perspective, the backcountry rebellion was emblematic of larger and more dangerous forces at hand: the subversive elements fomented by the Democratic–Republican societies so closely associated with the French Revolution and Jacobinism. It certainly did not help the rebel cause when, following the Battle of Bower Hill, David Bradford publicly praised the French terrorist Robespierre.[33] In the face of revolutionary fervor spreading throughout Europe and the Caribbean, and the growing popularity of French revolutionary principles, the Federalists, as "friends of order," needed to suppress the disturbances decisively and with finality. The government thus demanded that the rebels renounce violence, refrain from obstructing all excise laws, and pledge their submission to federal laws. Amnesty would be granted to all who complied. They further insisted that the western counties hold a popular referendum to determine the willingness of the citizenry to support these demands. The negotiating committee agreed to the terms and, after contentious deliberations, a standing committee of the Parkinson's Ferry convention voted 34–23 in favor of submission to the federal government. The referendum was held on September 11 and also produced mixed results: the overall trend was now toward submission, but many communities maintained their defiant positions toward federal authority. At some polling places, insurgents violently disrupted the polls by threatening voters and taking possession of ballot boxes.[34] Consequently, the referendum fell far short of the unequivocal submission that the Washington administration had demanded. As a result, the final report of the president's peace commission recommended the use of federal troops to enforce the laws in western Pennsylvania.

As developments would soon reveal, the federal army would not be necessary, for the rebellion it was meant to suppress had already begun to collapse. Despite continued defiance from some radicals, the moderate viewpoint had finally begun to prevail in the Forks. The president's mobilization of federal troops and the appearance of inflammatory anti-rebel editorials in eastern newspapers (some written anonymously by Alexander Hamilton) helped generate patriotic support for the administration. As many in the Forks began to see clearly, further resistance to the federal government would be futile and disastrous. On October 2, delegates to a second convention at Parkinson's Ferry unanimously swore submission and allegiance to the federal government and dispatched two representatives eastward to inform the president that his advancing army was no longer needed to enforce his authority in the Forks. The newly empowered federal government had met its first serious challenge by suppressing another civil insurrection, but not before radicals briefly employed terrorist tactics as a way of promoting and enforcing their political vision of western Pennsylvania. The rebellion's violence, first manifested in isolated acts against selected government officials, was eventually directed against the larger community of the Forks. Tom the Tinker became the chief rebel propagandist, and the Mingo Creek Association provided a ready-made organizational hierarchy. The establishment of extralegal courts reinforced their status as outsiders. In his study of the rebellion, James Roger Sharpe, citing Pauline Maier, likened the violence to earlier colonial uprisings, in that armed resistance in the Forks was *extra-institutional* rather than *anti-institutional,* since it provided citizens with an "instrument for action" in the absence of government cooperation. In doing so, the whiskey rebels cast light on very basic issues confronting the new republic: how and in what form should opposition to government authority be manifested? In essence, the rebels, through armed resistance, were testing the limits of legitimate opposition in a democratic society.[35] The sporadic use of terror that eventually emerged did not represent, however, the primary strategy of the insurgency, which was ultimately founded on conventional military strength and battlefield confrontation. Terrorizing neighbors helped obstruct the collection of taxes and briefly coerced community compliance with the rebel agenda, but nothing short of an army of thousands engaged in traditional warfare could hope to supplant federal authority. Only secondarily then, did the whiskey rebels employ terrorism, and even then the intercession of the federal government brought that campaign to a quick end.

On October 9, the two Parkinson's Ferry representatives met with President Washington and Secretary Hamilton, who had departed Philadelphia to review the northern half of the advancing federal army in Carlisle, Pennsylvania. Despite assurances that western Pennsylvania had reverted from rebellion to total submission and that the federal army would likely be unopposed in the Forks, a wary Washington refused to turn back or dismiss his troops. Raising and marching his army had been fraught with difficulty. Anti-draft riots, widespread desertions, and rampant pillaging had plagued the expedition from the very beginning, and the president was determined that his maligned army would march triumphantly into the Forks to arrest traitors and reinforce his unquestioned authority. The dispirited representatives returned home, and, a few days later, Washington, after reviewing his army's southern wing in Maryland, turned command of his federal troops over to Henry "Lighthorse" Lee and rode back to Philadelphia. Hamilton, who held no official military office, stayed with the army to help oversee the entire operation. In late October, General Lee and his army of 12,950 troops entered the Forks, after inflicting two fatalities in separate incidents that a judge later ruled as unfortunate accidents. Lee's army encountered hostile and resentful citizens along the way, but no violence and few if any armed insurgents. Left with no active militants to engage, the federal troops began to arrest those accused of federal crimes, but, because most of the rebel leaders had already fled the Forks along with hundreds of other insurgents, most of the 150 detainees were obscure, low-profile targets. After further investigation, the federal government was left with but 20 defendants, including the unfortunate Hermon Husband, who were brought back to Philadelphia to stand trial.

On November 19, the federal army began to withdraw from the Forks, and, on Christmas Day, the first bedraggled prisoners were marched through the streets of Philadelphia, lined with 20,000 curious onlookers. Nearly five months later, the trials began, but, because they were rife with inconclusive evidence, jury tampering, mistaken identities, and biased judges, only ten cases were brought to trial. Two defendants were eventually found guilty and sentenced to die by hanging, but received pardons from the president. Hermon Husband was exonerated but ultimately fell victim to pneumonia, likely contracted during the difficult journey from the Forks, and died while departing Philadelphia. Back in the Forks, General Lee issued general pardons, while former whiskey rebels submitted loyalty oaths and dutifully registered their stills. Although Lee's federal army succeeded in suppressing the rebellion and the Washington administration would be widely praised for acting decisively, collection of the whiskey tax would remain largely elusive until the new Republican administration repealed the excise in 1802. In retrospect, the Whiskey Rebellion, as with some earlier civil insurrections, managed to incorporate some limited elements of terrorism before these were ultimately eclipsed by traditional military tactics. The rebellion also made it clear that, despite the new Constitution and its empowerment of the federal government, the experiment in republicanism was still very much a work in progress and that the limits of both legitimate protest and government tolerance were still to be determined.

IV.   Fries's Rebellion

The reverberations from the Whiskey Rebellion would be felt for many years. It helped exacerbate the political polarization that ultimately resulted in the evolution of the two major parties of the era, the Federalists and the Republicans, and it also established a precedent for how the federal government might respond to civil insurrections. These lessons were not lost on John Adams, who had succeeded George Washington as president and was now embroiled in his own crises, domestic and international. Increasing public opposition to Federalist policies had prompted the passage of the Alien and Sedition Acts, which criminalized popular dissent and granted the president broad powers to prosecute protesters. Moreover, the Quasi-War with France necessitated an enlarged army and navy that would require additional financing. In 1798, Adams and Congress passed the Direct Tax Act, or "house tax," a progressive levy on land, slaves, and dwelling houses. The tax on houses was to be determined by the size and number of windows. As with the whiskey excise, the house tax was considered exceedingly burdensome, excessive and discriminatory. Farmers who worked hard to improve their lands were taxed accordingly for those betterments, while absentee speculators who possessed idle land were not. There were concerns that the house tax was a precedent for future taxation, and many were offended by the inquisitorial nature of an act that required officials to snoop around private property, counting windows.[36]

Although opposition to the house tax was somewhat scattered, flaring up in some western counties, the most significant resistance came from Northampton and Bucks counties in southeastern Pennsylvania, home to large numbers of German Americans. In the standard scholarly study of the rebellion, Paul Douglas Newman discovered that the rebellious protesters were mostly German Lutherans and the German Reformed, who referred to themselves as the *Kirchenleute* (Church People) in order to distinguish themselves from German Sectarians and English-speaking Quakers, groups with whom they tended to have strained relations.[37] The widespread construction of liberty poles across the state in late 1798 was the first public sign of protest. Just as the Federalists had branded similar poles raised by the whiskey rebels as "anarchy poles," they now referred to such poles as "sedition poles." Reviving memories of the Whiskey Rebellion, one pole that appeared in Greensburg was adorned with a message: "The father is gone to the Grandfather, and will come again and bring with him 70,000 men. In the year 1799. Tom the Tinker."[38] Another pole harkened back to the Stamp Act crisis, the Whiskey Rebellion and tax collector Benjamin Wells:

> Tone the Tinkerer, author.
> Liberty and No excise and No Stamp Act.
> Mr. Wells you are a cheating son of a Bitch.
> Huzza for Liberty and No Excise and No Stamp Act.
> This Liberty Pole is erected by Tone the Tinkerer and
> whoever cuts it down or demolishes it shall have his house
> torn down and demolished.[39]

Despite the ominous interjection of the infamous Tom the Tinker, there would be no repeat in eastern Pennsylvania of the whiskey violence. This was, however, not readily apparent when Jacob Eyerle, the Direct Tax commissioner, first attempted to appoint tax assessors for Northampton County. Cognizant of the groundswell of angry opposition to the house tax, most potential appointees refused to accept the position for reasons very similar to those of Nicholas Michael, who pleaded with Eyerle to "put me to jail so that I may be secure of my life, for if I inform against these people, I and my family will be ruined."[40] Despite such concerns about violent retribution, the rebellion would eventually prove noteworthy for its remarkable restraint and lack of rioting, as the Kirchenleute were bound and determined to avoid the inglorious fate of the whiskey rebels. Consequently, while hostile confrontations, threats, and other forms of verbal abuse were common, there would be a general absence of physical or ritualistic violence. Although stories circulated that women were driving assessors off property by dousing them with boiling water, thus prompting widespread ridicule and the derisive title "Hot Water War," there are conflicting opinions as to whether or not anyone was actually scalded in such fashion.[41] Nevertheless, Newman noted several reasons why a general policy of nonviolent resistance was possible. First, most of the assessors who eventually accepted the positions were active members of their community at large whose primary objective was to protect collective values, not to inflict harm and violence upon one another. Second, because many of the assessors were Quakers and Moravians, their pacifist attitudes also demanded an avoidance of violent confrontations.[42] Consequently, protesters first concentrated on their First Amendment rights, organizing public meetings and drafting petitions against the house tax.

While tax resisters began their campaign for reform, Jacob Eyerle's assessors also began their work. In early January 1799, John Wetzel, Jr., and John Butz began inspecting houses in Northampton County. They made three stops on January 2 in Macungie Township, and each time they were greeted by angry residents who, convinced that the house tax was somehow a hoax, threatened them with firearms and promises of physical harm should they continue with their rounds. The assessors decided to halt their inspections until further consultation with Eyerle. Two days later, in Upper Milford Township, Christian Heckenwelder attempted to inspect houses with the assistance of John Mumbower, a local tavern owner, until a group of Mumbower's neighbors threatened to kill him if he persisted in helping the assessor. That same day, in Northampton County, Michael Bobst was not only similarly obstructed from inspecting houses, but his neighbors also agreed to boycott his merchandise store and his son's tavern and additionally assessed a $10 penalty on anyone doing business with his family.[43] Even after learning of the law's legitimacy, protesters would continue to obstruct the tax and defiance would spread to nearby Bucks County, home to John Fries, a Revolutionary War veteran and an emerging leader of the resistance movement. Ironically, only four years earlier, Fries had marched with General Henry Lee's army to put down the Whiskey Rebellion. Now, despite his rather late appearance on the political scene, he would help lead another tax revolt that would eventually bear his name.[44]

Throughout January and February, tax assessors along the borderline separating Northampton and Bucks counties were prevented from conducting their work by defiant but nonviolent homeowners and crowds. Ever mindful of the heavy-handed government reprisals during the Whiskey Rebellion, the Kirchenleute resisters were challenging peacefully, not federal authority, but the constitutionality of the Direct Tax. One singular and culminating event would soon test the limits of this commitment to nonviolent resistance. Beginning on March 2, U.S. Marshall William Nichols began to arrest resisters in Northampton County and within days had detained nearly two dozen in a Bethlehem tavern. On March 7, a crowd of resisters that eventually swelled to nearly 400, approximately 130 of whom were armed militia, appeared in Bethlehem to secure the release of the prisoners. For several hours, John Fries negotiated with Nichols, attempting to post bond for the prisoners and to secure trial, not in Philadelphia before an Anglo American jury, but in Northampton County before a jury of German American peers. Despite being badly outnumbered by a hostile and inebriated crowd and facing seemingly insurmountable odds, Nichols refused to surrender the prisoners. Up to this point, Fries's Rebellion had assumed the familiar pattern established by past rebels and insurrectionists. A rescue riot appeared inevitable. But Fries remained as vigilant as Nichols, summoning impressive abilities to avoid violence, even as the confrontation wavered perilously close to a bloody riot. Finally, with pressures mounting and few options, Nichols allowed Fries and his militia to take the prisoners, and, with that gesture, Fries's Rebellion came to an anti-climactic but peaceful end. As with previous confrontations, there were plenty of harsh words, vile threats, demonstrations of force, and, at worst, punches thrown in anger, but the Bethlehem riot, if it can be so labeled, concluded with no bloodshed, injuries, or gunfire.[45]

From beginning to end, the resistance movement lasted a mere seven months, and Fries was only actively involved as a leader for about half that time. And because the rebellion was nonviolent, it remains fairly obscure; most American history survey textbooks fail to mention it. However, it is this nonviolent characteristic that is of particular interest here because it raises an interesting question: is it possible to terrorize people without actually resorting to violence? Given the definition offered in this study's Introduction and given the analysis of definitions conducted by Schmid, the mere *threat* of violence is enough to intimidate and thus terrorize.[46] Did this make Fries and his fellow resisters terrorists? They did intimidate tax assessors, and, because of that threatening behavior, taxes went uncollected and assessors were hard to come by, and those who did agree to work for Jacob Eyerle were often unreliable and unwilling to confront their angry neighbors. The fact that Federalist officials tended to select Quakers and German Sectarians to do their tax assessing only aggravated an already volatile social situation. But despite the air of intimidation, it was not necessarily directed beyond those who agreed to be tax assessors, and the Bethlehem riot was essentially directed at one man, William Nichols, who singularly defused the rebellion with one tortured and deliberate decision. Moreover, there were no accompanying public relations or propaganda campaigns other than the raising of liberty poles, although their appearance and impact should not be underestimated. In short, the rebellion was finished before the primary characteristics of terrorism, however benign they might have been, had a chance to evolve, leaving a movement founded upon extremely militant but nonviolent coercion.

While the tax resisters conducted their campaign with the lessons of the Whiskey Rebellion clearly in mind, those same lessons were not lost on the Adams administration as it planned its response to what Federalists, in an exaggerated state of heightened anxiety, called the "Northampton Insurrection." Because relations with France continued to deteriorate, Federalists regarded the backcountry resistance movement as yet another part of a larger French conspiracy to undermine the administration through the export of revolutionary tactics. Consequently, on March 12, Adams issued a proclamation, demanding that the Kirchenleute resisters cease their "treasonable proceedings" and retire peacefully to their homes.[47] No one in Philadelphia seemed to know that the resisters had already done so on their own. The "insurrection" had ended the moment that Marshall Nichols released his prisoners. To stress this point, on March 18, John Fries held a public meeting in which attendees unanimously agreed to abide by the president's proclamation, and swore not to obstruct future assessors in their duties. Despite the unanimity of the Kirchenleute submission, Adams, goaded by the bellicose Federalist press and ever mindful of Washington's response to the whiskey rebels, called forth a Federal army to suppress a tax rebellion that no longer existed. On April 4, a combined force of 1,000 federal troops and state militia marched from Philadelphia into Kirchenleute territory and, after encountering absolutely no opposition, served instead 27 indictments against a total of 91 persons, including John Fries, for criminal conspiracy, rescue, obstruction of process, and treason. After a series of trials, often with stacked juries, 32 resisters were convicted of crimes under the Sedition Act, and most were slapped with fines and prison sentences.[48] Three, including Fries, were found guilty of treason and sentenced to hang, but on May 21, 1800, Adams, perhaps again mindful of Washington's prior actions, issued a blanket pardon to all involved in the tax rebellion. Interestingly, his pardon extended to David Bradford, the only whiskey fugitive not covered by Washington's original pardon. Given the noninjurious character of the resistance movement and Fries's dogged determination to avoid violence, executing him and his fellow resisters would have constituted a gross overreaction on the part of the Adams administration. Yet, in the face of heated intraparty opposition, Adams' pardon was viewed as nothing less than an act of betrayal by the Hamiltonian wing, setting the stage for a division with the Federalist Party that would ultimately contribute to its loss of power and the ascension of the Jefferson–Madison Republican Party.

V. Antebellum Riots

As the three aforementioned civil insurrections demonstrate, independence did not necessarily douse the spirit of anti-authoritarianism in America. These insurrections tested the limits and strengths of America's newly born democracy and very much set a precedent for other violent episodes that would continue to mark the first decades of the new republic. The first half of the 19th century was witness to numerous wars, riots, uprisings, and conflicts, all part of a vulnerable and volatile political environment in which domestic terrorism would continue to emerge as a desperate but viable tactic. In this regard, methods of conflict and popular protest during the decades preceding the Civil War were part of a continuum that stretched back to the early colonial years, but which were seemingly given the stamp of approval during the years of the American Revolution when extralegal crowd action helped undermine British authority. Moreover, as Paul Gilje noted in his analysis of rioting, the Revolution encouraged greater political participation and popular protest as the American commitment to corporatism and the ideal of a single-interest society, so prevalent during the colonial years, gave way to egalitarianism and individual self-interest. The common interest once binding the components of society together disintegrated, thus generating greater social conflict and opportunities for domestic violence.[49] As with the colonial period, this antebellum violence came in many forms. Beyond the continuing pattern of domestic disturbances, the United States also fought major wars against Great Britain and Mexico during this period and engaged a number of native tribes, as well, including the Seminoles, Creeks, Shawnees, and Black Hawks. The nation was also involved in undeclared hostilities against France and the Barbary States. Interestingly and inaccurately, one historian recently dubbed Thomas Jefferson's campaign against the Barbary States as "America's first war on terror."[50] The Barbary States employed blackmail, piracy and kidnapping but not terrorism, for they sought no political objectives, just the extortion of money. Nonetheless, the Barbary hostilities and other wars, openly declared or otherwise, helped pave the way for the most deadly civil conflict in our nation's history.

As with warfare, diverse forms of rioting were just as prevalent during the first half of the 19th century as they were during the colonial period. There were, however, subtle distinctions between the two eras. Gilje noted that while pre-Revolution riots tended to be relatively benign and represented a sense of community solidarity, antebellum riots were more destructive and revealed tensions and strains *within* a community.[51] But early 18th-century riots also had a clear tone of anti-authoritarianism, directing much popular resentment toward government policies regarding tobacco, food, pine trees, impressment, or land ownership. In this sense, riots enabled the growth of American terrorism, as citizens developed a willingness to resist government policies and to employ increased levels of violence as a form of popular protest. In the aftermath of the three civil insurrections discussed above, however, most early-19th-century riots were less anti-authoritarian in nature and more personal and race/ethnicity oriented, resulting in the widespread persecution of Catholics, Mormons, and nonnative victims. These antebellum riots can be categorized into several types.

Nativism and Religious Riots

With population growth and increasing social diversity came the nativist clamor that newly arriving outsiders and non-Protestants were subverting American institutions. As early as 1642, Virginia had enacted legislation discriminatory against Catholics, but, beginning with the Antebellum Era, Irish Catholics, long discriminated against by English Protestants, were increasingly targeted for abuse by nativists, as refugees from the Irish potato famine flocked to the shores of America. Other significant anti-Catholic rioting occurred in New York (1825, 1831), Charlestown, Massachusetts (1834), Boston (1837), and Philadelphia (1844). Nativist riots directed at non-English sailors in American seaports were fairly common, but, after the acquisition of California and the subsequent discovery of gold there, riots against Chinese, Mexican, Chilean, and other non-American prospectors also became commonplace. Riots against the Mormon Church were also frequent during the 1830s and, following the murder of Joseph Smith in 1844, eventually drove its members to seek security on the faraway banks of the Great Salt Lake. Nativism became such an emotional and politically charged cause that it eventually found expression in the formation of the Know-Nothing Party during the 1850s. The Know-Nothings were short-lived, but unfortunately discrimination and violence against non-natives and non-Protestants, popularized during the antebellum period, would persist into modern times.

Vigilante Riots

The antebellum period gave rise to a number of vigilante movements that quickly multiplied following the Civil War. Richard Maxwell Brown, in his study of American violence, identified at least 100 vigilante groups that operated before 1860. Initially inspired by the South Carolina Regulators, vigilantism was necessitated in large part by the effective absence of law and order in frontier regions. A requisite to social stability in these areas, vigilantism, according to Brown, "was a sanctification of the deeply cherished values of life and property." It was also extremely violent at times, as victims were routinely assaulted, flogged, expelled, and, on many occasions, killed in the name of law and order. Brown estimated that antebellum vigilante movements took the lives of at least 200 persons.[52] Yet, conversely, many vigilante movements were nonviolent and had a salutary impact on their communities. The largest and perhaps most influential vigilante movement was the San Francisco Committee of Vigilance, who, in 1856, responded to the murder of a newspaper editor by mobilizing more than 6,000 mostly Protestant supporters and taking down the culpable and corrupt Irish American/Democratic Party political machine that had dominated the city's politics. Because the pursuit of justice through extralegal means was consistent with the terrorist mindset, vigilantism made its own significant contribution to the ongoing evolution of American terrorism.

Labor Riots

Although labor riots are usually associated with the latter half of the 19th century and the early 20th century, violence surrounding organized labor predates the Civil War. As early as the 1820s and 1830s, New York City dockworkers engaged in hostile strikes against management, while sailors violently protested wage reductions. During those years, organized riots were further employed by stonecutters, cabinet makers, and ropemakers.[53] The burgeoning textile industry also witnessed violent confrontations between striking weavers and strikebreakers in New York during the 1820s and in Philadelphia during the 1840s. In New England, armed women often engaged in acts of destruction to protest oppressive working conditions in the textile mills. Eventually, labor disturbances would plague the coal fields of central Pennsylvania as an unprecedented wave of murders, beginning in the midst of the Civil War, were committed by a band of Irish coal miners called the Molly Maguires. The Industrial Revolution would certainly usher in a new era of labor discord by the turn of the 20th century, but by then a legacy of labor-induced violence had been well established.

Anti-Abolitionist Riots

During the 1830s, riots against abolitionists were the most common form of collective violence. Largely confined to the north, abolitionism represented the worst fears of many Americans: a subversion of the Union and Constitution, the emancipation of millions of uneducated black workers, and the social prospect of "sexual amalgamation." Consequently, hundreds of attacks were conducted against abolitionists by mobs that often included community leaders and upper-class citizens.[54] Whether spontaneous or planned, these attacks could prove extremely dangerous, as the murder of newspaper editor Elijah P. Lovejoy in 1837 would indicate. In many cases, attacks on abolitionists turned into spontaneous and destructive assaults on black communities, as in New York City (1834), Cincinnati (1836), and Philadelphia (1838). As with acts of terrorism, many anti-abolitionist riots also assumed elements of theater and *charivari*, as participants blew tin trumpets and bombarded abolitionists with rotten eggs. No wonder then that many abolitionists traveling throughout the country were forced to do so surreptitiously.

Race Riots

In addition to riots directed against those who would rely on political institutions to abolish slavery, violent confrontations were also motivated by issues related exclusively to race. Between 1800 and 1860, Richard Maxwell Brown documented at least 80 episodes of collective black-white violence, including riots, slave rebellions, and lynchings.[55] Although, early on, the majority of attacks took place in the south, by the 1830s, the focus of this violence shifted to the north, where many communities of free blacks were seemingly under constant assault by intolerant whites. The 1829 destruction of Cincinnati's "Bucktown" established a familiar pattern of black–white violence: whites invaded a black neighborhood, assaulted black victims, destroyed homes and public buildings, drove residents into exile, and redoubled their rage when blacks dared defend themselves.[56] Indeed, in many northern cities, blacks willingly resorted to retaliatory violence in order to protect their homes and families. The occasional slave conspiracy or uprising was further testimony of the growth of collective black resistance. The infamous plots of Gabriel Prosser and Denmark Vesey in 1800 were discovered before any blood was shed, but Nat Turner's deadly conspiracy in 1831 took the lives of 60 whites, women and children included. As the Civil War approached, it was becoming increasingly evident that many blacks were willing to stand ground and defend themselves against white provocations with equal determination and rage.

Any consideration of antebellum race-based violence should include John Brown and his devoted followers, fanatical abolitionists responsible for the murder of five pro-slavery southerners in the infamous Pottawatomie Massacre in May 1856, and the failed raid on a federal arsenal at Harper's Ferry in 1859, which left another 14 dead. The Pottawatomie episode was ostensibly in retaliation for a raid by pro-slavery forces on the "free soil" settlement of Lawrence, Kansas, and Brown's subsequent attempt to seize the federal arsenal in Virginia was a prelude to what he had hoped would be an armed exodus by slaves that would ultimately "purge this land with blood." Two of Brown's sons were killed at Harper's Ferry, and Brown would ultimately hang in December 1859 for his role in the deadly affairs. Because of Brown's violent and fanatical behavior, Americans have long had difficulty assessing his legacy. Although, in the aftermath of his execution, abolitionists, northerners, and writers were quick to defend his noble charac-ter and righteous motives if not his extreme methods, by the mid-20th century, historical perceptions began to shift. James G. Randall, Ray A. Billington, James Malin, and Robert Penn Warren, among others, portrayed Brown at various times as a charlatan, horse thief, opportunistic brigand, or homicidal madman, leav-ing Americans with conflicting interpretations of the man many believed was responsible for the outbreak of the Civil War. By the 1970s, biographers such as Stephen B. Oates and Jules Abels acknowledged the contradictions that Brown seemingly embodied, thus evoking both empathy for, and criticism of, the radi-cal abolitionist.[57] The controversy over Brown's legacy was revived in 2000, two centuries after his birth, when Ken Chowder wrote an essay for *American Heritage* in which he proclaimed Brown "the father of American terrorism," admired by extremists from both the political right and left.[58] Five years later, in a major biography, David S. Reynolds appeared conflicted by Brown's contradictions, but explained away the conundrum by proclaiming him a hero *and* a terrorist. Reynolds referred to Brown as a "good terrorist" who committed "self-sacrificing terrorism" or "anti-slavery terrorism" that was justified by social injustice. In an unbefitting display of chauvinism, Reynolds attempted to distinguish between good and bad terrorism by suggesting that Brown differed greatly from bad or "modern" terrorists because he was an *American* terrorist in that he possessed "breadth of vision" and a particular "eloquence."[59] James Gilbert, a criminologist influenced by theories of psychopathology and sociopathic personalities, concurred that Brown was a terrorist, but offered a different rationale. Insisting on the need to provide definitional standards of terrorism devoid of emotional or mythical distortions such as those that have traditionally deified Brown, Gilbert provided a terrorism paradigm based not on one's deeds or beliefs, but rather on one's motives or "deep-seated personal and cultural pathologies." Thus, terrorism is not a strategy but a state of mind, and Brown's "classic messianic psychopathic rationalization" clearly defined him as "undoubtedly a terrorist to the core."[60]

The debate over Brown's credentials as a terrorist intensified in 2009, the 150th anniversary of the attack at Harper's Ferry. In op-ed pieces in the *New York Times,* Tony Horowitz referred to Brown as the "most successful terrorist in American history" and drew comparisons between Harper's Ferry and Al Qaeda's attacks on the World Trade Center on 9/11. David S. Reynolds again weighed in, and, although he surprisingly skirted the "terrorist" issue, he urged that Brown be granted a presidential pardon and be thereby rescued from the "looney bin of history."[61] In his 2010 study of terrorism in America, Michael Fellman agreed with Reynolds that Brown was a terrorist, referring to the zealot as a "professional revolutionary terrorist," although he did take issue by suggesting that, "extremists sometimes cut to the central point of a cultural contradiction, but this never makes them 'good' extremists." Fellman went on to describe Brown and his militia as "a small band of dedicated terrorists who would trigger the destruction of the tyrannical slave system. Here was born a classic case of revolutionary terrorism, political ideology linked to a plan for direct and violent action."[62]

As befitting the twists and turns surrounding Brown's overall historical legacy, perceptions of his alleged "terrorism" may be shifting as well. In a 2011 journal article, Paul Finkerman denied that Brown was a terrorist, pointing out that Brown did not kill indiscriminately, did not act in secrecy, did not wantonly destroy property, and did not kill innocent bystanders. Although one might argue with Finkerman's criteria, which differ from those established above, he concluded that Brown waged a campaign not of terror but of revolutionary guerrilla warfare, an assessment consistent with the position taken here as it pertains to most of Brown's activities.[63] The shocking attack at Pottawatomie, where the five victims were hacked to death with broadswords, was retributive homicide, although there is some speculation that Brown was acting partly to prevent attacks on his own family.[64] But methods and motivation notwithstanding, the one-and-done murders were not part of a sustained campaign of terror by Brown, and neither were his subsequent armed engagements against pro-slavery Missourians at Black Jack and Osawatomie, which more closely resembled traditional guerrilla skirmishes. The bloody episodes were his personal contributions to a wider guerrilla war waged between pro- and anti-slavery forces to establish not psychological manipulation but territorial control in "Bleeding Kansas," civil hostilities that ultimately claimed more than 200 lives in 1856. The Harper's Ferry episode was even less about generating terror and more about enabling a guerrilla army of liberated slaves to fight its way out of Virginia in order to establish a colony of free blacks in the mountains out west. In a country where racial divisions remain a thorny social issue, John Brown continues to represent many things to many people, including martyr, madman, messiah, and murderer, but, according to the academic parameters presented here, he was not a terrorist.

Miscellaneous Riots

Beyond the broad typologies above, there were many other types of special-ized riots that tend to be obscured by the larger picture of antebellum violence. Riots, for example, ensued during the 1830s and 1840s over election fraud, and the Know-Nothings were accused of establishing a "reign of terror" to obstruct immigrants from voting during the mid-1850s.[65] There were also occasional riots involving bank failures, food supplies, fire companies, gambling, prostitution, the-aters, opera houses, and even faculty–student relations on college campuses.[66]

Despite the intensity and diversity of rioting during the antebellum period, as with the colonial era, the vast majority of riots did not sink to the level of terrorist activity. The unlawful use of violence was usually an end in itself, with no victim-target differentiation or psychological manipulation. Rioters tended to lack both an organizational hierarchy and a reasoned propaganda campaign to accompany orchestrated violence. Some antebellum riots had absolutely no political motiva-tion, such as those employed to reinforce community morals. There was, however, one category of rioting that did, on occasion, ultimately assume the characteristics of terrorism. This one exception was the collective violence associated with land ownership controversies, a contentious subject of much consequence everywhere.

The American Revolution had a tremendous but underappreciated impact on issues related to the ownership of land. As far back as 1926, J. Franklin Jameson, in his landmark monograph on the social ramifications of the American Revolu-tion, posited the notion that, because the acquisition of land was "the chief task of manhood," the "relations of the American to the land were of the very first conse-quence" of the Revolution. In essence, confiscation, the end of primogeniture and entail, the end to quitrents and the lifting of royal restrictions all contributed to more democratic forms of landholding.[67] Consequently, during the early years of the new republic, the wider distribution of land held out the promise of a brighter future for yeoman farmers and for the country as a whole. But in select areas, this egalitarian vision was undermined by conflicting concepts of how private prop-erty was legitimately created and properly defended. On the one hand, there was an entrenched and powerful class of "gentlemen of property and standing," leaders of the Revolution who believed in the centralization of political power and in establishing safeguards to protect pre-Revolution contracts, especially large land grants bestowed by sovereign authority. These patrician landlords, many of whom had formed alliances with plebians during the Revolution to generate crowd activity, now viewed extralegal resistance as a threat to the country and their own social standing. Opposing the landed gentry were the agrarians, who not only sought a wider and more equitable distribution of land but who also claimed property ownership, based either on conflicting deeds or on their own hard labor and improvement of the land.[68] Consequently, it would be conflicts involving land ownership that would motivate certain groups of radical agrarians to subvert the law and engage in terrorist activity. Nowhere did these conflicting concepts of property ownership have more severe consequences than in New York and the hinterlands of Maine—at the time, part of the Commonwealth of Massachusetts.

Notes

1. John Shy, *A People Numerous and Armed: Reflections on the Military Struggle for American Independence* (Ann Arbor: University of Michigan Press, 1990), 249–250.
2. James Kirby Martin and Mark Edward Lender, *A Respectable Army—The Military Origins of the Republic, 1763–1789* (Wheeling, IL: Harlan Davidson, Inc., 2006), 20–27.
3. Robert E. Moody, "Samuel Ely: Forerunner of Shays," *New England Quarterly,* vol. 5, no.1 (January, 1932): 116.
4. Leonard L. Richards, *Shays's Rebellion—The American Revolution's Final Battle* (Philadelphia: University of Pennsylvania Press, 2002), 60–61.
5. David P. Szatmary, *Shays' Rebellion—The Making of an Agrarian Insurrection* (Amherst: The University of Massachusetts Press, 1980), 60–63.
6. Richards, *Shays's Rebellion,* 58; Szatmary, *Shays' Rebellion,* 75.
7. Szatmary, *Shays' Rebellion,* 83–84.
8. Ibid., 94.
9. Ibid., 76.
10. Ibid., 119.
11. Richards, *Shays's Rebellion,* 35–36; Szatmary, *Shays' Rebellion,* 109–114.
12. William Hogeland, *The Whiskey Rebellion—George Washington, Alexander Hamilton, and the Frontier Rebels Who Challenged America's Newfound Sovereignty* (New York: Scribner, 2006), 70.
13. Dorothy E. Fennell, *From Rebelliousness to Insurrection: A Social History of the Whiskey Rebellion, 1765–1802* (University of Pittsburg Press, 1981), 6–7.
14. Hogeland, *The Whiskey Rebellion,* 103–104.
15. Thomas P. Slaughter, *The Whiskey Rebellion—Frontier Epilogue to the American Revolution* (New York: Oxford University Press, 1986), 109.
16. Ibid., 115.
17. Ibid., 125–127; Hogeland, *The Whiskey Rebellion,* 126–129.
18. Slaughter, *The Whiskey Rebellion,* 151.
19. Hogeland, *The Whiskey Rebellion,* 131.
20. William Findley, *History of the Insurrection: In the Four Western Counties of Pennsylvania in the Year MDCCXCIV; With a Recital of the Circumstances Specially Connected Therewith, and an Historical Review of the Previous Situation of the Country* (Philadelphia: Samuel Harrison Smith), 65.
21. Fennell, *From Rebelliousness to Insurrection,* 113.
22. Ibid., 144.

23. Ibid., 61, 144–145.
24. Hogeland, *The Whiskey Rebellion,* 142.
25. Fennell, *From Rebelliousness to Insurrection,* 109.
26. Slaughter, *The Whiskey Rebellion,* 179.
27 Hogeland, *The Whiskey Rebellion,* 100.
28. Ibid., 154.
29. Slaughter, *The Whiskey Rebellion,* 186; Hogeland, *The Whiskey Rebellion,* 169.
30. Slaughter, *The Whiskey Rebellion,* 276.
31. Hogeland, *The Whiskey Rebellion,* 71–95.
32. Ibid., 195; Slaughter, *The Whiskey Rebellion,* 198.
33. Hogeland, *The Whiskey Rebellion,* 163.
34. Fennell, *From Rebelliousness to Insurrection,* 72.
35. James Roger Sharpe, "The Whiskey Rebellion and the Question of Representation," in Steven R. Boyd, ed., *The Whiskey Rebellion: Past and Present Perspectives* (Westport, CT: Greenwood Press, 1985), 123–125.
36. W.W.H. Davis, *The Fries Rebellion, 1798–99* (Doylestown, PA: Doylestown Publishing Co., 1899), 3–4; Jeffrey S. Dimmig, "Palatine Liberty: Pennsylvania German Opposition to the Direct Tax of 1798," *American Journal of Legal History,* vol. 45, no. 4 (2002): 371–390.
37. Paul Douglas Newman, *Fries's Rebellion—The Enduring Struggle for the American Revolution* (Philadelphia: University of Pennsylvania Press, 2004), 2.
38. Paul Douglas Newman, *Fries's Rebellion,* 90, 93.
39. Simon Newman, "The World Turned Upside Down: Revolutionary Politics, Fries' and Gabriel's Rebellions, and the Fears of the Federalists," *Pennsylvania History,* vol. 67, no.1 (Winter, 2000): 7.
40. Paul Douglas Newman, *Fries's Rebellion,* 96.
41. Peter Levine, "The Fries Rebellion: Social Violence and the Politics of the New Nation," *Pennsylvania History,* vol. 40, no.1 (July, 1973): 241–258.
42. Paul Douglas Newman, *Fries's Rebellion,* 96–97.
43. Ibid., 108.
44. Davis, *The Fries Rebellion,* 8–10; Paul Douglas Newman, *Fries Rebellion,* 112–119.
45. Davis, *The Fries Rebellion,* 63–66; Paul Douglas Newman, *Fries Rebellion,* 140; Levine, "The Fries Rebellion," 250.
46. Alex P. Schmid, Albert J. Jongman, et al., *Political Terrorism: A New Guide to Actors, Authors, Concepts, Data Bases, Theories, and Literature* (New Brunswick: Transaction Books, 1988), 5–6.
47. Davis, *The Fries Rebellion,* 69.
48. Paul Douglas Newman, *Fries Rebellion,* 180; Davis, *The Fries Rebellion,* 78.
49. Paul A. Gilje, *Rioting in America* (Bloomington: Indiana University Press, 1996), 63.
50. Joseph Wheelan, *Jefferson's War—America's First War on Terror* (New York: Carroll and Graf Publishers, 2003).
51. Gilje, *Rioting in America,* 63.
52. Richard Maxwell Brown, *Strain of Violence—Historical Studies of American Violence and Vigilantism* (New York: Oxford University Press, 1973), 305–319, quote from p. 97.
53. Paul A. Gilje, *The Road to Mobocracy—Popular Disorder in New York City, 1763–1834* (Chapel Hill: University of North Carolina Press, 1987), 185.
54. Michael Feldberg, *The Turbulent Era—Riot and Disorder in Jacksonian America* (New York: Oxford University Press, 1980), 43.
55. Brown, *Strain of Violence,* 320–326.

56. Feldberg, *The Turbulent Era,* 38–39.
57. For the best overview of the literature concerning Brown, see Merrill D. Peterson, *John Brown—The Legend Revisited* (Charlottesville: University of Virginia Press, 2002).
58. Ken Chowder, "The Father of American Terrorism," *American Heritage,* vol. 51, no. 1, (Feb/March 2002): 81–91.
59. David S. Reynolds, *John Brown, Abolitionist—The Man Who Killed Slavery, Sparked the Civil War, and Seeded Civil Rights* (New York: Alfred A. Knopf, 2005), 500–504.
60. James N. Gilbert, "A Behavioral Analysis of John Brown: Martyr or Terrorist?" in Peggy A. Russo and Paul Finkleman, *Terrible Swift Sword: The Legacy of John Brown* (Athens: Ohio University Press, 2005), 112–115.
61. *New York Times,* December 1, 2009.
62. Michael Fellman, *In Name of God and Country—Reconsidering Terrorism in American History* (New Haven: Yale University Press, 2010), 28.
63. Paul Finkleman, "John Brown: America's First Terrorist?" *Prologue,* vol. 43, no. 1 (spring, 2011): 16–27.
64. Reynolds, *John Brown, Abolitionist,* 144–166.
65. Feldberg, *The Turbulent Era,* 59.
66. Gilje, *Rioting in America,* 73.
67. J. Franklin Jameson, *The American Revolution Considered as a Social Movement* (Princeton: Princeton University Press, 1926), 29.
68. Alan Taylor, *Libertymen and Great Proprietors—The Revolutionary Settlement on the Maine Frontier, 1760–1820* (Chapel Hill: University of North Carolina Press, 1990).

6

THE WHITE INDIANS OF MAINE

I. Background

Between the mid-1790s and a local affair in 1809 known as the Malta War, the frontier of Maine was plagued by a wave of violence attributed to a group of dissident agrarians known as the White Indians. Sometimes disguised (quite unconvincingly) as natives, these extremists were also known at various times as Liberty Men, Regulators, and Anti-Renters. However, by 1800, the term "White Indians" was popularly applied to these dissidents, who employed violence and intimidation to oppose the interests of the great absentee proprietors who claimed title to the frontier lands on which they lived and farmed. This resistance movement, played out in the distant wilderness of Maine, some 100 miles from Boston, represented more than just a local problem with squatters. Post-Revolution agrarian resistance movements in Maine, as well as New York, concentrated on issues seemingly tied to the ownership of property, but in many ways represented a larger, more significant philosophical divergence over nothing less than the meaning of the American Revolution itself. As with the ongoing political battle between Federalists and Republicans, the confrontation between White Indians and proprietors was founded on differing viewpoints on the nature of republicanism—and on whether ownership of the untamed wilderness was the product of dubious title or actual occupation. The themes that played out in Maine—the distribution of land, class warfare, and the legitimacy of violent dissent—were recurring themes throughout the Post-Revolution Era and helped define the parameters of freedom within the new republic.

These broader issues were, of course, not readily discernible when the violence first erupted in Maine. In fact, because there was no climactic showdown between opposing forces, the provocations of the White Indians were largely overlooked by outside observers then, as well as by historians today. Until 1990, there existed no detailed, scholarly analysis of Maine's White Indians, despite a plethora of primary source materials. The White Indians made the pages of history only as part of the broader histories of Maine. James W. North's history of Augusta, published in 1870, surprisingly offered a fairly detached and objective consideration of the agrarian rebels, to whom North simply referred as "squatters" or "Indians." North detailed various violent provocations and acknowledged that the "guerilla warfare" committed by these squatters "was worse than open and formal insurrection," but he also carefully avoided demonizing the rebels, depicting them instead as misguided members of a relatively close-knit community.[1] Some of the aggrieved proprietors later published their memoirs concerning the land disputes, including R. Hollowell Gardiner, whose memoirs also offered a benign treatment of the White Indians and characterized the contentiousness as a simple disagreement over the price of land.[2] Robert E. Moody's study of Samuel Ely, published in *New England Quarterly* in 1932, was one of the first scholarly attempts to focus on the agrarian rebels, but no book-length treatment would exist for another six decades.[3] This sorry state of historical neglect was made all the more evident by the fact that of the two most-detailed studies of the resistance movement one was an unpublished doctoral dissertation submitted to Boston University in 1959 and the other an unpublished master's thesis submitted to the University of Maine in 1976.[4]

This conspicuous void was finally filled single-handedly by Alan Taylor, a noted historian of colonial America. First in a paper delivered in 1986 to the Bicentennial Conference on Shays's Rebellion and later with the 1990 publication of *Liberty Men and Great Proprietors,* Taylor provided not only the first major historical investigation of the White Indians but most likely the last as well. His exhaustive research, detailed narrative, and penetrating analysis ensure that any serious discussion of the Maine rebels will be based, in large measure, on his significant contributions. And Taylor made it clear that the White Indians, or Liberty Men, represented unshakable evidence that, even after 1783, the American Revolution was still a work in progress, that as long as the meaning of liberty could be subverted by questionable entitlement and the monopolization of property, then certain social ends of the Revolution could still be lost.[5]

II. Early Origins

The French began settlement activity in Maine in 1604, but were later repelled by English colonists from Virginia. Permanent English settlers arrived a few years later, but very little is known about them. Nor do historians know how the area was named. Maine eventually became the property of Massachusetts in 1677, but did not enter the union as a separate state until the Missouri Compromise of 1820–1821. The two centuries between settlement and statehood were largely marked by ongoing land disputes that began when the first white settlers encountered the coastal Indians, who were quite willing to sell identical deeds of land to different buyers. Millions of acres of untamed wilderness, bountiful fishing grounds, and a variety of furbearing animals attracted farmers, fishermen, and fur traders, as well as wealthy speculators who sought proprietary control of the Maine wilderness. In 1620, the English Crown granted a patent to the Council of New England, a group of proprietors who thus became the sole owners of the frontier stretching from the Chesapeake to the Penobscot River. The Council would eventually dissolve in 1635, but not before granting three major proprietary claims that together covered nearly 4 1/2 million acres of Maine: the Pejepscot, Plymouth, and Waldo patents. Unfortunately, not only were these three patents vague and overlapping, but they also conflicted with ten other existing land claims, nine of which were based on extremely dubious Indian deeds. Little wonder, then, that many would argue from the very beginning that the proprietors never held clear title to the three patents.[6]

The land claims controversy became further complicated every time the various proprietors subdivided and sold off lots that were located within the disputed areas. Fearful of having their claims subjected to a legal decision, the proprietors were reluctant to sue one another in court; this did not, however, prevent them from bringing suit against the settlers who had purchased deeds from competing proprietors. Compounding these problems, in 1661, the Plymouth patent was sold to a group of four merchants based in Boston, a move that signaled an eventful economic and political conquest of Maine by proprietors and other political forces of Massachusetts Bay. In his *History of Maine,* Charles E. Clark referred to this takeover as "the first American imperialism."[7] The acquisition became complete in 1677, when Massachusetts secured clear title by purchasing the proprietary rights to Maine. The land disputes, however, were over 130 years away from any type of long-term resolution.

The stakes in Maine multiplied as the settler communities grew and the area north of the Androscoggin River became more heavily populated. Most of the new arrivals squatted on uninhabited tracts of land, built crude houses, farmed the lands, and settled in for the long haul. In their minds, this was untamed wilderness, which could only be possessed by those who occupied and improved the lands—as long as they claimed only that which could comfortably support their families, now and in the future. Ownership of these lands by absentee proprietors undermined the occupants' freedom and reduced them to tenancy, a condition that had caused many of them to desert Europe for America. During this colonial era, violence was relatively rare and sporadic. A brief resistance movement by the settlers did appear in 1731, when Colonel David Dunbar led a band of agrarian rebels on raids against the property of what Alan Taylor called the "Great Proprietors"—the most propertied and powerful of the various land speculators. In defiance of both the jurisdiction of Massachusetts and the title claims of the Great Proprietors, Dunbar hoped to create a new colony located along the coast of mid-Maine. Toward this end, he and his followers destroyed sawmills, boats, and garrison houses owned by the proprietors, until the Board of Trade convinced Dunbar to cease and surrender.[8] Violent resistance, however, would reappear during the 1760s, when bands of men, often disguised as Indians, destroyed property belonging to the proprietors and their local supporters. Meanwhile, attempts to resolve the controversy remained largely stonewalled. Many of the Great Proprietors, because of legal issues, preferred selling quitrent deeds, which were contestable in court. Those who were willing to sell freehold titles had problems coming up with prices agreeable to the settlers.[9] Until the outbreak of the American Revolution, the Great Proprietors would continue to press their claims to Maine's central coast, while the settlers continued to squat and defy the proprietary claims.

During the Revolutionary War, the squatter violence and the legal tactics of the proprietors were temporarily suspended, but the Revolution ultimately brought about two significant developments in mid-Maine. First, because of population shifts during the war, thousands of newcomers arrived, most of whom settled in the backcountry. Between 1775 and 1790, the population of Maine tripled to nearly 100,000. Second, because most of the Great Proprietors who claimed title to these lands had remained loyal to the Crown during the war and now faced potential confiscation of these lands by the Commonwealth of Massachusetts, these newly arriving settlers assumed that the backcountry was free for the taking.[10] These assumptions were not merely wishful thinking. The republican ideology on which the Revolution was founded often meant different things to different people, but there was one social dimension that was undeniably an important ingredient to many: a spirit of egalitarianism based in large measure on the concept of social "leveling"—the creation of an equal economic playing field that could only be brought about by the dissolution of large land holdings in the interest of decentralized wealth and privilege. In Maine, this was not to be.

In 1779, a proposed draft for the Massachusetts state constitution required the confiscation of all landholdings in excess of 1,000 acres, but was defeated by conservative forces sympathetic to the Great Proprietors. In the end, Massachusetts failed to confiscate the claims of the proprietors, who skillfully exploited their political connections in order to finagle legislative confirmation of their claims. In 1788, the General Court of Massachusetts followed suit and confirmed the validity of the Waldo Patent, then controlled by the powerful Henry Knox, as well as the Plymouth Patent, controlled by a group of Kennebeck Proprietors. A legal hold-up would delay the confirmation of the Pejepscot Patent for another 25 years. Had the General Court also mandated that the proprietors grant small farms at token prices, as it had in northeastern Maine, chances are most of the agrarian disturbances along the central coast would have ceased. Unfortunately, the Great Proprietors opposed this policy known as "quieting."[11] Despite these legal proceedings, many continued to argue that the proprietors, from the very beginning, lacked clear title to lands now claimed by the squatter communities. While many of the proprietors readied for continuing legal battles from the comfort of their mansions far removed from the Maine wilderness, hostile squatters were preparing their own tactics conducive to the Maine frontier—tactics that relied not on the letter of the law but on methods that can only be described as terroristic.

III. The White Indians Strike

Once it became clear that widespread confiscation was but a mere illusion and that the egalitarianism of the Revolution was being subverted by the continued monopolization of property, the squatters once again turned to hostile methods to forestall the attempts by the proprietors to establish their legal authority in the backcountry of Maine's central coast. In his study of the resistance movement, Alan Taylor compiled a lengthy list of approximately 140 incidents of extralegal violence in the disputed areas between the years 1790 and 1810.[12] The vast majority of these episodes involved armed attempts by the White Indians to prevent surveyors of the Great Proprietors from running survey lines through the disputed areas. This backcountry violence took a new turn in 1792, when the squatters within the Waldo Patent were joined by Samuel Ely, the itinerant preacher with an infamous past. The Great Proprietors could not have been thrilled with Ely's appearance, for here was the man responsible for "Ely's Rebellion," the 1782 insurrection of agrarian rebels in Hampshire County, Massachusetts, a precursor of Shays's Rebellion by four years. He was now back at it again, this time in Maine, exhorting disenchanted squatters into violent acts of defiance and personally leading attacks against persons and property associated with the Great Proprietors.[13]

Typical of the White Indian attacks was the confrontation with Ephraim Ballard, who was hired in late 1795 by the state of Massachusetts to run survey lines partly separating the Waldo and Plymouth patents. While conducting his survey near Balltown, he and his team bunked at the home of Jonathan Jones, a local supporter of the Kennebeck Proprietors. According to Ballard, upon entering the backcountry, he and his assistants were confronted with "much abuse and repeated insult." On the night of November 12, his team was awakened by gunshots whizzing by their heads, and Ballard was immediately confronted by four armed men with blackened faces, one of whom stuck a pistol against the surveyor's chest. The men demanded Ballard's papers and survey tools, on threat of death. After confiscating his papers and destroying his compass, the attackers left. As they fled the scene, some were recognized by members of the Jones family, which had set out to protect Ballard. The witnesses, however, refused to divulge the identities of the attackers because, as one would later testify, "we are threatened that our lives and our families with our houses shall be destroyed if we give any information against them."[14] Their fears were not unwarranted. Three days later, the barn of Jonathan Jones, which reportedly held more than 60 tons of hay, was set afire by what he described as "wicked and lawless men."[15]

A few months later, another similar episode revealed the extent to which the White Indians had instilled fear not only in the Great Proprietors but also with members of the local community who sided with the proprietary claims. On July 8, 1796, John Trueman, an agent for a proprietary company, was summoned by Isaac Prince to discuss terms of a suit brought against Prince by Trueman's employers. On his way to New Milford, Trueman was ambushed by a group of "banditti and thieves" with blackened faces, who dragged him from his horse, stripped off his clothing, beat him with sticks, slashed his ears with a small knife, and robbed him of his belongings, all the while verbally abusing him with threats of instant death. Trueman repeatedly begged for his life and was allowed to escape, but only after he was able to identify Prince as one of his attackers.[16] An investigation eventually led to the arrests of three suspects in March 1797, who were subsequently jailed in nearby Wiscasset. Meanwhile, the local gossip mill began to spin. Word circulated that Asa Andrews, one of the attackers, had turned informant and that his life was now in great peril. Andrews had been a reluctant conspirator and had participated in the assault only because Prince had forced him. There were also reports that the White Indians and their supporters would shortly attempt a rescue riot. Two local militia companies were subsequently dispatched to protect Wiscasset's flimsy wooden jail. Regardless, on the morning of March 21, an armed crowd estimated at between 200 and 300 men marched into Wiscasset and boasted of their intent to free the three suspects. Convinced that the jail could not be protected without a bloody confrontation, the local magistrates sent the militia home, in essence surrendering the prisoners. The next afternoon, the mob descended on the jail and, at gunpoint, forced the jailer to release the suspects. The Trueman affair would prove to have lingering aftereffects. After the rescue, several of the conspirators fled the area, never to return. A few weeks later, mysterious notices appeared in the Wiscasset area, which, according to Manassah Smith, warned that, should any of the Trueman conspirators be further identified, the White Indians "will destroy [Wiscasset] by poisoning the provisions, water, etc., and by burning all the buildings . . . and all those who shew themselves on the side of government." Smith, a local proprietary attorney, also lamented that "this is the way we are to be governed by mobs, highway robbers and thieves . . . God deliver us from such a banditti of Devils."[17] Fearing for his life, Asa Andrews fled to Westford, Massachusetts, but failed to escape White Indian justice; he later reported that "rioters" had tracked him down and "ambushed" his home. For his role in the Trueman affair, Andrews would later maintain that he never again "went to bed without fear and never went abroad without apprehension of danger."[18]

As fate would have it, Asa Andrews's next door neighbor for a brief period was none other than Samuel Ely, who in 1797 wrote a pamphlet entitled *The Deformity of a Hideous Monster, Discovered in the Province of Maine, by a Man in the Woods, Looking After Liberty*. Reportedly printed "near Liberty Tree," Ely's pamphlet made a case on behalf of the squatter communities by challenging the legality of the Plymouth Patent, which, according to Ely, had been subjected over many years to invalid Indian deeds, legal indiscretions, disputed borders, bribery, and the unfulfilled promises of the American Revolution. Ely argued that ownership of land should be held only by the "first possessor" and that the "hideous monster," that is, the local courts and Great Proprietors, had no legal basis to adjudicate title. Should the proprietary claims be upheld, the squatters would be ruined, leaving them with no alternative other than the type of violent resistance experienced by Ephraim Ballard. Mixing biblical parables into his treatise, Ely maintained the right of the people to resist unjust laws. Just as they had fought British despots to protect liberty, they would do the same to protect their homes against the equally despotic proprietors, who, by undermining freedom, were subverting the very meaning of the American Revolution. Ely warned that should "an army be sent here to destroy us, do the Court think that we should die like dogs? No, if we must be killed, we will die like men."[19]

A year later, many of these same themes appeared, albeit in more sophisticated form, in an equally significant pamphlet produced by James Shurtleff, who managed an even lengthier title than that claimed by Ely: *A Concise Review of the Spirit Which Seemed to Govern in the Time of the Late American War, Compared with the Spirit Which Now Prevails; With the Speech of the Goodness of Freedom, Who Is Represented as Making Her Appearance upon the Alarming Occasion.* A devotee of John Locke and Adam Smith, Shurtleff resided in Litchfield, located along the disputed border between the Pejepscot and Plymouth patents. Primarily a farmer, he also served as a land surveyor, church elder, school teacher, and representative to the General Court. Like Ely, Shurtleff lamented the apparent passing of the Revolution's patriotism and the rise of "self-love, the assailant of virtuous liberty and parent of every vice." The patriots who won the Revolution had been "tutored in the school of freedom . . . and cannot easily forget the interesting lessons they have been thus taught." In Shurtleff's mind, monopolizing wild lands was a form of tyranny, reducing settlers to lifelong slaves. Title to wild lands could only be established through occupation and improvement. This was a basic right, established, in large measure, by the sacrifices made by settlers, many of whom were now squatters in Maine, who had fought and won the Revolution. As opposed to the proprietors, who had no intent to improve the lands, the settlers deserved praise for their contributions to the burgeoning population of mid-Maine. Instead of living in the urban seaport towns where they would have constituted a social burden, the settlers, by virtue of their improvement of wild areas, prevented the "Lords of Soil" from "engrossing uncultivated land." Shurtleff did not justify or threaten violence to the extent that Ely did, proposing instead that the settlers be allowed to purchase the disputed lands at reasonable prices. He did, however, suggest that the settlers had every right to defy unjust laws and that "those who encourage mobs, may be destroyed by mobs."[20]

Ely and Shurtleff accurately articulated the sentiments and legal positions held by the defiant elements within the settler communities. This was particularly significant because the backcountry residents, partly owing to their geographical accordingly. Well-publicized Klan murders in Alamance and Caswell counties forced Holden to declare martial law and to suspend the writ of habeas corpus in those two counties in July 1870. Together with ex-U.S. Army Colonel George Kirk, who commanded a volunteer militia of about 200 recruits, Holden conducted an ambitious but occasionally illegal campaign, dubbed the "Kirk–Holden War," against the Ku Klux Klan. Not a real war in the traditional sense, the campaign was actually a human dragnet that collared more than 100 suspected Klansmen; however, all cases were undermined by local authorities, all suspects were released on bond, and none received punishment of any kind. Instead, Klan suspects sued Kirk and Holden for false arrest, state courts indicted Holden for having ordered military arrests, and, when Democrats took over the state legislature in late 1870, Holden had to flee the state to avoid prosecution. Kirk fled home to Tennessee, escaping an attempt on his life. In early 1871, Holden was expelled from office by the state senate, thereby becoming the second state governor in American history to be impeached, but the first to be convicted and removed from office.[103] Although seemingly a stinging defeat for the anti-Klan forces, the Kirk–Holden War actually hastened the demise of the hooded order in Alamance and Caswell counties as dozens of Klansmen, intimidated by the growing military presence and pressured to disavow connections to terrorism, either confessed their complicity or seized the opportunity to disband. Still, the confrontation in North Carolina did not bode well for state efforts to combat the Klan, leaving only the federal government to battle the hooded terrorists.

Reliance on the federal government offered little reassurance to the anti-Klan forces. The power of state-rights prevented Congress from taking a more forceful hand in clamping down on what was widely perceived to be issues strictly limited to local and state jurisdiction. Nonetheless, in May 1870, Congress passed the Enforcement Act, meant to give teeth to the 15th Amendment, passed in early 1869, which had prohibited the denial of suffrage. Significantly, the Act also contained a section, similar to provisions adopted in some states, that made it illegal for disguised persons to conspire with intent to deprive a person of citizenship rights. Unfortunately, Congress had no authority to uphold the Act, and its impact was negligible. Presidents Andrew Johnson and U.S. Grant, who did possess the authority, used federal troops on a limited basis to police areas plagued by Klan outrages, but this alone constituted federal intervention prior to 1871. At least one state, however, was unwilling to wait for Washington to take the initiative. In Mississippi, U.S. Attorney G. Wiley Wells, applying the new Act, issued more than 200 indictments of suspected Klansmen by September 1870. While awaiting trial, the suspects were released on bond. Only through the combined efforts of several individuals did the Grant administration finally take more aggressive action in the campaign against the Ku Klux Klan beginning in early 1871: Grant's Attorney General Amos Akerman; U.S. Army General Alfred Terry, Commander of the Department of the South; South Carolina governor Robert K. Scott; and the aforementioned Major Lewis Merrill, a veteran of guerrilla wars against the

Plains Indians. Scott had grown weary of Klan terrorism, appealing to Washington time and time again for relief of any kind, preferably in the form of federal troops. Congress, in the meantime, had continued to search for ways to enforce its radical agenda, passing a Second Enforcement Act, which provided for the use of federal troops during elections. Finally, Grant, generally supportive of freedmen's rights, and Akerman, determined to uphold the law in the South, became convinced that only federal intervention could restore the rights of freedmen that the Klan had so fanatically denied. Their strategy, given the vast numbers of conspirators involved with the Invisible Empire, made the most practical sense: arrest, prosecute, and punish only high-ranking Klansmen in one concentrated area, hoping that depriving several dens of their leadership would deter and diminish Klan terror in that region, thereby leading to a "snowball" effect on the extended Klan. In consultation with General Terry, it was decided that Scott and South Carolina would finally receive the long-sought relief and that federal troops would be dispatched to York, Spartanburg, and Union counties, scenes of some of the most notorious Klan outrages ever, including the beating of Elias Hill and the lynching of Jim Williams. Perhaps no other community was as thoroughly infiltrated with Klansmen as was York County. Allen Trelease calculated that of 2,300 adult white males in the county 1,800 were sworn members of the Klan, comprising about 45 dens.[104] Jerry West, however, later took issue with these numbers, suggesting instead that no more than 1,400 Klansmen and about 30 dens called York County home.[105] Either way, it would appear that even the most moderate of estimates placed at least half of the adult men of York County within the realm of the Invisible Empire.

In March, General Terry redeployed Major Merrill and three companies of the Seventh Cavalry from Indian duty in the Great Plains to South Carolina. Several years later, the Seventh, led by their indomitable commander, Lieutenant Colonel George Armstrong Custer, would ride into infamy at the Little Big Horn. Also in March, the senate received a report on the North Carolina Klan prepared by John Scott, the senator from Pennsylvania, which confirmed the existence of the hooded order in the Tar Heel state, giving further credence to what many still maintained were but vicious rumors spread by ignorant freedmen and immoral Republicans. Merrill established his headquarters in Yorkville and set about investigating what he personally believed to be much-exaggerated rumors. It didn't take him long to discover otherwise. In April, Congress approved the Third Enforcement Act, an anti-Ku Klux bill authored by Benjamin Butler, the Radical Republican congressman from Massachusetts and former Union general. More popularly known as the Ku Klux Klan Act or Force Bill, this last of the Enforcement Acts had several key elements. The Act made it illegal to deny a citizen's right to participate in political life, to own property, to vote, or to serve on juries. It made it illegal to use a disguise in the act of obstructing a person's equal rights under the law, and additionally bestowed upon the President powers to suspend the writ of habeas corpus. On the day that the Ku Klux Klan Act became law, Congress also created the Joint Select Committee, consisting of seven senators and 14 representatives and chaired by John Scott, who had directed the earlier investigation in North Carolina. This committee, composed of 13 Republicans and eight Democrats, first convened in April and conducted various hearings until September, including those held before subcommittees in North and South Carolina, Georgia, Florida, Mississippi, Alabama, and Tennessee. Witnesses included blacks and whites, radicals and conservatives, and even the Grand Wizard himself, Nathan Bedford Forrest, who made his own particular contribution to the many lies, distortions, half-truths, and convenient memory lapses that ran rampant throughout the testimony, most of which was offered by hostile witnesses. Nonetheless, most of the committee testimony contained an endless litany of riveting stories that were and still are difficult to refute; hence, the committee's findings, stretching over 13 volumes and 8,000 pages of fine-print testimony, contained an amazing record of the Ku Klux Klan and remains the most indispensable resource on the Invisible Empire. Thousands of pages are devoted to documenting hundreds and hundreds of outrages committed against blacks and white radicals at the hands of hooded terrorists.

Interestingly, the summary report contained a dissenting, minority report signed by the eight Democratic members of the Committee.[106] In an attempt to whitewash the committee's investigation, the minority report provided a vigorous defense of the South, maintaining that the outrages there had nothing to do with any type of organized structure and that law-abiding southerners condemned them all. It claimed that stories of roving bands of disguised miscreants were grossly exaggerated by radicals seeking to justify federal policies meant to rob and malign the good people of the South. The real crime in America was the recent Ku Klux Klan bill, according to the minority report, which characterized the bill as "the grossest outrage, the foulest calumny, ever perpetrated or circulated upon or against a helpless people by their rulers."[107] The testimony from hundreds of witnesses before the politically divided Joint Select Committee closely resembled court testimony pitting prosecution or majority witnesses against defense or minority witnesses. The question and answer exchanges between committee members and witnesses often assumed adversarial tones, and provided minority witnesses and Klan defenders with convenient forums in which to deny Klan outrages and to condemn the committee's investigation as a travesty of justice. Their testimony was especially instructive: by providing a collective but flimsy defense of the Ku Klux Klan, they set new standards of disingenuous palliation. Black schools and churches, they argued, weren't destroyed by the Klan, but rather were all victims of unfortunate accidents caused mostly by blacks; the hooded nightriders terrorizing black communities were actually blacks themselves, committing outrages and framing innocent Klansmen in the process. Even those who acknowledged rough treatment of blacks downplayed the violence. Witnesses claimed that whippings were basically harmless, and one described a particular beating as "a few licks," rationalizing, "I never understood that the beating was very serious."[108] Many witnesses concurred with the testimony offered during an investigation into the tainted 1868 elections when one conservative witness remarked, "it seemed a very light thing to kill a negro in my section—scarcely worth burying when found."[109] One minority witness claimed that, in general, carpetbaggers were "treated with every idea of kindness, courtesy, and hospitality," and argued that blacks voted without impediments of any kind.[110] Another witness testified about a "known principle existing in the minds of the negroes to seek intercourse with the superior race."[111] Teachers from the north were widely described as possessing immoral character. Although Anna Davis, the gun-toting schoolteacher who courageously held the Klan at bay, was described by acquaintances as a virtuous, Christian woman, white conservatives described her as a "strumpet," a woman "of easy virtue" who allegedly lived in sin.[112]

The testimony of witnesses led to many heated and evasive exchanges, but perhaps none as bizarre as the following excerpts, which took place during testimony held in Washington between Republican John Pool and a white conservative witness from Mississippi:

Pool: Do you believe there was ever in the State an organization of what is publicly known as the Ku-Klux?

Witness: I have known no such organization.

Pool: I did not put the question in that form. I asked you if you believe that there ever existed, in the state of Mississippi, since the surrender, such an organization as is popularly termed Ku-Klux?

Witness: That is a very general term. What do you mean by "popularly termed Ku-Klux?" What kind of organization is that? If you will be more specific, I will give a definite answer to the question.

Pool: Do you not understand what is generally meant by the term Ku-Klux organization?

Witness: If it means an organization that is in disguise, I will state in answer to that question, that I have known of a political organization in 1868, in which they wore disguises. If it is asked whether I know anything of an organization in the State that committed outrages, whether in disguise or not, I will state that I know of no such organization.

Pool: How extensive was that organization in your state?

Witness: I know nothing of it beyond my own village; and I know nothing of that particular organization except for two or three weeks.

Pool: Do you know if there is such a city as London?

Witness: I have heard so.

Pool: I asked if you knew it.

Witness: I do not.

Pool: Do you believe there is?

Witness: I believe there is.[113]

Verbal sparring of this nature was common. Even though minority witnesses were identified as such in the committee report (as were "colored" persons), in many cases, the questions and responses themselves provided enough verbal cues to reveal which side of the partisan fence witnesses stood. The minority report and testimony notwithstanding, the committee's final report made it abundantly clear that the Ku Klux Klan was no myth and their outrages no fabrication, declaring that the hooded order "demoralized society and held men silent by the terror of its acts and by its powers for evil."[114]

While the Joint Select Committee was busy conducting its summer hearings, Major Lewis Merrill was making headway in his investigation of the Yorkville Klan, courtesy of a number of informants, or "pukers," who provided a wealth of inside information. Community leaders in York had assured Merrill that the outrages would stop, but, as if to taunt him and his troops, the Klansmen continued their violence undeterred. Finally, in June, Merrill submitted his findings to General Terry, who was stunned not only by the depth and breadth of the report but also by the sheer number of Klan outrages documented therein. Merrill provided undeniable evidence of a wide violent conspiracy to deny freedmen their rights, and, when a Joint Select Subcommittee arrived in South Carolina in late June to conduct local hearings, members had his report in hand. Despite the mounting evidence against the Klan, subcommittee Democrats remained skeptical, even after a local constable, also a Democrat, pumped five bullets into a black musician who was entertaining subcommittee members. The victim, who survived the attack, was accused of obstructing the sidewalk and was shot while resisting arrest.[115]

By now, Major Merrill had become convinced that South Carolina's courts would not aggressively prosecute Klansmen. His biggest problem was that his orders were to assist civil authorities, not displace them; unless these authorities were willing to take the initiative, the Army had no recourse but to sit and watch in frustration. Still, Merrill hoped to spur authorities to action and, accordingly, sought to submit incriminating evidence about the Ku Klux Klan before the civil courts. When the fall session began in September, Merrill found his efforts subverted by the presiding judge, who was sympathetic to the Klan, and the Grand Jury, who turned Merrill's presentation into a 10-day farce by belittling his report and questioning his evidence. Only later did Merrill discover that as many as one-third of the Grand Jury members were Klansmen.[116] But while Merrill failed to motivate local authorities, his report certainly made a great impression on Attorney General Amos Akerman, who came to the same conclusions as did Merrill: as long as the military authorities operated at the behest of civil authorities in York County, the Klan would continue to dominate and violate laws. After further consultation with Merrill and Governor Robert K. Scott, Akerman decided the time had come for President Grant to invoke the authority of the Ku Klux Klan Act. On October 12, 1871, he issued a preliminary proclamation in which he ordered all persons involved in criminal activities in nine South Carolina counties to surrender all arms and disguises within five days. Instead, many Klansmen began to flee South Carolina, some going so far as to leave the country. Most, however, chose to ignore Grant's edict. Consequently, on October 17, at Akerman's recommendation, Grant took the ultimate step by suspending the writ of habeas corpus in the nine counties, thereby giving the military authorities the powers they needed to act. The impact on York County, where almost every adult white male was or knew a Klansman, was sudden and transformative. Beginning on October 19, federal troops began to comb the countryside, arresting hundreds of suspected Klansmen, while dozens more continued to flee. By the end of the month, 79 suspects had been detained, and, by the end of the following April, the number had risen to 533. Surprisingly, dozens more voluntarily surrendered. Yorkville, which had once been a bustling community, now had a vacant and lonely look to it.[117] Eventually, most of the defendants were released on bail to await trial.

The federal government's prosecution of South Carolina Klansmen commenced in the 4th Federal Circuit Court in Columbia, beginning with the November 1871 term. The bulging docket of cases would be heard by two federal judges: Hugh Lennox Bond, originally from Maryland, who, despite his Republican predilections, was known as a fair, impartial judge, and George Seabrook Bryan, a South Carolina native and Whig-turned-Democrat who frowned on Klan activities but demonstrated a clear pro-southern bias, nonetheless. The government's prosecution team consisted of U.S. Attorney for South Carolina David Corbin and South Carolina Attorney General Daniel Chamberlain, both from the north and, hence, carpetbaggers in the minds of white conservatives. They would be opposed by two former U.S. attorneys general who would represent all of the defendants: Henry Stanbery, an Ohio Democrat and critic of Radical Reconstruction and, the star of the proceedings, Reverdy Johnson, also a former Whig senator from Maryland, who earned his reputation by successfully representing the slaveholder in the landmark Dred Scott decision of 1857. Key to the prosecution's case was the make-up of the Grand Jury, and, because whites failed to respond to the jury summons, 15 of the 21 Grand Jurors were black. The opposing strategies were fairly straightforward. The prosecution sought to reverse a long-standing tradition whereby the federal government refused to adjudicate state violations of Constitutional rights. Essentially, Corbin and Chamberlain sought to apply the protections guaranteed under the Bill of Rights to state action via the 14th Amendment, arguing that state authority was superseded when the actions of defendants were tantamount to acting under the color of state law, a position, if upheld, that would significantly alter the nature of federalism in America. Their reading of the 14th Amendment was based in large measure on an Alabama case tried that May, *U.S. vs. Hall,* in which Circuit Court Judge William B. Woods ruled in favor of the broad nationalization of political and civil rights they sought. The defense, conversely, vehemently opposed any such broad interpretation of the 14th and 15th Amendments and the three Enforcement Acts.

The Federal government had so many cases to try and each individual case took so long to hear that by the end of the court term in January 1872, only four trials had been held over a six-week period, leading to a total of five convictions.

But because 49 defendants waived their right to a trial and pled guilty, 54 defendants were eventually sentenced for their crimes, which, during the first term, ranged from a minimum sentence of one month in prison and a $10 fine to a maximum sentence of five years and a $1,000 fine. There were still more than 400 defendants awaiting trial when the next court term began in April. By then, the determination of the Justice Department had begun to wane. Attorney General Amos Akerman had resigned the previous December and been replaced by George H. Williams, who was decidedly less enthusiastic than his predecessor about prosecuting southern resistance leaders. The reasons behind Akerman's resignation have never been fully explained, and there appears to be a difference of opinion regarding Williams's motivation, or lack thereof. J. Michael Martinez claimed that Williams, by backing off the Klan, was merely "in step with his times" by contributing to a "wholesale retreat from Reconstruction."[118] Lou Falkner Williams, however, suggested, as did Everette Swinney, that Williams was acting out of his sensitivity to public charges that he was guilty of excessive use of federal troops in the South. A rollback of Reconstruction notwithstanding, this need to assuage public opinion likely appeared to be the more direct reason for the diminished determination in the Department of Justice. Legal scholars had criticized Williams's appointment, finding him "wanting in those qualifications of intellect, experience and reputation which are indispensable to uphold the dignity of the National court," and the national press had recently uncovered scandals involving his private use of Justice Department funds.[119]

The arrests of Klan defendants from York County continued through the summer of 1872, but Williams obstructed subsequent convictions at nearly every opportunity, forcing Corbin and Chamberlain to change their prosecution tactics, negotiating as many plea agreements as they could. They also concentrated on egregious murder cases, seeking stiffer sentences than those meted out during the previous winter session. During the April term, another 18 cases were tried and a total of 96 cases were terminated, leaving more than 1,200 still remaining. The maximum sentence received was ten years in prison and a fine of $2,000. By then, as one observer put it, the much-ballyhooed South Carolina Ku Klux trials were coming to an anticlimactic end, "not with a bang, but with a whimper." In September, Williams began to consider a clemency request from Alexander Stephens, former vice-president of the Confederacy, leading to vehement protests from Major Merrill, who countered that "the causes from which Ku Kluxism sprung are still potent for evil."[120] Regardless, all arrests and prosecutions under the Enforcement Acts ended by early 1873. By Corbin's own account, the final prosecution scorecard read as follows: 1,355 indictments, 27 convictions, 75 guilty pleas, 5 acquittals, and 54 cases where the government was unwilling to prosecute.[121] The approximately 1,200 cases which were still pending were either discontinued or indefinitely postponed. National apathy had begun to set in and, as Martinez noted, people north and south wanted to move beyond Radical Reconstruction, even if it meant whitewashing the Klan's terrorist past. The collapse of the federal efforts to combat the Ku Klux Klan were sadly reflective of the government's vacillating policies toward the Invisible Empire, which had always been intimately connected to congressional Reconstruction. By 1873, however, even northerners had grown weary of divisive politics, and the Republican Party began to focus less on the plight of freedmen and more on issues related to industrial and corporate growth. When President U.S. Grant, at Williams's behest, began quietly to pardon certain convicted Klansmen in early 1873 and when, during that summer, he announced his willingness to extend clemency to all convicted Klansmen who applied, barely a whimper of protest was heard.

V.   From Resistance to Retreat

Although South Carolina was the primary focus of federal attempts to suppress Ku Klux Klan terrorism, a few other states were also witness to indictments based on the Enforcement Acts, though ensuing trials were rare. In North Carolina, where the very first federal trials actually began in June 1871, a total of 763 indictments were handed down, resulting only in 24 convictions, 23 guilty pleas, 13 acquittals, and nine dropped cases. Mississippi, which had earlier issued more than 200 indictments, eventually disposed of more than 300 cases, leading to 262 convictions in the northern section of the state alone; all defendants were given suspended sentences, even those indicted for murder.[122] Alabama indicted more than 150 suspected terrorists, but, because of a shortage of court personnel, no trials were ever held. In Florida, there was one conviction and one acquittal. Taken as a whole, the federal Ku Klux Klan trials left a legacy of mixed success. When one considers the sheer number of indictments versus the end number of convictions, the trials appear to have failed, a clear case of the government taking on far more than it was capable of handling. Grant's clemency policy would tend to support the perception that the trials were a tremendous waste of time, effort, and money. Yet, the federal crackdown had a salutary impact. The well-publicized trials cast a huge spotlight on Klan terrorism, causing many influential Democrats to distance themselves from the Invisible Empire. Many leading Klansmen were either now serving time or were still on the run as fugitives from justice. And although the Klan had already died out in states such as Virginia, Arkansas, Tennessee, Texas, and Louisiana, partly because Democratic control of their legislatures precluded the need for Klan activism, the trials and the attendant military response hastened the Klan's demise in the Carolinas and elsewhere by the end of 1871. In Alabama, a combination of public disapproval and mass indictments helped undermine the Klan, and in Kentucky federal prosecutions, limited as they were, contributed to diminishing Klan violence. Sporadic outrages committed by scattered Klansmen would continue until 1873, but, for all practical purposes, the Invisible Empire ceased to exist, though certainly other smaller and more isolated secret societies continued to night ride.

Surprisingly, new cases continued to be prosecuted by Washington under the Enforcement Acts, resulting in a number of convictions, but, by the end of 1875, most defendants had either served their sentences or received pardons.[123] The

Civil War was now ten years in the past, and Radical Reconstruction had run its course. Southern conservatives who had fought and lost the war won the peace, partly because of political intransigence and partly because Klan terrorism had helped preserve white supremacy and racial segregation in the South. The social revolution so eagerly sought by Radicals would have to wait another century, not due solely to the failed efforts of Congress or the White House. In the aftermath of the federal trials, the Supreme Court began to weigh in as well on the paramount issues of race and the Constitution. The Alabama case *U.S. vs. Hall* and the legal arguments offered by the government's various prosecution teams had cried out for Supreme Court interpretation of the 14th Amendment. In a series of landmark decisions beginning with the *Slaughterhouse* cases in 1873, the *Cruikshank* decision in 1876, and culminating in *Plessy vs. Ferguson* in 1890, the nation's highest court invalidated a broad construction of the 14th Amendment, ruling that it failed to nationalize the Bill of Rights. In essence, the 14th and 15th Amendments would protect blacks only from infringement of their civil rights by state officials, not by private parties; moreover, the failure of a state to protect its citizens could not be construed as justification for federal intervention. The *Cruikshank* ruling, which reversed the federal convictions of 300 Louisiana terrorists linked to a massacre of more than 100 freedmen, transformed most of the South into what one historian called "a free-fire zone for terrorists . . . "[124] The Court's interpretation of the 15th Amendment was slightly more amenable to federal intervention, but, as Lou Falkner Williams pointed out, the negative wording of the Amendment foreshadowed the eventual disenfranchisement of most black citizens.[125]

The Compromise of 1877 is generally acknowledged as the final act of Reconstruction, but the federal rollback had begun much earlier, and the Ku Klux Klan played no small part in Washington's retreat from the vision of black equality that the Civil War victory seemed to have promised. In his study of Reconstruction violence, George Rable contended that terrorism was a significant element in a conservative counterrevolution in the South that ultimately subverted the "revolutionary" agenda of northern Republicans. Yet, curiously, Rable also maintained that in the end the Ku Klux Klan played but a small part in this counterrevolution, having proven to be weak, disorganized, and ineffectual.[126] Clearly, the impact of Ku Klux Klan terrorism was staggering. Terrorists had established an unprecedented level of extralegal authority, dominating local politics in certain areas and establishing a shocking degree of social acceptance that even today is difficult to comprehend. The Klan might have failed to entice black voters to join the Democratic Party en masse, but it did contribute mightily to undermining the Republican Party in the South, murdering and intimidating party officials and scaring away potential voters. Employing similar tactics, Klansmen also helped break up southern chapters of the Union League. Night raiding robbed many freedmen of their arms, leaving them defenseless against attacks and contributing to the demise of the black militias. Klan outrages against schools and teachers delayed black education throughout the South. Attacks against black businessmen, farmers, and contracted laborers undermined their economic independence and further established black dependency on the financial good will of whites. The psychological repercussions from Klan terrorism on thousands of black and white victims were immeasurable. Klan terrorism subverted the electoral process, making it nearly impossible to conduct free and honest elections in many areas. In the end, the efficacy of Ku Klux Klan terrorism cannot be so simply dismissed, for it ultimately helped undermine Reconstruction's promise of an egalitarian society by violently perpetuating white supremacy in the South. Although a century and a half removed from the advanced military technology of today's world, replete with endless ways to injure the human body and mind, the Reconstruction Ku Klux Klan, despite its many later permutations, remains the most notorious, influential, and violent domestic terrorist group in American history.

Notes

1. Richard Maxwell Brown, *Strain of Violence—Historical Studies of American Violence and Vigilantism* (New York: Oxford University Press, 1975), 16–17.
2. M. D. Scalpel (Dr. Edward H. Dixon), *The Terrible Mysteries of the Ku Klux Klan* (no publisher listed, 1868).
3. Albion Tourgée, *The Invisible Empire* (1880, reprinted by Louisiana State University Press, Baton Rouge, 1989); Albion Tourgée, *A Fool's Errand by One of the Fools* (New York, 1879).
4. John Patterson Green, *Recollections of the Inhabitants, Localities, Superstitions, and Kuklux Outrages of the Carolinas* (no publisher listed, 1880), 135.
5. J. C. Lester and D. L. Wilson, *Ku Klux Klan—Its Origin, Growth and Disbandment* (1884, reprinted by Neale Publishing Company, New York, 1905), 72, 74.
6. Ibid., 107.
7. Ibid., 78.
8. Lester and Wilson, *Ku Klux Klan* (1905 reprint), 155.
9. Thomas Dixon, *The Clansman* (New York: Grosset & Dunlap, 1905).
10. S.E.F. Rose, *The Ku Klux Klan or Invisible Empire* (New Orleans: L. Graham Co., 1914), 17.
11. Rose, *The Ku Klux Klan;* Susan L. Davis, *Authentic History of the Ku Klux Klan, 1865–1877* (New York: American Library Service, 1924); Mr. and Mrs. W. B. Romine, *A Story of the Original Ku Klux Klan* (Pulaski, TN: Pulaski Citizen, 1934).
12. Stanley F. Horn, *Invisible Empire* (1939, reprinted by Gordon Press, New York, 1972).
13. Eric Foner, *Reviews in American History,* Vol. 10, No. 4 (December, 1982): 82–100.
14. William Peirce Randel, *The Ku Klux Klan* (New York: Chilton Books, 1965), 17.
15. David M. Chalmers, *American Historical Review,* Vol. 71, No. 2 (January, 1966): 702–704.
16. Everette Swinney, *Suppressing the Ku Klux Klan: The Enforcement of the Reconstruction Amendments, 1870–1877* (New York: Garland Publishing, Inc., 1987), 40.
17. Allen W. Trelease, *White Terror—The Ku Klux Klan Conspiracy and Southern Reconstruction* (Baton Rouge: Louisiana State University Press, 1971).
18. JSC, North Carolina, 160.
19. Trelease, *White Terror,* 184.

20. Wyn Craig Wade, *The Fiery Cross* (New York: Oxford University Press, 1987).
21. Lenwood G. Davis and Janet L. Sims-Wood, *The Ku Klux Klan—A Bibliography* (Westport, CT: Greenwood Press, 1984).
22. Lou Falkner Williams, *The Great South Carolina Ku Klux Klan Trials, 1871–1872* (Athens: University of Georgia Press, 1966); Jerry L. West, *The Reconstruction Ku Klux Klan in York County, South Carolina, 1865–1877* (Jefferson, NC: McFarland & Company, 2002); J. Michael Martinez, *Carpetbaggers, Calvary, and the Ku Klux Klan* (New York: Rowman & Littlefield Publishers, 2007).
23. Stephen Budiansky, *The Bloody Shirt—Terror After Appomattox* (New York: Viking, 2008).
24. Kwando Mbiassi Kinshasa, *Black Resistance to the Ku Klux Klan in the Wake of Civil War* (Jefferson, NC: McFarland & Company, 2006).
25. Tourgée, *Invisible Empire*, 37; Davis, *Authentic History*, 16–34.
26 Trelease, *White Terror*, 64.
27. JSC, Mississippi, 237, 1075.
28. Trelease, *White Terror*, 294.
29. KKK, 441.
30. Ibid., 7.
31. Scott Reynolds Nelson, *Iron Confederacies: Southern Railways, Klan Violence, and Reconstruction* (Chapel Hill: University of North Carolina Press, 1999).
32. KKK, 85. As the report argued, this would be accomplished by "each member providing himself with a pistol, a Ku-Klux gown, and signal instruments."
33. JSC, South Carolina, 387; JSC, Georgia, 75; KKK, 44–47. Stricken with rheumatism at the age of seven, Hill was crippled in both legs and arms and had to be fed and cared for by others.
34. HMD, 41st Congress, 2nd sess., no. 154, serial 1435, 161–162.
35. HMD, 41st Congress, 1st sess., no. 13, serial 1402, 36.
36. HMD, 40th Congress, 3rd sess., no. 23, serial 1385, 39.
37. Trelease, *White Terror*, 154.
38. KKK, 18.
39. HMD, 41st Congress, 2nd sess., no. 154, serial 1435, 542.
40. HMD, 41st Congress, 1st sess., no. 12, serial 1402, 14. The witness added that "there was a complete reign of terror existing in that parish . . . and most of the prominent Republicans were forced to leave the parish to save their lives, as in many instances, notices had been served upon them by the KKK to that effect."
41. Trelease, *White Terror*, 150.
42. HMD, 41st Congress, 2nd sess., no. 154, serial 1435, 153.
43. JSC, Florida, 268.
44. KKK, 69.
45. HMD, 41st Congress, 1st sess., no. 18, serial 1402, 54.
46. JSC, Alabama, 1431.
47. JSC, Florida, 261.
48. Kinshasa, *Black Resistance*, 88.
49. Lisa Cardyn, "Sexualized/Gendered Violence: Outraging the Body Politic in the Reconstruction South," *Michigan Law Review*, vol. 100 (February, 2000): 704.
50. Nelson, *Iron Confederacies*, 111.
51. Wade, *Fiery Cross*, 76.
52. Cardyn, "Sexualized/Gendered Violence," 727.
53. JSC, Georgia, 1120.

54. Cardyn, "Sexualized/Gendered Violence," 704.
55. Williams, *Ku Klux Klan Trials,* 36. Williams further maintained that white male authority was the "driving force behind the entire value system of Reconstruction South Carolina."
56. Cardyn, "Sexualized/Gendered Violence," 863.
57. Martha Hodes, "The Sexualization of Reconstruction Politics: White Women and Black Men in the South After the Civil War," *Journal of the History of Sexuality* (1993): 402–417.
58. JSC, Alabama, 675. The victim's attackers were later arrested, but jumped bail and reportedly fled to Arkansas.
59. Ibid., 1205.
60. JSC, Mississippi, 207; JSC, Georgia, 1098.
61. JSC, South Carolina, 999; Nelson, *Iron Conspiracies,* 126.
62. Budiansky, *The Bloody Shirt,* 8.
63. George C. Rable, *But There Was No Peace: The Role of Violence in the Politics of Reconstruction* (Athen: University of Georgia Press, 1984).
64. Budiansky, *The Bloody Shirt,* 7.
65. Kinshasa, *Black Resistance,* 29; Edward Magdol, *A Right to the Land: Essays On the Freedmen's Community* (Westport, CT: Greenwood Press, 1977), 136.
66. Williams, *Ku Klux Klan Trials,* 45.
67. KKK, 72.
68. JSC, Georgia, 209.
69. Ibid., 199.
70. Martinez, *Carpetbaggers, Cavalry,* 4.
71. JSC, Mississippi, 793.
72. Rable, *But There Was No Peace,* 74.
73. Ibid., 73.
74. HMD, 41st Congress, 1st sess., no. 13, serial 1402, 49. During the same hearing, a member of the Board of Supervisors of Registration in New Orleans spoke of "a feeling of terror existing in the minds of the Republicans in the ward."
75. JSC, Florida, 329.
76. Martinez, *Carpetbaggers, Calvary,* 146.
77. Trelease, *White Terror,* 120.
78. KKK, 21. Concerning collusion between the courts and Klan defendants accused of murdering blacks, Howard added that "in many cases of brutal murder brought before the civil authorities, verdicts of justifiable homicide in self-defense have been rendered."
79. Trelease, *White Terror,* 315.
80. KKK, 18.
81. Freedman's Bureau Report, August 8, 1866, Record Group 105, M999, roll 34, 00129, NA.
82. KKK, 20.
83. Ibid., 21.
84. HMD, 41st Congress, 2nd sess., No. 17, serial 1431, 18.
85. KKK, 31. The following notice was submitted to the Joint Select Committee as a typical example of the published renunciations:

Mr. Editor: I desire to make this public announcement of my withdrawal from all affiliation with the republican party, with which I have heretofore acted. I am prompted to take this step from conviction that the policy of said party, in encouraging fraud, bribery, and excessive taxation, is calculated to ruin the country; and that I did not vote at the last election, because I entertained my present opinion of the republicans, and have been so for the last twelve months.

86. JSC, South Carolina, 929.
87. Trelease, *White Terror,* 61–62.
88. Ibid., 60.
89. Green, *Recollections,* 155–163.
90. JSC, South Carolina, 1215.
91. John Hope Franklin, *From Slavery to Freedom,* 4th ed. (New York: Alfred A. Knopf, 1974), 185.
92. JSC, North Carolina, 86.
93. JSC, Mississippi, 823.
94. Kinshasa, *Black Resistance,* 21.
95. Ibid., 69.
96. Paul A. Gilje, *Rioting in America* (Bloomington: Indiana University Press, 1996), 95.
97. Kinshasa, *Black Resistance,* 77.
98. Joel Williamson, *After Slavery—The Negro in South Carolina During Reconstruction, 1861–1877* (Chapel Hill: University of North Carolina Press, 1965).
99. JSC, North Carolina, 253; Kinshasa, *Black Resistance,* 77; Green, *Recollections,* 67–70. According to testimony, the Lowrie (or Lowry) family dated back to the days of the American Revolution and during the Civil War, several relatives fighting for the Confederacy were captured, but managed to escape from a federal prison.
100. Melinda Meek Hennessey, "Racial Violence During Reconstruction: The 1876 Riots in Charleston and Cainhoy" (Paper, Southern Historical Association, 1983), quoted in Herbert Shapiro, *White Violence and Black Response* (Amherst: University of Massachusetts Press, 1988), 11–13.
101. Kinshasa, *Black Resistance,* 78.
102. Trelease, *White Terror,* 277–278.
103. Ibid., 225.
104. Ibid., 363
105. West, *Ku Klux Klan in York County,* 41.
106. KKK, 289–588. Regarding disguised criminals and their campaign of terror, the Minority Report argued that "we deny that these men have any general organization, or any political significance, or that their conduct is indorsed (sic) by any respectable number of the white people in any state . . . they furnish the men in power at Washington the only excuse left to make war upon them, and to continue the system of robbery and oppression which they have inaugurated."
107. Ibid., 292.
108. JSC, Mississippi, 655.
109. HMD, 41st Congress, 2nd sess., no. 154, serial 1435, 78.
110. JSC, Georgia, 623.
111. JSC, Mississippi, 560.
112. Ibid., 823.
113. JSC, Mississippi, 215–216.
114 KKK, 28.
115. Martinez, *Carpetbaggers, Calvary,* 142.

116. Ibid., 146.
117. Ibid., 150.
118. Ibid., 200.
119. Williams, *Ku Klux Klan Trials,* 124.
120. Martinez, *Carpetbaggers, Calvary,* 198.
121. West, *Ku Klux Klan in York County,* 116.
122. Trelease, *White Terror,* 408.
123. Ibid., 417.
124. Michael Newton, *The Invisible Empire: The Ku Klux Klan in Florida* (Gainesville: University Press of Florida, 2001), 26.
125. Williams, *Ku Klux Klan Trials,* 141.
126. Rable, *But There was No Peace,* 110–111.

9

THE MOLLY MAGUIRES

I. Background

No episode of American terrorism has generated as much mystery as the violence that plagued the Pennsylvania coal fields during the middle decades of the 19th century. Most of the violence, in particular the murder of 16 persons between 1862 and 1875, was attributed to the Molly Maguires, a secret society of Irish miners with loose ties to the Irish fraternal association called the Ancient Order of Hibernians. The Molly Maguires, it was said, could trace their terrorist roots back to Ireland, where a long legacy of violence between landlords and peasants had been established. In America, the Molly Maguires found a different adversary, in the form of abusive capitalists who controlled the coal and railway industries in eastern Pennsylvania. Through murder and industrial sabotage, the Mollies created an image that to this very day presents problems in separating myth from reality. What is undisputable is that the rash of violence, directed mostly against mine officials, led to the assignment of an undercover Pinkerton agent who successfully infiltrated the Mollies and helped bring them down after a series of high-profile trials. In the end, 20 persons were found guilty of murder and subsequently executed. Virtually all other details surrounding the Molly Maguires are shrouded in contention and controversy. Count historians among those who cannot reach a consensus about who the Mollies were, what they were all about, and if they even existed at all. The primary problem is that the Mollies left behind no indisputable evidence of their existence. Aside from notorious coffin notices, the Mollies produced no other documentation that attempted to justify their alleged atrocities or delineate their goals and objectives. Consequently, as Kevin Kenny noted in his exhaustive study of the Mollies, because most of the contemporary accounts tended to be hostile and biased, "historians can never know for certain who and what the Molly Maguires were."[1]

Despite these drawbacks, or perhaps because of them, the Molly Maguires constitute an interesting study in the evolution of American terrorism. For their legacy, however cloudy it might be, cannot be understood apart from a reading of several historical, political, and social forces that converged in the heart of Pennsylvania coal country in the mid-19th century. A historiographical introduction reveals the complex layers involved in attempting to make sense of the Mollies. Contemporaneous accounts helped create the standard portrayal of the Molly Maguires as evil, bloodthirsty terrorists who were brought to justice through the heroic efforts of Franklin Gowen, the president of the Philadelphia and Reading Coal Company, and James McParlan, the Pinkerton agent who risked his life to infiltrate the Mollies. These early accounts were first provided by newspapers, in particular, the *Miners' Journal* and the *Shenandoah Herald,* both unabashedly hostile toward the Mollies. Regardless, anyone still wishing to research the Mollies is necessarily drawn to their pages.

The first two book-length treatments of the Molly Maguire episode were both published in the immediate aftermath of the trials in 1877 and were written by none other than Allan Pinkerton, founder and owner of the renowned detective agency that helped crack the case, and Francis Dewees, an attorney for the Philadelphia and Reading Coal and Iron Company. Both books relied extensively on McParlan's court testimony and predictably demonized the Mollies. Although Pinkerton claimed that his book "strictly follows the truth" in a "constant endeavor to adhere closely to facts," his account was more semi-fictional than factual and concerned itself almost exclusively with romanticizing McParlan's undercover exploits.[2] In Pinkerton's mind, the Molly Maguires not only were responsible for virtually all acts of violence in the eastern Pennsylvania coal fields, but also manipulated state politics and were active everywhere from Maine to Georgia. And although Dewees claimed to have treated the Mollies "without prejudice and without bias," he also acknowledged that the "effort may not have been successful."[3] It wasn't. Dewees did a slightly more credible job than did Pinkerton, noting the historical connection between the Mollies in America and the earlier version in Ireland and thereby touching on the broader transatlantic issues of ethnicity and religion. In the end, however, both Pinkerton and Dewees maintained similar degrees of moral indignation toward the Mollies. This basic storyline was upheld by other contemporaneous accounts, including Edward Winslow Martin's *History of the Great Riots and of the Molly Maguires,* published in 1877, and the 1881 *History of Schuylkill County,* which referred to the Mollies as a "malignant social cancer" guilty of creating a "reign of terror" in Pennsylvania's coal country.[4] Only an account written by E. H. Heywood and published by the pro-labor Co-Operative Publishing Company in 1878 dared defend the Mollies, describing them as "labor reformers" who were martyred on the "gallows of capitalism."[5]

As Kevin Kenny noted in his study of the Molly Maguires, the 1930s would witness a revisionism of sorts, largely inspired by Depression-era politics. Leftist-leaning historians, sympathetic to organized labor, were more willing to consider the Mollies within a broader context of violence between workers and capital, a long-standing confrontation fraught with timely implications. Published in 1943, Anthony Bimba's *The Molly Maguires* was a sympathetic portrayal of the Pennsylvania coal miners, who had been reduced to "feudal bondage" by a collusion of the mine owners, headed by the powerful Pennsylvania and Reading Coal and Iron Company, an arm of the Pennsylvania and Reading Railroad. But Bimba didn't stop there. He further maintained that the Mollies, as a group, did not actually exist, that they were but a fiction maintained by the mine owners to deflect attention away from their own brand of corporate terrorism. Individual and isolated acts of terrorism that may have been conducted by Irish renegades were but a natural response to the sustained terrorism conducted against the Irish mine workers by a combination of Pinkerton agents, Coal and Iron Police forces, and various corporate provocateurs. Even the trials were terroristic, in that the Coal and Iron Police were said to have intimidated witnesses. Random murders attributed to the Molly Maguires were but symptoms of a wider class war to avenge what Bimba called "ruling class murder."[6] Four years later, J. Walter Coleman's *The Molly Maguire Riots* reinforced many of Bimba's themes. According to Coleman, not only were the Mollies a capitalist fabrication, but also the coal country violence was actually the work of several different gangs working the coal mines. The one true villain in Coleman's melodrama was James McParlan, the agent provocateur who, while undercover with the Mollies, used his position to save property from destruction but not to warn persons whom he knew were murder targets. If the Mollies were as bloodthirsty as most have claimed, Coleman asked, how was it that McParlan managed to survive? Although Coleman suggested that the Mollies should be considered within the context of a class and racial struggle, he never really elaborated on the race issues.[7]

These issues related to race were largely ignored until the publication of Wayne Broehl, Jr.'s *The Molly Maguires* in 1964. Although Kenny wrote that Broehl's work was regressive and guilty of "epistemological naiveté," it did elaborate on the early Irish roots of the Molly Maguires, placed the anti-Molly movement within the wider context of anti-Irish nativism, and described the ambivalence of the Catholic Church toward Irish-instigated terrorism.[8] In general, the sympathetic tone toward the Mollies would continue throughout the 1960s and 1970s. Charles A. McCarthy's *The Great Molly Maguire Hoax* (1969) referred to Franklin Gowen as a "disciple of the devil," and Sidney Lens, in *The Labor Wars* (1973), claimed that the Molly Maguires were no more real than "fairies or hobgoblins."[9] Harold W. Aurand's *From the Molly Maguires to the United Mine Workers* (1971) provided a slightly more neutral account of the Mollies, but lamented that Gowen and the mine owners were able to besmirch labor with the stigma of terrorism.[10] Adding a cinematic perspective to the discussion was the 1970 film *The Molly Maguires,* directed by Martin Ritt and starring Richard Harris as McParlan and Sean Connery as John Kehoe, the alleged ringleader of the Mollies. Sadly, the film reduced the entire Molly episode to a confrontation between two Irishmen, Kehoe and

McParlan, thereby excluding virtually all of the other complexities involved in the real story. While offering a grim portrayal of life deep in the coal mines, the film assumed a tone of moral ambiguity when it came to the antagonists, refusing to brand either as good or evil. Perhaps the film's indecisiveness contributed to its failures. Panned by the critics, it returned less than $2 million at the box office—a far cry from the $11 million in production costs.[11]

This is where the Molly Maguire literature stood for the next 25 years. Thus, by the late 1990s, all that existed were but a few older books with divergent interpretations, none of which were based on objective research methodologies capable of passing the rigorous standards of modern academia. Then, in 1998, came Kevin Kenny's extensive scholarly work, appropriately entitled *Making Sense of the Molly Maguires*. Without doubt the most comprehensive and widely researched work on the Molly Maguires, it leaves little more to be said about the infamous renegades. Renegades they were, for Kenny maintained that, while the Mollies might not have constituted the vast and ominous conspiracy portrayed by contemporaries, "as a pattern of violence by certain Irishmen under certain circumstances, they certainly did exist."[12] Kenny did well to "make sense" of the many mysteries surrounding the Mollies. There was indeed some overlap in membership between the Mollies and the Ancient Order of Hibernians (AOH) as well as the Workingmen's Benevolent Association (WBA), but participation in these associations was distinct and separate. And although Kenny described in great detail the origins of the American Mollies, which were rooted in the early Whiteboy, Ribbonmen, and Molly Maguire movements in Ireland, he maintained that no pre-existing Irish Mollies were exported to the United States. The Mollies in America evolved from a meeting of two worlds: a distinctive Irish culture seeped in the tradition of resistance to social injustice, mixed with a distinctive working class culture of the eastern Pennsylvania anthracite region. Kenny also took McParlan to task for allowing murders to proceed without warning and emphasized the incompetence of the Molly defense team. The judicial irregularities and suspect testimony that marked the trials were seemingly insignificant, for their legality was not an issue. Public passions had been stirred to the point where someone needed to be punished in order to save society. Consequently, the trials and subsequent hangings served an ideological purpose, transcending the original acts of violence, which may or may not have been committed by those executed.

Although a few specialized monographs have since appeared by Molly Maguire "enthusiasts," given the exhaustiveness of Kenny's study, all that seemingly remains regarding the Molly Maguires is to consider the historical impact of their terrorist ways.[13] For, make no mistake, regardless of the many uncertainties surrounding the Mollies, contemporaries were very clear about the atmosphere created by the violence attributed to them. The *Miners' Journal* reported that the Molly Maguires "dominated and terrorized the entire coal regions."[14] The *Philadelphia Ledger* argued that the primary purpose of the Mollies "was terroristic and revenge . . . accompanied by brutal beatings, incendiary forces, and assassination."[15] Samuel T.

Wiley's study of Schuylkill County declared that the Mollies "held the anthra-cite coal regions in a state of terror for many years."[16] Even the *Catholic Standard* described the Molly Maguires as "a society rendered infamous by its treachery and deeds of blood—the terror of every neighborhood in which it existed."[17] These types of characterizations can be found throughout the literature, thereby suggesting that the atmosphere of terrorism associated with the Molly Maguires deserves a closer analysis.

II. Irish Origins

As many have noted, Molly Maguire terrorism can best be understood as part of a long legacy of agrarian violence that plagued Ireland for generations. Irish ban-ditry can be traced back to the early 1700s, when defiant peasants began a violent campaign against English conquest and consolidation of power. Between 1711 and 1713, a band of Irish bandits, said to be organized under distinctive leader-ship, began to slaughter hundreds of cattle and sheep. Dressed in white shirts with white linen bands around their heads, they disappeared and were never heard from again. These events were but a precursor of what was to follow 50 years later: two major phases of peasant disturbances stretching over nearly 100 years. These disturbances originated in the most impoverished areas of north-central Ireland, lands stricken with famine and economic dislocation. As Michael Beames pointed out in his study *Peasants and Power,* the first phase lasted from about 1760 to 1800 and witnessed the appearance of the Whiteboy movement.[18] Emerging during the winter of 1761, the Whiteboys, so called because of their distinctive garb, rose in opposition to landowners who had increased rents and enclosed grazing lands thought to be commonly held. Many of these landowners were British, but some were Irish as well. By the end of the 18th century, several other Irish peasant movements had surfaced: fellow Catholic groups such as the Right Boys and the Defenders, Protestant groups such as the Peep O'Day Boys and the Orangeboys, and Presbyterian groups such as the Hearts of Oak and the Hearts of Steel. These Irish bandits did not seek revolution or destruction of the existing system. Their motivation was fairly simple: to defend the interests of the agrarian peasant class against the all-pervasive power of landed capital. As Kenny noted, the chief source of conflict was not Irish nationalism, but rather the occupation and control of land, and therefore such resistance needs to be considered in local, not national, terms.[19] The Whiteboys and others demon-strated little restraint when it came to their particular brand of violence. They tore down fences and destroyed property; they drove off or mutilated livestock. And they intimidated, abused, or killed those perceived as enemies: informers in their midst, agents of the landowners, or supplanters of evicted tenants. For many of these young and defiant men, conspiracies, drinking, storytelling, and fighting constituted the very fabric of their existence, a response to mounting frustrations with life's injustices.

By 1800, only the Whiteboy movement had survived, and Irish agrarian banditry began to assume new shapes and forms, beginning with movements such as the Threshers (1806–1807), the Terry Alts (1831–1847), the Ribbonmen (1819–1820), and, ultimately, the Molly Maguires (1844–1847). These groups, which collectively represented what Michael Beames called the second phase of agrarian disturbances, had similar characteristics. Their memberships were secret, they administered oaths establishing bonds of solidarity, and they created separate cells in order to shield one another from charges of complicity in criminal activity. They also agreed to travel outside their home territories to conduct acts of terror for one another, a system of reciprocity that protected local bandits from being recognized. The Whiteboys, perhaps numbering in the thousands, continued to destroy property, mutilate livestock, and murder opponents, and also broadened the scope of their transgressions to include arson, robbery, and burglary. They also earned a reputation for cropping off ears, cutting out tongues, and severing fingers and arms.[20] The Whiteboys were also notorious for distributing coffin notices that often explained political objectives, claimed the legality of their actions, or threatened recipients with injury or death, usually symbolized through drawings of coffins, guns, and skeletons. The larger motivating force behind the Whiteboys, as well as other resistance movements, was what some scholars call "retributive justice."[21] Terrorist tactics were meant to not only manipulate public behavior, but also to punish those deemed guilty of crimes against the people.

In his study of the pre-famine Irish underground, Tom Gavin noted an institutional lineage that extended from the Defenders to the Ribbonmen and finally to the Molly Maguires, the last of the agrarian renegades to terrorize Ireland during the first half of the 19th century.[22] The Mollies, who first appeared in 1843 in the areas surrounding south Ulster and east Connaught, also assaulted agents of the landowners, as well as animals and livestock. In grazing areas, they concealed needles, which were then swallowed and consumed by cattle. They mutilated horses and dogs, but avoided attacks on pigs, an essential mainstay of the peasant economy. The Mollies, who were Catholic, also maintained many of the traits established by earlier resistance movements, including the cultural association with mythical women. It is not known whether or not there was an actual Molly Maguire, but various speculations, all rooted in Irish folklore, abound. Some say that Molly was a poor and feeble widow in County Atrim who was abused and then evicted from her home by her landlord's agent in 1839. Others claim that Molly used her home as a meeting place where she and others plotted nefarious deeds. Some maintain that she was a huge, ferocious woman, who strapped pistols to her thighs and led men dressed in women's clothing on nighttime raids against landlord agents and government officials. Whether Molly actually existed is less pertinent than this common 19th-century Irish allegiance to mythical women. The men who conducted violent acts on behalf of the Mollies and other resistance movements were known to disguise themselves as women and blacken their faces. In his history of Ireland, W.E.H. Lecky argued that this custom began as early as the 1660s, when a secret militia in Kerry dressed in women's clothing, blackened their faces with burnt cork, and attacked its enemies with hazel sticks.[23] By the 1830s, resistance groups such as the Lady Rocks and the Lady Clares wore bonnets with veils. As both Kevin Kenny and James Donnelly, Jr., have observed, the use of women's clothing served a purpose beyond disguise; it also endowed the agrarian bandit with legitimacy, investing him with the character of a higher authority as a "daughter" of Molly Maguire.[24] When, in 1848, ominous coffin notices, many of which were signed "One of Mollie's Children," began to appear in the eastern Pennsylvania coal regions, many among the recently arrived Irish immigrants well understood their meaning.

III. The Molly Maguires in America

If the Molly Maguires in America can best be understood as a fusion of two worlds, then the life of Irish coal miners in eastern Pennsylvania requires particular consideration. Their collective story entails sociological, economic, and political issues very much reflective of America's Gilded Age: the immigrant experience in the face of intense nativism, the growing power of industrial capital, and the exploitation and attendant militarization of workers. These were the forces that, combined with the customs of Irish banditry, would shape the lives of those who came to be known and feared as the Molly Maguires.

It was the deadly Irish potato famines of the mid-1840s that multiplied the number of those leaving the Emerald Island and heading for the United States. During the last eight months of 1847, nearly 53,000 Irish immigrants arrived in New York City alone. During the same period, about 18,000 made their way to Boston.[25] Concentrating in the northeastern states, many found jobs as industrial workers or miners. These Irish immigrants also discovered something else upon arrival in America: hostile anti-Catholicism, an irrational response caused partly by what was then only the beginning of an eventual flood of Catholic immigrants from parts of southern and eastern Europe. In the 1850s, this anti-Catholicism blended with a general assault on foreigners, contributing to the formation of the Know-Nothings, a nativist order that began with secret membership but abandoned its protective cover in order to campaign openly during public elections. It was also during the 1850s that rumors began to circulate in eastern Pennsylvania of a secret order of Irish workers known as the "Buckshots" or "Black Spots." In 1857, Benjamin Bannan, editor of the *Miners' Journal,* first linked the Molly Maguires to election fraud during the preceding year.[26] Bannan, a staunch supporter of the Republican Party, and the *Journal* would continue their sensationalized reporting of the Mollies for the next 20 years. The Molly Maguires were also said to be responsible for disturbances around the coal fields of Cass Township in 1862, a form of collective protest against conscription into the Union Army. Hostilities toward the Irish increased following the draft riots in New York City in 1863, when thousands of Irishmen took to the streets to protest conscription. Those four sad days of rioting obscured the fact that only two weeks prior, Irish troops had fought courageously on behalf of the Union cause at Gettysburg. Unfortunately, Irish immigrants, based upon their faith and birthplace, would find themselves largely excluded from America's social mainstream throughout the post–Civil war era.

Aside from the upswing in immigration, Gilded Age America also witnessed the explosive growth of industry, a phenomenon that transformed not only the economy but also social relationships as well, in particular, those between capital and labor. The problems associated with corporate power and labor violence, as well as with nativism and anti–Catholicism, would play themselves out deep in Pennsylvania's anthracite regions. There, without question, economic life was dominated by the mighty Philadelphia and Reading Railroad, which controlled the transportation of coal and later, through its subsidiary the Philadelphia and Reading Coal and Iron Company, stockpiled ownership of more than 65,000 acres of coal fields.[27] Franklin Gowen, who began his career as the district attorney in Pottsville, joined the P & R Railroad (commonly known as the Reading Railroad) as legal counsel in 1867 and eventually became president of both firms in 1871. Early accounts of the Molly Maguires portrayed Gowen as a visionary, the type of enterprising capitalist who helped build modern America. Revisionists saw him as the prototypical robber baron, who built a corrupt empire on the exploitation of workers and manipulation of the political system. The truth, as is commonly said, probably lies somewhere in between. What is certain is that Gowen devoted much of his time and many of his resources to battle and suppress the Workingmen's Benevolent Association (WBA), the trade union that represented mine workers of different ethnic and craft backgrounds.

Although the first labor disturbances in the coal region occurred in 1842, the first attempt to organize miners didn't occur until 1849, when John Bates organized a union, called a strike, and then absconded with the union treasury.[28] The WBA was formed in 1868 as a benevolent association in order to circumvent laws that made labor combinations illegal. During its early years, the WBA's dominant voice was that of its president, John Siney, and, although he would personally favor non-violent strategies of negotiation and compromise, he would constantly battle forces within the union calling for more violent and subversive tactics. Workers' pay cuts in face of rising freight and coal costs eventually led to a series of labor disputes, culminating in the WBA's "Long Strike" of 1875, which lasted six months and precipitated new rounds of violence. The strike, which exacerbated the impoverished condition of the miners, was but another hardship necessarily endured, compounding the adversities of life. Tensions already existed between the Irish, who held the lowest paying jobs, and the English, Welsh, and Scots, who held the higher-paying miner and supervisory positions, thereby restoring adversarial relationships that had existed in pre-famine Ireland. Life in the mines was dirty and dangerous: between 1869 and 1950, more than 35,000 men lost their lives while working the anthracite fields of eastern Pennsylvania.[29] Miners usually worked 12 hours a day, six days a week, for about $50 to $60 a month in wages. Company stores, which miners were required to patronize, sold goods at inflated prices. The miners who scratched out a living under these trying circumstances usually lived together in small settlements called "patches," which were hastily built near the coal breakers.

Adding to the confrontation between labor and capital was the formation of the Reading Railroad's Coal and Iron Police, established through a series of laws passed by the state legislature in the mid-1860s which not only created additional public police forces for the anthracite regions but permitted privately owned railroads to hire their own law enforcement agents. The Coal and Iron Police, though privately employed, were granted broad and unusual powers to uphold public law and order, creating either a very efficient security force or an army of thugs, depending on one's viewpoint. Detractors note that many of the Coal and Iron Police had criminal records and no compunction about employing strong-arm tactics to coerce strikers. Contributing to this volatile environment were ethnic gangs, who often found themselves at war with one another. Rival groups such as the "Modocs," an alliance of Welsh and German Protestants, and the "Sheet Iron Gang," a ring of skilled miners from Kilkenny, clashed throughout the 1870s, often engaging in drunken melees.[30] Though Irish, the Sheet Iron Gang, also known as the "Iron Clads" or the "Chain Gang," found itself at odds with the other major Irish gang said to stalk the Pennsylvania coal country: the infamous Molly Maguires.

Although faint traces of Molly Maguire activity had been reported prior to the 1860s, it wasn't until the Civil War that the Mollies were first blamed for instigating a "reign of terror" throughout the areas surrounding Schuylkill County. Despite the fact that no proof had yet surfaced to confirm their existence, by the end of the Civil War, the Mollies stood accused of complicity in virtually every major social disturbance in the Schuylkill area, including a series of riots in Cass Township to protest wages and the passage of the Militia Act of 1862. The Act, a piece of federal legislation authorizing state conscription, eventually led to the appointment of Schuylkill County's draft commissioner: none other than Benjamin Bannan, editor of the *Miners' Journal*. Bannan and the *Journal* insisted that the Molly Maguires, the infamous bandits who had terrorized pre-famine Ireland, had indeed resurfaced in America and were now largely responsible for the crime wave sweeping the entire coal region of eastern Pennsylvania. And what a crime wave it was: assault, arson, industrial sabotage, and murder. The *Miners' Journal* documented more than 50 murders between the years of 1863 and 1868 alone.[31] Of those 50, six would eventually be attributed to the Mollies, apparently a by-product of either Civil War issues or downright robbery. But all six victims also had connections to the coal mines. On June 14, 1862, F. W. Langdon, a mine foreman, was beaten and stoned to death by a crowd following a public altercation with a group of Irish miners that included John Kehoe. Kehoe, who would later become publicly known as the "King" of the Molly Maguires, worked in

Langdon's mine and had made previous threats against him. Although Langdon's death was not then directly tied to the Mollies, questionable court testimony 15 years later would link Kehoe to this crime and result in his execution. On November 5, 1863, George Smith, a mine owner, was killed when a gang of men with blackened faces stormed into his home and shot him to death in front of his family. George Ulrich, one of Smith's employees, was on the scene and managed to return fire; when news circulated that a Molly Maguire funeral had been held shortly thereafter, it was widely assumed that Ulrich had exacted some measure of retaliation for Smith's death. The reasons for Smith's assassination are complex. He and at least three other local victims were shot on "Guy Fawke's Night," the traditional night of ritualistic displays of anti-Catholicism in both England and America, a stark reminder of the ethnic hostilities that still existed in America between the Irish and English. Moreover, Smith stood accused of two further transgressions: he had recently fired a number of Irish miners and submitted to the government the names of miners who had not yet registered for the draft. Other accounts suggest that Smith's killing might have been an attempt to halt the production of coal, another act of industrial sabotage meant to undermine the Union war effort.[32]

The murders of Langdon and Smith, together with the next four murders attributed to the Molly Maguires, define a first phase of Molly terrorism (1862–1868) in America, which was largely motivated by robbery or conscription issues, and involved victims who worked for the mines in some authoritative capacity. Both David Muir, who was assassinated on August 25, 1865, and Henry Dunne, who was similarly killed on January 10, 1866, had been mine superintendents in Cass Township during the conscription disturbances. Muir was killed in broad daylight during his morning walk to the mines. Two or three men were seen fleeing the scene, only to escape into the woods. Dunne was riding in his carriage during the early evening when he was attacked on the road from Pottsville to Minersville. He was shot four times, dragged from his carriage, and shot again in the face. His assailants, about five in number, laughed loudly as they casually walked away down the main road.[33] No one was ever arrested for the Muir and Dunne murders, and it remains unclear why they were killed. William Littlehales, who was shot to death on March 15, 1867, and Alexander Rea, who was killed on October 17, 1868, however, were victims of highway robbery, a common Molly Maguire misdeed. Both were mine superintendents, and both were shot while in possession of payroll monies. No arrest was ever made in the Littlehales murder, but three Mollies would eventually march to the gallows for killing Rea, another outcome of testimony that emerged during the Molly Maguire trials of 1877. During these trials, Daniel Kelly, a.k.a. Manus Cull or "Kelly the Bum," would confess to killing Rea, but manage to evade prosecution by turning state's evidence, which ultimately resulted in the execution of Patrick Hester, Peter McHugh, and Patrick Tully.[34] A brief lull in criminal activity followed for a short period, partly owing to the pacification efforts of the newly created Coal and

Iron Police. The emergence of the WBA also contributed to this general quietude, which would, unfortunately, be followed by a second, more lethal round of Molly terrorism. But in the meantime, the legend of the Molly Maguires continued to grow, the beneficiary of community gossip and continued reporting from the *Miners' Journal* and other periodicals emanating from Pennsylvania's coal country. People began to ask questions. Who were these men known as the Molly Maguires? Whence did they come? What did they want? Then and now, these questions are not easily answered. There was, however, no shortage of those who believed they knew the answers.

IV. The Molly Maguires: Legend and Reality

In its first story about the Molly Maguires, the *Miners' Journal* reported that the Mollies, "a new and exclusively Irish Catholic secret organization," had originated in Boston as a political response to "Know-Nothingism." According to the *Journal,* the Mollies were also connected to the Locofocos, the labor wing of the Democratic Party.[35] This was a negative association, for the Locofocos had been implicated in the "flour riots" of 1837, when, in the midst of a severe depression, angry mobs stormed and attacked flour dealers. In the end, the *Journal* described the Mollies as a secret band of assassins, "which dealt in death as merchants deal in goods."[36] Edward Winslow Martin claimed that the Mollies had been imported from Ireland to safeguard the miners but had instigated instead "a constant state of terror."[37] He further charged that, within the coal region of Pennsylvania, the Mollies constituted the driving force behind the Ancient Order of Hibernians (AOH), the Irish fraternal organization that first appeared in America in the late 1830s. This allegation was nothing new. Since the 1850s, many had assumed that the AOH and the Molly Maguires were one and the same. It certainly did not help that Catholic clergymen in Schuylkill County reinforced this contention. Father Daniel McDermott of Philadelphia, an outspoken critic of the Molly Maguires, condemned all societies, including the AOH, asserting that it "sympathized with and aided murders."[38] After spending two and a half years infiltrating the Molly Maguire underground, James McParlan continued to make this assertion. Consequently, contemporaries knew of the Molly Maguires only in vague and hostile terms: as transplanted Irish terrorists, who, after assuming identities such as the AOH or WBA, continued to plot death and destruction in America—either for politics, revenge, or money.

Kevin Kenny has provided the only in-depth sociological analysis of those Irishmen in America who came to be known as the Molly Maguires. Tracing the family roots of known Mollies, as well as those of their associates, Kenny noted that the vast majority had emigrated from nine counties in north-central and north-western Ireland: Monaghan, Caven, Fermanagh, Longford, Leitrim, Roscommon, Sligo, Mayo, and Donegal. The nucleus of the Molly Maguire leadership had come from the Irish-speaking population of County Donegal. The designation

"Irish-speakers" is especially noteworthy because, as Kenny pointed out, significant numbers of Irish immigrants in Pennsylvania came from a preliterate Gaelic culture, which distinguished them from the non-Irish speakers of eastern and southern Ireland. Consequently, because of their distinctive language, culture, and customs, the Irish-speaking Mollies of America "were the archetypical 'wild Irish,' noticeably and ominously different from the mass of Irish immigrants."[39]

As for charges that the Molly Maguires and the AOH were indistinguishable, there certainly was some overlapping membership, but peaceful members of the AOH tried desperately to disassociate themselves from the Mollies. When the *Pilot,* an Irish-American newspaper, accused the AOH of "Molly Maguireism," angry protest letters from the AOH appeared immediately. Readers were reminded that the AOH stood for "friendship, unity, and true Christian charity" and that "if any member of the Order be convicted of robbery, perjury, or any other atrocious offense, he shall be excluded from the Order for life."[40] Yet, the allegations would persist for reasons easily understood. Firstly, the AOH was also an Irish secret society, one that been involved in New York City riots during the early 1870s that resulted in 68 deaths and hundreds of injuries. Secondly, the AOH lodges in the Schuylkill area were dominated by men from County Donegal who were very familiar with the legacy and strategies of political violence. While the AOH in general did not participate in or condone violence, in all probability certain Mollies did use AOH lodge facilities to plot their nefarious activities. And the AOH did provide an organizational structure that helped define the Molly Maguire hierarchy. AOH chapters were referred to as divisions, and each had an elected leader called a bodymaster, as well as a secretary and treasurer. During the Molly Maguire trials of 1876–1877, Jimmy Kerrigan, a former Molly turned informer, would testify that the Molly leadership came from a core of AOH bodymasters. Of the 16 Mollies eventually sentenced to death, five were bodymasters, one was a division treasurer, one a division secretary, and five others had affiliations with the AOH.[41] In one of the few existing primary sources attributed to a Molly Maguire, in a letter to the *Shenandoah Herald,* John Kehoe denied any connection between the Mollies and the AOH.[42] Only in the late 1870s, after the trials and subsequent executions, was the AOH able to distance itself from the Molly Maguires. Even then, it took a new AOH constitution and an organizational overhaul to purge the fraternal society of this disreputable association.

Charges that the Workingmen's Benevolent Association was similarly implicated in Molly Maguire activity were even more tenuous, despite the fact that the miners' union certainly included Mollies among its members. The WBA leadership never wavered in its condemnation of Molly Maguire violence, but was constantly undermined by public association of the Mollies with trade unionism, tarring all unionists as if they somehow represented a monolithic movement. Franklin Gowen and Benjamin Brannan were particularly forceful in their insistence that the concurrent leadership of the WBA and the Molly Maguires was responsible for "terrorism and tyranny," prompting John Siney, president of the

WBA, to complain that his union had been unfairly "stigmatized as a band of assassins."[43] In reality, the WBA was an ethnically diverse union, which counted among its membership not only the Irish but also significant numbers of English, Welsh, German, Dutch, and native-born American miners. And while the Mollies, without question, evolved in response to labor issues associated with the Pennsylvania anthracite region, their concept of trade unionism varied significantly from that of the WBA leadership, which was dominated early on by the English and, to a lesser extent, the Welsh.[44] The WBA preferred labor strategies based on negotiation and compromise; the Mollies relied on terror.

In a discussion regarding the infamous Molly Maguires, historian Kenneth Jackson acknowledged that, given the long-standing historiographical controversies surrounding the Mollies, "some see them as brutal terrorists and others as martyred heroes."[45] Though seemingly on the mark, his assertion is more complicated once the tactics of the Mollies are more closely scrutinized. A long list of Molly Maguire transgressions reveals two distinct categories: industrial sabotage and murder. Acts of industrial sabotage were directed primarily against railroads and coal companies, in particular, the Philadelphia and Reading. In testimony before the Pennsylvania state legislature, Franklin Gowen listed 88 alleged incidents of industrial sabotage in the Schuylkill and Shamokin regions during the first six months of 1875 alone.[46] Little wonder that Gowen made eradicating the Molly Maguires his life's crusade. Early reports of the Mollies centered on their attempts to wreak havoc on the railway lines leading in and out of the coal region. The Mollies were accused of destroying bridges, misplacing rail switches, plundering warehouses, assaulting watchmen, and obstructing tracks, often by moving sidetracked cars back onto the main lines. A disaster near Mahanoy City was narrowly averted in 1875 when a passenger train was nearly derailed. In a clandestine report to Allan Pinkerton, James McParlan fingered John Gibbons, Mike Murphy, John Thompson, "and a man named Doyle"—all known Mollies—as those responsible for the near calamity. According to the undercover agent, Gibbons let a sidetracked car loaded with iron onto the main line in hopes of causing a collision with a carload of passengers scheduled to pass through that night. Luckily, railroad officials spotted the iron car and were able to telegraph a warning to Mahanoy City before the passenger train departed.[47] The Mollies were further accused of setting fires in coal mine shafts and inciting labor riots among the miners. When a fire broke out in the Steuben Shaft near Avondale in 1869 and 110 miners died of suffocation, the coal miners accused the Molly Maguires. For that matter, just about every major coal mining disaster was blamed on the Mollies. Yet, despite the widespread accusations and the presumptions of guilt regarding acts of industrial sabotage, no Molly was ever indicted for such an act.

The same, of course, cannot be said regarding the complicity of the Molly Maguires in the wave of murders that terrorized the Pennsylvania coal country during the 1860s and 1870s. The *Miners' Journal* counted at least 50 murders in Schuylkill County alone during a five-year period beginning in 1863. Although many of these murders were explicable (two women were killed by their husbands), most were not. As vicious as this period was, it doesn't include the murders committed during the second phase of Molly Maguire violence, which covered the years 1870–1875. We can never know for sure how many murders the Molly Maguires committed. What we do know is that the Mollies were ultimately held accountable for 16, ten of which occurred during this second phase. Consequently, this is the image most associated with the Molly Maguires—a band of assassins. Even for those who continue to sympathize with the Molly Maguire cause, this is a historical record that is difficult to deny.

The Molly Maguires demonstrated several characteristics of a terrorist campaign. A Molly Maguire bodymaster had the power to sentence enemies to death. He could then request the bodymaster of another lodge to provide assassins to do the dirty work, an arrangement popularized among the Whiteboys and other terrorist groups of pre-famine Ireland. Contracting outside killers insured the anonymity of local Mollies and provided further evidence of a conspiratorial element involving organizational chains of command. Aside from outright murder, the Molly Maguires also employed coffin notices, partly to terrorize certain individuals psychologically and partly to add to their public aura of mystery. In his testimony before the state legislature during the infamous "Long Strike" of 1875, Franklin Gowen presented a collection of 14 such notices. Although it is understandably difficult to establish the authenticity of these coffin notices, Kevin Kenny suggested that, based on the orthography employed, they are likely the genuine articles.[48] These notices, crude drawings included, also appeared in Francis Dewees's treatment of the Mollies that appeared in 1877. Of the 14, 11 contained specific threats to their recipients. Some threatened to destroy property. One, not mincing words, warned, "you will die." Five were specifically directed at "Blacklegs," another term for strikebreakers, and included threats such as these:

> Mr. Black-legs if you don't leave in 2 days time you meet your doom their will Bee an open war.

> Any blackleg that takes a Union mans job while He is standing for His rights will have a hard Road to travel and if He don't he will have to Suffer the consequences.

> Black legs take Notice—that you are in danger of your Life by working in the mines without the Consent of the union men of Swatara Branch 14 Dis at Middle Creek Mines.[49]

Oddly, three of the notices contained relatively civilized declarations regarding labor issues and were accompanied by signatures: two requested temporary adjustments of working hours and one announced the beginning of a strike. Seven were accompanied by drawings: two were adorned with pistols, two with coffins, and three had drawings of both. None were specifically signed "Molly Maguires," although one was signed "M.M.N." and another "M.M.H.S.T." By no means were coffin notices restricted to those associated with the coal mines or railroads. Thomas Foster, editor of the *Shenandoah Herald* and outspoken critic of the Molly Maguires, received a notice prefaced with a sketch of skull and crossbones that read, in part:

> Mr Edtore wie wil give ye 24 hurse to go to the devil
> We aint done shooting yet
>
> P. Molley[50]

These coffin notices provided brief but important clues about the motivating factors behind Molly Maguire violence, a subject not easily discernable given that the Mollies left behind so few indications of their collective state of mind. Most of the notices provided by Gowen appeared during the "Long Strike," so it should come as no surprise that they were directly related to labor issues: either to warn strikebreakers away from the mines or to demand fair treatment for workers. Labor issues were also the focal point of a letter signed by "A Molley" and published in the *Shenandoah Herald* on October 2, 1875. The primary purpose of the Mollies, according to the letter, was to secure the objectives of the recently collapsed trade union: just wages and safe working conditions. "I am against shooting as mutch as ye are," the letter asserted, "but the union is broke up and we have got nothing to defind ourselves with But our revolvers . . . I have told ye the mind of the children of mistress Molly Maguire, all we want is a fare Days wages for a fare days work."[51] While neither a sophisticated nor articulate political pronouncement, the letter, along with the coffin notices, does confirm what some have long maintained about the Molly Maguires: that, above all else, the Mollies represented a form of trade unionism, albeit a *violent* form of unionism that differed significantly from the unionism of the WBA, which was based on a model of compromise and negotiation. Consequently, beyond the murder and mystery, the Molly Maguires did represent a political viewpoint, a perspective shaped by and adapted to the conditions shared by the Irish coal miners in eastern Pennsylvania.

If newspaper editorials, public denunciations, and early historical accounts are to be believed, then the trail of Molly Maguire murder, sabotage, and psychological terror certainly took its toll upon the law–abiding folks whose lives revolved around the coal mines and railroads. Benjamin Bannan and the *Miners' Journal* warned that the Molly Maguires had established "a reign of terror in Schuylkill County, and that the time has arrived when the ruffians must be brought to justice or driven out, or life and property in this County in the future will not be worth a bauble."[52] The *Journal* later went on to assert that the Mollies had "dominated and terrorized the entire coal regions."[53] Samuel Wiley's history of Schuylkill County concurred with this assessment, insisting that the Mollies "held the anthracite coal regions in a state of terror for many years."[54] Francis Dewees, in his slanted account of the Molly Maguires, argued that during the Molly "reign of blood, . . . no monarch was more potent, no Eastern despot more cruel and merciless" than the Mollies, and they "held communities terror-bound, and in wanton malice defied law, destroyed property, and sported with human life."[55] Franklin Gowen would later suggest that miners lived in fear and had trouble sleeping at night for fear of assassination. So real was the perceived threat of Molly Maguire vengeance that, in Shenandoah, mine bosses routinely employed bodyguards equipped with shoulder-hoisted carbines.[56]

Perhaps just as menacing to the wider public was the idea that, as was widely believed, the influence of the Molly Maguires extended deeply into local politics in a conspiracy of immense proportions. The Mollies were widely accused of dominating the local Democratic Party, and any number of county commissioners, constables, school superintendents, and police chiefs were said to be members, constituting what A. Monroe Aurand called "a state within a state."[57] In Schuylkill County, the Mollies allegedly held the offices of county commissioner and tax collector, while in Carbon County, according to similar allegations, one Molly held the position of county commissioner and another held a seat in the state legislature.[58] Allan Pinkerton went one step further, maintaining that the Molly Maguires controlled the Pennsylvania state finances.[59] Most of these accusations were undoubtedly based on the mistaken assumption that the Molly Maguires and the AOH were identical organizations, for AOH membership was widespread and many reputable associates did hold various public offices. However, whether or not the Mollies actually manipulated local politics is not as significant as the common perception that they did. For, as we have seen, when it comes to terrorism, *perception* is sometimes as effective as *reality*. If people believe they are being terrorized, then they are, regardless of whether the threat against them is real or imagined. And the evidence suggests that the people of Pennsylvania's coal region believed resolutely that their lives were endangered and manipulated by shadowy terrorists called the Molly Maguires. If the six murders and other acts of sabotage attributed to the Molly Maguires between 1862 and 1868 are any indication, the Mollies were certainly unyielding in their attacks on the coal and railroad interests. But no one could have known at the time that the Mollies were just getting started, for their second phase of violence would far surpass the atrocities of the first, creating more terror and contributing further to the mythological proportions of the legacy of the Molly Maguires.

V. A Spy Infiltrates the Molly Maguires

Following the murder of Alexander Rea in October 1868, there was a lull in terrorist activity until 1874, partly because of the pacification efforts of the Coal and Iron Police and partly owing to the work of the WBA, which made noble efforts to curtail the violence. However, during this transition period, on April 15, 1870, Patrick Burns, a mine foreman from Tuscarora, was shot and killed. As with all of the earlier murders, no one was arrested at the time, although the dark role of the Molly Maguires would eventually become apparent. Court testimony eight years later would reveal that Burns had been shot by Martin Bergin at the behest of John Kane, who had embezzled company funds and was embroiled in a series of labor disputes with Burns, who had discovered Kane's improprieties. Bergin would later hang for the shooting, but Kane would escape prosecution for lack of corroborating evidence. A year and a half later, in December 1871, Morgan Powell, a Welsh mine superintendent who apparently discriminated against Irish miners, was assassinated. True to form, no one was immediately arrested, but subsequent court testimony would lead to the execution of three Mollies: Alexander Campbell, John Donahue, and Thomas Fisher. Two other Mollies, Patrick McKenna and Patrick O'Donnell, would receive prison terms for complicity in the Powell murder. These two murders notwithstanding, there was a noticeable drop in terrorist activity until late 1873, which, coincidentally or not, is the same time when one James McKenna arrived in the coal region. Members of the Molly Maguires who quickly befriended McKenna and initiated him into their ranks could not have known that he was, in fact, James McParlan, a Pinkerton undercover agent sent to infiltrate the infamous terrorists. A new chapter in the Molly Maguire saga was about to unfold.

In October 1873, Allan Pinkerton, founder and president of the renowned Pinkerton Detective Agency, received a letter from Franklin Gowen proposing a meeting between the two. Born in Scotland, Pinkerton had established a reputation here in America during the Civil War, when he directed the intelligence network of Union General George B. McClellan. Now he headed his own agency, one that specialized in the tactics of infiltration and hired informants. Gowen, meanwhile, was anxious to put a halt to the Molly Maguires and their terroristic ways. During their first meeting in Chicago, Gowen elaborated on the Mollies and, according to Pinkerton's own account, described the objective of the Philadelphia and Reading: "We want people to sleep unthreatened, unmolested in their beds, undisturbed by horrid dreams of midnight prowlers and cowardly assassins. We want the miner to go forth cheerfully to the slope, or the shaft . . . void of the fear in his heart when he parts from his wife, that it may be their last farewell on earth."[60]

Together, Gowen and Pinkerton hatched a plot that would ultimately bring down the Molly Maguires, a bold and risky mission that required a covert agent to infiltrate the Mollies and secure sufficient evidence to bring them to justice. But where could one find such an agent? Pinkerton thought first about scouting the coal districts of southern Illinois and Ohio in hopes of finding someone with mining experience. But he soon realized that he could not place his full confidence in a new acquaintance, especially one without formal Pinkerton training. Then one morning while riding a streetcar along Chicago's Fifth Avenue, Pinkerton recognized one his agents, who was then working undercover for the transit system. He was James McParlan, a 29-year-old born in Ireland who had been an employee of the Pinkerton Detective Agency for about a year. Having arrived in the United States in 1867, McParlan had held a series of odd jobs before enlisting with the Pinkertons. Though only passably educated, McParlan was held in high regard by his employers, who admired his honesty, tact, shrewdness, and perseverance. That same day, Pinkerton met with McParlan and offered him the undercover assignment. Despite the obvious risks involved, McParlan accepted without any apparent reservations, partly because Pinkerton promised him that he would never have to testify in court about the Molly Maguires and his covert activities. The two agreed that, while undercover, McParlan would provide regular reports of his activities, usually to Benjamin Franklin, head of the Pinkerton offices in Philadelphia. Thus began a fascinating tale of industrial espionage. Whether one sees McParlan as a courageous hero or an unscrupulous agent provocateur, it cannot be denied that his two and a half years undercover were fraught with danger at every turn.[61] That he was able to ruin the Molly Maguires and still survive, even after his cover was ultimately blown, justified the faith placed in him by Alan Pinkerton. It does not, however, necessarily justify the methods he employed while undercover, methods that to this day have generated endless debate among those familiar with the Molly Maguire story.

On October 27, 1873, McParlan, assuming the alias James McKenna, entered the coal region and, for a few weeks, traveled from town to town, striking up conversations, listening to rumors, and absorbing all he could about the infamous Mollies. Convinced that the Molly Maguires were real and not myth, he settled on Pottsville, the business center in Schuylkill County, as his base of operations. There, he set about winning the confidence of the local Irish community. Aware that the town taverns were the focal points of social activity, as well as the primary meeting places of secret societies, McParlan began to ingratiate himself with the local drinkers at the Sheridan House, a known hangout for "sleepers," a term used to describe the Molly Maguires. The Sheridan House was owned and operated by Patrick Dormer, a former county commissioner and known sleeper. McParlan impressed his early acquaintances with his ability to drink, sing, drink, dance, and drink again. In reality, one of McParlan's most useful skills was his ability to drink less than he appeared to and to feign drunken stupors in order to eavesdrop on conversations. McParlan also used these drinking occasions to fashion an elaborate cover story. He was James McKenna, a Civil War veteran and AOH member from Buffalo but now a fugitive, having killed a man over a labor dispute. His seemingly endless supply of money was attributed to a government pension and "shoving the queer," or passing counterfeit money. Now, he was looking for work in the mines. In January 1874, Dormer referred McParlan to Michael "Muff" Lawler, tavern owner and bodymaster of the Shenandoah chapter of the AOH. By April, McParlan had relocated to Shenandoah and was sworn into the local AOH. After becoming secretary three months later, he became part of the AOH inner circle of bodymasters and officers, many of whom were Molly Maguires.

isolation, had very little political representation in the General Court and consequently few opportunities to make their official arguments known. The White Indians, however, needed no further encouragement when it came to provoking fear and intimidation.

IV. Methods and Strategies

Similar to rioters elsewhere, Maine's agrarian rebels adopted the mock-Indian persona to disguise their true identities. This was especially true after 1800. During attacks, they usually blackened their faces, wore ragged Indian blankets and moccasins, and sometimes spoke in mock-Indian dialects. The White Indians created a distinctive underground culture, complete with elaborate costumes, songs, flags, and military-type discipline. They also selected chieftains, evidence of a leadership element. In his valuable list of extralegal incidents of violence in mid-Maine, Alan Taylor noted that about 40% involved attempts to intimidate proprietary supporters. This included burning barns, shooting or mutilating livestock, stealing tools, torching haystacks, toppling fences, and "besetting houses at night with cowbells, gunshots, hurled stones, and bloodcurdling yells." The other 60% involved the obstruction of deputies, surveyors, and land agents from intruding into the disputed backcountry.[21] As with other terrorists, Maine's White Indians had a definite method to their insurrectionary activities. Their campaign against the proprietary interests certainly incorporated a degree of psychological warfare. The Indian disguises, however crude they might have been, were certainly meant to provoke fear as well as to provide anonymity. Following his own unpleasant confrontation with approximately 75 terrorists, Pitt Dillingham described what he saw: "They were dressed with caps about three feet high, masks, blankets, moccasins on their feet. Their caps and masks were decorated with the most uncouth images imaginable. The masks were of bearskin, some sheepskin, some stuck over with hog's brisills . . . the frantic imagination of a lunatic in the depths of desperation could not conceive of a more horid or ghastly spectre. Their savage appearance would strike terror to the boldest heart . . . their appearance shook every fiber of my frame."[22]

Dillingham was no mere easily intimidated settler; he was a deputy sheriff. As part of their campaign of terror, White Indians were known to kill, roast, and devour horses as their owners looked on in horror. They placed coffin notices on doorsteps and left an actual open coffin on the porch of the Lincoln County sheriff. They also distributed letters written in blood.[23] Other testimony confirmed this atmosphere of fear and exposed the feelings of helplessness experienced by those supportive of the Great Proprietors. George Ulmer, an agent for Henry Knox, complained that "this combination . . . is too powerful and the individuals who compose it too numerous to be suppressed by the ordinary exercise of civil authority, without an armed force."[24] Knox himself referred to the insurgents as "audacious and bloodthirsty villains that ever disgraced the surface of New England."[25] Philip Bullen, a surveyor for the Kennebeck

Proprietors, complained of "hardships, suffering, dangers, and fears" every time he attempted to draw survey lines, for fear of "being fired upon, if not killed" by the "evil disposed inhabitants" of the backcountry.[26] Lemuel Paine, an attorney, likewise condemned the "untranquil and seditious spirit" created by the insurgents and, in a letter to the Commonwealth's attorney general, suggested, "The menaces and threats which they utter, the intentions they avow, and the repeated acts of violence, injustice, and outrages which they continue to approbate and commit indicate the depravity of their hearts . . . the most prominent feature in their character is a violent and implaceable hatred. So great is the terror which their conduct and menaces have inspired . . . they are as deaf to voice of reason and persuasion as is the tempest—or the billows to the ocean."[27] John Merrick, a proprietary land agent, bemoaned the actions of "unknown men, who dare not *name* or *shew* themselves . . . who are one day said to be *many and powerful*, when it is designed that they shall *inspire terror*, and the next day are represented as *few and contemptible*, when it is intended to *prevent any force from being kept up against them*."[28]

Merrick's statement raised a relevant question: just how many of "them" were out there? Establishing the numbers involved in a secret conspiracy like the White Indians was, of course, extremely difficult, especially for a movement decentralized over thousands of acres of Maine's central coast and backcountry. As one surveyor put it, "They appear in their disguise, commit an outrage and disappear. I think if the sheriff, officers and magistrates should go into that section of the county they would not find any body of armed men . . . all would appear in peace."[29] And there is also the possibility that inclusion in White Indian activities by particular individuals was never constant. As the Asa Andrews episode indicated, settlers who were reluctant to get involved were sometimes coerced into participation; their personal culpability was a form of insurance that they would not run to authorities with incriminating information. Consequently, while victims of specific assaults might have been able to provide fairly reliable numbers regarding their attackers, no one really seemed to know how many true insurgents were active in Maine. John Merrick estimated the number of White Indians in Kennebec County alone to be approximately one thousand but had no way of confirming his allegation.[30] This uncertainty behind the numbers only contributed to the mysterious aura surrounding the White Indians. Moreover, partly because of the physical isolation of many of the communities and partly due to logistical barriers, the White Indians scattered throughout Maine did not represent any type of unified, monolithic movement directed by a centralized authority. More likely, those who called themselves White Indians constituted local bands of terrorists, directed by chieftains, who could muster anywhere from 30 to 300 armed allies on short notice.

Despite their attempts at anonymity, the identity of some White Indians was widely known. Names such as Daniel Brackett, Isaac Prince, David Hildreth, and Josiah Dill figure prominently in primary documents that also reveal other names, such as William Hoge, Enoch Hill, Samuel Crockett, or Levi Hamblin. This should come as no surprise. As one traveled further into the backcountry, the communities became more isolated and insular. For better or worse, everybody seemed to know everybody else. Secrets were hard to keep. Despite being "outed" by nosy neighbors or agents of the Great Proprietors, many of these insurgents operated with seeming impunity, and understandably so. While charges were filed against some White Indians, most were well aware that the prevailing climate of intimidation and reprisal, the reluctance of sheriffs and officials to enter the disputed areas, and the constant threat of rescue riots meant that traditional methods of law enforcement were futile.

The case of Daniel Brackett is especially interesting. Much of what we know about the White Indian subculture can be traced to a recruiting notice crudely written by one "Teckarb Leinad." One wonders how long it took for the authorities to reverse the letters and identify Brackett as its author. A veteran of the Continental Army, the 50-year-old Brackett had settled in Fairfax County after the Revolution. Now, he and his only son were directing attacks on the proprietary interests. In his notice, Brackett invoked the White Indian myth about a native deliverer who could come to defend the settler cause. As part of his recruiting pitch to potential insurgents, Brackett pleaded, "We poor Indians pitty you and was willin' to spend our life for you because we all won brother; and our Indian king beggs a favor of every settler and inhabbatant that is infringed upon or like to be: that is to tell every Indian that you see that Their king desires them to aquipp themselves with a Capp and blanket and a gun and tomahawk and Visit him . . . and take Directions: for he means to Cut Down all poopery and kill the Devil and give the world of mankind some piece by stopping the progres of Rogues and Deceivers and helping every man to his right and privilidges and libertys: the same as our Indian nation enjoys."[31] Brackett's broadside underlined an identity separate from the social mainstream, thereby providing a context for extralegal authority. But it also suggested an environment of intimidation generated by his fellow insurgents, a precarious situation that would continue to evolve and greatly impact life along Maine's frontier.

V.   The White Indian as Terrorist

It is evident that Maine's White Indians demonstrated all of the characteristics of terrorists. Aside from their economic concerns regarding the possession of "wild lands," they clearly had political motives, based in large measure on the Revolution's republican ideology, or at least as they understood it. The circulars published by Ely, Shurtleff, and Brackett helped define the parameters of these political convictions. But as Thomas A. Jeffrey pointed out in 1976, the battle between insurgents and proprietors involved broader political viewpoints. Jeffrey noted that during the 1790s, the squatter communities in Maine tended to lean toward the emerging Democratic–Republican Party, which was then coalescing under the leadership of Thomas Jefferson.[32] Jefferson's party was particularly attractive to farmers, mechanics, seamen, artisans, small merchants, and others who tended to be non-propertied, uneducated, and underprivileged. The Great Proprietors, on the other hand, tended to rally around the Federalist Party directed by Alexander Hamilton, first, and then John Adams, and usually came from the ranks of the urban, educated and propertied classes with ties to large business concerns. Apart from their clear class distinctions, Republicans (as the Democratic–Republicans came to be known) and Federalists differed over their vision of what America should be. Republicans aspired to a more egalitarian, agrarian society, with decentralized power emanating from a government devoted to protecting people's liberties. Federalists argued on behalf of a more hierarchical society based on commerce and big business, all promoted by a centralized government devoted to the protection of private property. From the squatter perspective, at stake in Maine were not only the future of their homes and families, but also the very direction of the newly established republic.

As far as the White Indians were concerned, these political beliefs and attitudes provided specific justification for the use of terror as a primary form of resistance to the Great Proprietors. As part of his argument for resisting the *Hideous Monster,* Samuel Ely also declared, "If (rulers) make or pass resolves that shall oppress or destroy my neighbor, I have no warrant to obey them; or if rulers make a law to dispossess me of my just property, I have a just right to resist; . . . while other parts of the union enjoy the great blessings of liberty and a very happy Constitution, we are tied up and bowed down under oppression, our rights are threatened and we have no liberty; we do not delight in war, but if it must be we will try it once more."[33] Similarly, Shurtleff, in his *Concise Review,* argued, "If a man has learning, money, wit, and sagacity, and uses them against his neighbor in an unjust cause, his neighbor had an equal right to use his faculties, which may be of a different kind, against him, contrary to law. To take the advantage of others . . . furnishes arguments to justify mobs."[34] Keeping in mind that it was Shurtleff who warned that "those who encourage mobs, may be destroyed by mobs," one can easily decipher what he meant when he justified faculties "of another kind . . . contrary to law."

Violence and terror were certainly crucial elements of the White Indian campaign against the proprietary interests, yet amazingly, until the death of Paul Chadwick in 1809, apparently no White Indian attack resulted in a fatality, either to the victims or the attackers. Alan Taylor suggested that this was by design: in order to retain their coalition, "the White Indians carefully avoided the acts of bloodshed that would drive the fence sitters into cooperation with the authorities as the lesser of two evils."[35] Given the tenuous relationship between the insurgents and the "fence sitters," this certainly makes sense at a certain level. It does not, however, account for the number of close encounters, survival of which can only be attributed to good fortune. In July 1800, Bradstreet Wiggins and his survey team, working for Henry Knox, were assaulted by a group of settlers disguised as Indians. Wiggins was shot in the shoulder, and Nathan Smith was seriously wounded by a bullet that entered his hip, passed through his testicles, and lodged in his groin. So serious were Smith's wounds that the first depositions listed him as a fatality.[36] Several months later, Josiah Little, the primary Pejepscot proprietor, who was visiting Lewiston, was wounded when a disguised crowd fired gunshots into the home of Ezra Purrinton, his host. In November 1807, after serving several writs, Deputy Sheriff Henry Johnson was assaulted in Fairfax County by White Indians in "hideous garb." His horse was shot out from under him and Johnson was struck by two bullets—one passed through his leg and another lodged in his foot.[37] Whether the sparing of lives was by design or luck, once the violence turned increasingly bloody in 1807, the insurgents would begin to lose credibility among the wider community of settlers.[38]

The lack of fatalities did not diminish the impact of White Indian terrorism. The previous testimony of Pitt Dillingham, Lemuel Paine, and others seemed to confirm that the violent provocations created a psychological impact upon the broader community, reaching far beyond the immediate victims of personal attacks. And, as noted earlier, 40% of the extralegal incidents involving the White Indians were directed not at the proprietors but at their supporters.[39] The nocturnal raids, bloodcurdling screams, coffin notices, and horse eating, as well as the "horrid visages" of their mock-Indian persona, were all meant to generate a constant environment of fear. And although it is improbable that the White Indians scattered throughout Maine were part of a unified command structure, there is evidence that local bands established an organizational hierarchy. Crowds of insurgents often performed coordinated military maneuvers, usually necessitating some type of rank and order. Chieftains were chosen and discipline instilled. And despite the element of secrecy, local firebrands such as Samuel Ely, David Hildreth, Daniel Brackett, and Nathan Barlow were known to have directed bands of insurgents. In 1808, the *Kennebec Gazette* reported that Barlow alone commanded nearly 150 "Barlow Indians."[40]

Despite the variety of terms used to describe the White Indians—they were referred to at various times as banditti, rioters, ruffians, house burners, cattle killers, and simply as the mob—they, as did earlier "crowds" in American history, exhibited a "mind" to their methods. They demonstrated restraint and, despite the number of injurious attacks, were seemingly cognizant of a line that was not to be crossed. Regardless, with or without the deliberate taking of lives, it is evident that the White Indians exhibited all of the elements of a terrorist movement.

VI. The Proprietors Respond

The Great Proprietors reacted to the wave of White Indian terror in different ways. Some continued to negotiate with disgruntled squatters and complete mutually agreeable arrangements to rent or sell. Some, such as Henry Knox and Charles Vaughan, cultivated patrons within the settler communities and used them as allies, representatives, and informants, which obviously did not endear these folks to their neighbors. George Ulmer, Ezekiel Dodge, and Thurston Whiting all served Knox before abandoning him during the early 1800s. Many proprietors sought legal redress and won eviction suits against squatters. Enforcing these legal decisions, however, was another challenge altogether. After the attacks on Pitt Dillingham and Henry Johnson, law enforcement authorities were decidedly unenthusiastic about entering the central coast backcountry to deliver writs. Arthur Lithgow, sheriff of Kennebec County, reported that nearly all of the 140 writs obtained by the Great Proprietors in his county were destroyed by bands of White Indians.[41] Consequently, in 1802, the General Court authorized the proprietors to employ state militia "for pursuing and taking up sundry persons concerned in riotous opposing and firing upon a surveyor and others."[42] Proprietors also invoked the Riot Act of 1786 to engage and arm civilians to disperse groups of men "routously, riotously, or tumultuously assembled."[43] In the immediate aftermath of the attack on Deputy Sheriff Henry Johnson and in response to continued threats from White Indians, law-abiding citizens of Augusta cited these legal precedents and formed a local militia that became known as the Augusta Patrol.

Still, Sheriff Lithgow remained unconvinced that he had the firepower to challenge the White Indians. In January 1808, he ordered Major General Henry Sewell of the state militia to detach 400 armed men to assist in the suppression of insurgents, because it was "no longer prudent or safe to attempt to execute the law or to enforce the regular administration of justice."[44] In this particular instance, Lithgow invoked the Law of 1787, passed in response to Shays's Rebellion, which allowed the sheriff to call out the militia whenever an insurrection threatened to subvert the Constitution and other laws of the land. He did not, unfortunately for him, appeal first to the governor of the Commonwealth. Upon receiving Lithgow's petition, Governor James Sullivan denied the request and ordered the militia disbanded, arguing that, because eight weeks had passed since the assault on Henry Johnson without further incident, no threat of insurrection existed in Kennebec County. Thus, the Law of 1787 was not applicable. Sullivan further admonished Lithgow for his failure to consult the governor and for his failure to employ the Riot Act of 1786, which allowed the use of local civilians, as opposed to first seeking relief from the Commonwealth. Lithgow was subsequently dismissed from his position.[45]

By 1808, the Great Proprietors had larger political issues to concern themselves with, beyond the squatters living on disputed lands. The Jeffersonian–Republicans had swept the 1807 Commonwealth elections, finally giving the squatters a legitimate path to political influence and leaving the Federalists and proprietors scrambling for ways to protect their landed interests. It soon became clear that the Republican administration and the Federalist-oriented proprietors would have to negotiate some resolution regarding the long-disputed land titles. Republicans needed to act quickly to maintain the allegiance of the backcountry settlers, and the proprietors needed to capitalize on the growing settler dissatisfaction with the increasingly violent resistance movement. Consequently, in 1808, the General Court approved the Betterment Act, legislation that allowed dispossessed long-term squatters to claim monetary reimbursement for whatever improvements or "betterments" they might have added to the land. Correspondingly, the Act conceded that the proprietors were entitled to the land's value "in a state of nature." Settlers who agreed to purchase land according to the terms of the Betterment Act were eventually given three years to repay their debts in full. Determined to suppress the White Indian insurgency, the General Court passed additional legislation that allowed local justices to call out the militia without first petitioning the governor. It also tacked on steep fines and lengthy jail sentences for persons caught donning Indian disguises in order to obstruct the work of deputy sheriffs.[46] In the end, the Betterment Act and its attendant legislation had serious flaws but would ultimately trigger events contributing to the demise of the White Indians.

Emboldened by the Betterment Act, the proprietors sent new teams of surveyors into the heart of the backcountry, instigating further provocations by the White Indians. Meanwhile, John Chandler was chosen to replace Arthur Lithgow as sheriff of Kennebec County and immediately set out to enforce the new legislation. When Chandler arrived in Augusta in March 1808, he found a community in turmoil. Thomas Jefferson's Embargo Act of 1807 had taken a severe toll on the many settlers who relied on the lumber industry. Debts and eviction notices began to mount. Defying the General Court, White Indians, operating in groups varying in size from five to 70, resumed their attacks on surveyors and sheriffs serving writs of ejection. A deputy sheriff, identified only as Col. Thatcher, found an empty coffin on his front porch late one night.[47] In nearby Litchfield, White Indian assaults increased significantly, and, across the Kennebec River from Augusta, towns such as Malta (now Windsor) and Balltown (now Jefferson) became centers of the resistance movement. On April 18, 1808, Moses Robinson, constable of Fairfax, arrested his neighbor, Daniel Brackett, a.k.a. the infamous "Leinad Tekcarb," for unpaid debts. Brackett, leader of the Fairfax White Indians, was quickly rescued by an Indian-attired crowd that also forced Robinson to surrender his writ. Robinson, however, obtained a new warrant and returned to re-arrest Brackett. Once again, Robinson was assaulted before he could deliver Brackett to the local magistrate, this time by Nathan Barlow and seven other Barlow Indians. They shot Robinson's horse out from under him, robbed him of his papers, carried him off to a neighboring house, stripped him naked, and beat him unmercifully with sticks and branches. They then turned him loose into the woods, where he wandered for three miles before reaching his family.[48]

The attack on Robinson further exasperated the deepening division between groups of backcountry settlers. The Betterment Act was partly responsible for this rift. Some settlers were able to use its terms to come to agreeable resolutions with the proprietors, but others were unable to capitalize on its terms, either because they hadn't established sufficient residency (six years) or could not meet financial obligations. The assault on Robinson angered the more moderate settlers, who had already expressed misgivings about the violent methods of the insurgents. John Chandler, high sheriff of Kennebec County, reported that many of the settlers who had "once countenanced the opposition . . . now see that they are not safe among themselves."[49] Further evidence of this widening division came when Nathan Barlow was arrested, convicted largely due to the testimony of his neighbors, and hurried off to serve a two-year prison term before his fellow insurgents could rescue him. Not only were the White Indians losing local support, but more and more of the settlers were also coming to financial terms with the Great Proprietors, signaling the inevitable end of the resistance movement.

VII.   The Malta War

The White Indian insurgency in Maine culminated with a series of events in 1809 known to the locals as the Malta War, although this so-called "war" really consisted of nothing more than a murder, a highly visible trial, and a failed rescue riot. The gravity of certain of these events, however, is hard to deny. A life was taken: the only known fatality of the insurrection in Maine. The murder of Paul Chadwick and the publicity accompanying the trial of his assailants would ultimately lead to the unraveling of the resistance movement. Following the trial, scattered incidents of violence would occur sporadically until 1825, but for all practical purposes, the White Indian insurrection would cease to exist after 1810.

The seeds of the Malta War were sown when Aaron Choate, a squatter living on a plot of land in Malta, agreed to purchase his lot from a proprietor. In conjunction with the Kennebeck Proprietors, Choate hired Isaac Davis to help draw survey lines. Davis, in turn, hired two assistants, John Pratt and Paul Chadwick. Chadwick had been a local insurgent, or "Malta Indian," but turned against his neighbors when the proprietors offered 100 free acres to someone who would assist Davis. Understandably, Chadwick's participation was to be kept a secret. Although an earlier attempt by Davis to survey in June 1809 had been obstructed by a band of armed Malta Indians, he decided to try again in the fall. On September 8, while walking in advance of Davis and his survey team, Choate heard suspicious noises in the bushes and nearby trees. Suddenly, eight Malta Indians, armed with pistols, muskets, and scythes, burst from the thicket. They were dressed in blankets, colored caps that extended down to their shoulders, and veils with holes cut out for their eyes and mouths. One of them struck a pistol against Choate's chest and told him, "If you speak a word, I'll blow you through." The eight formed a line and confronted the approaching survey team. One of the Indians ordered the others to "fire low," while another demanded of Chadwick, "Damn you, how came you here? This is good enough for you." At that, three of the assailants discharged their muskets, hitting Chadwick in the leg, shoulder, and torso. The Indians then turned Chadwick's body over as he lay weltering in blood and boasted, "What he had got was good enough for him." The attackers then fled; the mortally wounded Chadwick was taken to the nearby house of David Leeman, Choate's father-in-law, where he languished for two days before dying.[50]

Before he died, however, Chadwick managed to provide testimony to a local justice and identified Elijah Barton and Jabez Meigs as two of his assailants.

Choate identified a third assailant, David Lynn. Eventually, warrants were issued for six other suspects: Prince Cain, Nathaniel Lynn, Jonas Proctor, Ansel Meigs, Joel Webber, and Adam Pitts. All hailed from Malta and all took to the woods, where they hid for several days before close friends and confidants convinced them to surrender. On September 15, all but Joel Webber, who had absconded, appeared before Justice James Brackett. Standing in court, several of the defendants began to weep and confessed to being present at the scene of Chadwick's murder. That was enough evidence to move forward with charges against the eight, and they were subsequently transferred to Augusta's new stone jailhouse to await word from a grand jury. Rumors, however, soon began to circulate that the Malta Indians were roaming the woods in preparation for a rescue riot to free the eight. There were also rumblings about the insurgents planning to torch government buildings and the homes of local proprietors and their agents. Meanwhile, Sheriff John Chandler made preparations to defend the town, ordering a small militia detachment under the command of Major General Henry Sewell to act as sentinels and to form patrols. In addition, a cannon from an old fort was mounted on wheels and moved to the west end of the Kennebec River bridge, pointing eastward toward Malta. Several tense days later, on October 3, the grand jury found sufficient evidence to indict the eight defendants and ordered the trial to begin in November.

Later that night, about 200 Malta Indians gathered along the east side of the Kennebec River, about a half-mile from the bridge. After a brief confrontation with some of Chandler's sentinels, the insurgents captured Abner Weeks, a major with the local militia. Weeks was released with a message for the authorities in Augusta: free the eight defendants within three hours or the insurgents would burn the town to the ground. Warning bells immediately began to ring throughout Augusta, and the streets began to fill with people running in all directions. Sheriff Chandler, mindful of the circumstances that had undermined his predecessor, Arthur Lithgow, had been reluctant to call out additional troops but now deemed it necessary to activate an additional 300 men to guard the jailhouse. Nothing further happened that night, but the next day, six additional militia companies arrived in Augusta, fully armed and ready for battle. The insurgents, however, seemingly disappeared. Nevertheless, for the next week, Augusta resembled an armed camp as women and small boys were recruited to mold bullets for the anticipated confrontation. The militias drilled throughout the day while government spies were sent into the Malta backcountry to report on the insurgents. None were to be found. Regardless, a poem entitled "The Malta War" soon appeared in the *Kennebec Gazette*. It read, in part:

> The great Stone Jug of Kennebec
> > Has Cost us many a crown,
> Yet Malta Indians do expect
> > To tear the building down

Or else to draw the stopper out
    And liberate their friends,
But they will find that we're so stout,
    They'll not obtain their ends.

We'll let them know that we are men
    That mean to do what's right,
And if the rebels do come on
    We'll have a bloody fight.

The Malta men do nought but brag
    And tell how stout they are
And think that their numerous hosts
    The soldiers they will scare

But they will find out their mistake
    If ever they come here,
To break the jug of Kennebec
    Whilst we are kept so near.[51]

Bold words, but then this war was far more rhetorical than real: the Malta Indians failed to make good on their threat, and talk of a rescue riot quickly dissipated. On October 10, the forces surrounding the Augusta jailhouse were reduced to a regular rotation of 100 men, which successfully maintained peace until the trial began in November. Chandler's show of force later won approval from the Commonwealth, grateful that his actions had preempted a violent confrontation.[52]

The trial for the murder of Paul Chadwick began November 16, 1809. Charges were brought against seven of the original nine defendants. Joel Webber remained a fugitive and was not tried. Jonas Proctor agreed to turn state's evidence in return for immunity against all charges related to the Chadwick case. The trial generated a great deal of local interest, and, fortunately, the proceedings and testimony were recorded in shorthand by John Merrick, a proprietary land agent, who later published the trial record.[53] The court was held by four judges: Theodore Sedgwick, Samuel Sewall, George Thatcher, and Isaac Parker. The defendants, unable to cover their court costs, were assigned legal representation by the court. Examining the trial and reading the testimony, one is struck by how similar this trial is to the modern-day trials with which we have grown accustomed, 200 years' separation notwithstanding. There were arguments between opposing legal teams over semantic issues, jury selection, charges of jury tampering, the credibility of witnesses, and the admissibility of evidence. A particularly contentious issue was the admissibility of Chadwick's deathbed testimony: was he of sound mind at the time? There was considerable wrangling over the confessions proffered by several defendants during their first court appearance back in early October. Nonetheless, several truths did emerge from the trial. Chadwick had not been a random target that fateful day. Several witnesses testified that the defendants, in Indian disguise, had specifically inquired as to the whereabouts of Chadwick the day of his shooting. One of the Indians reportedly boasted, "Chadwick has crooked eyes and I mean to straighten them."[54] This line of testimony provided a motive for the shooting: Chadwick, by accepting the survey assignment, had earned the enmity of his neighbors. The defendants, all of whom pleaded not guilty, argued that the testimony against them was biased or inadmissible. Chadwick's testimony was unreliable, they maintained, as was that of Aaron Choate and other prosecution witnesses; the confessions had been coerced with promises of preferential treatment. They had fled to the woods, they claimed, not because of their guilt but because they were afraid. Further, several defendants offered alibis for the day of the murder. Despite this rigorous defense, the prosecution was able to present compelling evidence that all seven of the defendants had been present at the scene of Chadwick's murder. What the prosecution could not establish was who among the seven had actually shot Chadwick. Compounding this huge problem was the decision by all seven defendants to stand trial as one, none agreeing to testify against the others. This was a calculated risk—it meant that those who had not discharged their weapons could be found guilty with those who had. The gamble paid off. Unable to establish the identity of the actual shooters and unwilling to punish innocent men along with the guilty, the jury shockingly acquitted all of the accused.

Robert H. Gardiner, a proprietor turned historian, albeit one with a transparent agenda, would later charge that, because the defendants were allowed to challenge the assignment of "respectable" jurors, "the trial was before a packed jury of squatters or the associates of squatters."[55] However, Thomas A. Jeffrey accurately noted that the jury members came from a wide geographic spread of home towns, many to the north of Kennebec County, thereby undermining the notion of a conspiracy or any connection between the jury and the Malta Indians.[56] In his history of Maine, James North offered an alternative explanation for the jury's acquittal. He asserted that "the mass of testimony and weighty arguments were too much for the feebly discriminating powers" of the jury.[57] As with Gardiner, North offered no evidence to support his charge, and, 200 years after the fact, there appears no way to determine exactly how feeble the jury's powers might have been, if at all. What we do know is that both Gardiner and North were notable members of Maine's Federalist Party. It is not unreasonable to assume that had the same jury returned a guilty verdict neither Gardiner nor North would have been as dismissive of the jury's membership or aptitude.

VIII. Epilogue

By all accounts—those of contemporary observers as well as latter day historians—the Malta War was the culminating event of the White Indian resistance in mid-Maine. Occasional acts of violence would erupt during the next few years, but, in general, a spirit of compromise evolved between the Great Proprietors and the squatter community, and, accordingly, the level of terrorist activity dropped precipitously. The Betterment Act had provided the means to lessen the political tensions, and the death of Paul Chadwick completely discredited the resistance movement. Although Robert H. Gardiner first thought that the trial had been "a mockery of justice," he also conceded that it ultimately produced a very favorable aftermath.[58] Thomas A. Jeffrey agreed that the trial had a "salutary effect," and James North noted that the trial's "surprising result" ended with "a favorable ending."[59] By the end of the trial, much of the White Indian leadership had been incapacitated, and, accordingly, resistance in Malta and elsewhere all but vanished. Nathan Barlow was doing hard labor for his part in the assault on Moses Robinson. Evading arrest for his participation in the Robinson affair, Daniel Brackett and his family fled Fairfax and moved about until finally settling in New York in 1815. Samuel Ely had long fled Maine, never to return. Only James Shurtleff would remain politically active as one of the area's prominent Jeffersonians.

Following the trial, the freed defendants went home peacefully, and many eventually made amends with the family and friends of Paul Chadwick. Some went on to become highly respectable members of the community. And while the trial itself brought no closure to the continued legal wrangling over property ownership, both squatters and proprietors exhibited a new willingness to compromise. The squatters had already exhibited a division within their ranks over the use of violent tactics. The trial hastened the decline of those who continued to preach resistance, as more and more of the fence-sitters distanced themselves from the insurgents. With the White Indian movement seemingly discredited, many of the more hostile, disaffected squatters abandoned their homes in search of opportunity elsewhere.

Meanwhile, the Great Proprietors, having had their day in court and seeing justice denied, were also encouraged to settle property issues more amicably. In March 1810, the General Court passed an amendment to the Betterment Act, which promised to ease the mortgage difficulties of the squatters. Before long, surveyors began to appear more frequently in Maine's backcountry, running survey lines and operating without fear. Beyond these local developments, larger national issues also contributed to defusing the once volatile environment. The country was moving toward war with Great Britain, and the economy was still suffering from the federal government's manipulation of foreign trade. In a few short years, Maine would be separated from the Commonwealth of Massachusetts and became a separate state, free to resolve all remaining property disputes.

In the end, the Great Proprietors would have their way. The resistance had crumbled, and, by the time of statehood in 1820, the proprietors continued to possess the best lands in mid-Maine. Many of the settlers, however, with good reason, thought of the White Indian insurrection as a success. The tactics of terror had bought squatters precious time in their efforts to accumulate enough resources to resolve their financial disputes. The resistance movement had forced the Great Proprietors, through legislation such as the Betterment Act, to moderate their pricing policies. And the White Indians had induced the court system to clear away title conflicts. By standing up on behalf of the squatters, the insurgents in Maine had helped establish the predominance of freehold tenure. But beyond that, through its orchestrated use of terror and the murder of Paul Chadwick, the White Indians helped define the parameters of socially accepted violence. Chadwick's murder had clearly crossed the line. The White Indians were also crucial in establishing the legacy of agrarian violence in the new republic. The promise of the Revolution demanded that tyranny be met with resistance. Thus, throughout the new nation, disgruntled farmers and squatters would continue to employ violence as a means toward a legitimate end. And especially in New York, contentious issues related to the ownership of land would continue to provoke disaffected citizens with a penchant for violent confrontation.

By 1822, not only had Malta's White Indians all but disappeared, but so too had Malta itself, at least in name. Because of the town's great shame associated with the resistance movement and the murder of Paul Chadwick, the state legislature eventually changed the name of the community to Windsor.

Notes

1. James W. North, *The History of Augusta* (Augusta, ME: Clapp and North, 1870), 354.
2. Robert Hallowell Gardiner, *Early Recollections of Robert Hallowell Gardiner, 1782–1864* (Hallowell, ME: White and Horne Co., 1936).
3. Robert E. Moody, "Samuel Ely: Forerunner of Shays," *New England Quarterly*, V, (1932): 105–134.
4. Lawrence Donald Bridgham, "Maine Public lands, 1781–1795: Claims, Trespassers, and Sales," (PhD dissertation, Boston University, 1959); Thomas A. Jeffrey, "The Malta War," (MA Thesis, University of Maine, Orono, 1976).
5. Alan Taylor, *Liberty Men and Great Proprietors*, (Chapel Hill: University of North Carolina Press, 1990).
6. For more on early Maine and the land dispute, see also Gordon Kershaw, *The Kennebec Proprietors, 1749–1775* (Portland, The Maine Historical Society, 1975); Richard W. Judd, Edwin A. Churchill, and Joel W. Eastman, eds., *Maine: The Pine Tree State from Prehistory to the Present* (Orono: University of Maine Press, 1995).
7. Charles E. Clark, *Maine* (New York: W. W. Norton & Co., 1977), 41.
8. Taylor, *Liberty Men*, 11.
9. Ibid., 13.
10. Ibid., 14–15.
11. Ibid., 20.
12. Ibid., 264–279.
13. Moody, "Samuel Ely," 117–134.
14. Philip Bullen to Kennebec Proprietors, January 1, 1796, Kennebec Proprietors Papers, Box 4, Coll. 60, Kennebec Purchase Records, MNHS. See also Philip Bullen deposition, Related Papers, Resolves—January 29, 1799, Chapter 92, MA; Jonathon Jones, John Jones, Thomas Grover, and Paul Jones deposition, January 5, 1796, Box 4, Coll. 60, Kennebec Purchase Records, MNHS.

15. James to Jonathan Trask, November 1795, Related Papers, Resolves—January 29, 1799, Chapter 92, MA.
16. John Trueman to Council, October 3, 1796, Box 10, Council Files, MA; Asa Andrews, Winter, 1797, Box 12, Council Files, MA.
17. Manassah Smith to John Trueman, May 6, 1797, Box 11, Council Files, MA.
18. Asa Andrews, July 12, 1800, Box 12, Council Files, MA.
19. Samuel Ely, *The Deformity of a Hideous Monster, Discovered in the Province of Maine, by a Man in the Woods Looking After Liberty* (1797), 9.
20. James Shurtleff, *A Concise Review of the Spirit Which Seemed to Govern in the Time of the Late American War, Compared with the Spirit Which Now Prevails; With the Speech of the Goddess of Freedom, Who is Represented as Making her Appearance Upon the Alarming Occasion* (1798), 6, 10, 39.
21. Taylor, *Liberty Men*, 118.
22. Pitt Dillingham to Arthur Lithgow, January 30, 1808, Related Papers, Resolves—1809, Chapter 55, MA.
23. Taylor, *Liberty Men*, 193; North, *History of Augusta*, 358.
24. George Ulmer and Robert Houston to Governor Caleb Strong, August 12, 1800, Related Papers, Resolves—1800, Chapter 63, MA. For further testimony regarding the climate of fear, see Ezra Purrinton deposition, January 27, 1801, Box 12, folder for 1800–1802, Pejepscot Proprietor's Papers, PEM; John Merrill deposition, January 31, 1801, Box 12, folder for 1800–1802, Pejepscot Proprietor's Papers, PEM.
25. Henry Knox to Governor Caleb Strong, August 15, 1800, Related Papers, Resolves—1800, Chapter 63, MA.
26. Philip Bullen to Charles Vaughan, November 26, 1801, Box 7, Kennebec Purchase Records, MNHS.
27. Lemuel Paine to James Sullivan, February 13, 1808, Box 16, Council Files, MA.
28. Taylor, *Liberty Men*, 199.
29. Ibid., 195.
30. Ibid., 195.
31. Arthur Lithgow papers, Box 16, Council Files, MA; reprinted in Taylor, *William and Mary Quarterly*, 102; and *Liberty Men*, 186.
32. Jeffrey, "The Malta War," 25–29.
33. Ely, *Deformity of a Hideous Monster*, 13.
34. Shurtleff, *Concise Review*, 38–39.
35. Taylor, *Liberty Men*, 196.
36. George Ulmer to Henry Knox, July 23, 1800, Related Papers, Resolves—November 15, 1800, Chapter 63, MA; Peter Smith deposition, August 11, 1800, Related Papers, Resolves—1800, Chapter 63, MA.
37. Henry Johnson deposition, February 15, 1808, Box 16, Council Files, MA. Johnson revealed that his attackers had masked faces and spoke in a mock Indian dialect.
38. Taylor, *Liberty Men*, 202.
39. Ibid., 118.
40. Jeffrey, "The Malta War," 60.
41. Arthur Lithgow to Governor and Council, February, 1808, Box 16, Council Files, MA.
42. Jeffrey, "The Malta War," 33.
43. Ibid., 44.
44. Arthur Lithgow to Henry Sewell, Eighth Division Orders, January 19, 1808, Box 16, Council Files, MA.

45. Taylor, *Liberty Men*, 196.
46. Jeffrey, "The Malta War," 5; North, *History of Augusta*, 354.
47. Taylor, *Liberty Men*, 193.
48. Moses Robinson account, February 14, 1809, Related Papers, Resolves—1808, Chapter 269, MA.
49. Taylor, *Liberty Men*, 201.
50. Trial testimony found in John Merrick, recorder, *Trial of David Lynn, et al., for the Murder of Paul Chadwick* (Hallowell, ME: Ezekiel Goodale Publisher, 1810).
51. North, *History of Augusta*, 383.
52. Jeffrey, "The Malta War," 66.
53. Merrick, *Trial of David Lynn*.
54. Ibid., 24.
55. Gardiner, *Early Recollections*, 72.
56. Jeffrey, "The Malta War," 70, fn.
57. North, *History of Augusta*, 381.
58. Quote located in Jeffrey, "The Malta War," 80.
59. Ibid.; North, *History of Augusta*, 382.

7

THE NEW YORK ANTI-RENT WAR

I. Background

Of all the land controversies that plagued colonial America and the new republic, none were as complex, expansive, or sustained as those along New York's Hudson River, home to princely manorial estates that stretched far up river and beyond both the eastern and western horizons. When the Dutch first settled the area, then known as New Netherland, the Dutch West India Company, in the name of the States-General, began in 1629 to grant huge tracts of land along the Hudson to various leading citizens, in order to stimulate further colonization. These fortunate grantees, or Lords of the Manor, were known as "patroons," and, after satisfying local Native American claims, they eventually became prosperous and powerful landlords to thousands of tenant farmers. At issue was not only the mere existence of these manorial estates but also the contractual agreements between the patroons and their tenant farmers—controversies that would endure for more than two centuries. Many patroons quickly understood that greater wealth and long-term political influence were to be accumulated through the collection of rents rather than through the outright sale of individual lots. Consequently, they created a system of leasehold tenure that guaranteed them fantastic sums of wealth in the form of rent, a throwback to the feudal estates of Europe.

The English takeover of New Netherland in 1664 had little impact on the patroons, for rather than dismantling the estates, the English simply emulated the Dutch model and created their own stately manors. Between 1670 and 1760, English governors granted tens of millions of acres to their own friends and associates. Some of these Dutch and English grantees decided to sell their lands, but many were able to expand their vast estates by adding additional tracts, often through suspicious if not outwardly fraudulent means. By the early 18th century, several wealthy and influential families held title to enormous tracts of land along the Hudson River: the Van Rensselaer family, descendants of diamond merchant Kiliaen Van Rensselaer and by far the largest land-holding clan, for example, collectively possessed more than 1 million acres in the area surrounding Albany, eventual home to more than 3,000 tenant families. Similarly, although on a somewhat smaller scale, the Philipse family held more than 200,000 acres, and Livingston Manor extended over 160,000 acres. Even the smaller estates, such as the Duanesburgh and Blenheim patents, extended over 60,000 and 40,000 acres, respectively.[1] By the 1810s, more than 2 million acres of Hudson Valley land were owned collectively by about two dozen leasehold estates, and, by the 1840s, more than 260, 000 tenants, or 12% of New York's population, lived and farmed on these estates.[2]

The leasehold tenure system was based on contracts that bound landlord and tenants together, often *in perpetuity*. Contracts varied but usually granted tenants access to and occupation of land in exchange for a combination of money, goods, and services to be rendered yearly after an initial grace period. The patroon maintained ownership as well as rights and privileges regarding repossession, natural resources, property access, improvements to the land, and other provisions that guaranteed a disproportionate transfer of wealth from tenants to landlords.[3] These debilitating conditions were often compounded by contractual obligations that compelled tenants to purchase goods from the patroon's commissary and to employ the patroon's mills, additional terms that together reduced tenants to a state of "voluntary slavery."[4] The monopolization of land and the great disparity of wealth created an untenable social structure along the Hudson that eventually spawned resentment, antagonism, and hostility. When a flood of New Englanders and southern New Yorkers infiltrated the Hudson Valley during the 18th century, new settlers and squatters, along with existing tenants, began to challenge the landlords' claims to the land. Thus began the infamous New York Anti-Rent War, a tenant revolt that would endure until well into the late 19th century. The prolonged controversy had two distinct periods of severe violence, one during the 1760s that coincided with the fervor of popular resistance during the Revolutionary Era, and the other during the antebellum/Civil War period, roughly 1839–1869. The enduring controversy would eventually garner broader national attention as anti-rentism became closely associated with the free-soil and national reform movements that would sweep the country, but the distressed tenants of the Hudson Valley seldom wavered from their primary objective: the abolition of the Hudson's manorial estates in order to create a more egalitarian society based on freehold tenure and a more equitable distribution of land.

II. 18th-Century Disturbances

The Hudson Valley, with its fertile soil and easy access to the Hudson River and New York City, was a popular destination that became home to a population as diverse as any in America. Alongside the English, Dutch, and various Stockbridge and Wappinger Indians, were German, Irish, Scot, and Welsh tenant farmers who grew oats, corn, wheat, rye, and livestock. The Hudson Valley tenants created tightly knit and often-defiant communities that periodically engaged in crowd action to prevent delinquent neighbors from being evicted, thus setting a precedent for collective action as a means of self-defense. The first large-scale rioting along the Hudson began to take root in Livingston Manor and Rensselaerwyck during the early 1750s, when Josiah Loomis and Robert Noble began to organize a resistance movement to defy their landlords.[5] Based on conflicting Indian and Massachusetts titles, insurgent tenants renounced their leases, refused to pay rent, and began to stake freehold claims to tracts owned by the Livingston and Van Rensselaer families. They also attempted to foment a wider rebellion by pressuring other tenants to join the anti-rent movement. When Robert Livingston, Jr., had Loomis evicted from Livingston Manor in 1751, Loomis brought suit in a New York court, the beginning of a long and tortuous legal nightmare of endless litigation by various parties concerning the disposition of Hudson Valley land. He and other insurgents also sent petitions to the Massachusetts Legislature as a means of contesting New York titles, which also set in motion a concurrent and convoluted political machination involving both state and party politics that would at various times disregard, embrace, or exploit the anti-rent cause. With some encouragement from Massachusetts, insurgent farmers continued to defy the landed gentry, and at least one threatened to kill Livingston personally.[6] The influence of Massachusetts should not be underestimated. Both Noble and Loomis were granted military commissions by William Shirley, governor of Massachusetts, which bestowed on the rebels a semblance of authority and credibility. In a revisionist study of New York's manorial society, Sung Bok Kim, discounting tenant impoverishment and class conflict in New York, argued that the anti-rent movement was actually the direct product of an unseemly land grab by greedy settlers from Massachusetts and the Bay Colony's General Court. Together, they instigated the entire resistance, according to Kim, leaving rebellious tenants but "a pawn in the contest between private speculators in western Massachusetts and the New York landlords."[7]

Whatever their motives, armed insurgents soon began to obstruct government agents from dispossessing tenants and arresting fellow rioters. They also made it clear to tenants that they would not tolerate a break in the ranks, arguing that anti-renters needed to stick together to present a united front to the landlords. One loyal tenant who dared join a landlord's posse was later shot and wounded by an insurgent. Most, however, got the message. Robert Livingston complained that many of his "easy and quiet" tenants were now reluctant to show him civility in public, and he feared that they would soon join the anti-rent forces.[8] Conditions became so precarious that one sheriff confessed to the lieutenant governor that "it is unsafe for me or any officer of this Government to execute Our Offices in these parts."[9] By February 1755, an angry John Van Rensselaer, reacting to scattered confrontations among defiant tenants, sheriffs, and landlord agents, decided to act forcefully and led a posse of loyal tenants into Claverack to detain an insurgent leader, William Rees. Rees resisted arrest and was shot and killed while attempting to escape.[10] Rather than intimidating the tenants into submission, Rees's killing only hardened their resolve, and a frightened Robert Livingston, Jr., reacting to rioters on Livingston Manor, lamented to the government, "I am daily in danger of my Life."[11] At one point, Margaret Livingston, his sister-in-law, feared that rioters would overthrow the manor and take his life.[12] In June 1757, a frustrated Livingston sent a posse headed by the sheriff of Albany County to arrest rioters who had assembled at the farm of Jonathan Darby, who was to be evicted. As the posse approached Darby's home, they began to exchange gunfire with the insurgents. Several of the rioters fled the scene but were captured and jailed.[13]

For the next several years, the violent rioting subsided while several parties, including the local Stockbridge Indians, continued to litigate in New York courts conflicting land claims against the Hudson landlords. In the meantime, while many loyal tenants, or up-renters, continued to honor their burdensome contracts as best they could, insurgents continued to mobilize, agitate, and withhold rent. Assessing the economic impact of the early anti-rent movement is difficult by any measure, but, in his study of the Hudson land controversy, Thomas J. Humphrey estimated that in any given year during the late colonial period, the Van Rensselaers usually collected between 50% to 70% of the rent owed and that the Livingstons collected approximately 70%.[14] The problem, of course, is determining how much of the uncollected rent was due to legitimate tenant hardship as opposed to outright insurgent defiance. Suffice it to say that the economic impact of the rent strike was significant, particularly for large landowners such as the Van Rensselaers, who had thousands of tenants on their land and ledger. For many landlords, the loss of profits was compounded by the defiant and hostile attitude of tenants, from whom a more deferential comportment was expected, if not demanded. Thus, in many ways, the anti-rent movement represented a direct threat to the hierarchical social relationships that had elevated the Hudson landlords into positions of political power.

By the fall of 1765, political and social conventions had changed significantly, not only in New York but also throughout the American colonies. That spring, Parliament had passed the Stamp Act, provoking unprecedented popular resistance and the eventual appearance of the Sons of Liberty. A democratizing spirit had begun to spread, and for many, notions of social leveling and widespread freehold tenure, already popular with Hudson Valley tenants, would become important elements of the emerging revolutionary mindset. Rioters along the Hudson had never disappeared altogether, and, in late 1765, Robert Noble and his insurgents revived their operations, attacking or intimidating families loyal to the landlords. This put many tenants in a difficult dilemma. If they sided with the rioters, they faced eviction or imprisonment. If they remained loyal to their landlords, they put the welfare of their families at risk. Rioters warned one such up-renter, Peter Witbeck, that if he stayed on his farm, they would "pull down his house and destroy his grain."[15] In June 1766, determined to rid their manors of rioters, the Van Rensselaer and Livingston families, accompanied by a county sheriff, organized a posse of about 130 men to arrest Noble. A roadside confrontation with Noble and approximately 30 insurgents quickly turned into a shootout that lasted nearly an hour and ceased only when the posse broke for the woods. One posse member was killed and several combatants were wounded on both sides, including Noble, who was shot in the back, and Henry Van Rensselaer, who took a shot in the arm. One month later, Jeremiah Van Rensselaer and 250 British troops marched throughout Rensselaerwyck, driving off rioters and apprehending others for arrest. From that point forward, violence along the upper Hudson began to wane; in the meantime, concurrent hostilities to the south were continuing to escalate.

In late 1765, in response to proposed changes in their leases, disgruntled downriver tenants of the Philipse Highland Patent began to rally around William Prendergast, an Irish immigrant. These insurgents also submitted petitions and filed suits, arguing that landlord claims were invalid, fraudulent, and superseded by tenant claims based on either Native American titles purchased from speculators or by tenant occupation and improvement of the land. When legal redress appeared hopeless, insurgents initiated attacks against tenants who had taken over the leaseholds of dispossessed anti-renters, further widening the target audience of their orchestrated violence. In November, nearly 40 rioters forcefully removed several such families and returned the disputed farms to their original tenants. Other anti-rent rioters intimidated or assaulted neighbors who failed to support the cause. The following spring, after several insurgents were captured and jailed in New York City, Prendergast and approximately 200 rioters mobilized on the outskirts of Manhattan and threatened to invade the island and free the prisoners. Seeking help from expected allies, Prendergast appealed to the local Sons of Liberty for assistance, only to be rebuffed. Many of the southern landlords were themselves prominent Sons, leading one cynic to note that the Sons of Liberty were "great opposers to these Rioters as they are of the opinion no one is entitled to Riot but themselves."[16] Rather than negotiate with or submit to the insurgents, New York Governor Henry Moore instead issued warrants for the arrests of Prendergast and other rebel leaders. With a reward on his head, Prendergast narrowly escaped capture, while the other rioters fled the field.

Although New York City was spared a rescue riot, violence began to escalate elsewhere along the southern Hudson. In May, landlord agents looking for her husband beat a pregnant woman, who miscarried three days later. Within a week, insurgents approached the home of George Hughson, who had taken over the farm of an evicted rioter. Although Hughson was missing, Prendergast verbally abused and threatened the tenant's pregnant wife, demanding that her husband abandon the lease but leaving her otherwise unmolested. When warrants were issued for the arrest and eviction of the insurgents, Samuel Peters, attempting to serve the writs, and Hughson himself were captured and detained by rioters. For several hours, the two prisoners were beaten, whipped, dunked in water, and forced to stand trial before Prendergast in a mock courtroom surrounded by 200 rioters. When Hughson questioned the legitimacy of such an extralegal gathering, Prendergast replied that, "mobs had overcome kings before." Hughson and Peters were also paraded on wooden horses before jeering crowds, a form of punishment known as "riding the stang."[17] After suffering much pain and degradation and swearing not to enter testimony against their captors, the prisoners were eventually released. Shortly thereafter, British troops were ordered to march against the poorly armed insurgents, who were completely overwhelmed by the king's army. Hundreds of rioters were arrested, but only 60 eventually stood trial. Prendergast was captured, tried by a stacked court for capital treason, and sentenced to death, but, when the county sheriff could find no one to conduct the execution, the king granted an official pardon.

Prendergast would return peacefully to his home and, despite occasional outbreaks of violence, the anti-rent rioting began to subside over the next few years. However, the American Revolution soon provoked additional riots along the Hudson, as partisan politics between patriots and loyalists further complicated the dichotomy between landlords and tenants. After the Revolution, those landlords along the lower Hudson who had remained loyal to the Crown had their landholdings confiscated and redistributed. Moreover, many landlords who had supported the patriot cause were ever-sensitive to the prevailing political winds and chose to sell their lands. Consequently, the number of freeholders increased significantly all along the Hudson Valley, especially in the south. The leasehold controversy, unfortunately, would remain unresolved for decades. Although aristocratic monopolization of land ran counter to the spirit of the Revolution, as evidenced by the abolition of primogeniture and entail, newly established courts and legislatures would continue to validate the original Dutch and English grants of patriot landlords, such as the Van Rensselaers and Livingstons, who together owned more than half of New York's leased land.[18]

III. Antebellum Violence Along the Northern Hudson

Despite a lingering resentment against the landed aristocracy and an occasional outbreak of violence, rioting along the Hudson Valley would dissipate for several decades following the Revolution. County sheriffs were killed in separate anti-rent disturbances in 1792 and 1813, yet an uneasy and tenuous peace would largely prevail. The economic outlook was mostly positive, new farming techniques made the lands increasingly productive, and a variety of available leases provided tenants with some measure of security. In a system founded on reciprocity, many benevolent landlords provided a variety of social services for their tenants, seeking deference and political allegiance in return. One such generous landlord was, oddly enough, Stephen Van Rensselaer III, who had inherited his family estate in 1769, when he was only five years old, but assumed control of the manor 20 years later. Known for his hospitality and humanitarianism, the landlord popularly known as "the Good Patroon" extended sympathy and understanding to his tenants, often postponing or waiving the rents of those who could not pay. A Harvard graduate, militia officer, noted politician at both the state and federal levels, and perhaps the richest man in America, Van Rensselaer was widely respected and considered "a true friend" to his tenants.[19] Such was his benevolence that many of his tenants believed that upon his death, the patroon would somehow grant them the rights to purchase their lots of land. Aristocratic landlords of his lofty status were becoming relics of the past, and the new inheritance laws guaranteed that he would be the last of the Van Rensselaer patroons. One can only imagine the shock and frustration when, upon his death in January 1839, his will bestowed the family estate on two of his sons and, further, demanded that all unpaid rents should be collected immediately, a cumulative debt that exceeded $400,000. With but a few exceptions, the will failed to grant any provisions for relief.

Stephen Van Rensselaer's will bequeathed the manorial lands east of the Hudson River to Stephen Van Rensselaer IV and the western lands to William P. Van Rensselaer, neither of whom inherited their father's social graces or his paternalistic instincts. They did, however, inherit his debts, which also approximated $400,000 and resulted in a desperate need to collect on tenant arrears. Their attempts to collect back rent triggered the second major phase of Hudson rioting, a period that would last about 25 years. The intensity of the renewed violence mixed with the complexity of partisan politics and social reform was such that most modern discussions of the New York Anti-Rent War concern this 19th-century episode. After Stephen Van Rensselaer IV distributed handbills demanding payment of debts, tenants throughout his manor, particularly those who lived in the vicinity of the Helderberg Hills, began to organize a collective response. That spring, a meeting of defiant tenants met in Berne and began to correspond with Van Rensselaer after he refused to meet with them personally. On July 4, tenants again met in Berne, drafted proposals to readjust their debts, and, after demanding the conversion of their leases into freeholds, issued a declaration of tenant independence from manorial landlords. That fall, after negotiations between Van Rensselaer and the tenants broke down, the landlord escalated the confrontation by securing writs of ejectment against delinquent tenants.

In late August, Amos Adams, undersheriff of Albany County, began to issue writs in several Helderberg townships, beginning at the farm of Isaac Hungerford, who defiantly brandished a knife and warned Adams not to proceed further, proclaiming the willingness of himself and others "to die in the cause of resisting any officer that would come there on the patroon's business."[20] Adams continued to deliver writs to distressed tenants, but later that night, while he was bunking at a local tavern, insurgents broke into his stable, destroyed his wagon, and sheared his horse's mane and tail. In September, Sheriff Michael Artcher received an anonymous letter that warned him not to deliver writs to Helderberg tenants: "You need not think this to be children's play, for the tenants have arisen in the name of justice, and it will need a stronger hand than you are aware to put them down. Their strength is fast gaining. If you come out in your official capacity, you come against great strength and I would not pledge your safe return. Therefore, if you come, you come at your own risk."[21] Sufficiently intimidated, Artcher did not go at first. He sent a proxy, Daniel Leonard, who was subsequently accosted by insurgents, manhandled, verbally abused, and forced to toss his legal papers into a barrel of burning tar. Over the next three months, Artcher, accompanied by posses, would personally make several forays into the hills surrounding Berne to serve writs and suppress the rebellion, a bloodless confrontation misnamed the "Helderberg War." Early attempts in October and November were met with similar responses: the sounds of tin horns blaring signals to mobilizing rioters throughout the countryside and the obstruction of roadways by armed mobs who quickly forced the sheriff to retreat. In December, the sheriff and a posse of more than 500 men approached Reidsville, but a hostile reception by a crowd of nearly 1,800 rioters sent the sheriff and his posse scurrying back to Albany. A week later, Artcher, accompanied by a state militia, once again marched on Reidsville, but, because Governor William Seward had promised to consider the anti-rent griev-ances, the rioters abandoned the field and could not be found when Artcher arrived to serve writs and make arrests. With no opposition or war to fight, the state militia quickly returned to Albany.[22]

A month later, in January 1840, during his annual state message, Governor Seward, sympathetic to the anti-rent movement, urged his fellow Whigs in the legislature to consider means of dismantling the Hudson's manorial estates, which he described as "oppressive, antirepublican and degrading."[23] In their various entreaties to the state legislature, anti-renters demanded several changes to state law. One alteration would sever a landlord's right of *distress,* or the power to seize and sell a tenant's personal property in order to recover unpaid rent. Anti-Renters also wanted the state to tax a landlord's income from rent, and, above all, they wanted a new law enabling tenants to challenge the validity of landlord titles when they were sued for nonpayment of rent. That March, the legislature ordered an investigation of the burdensome leasehold system and arranged to negotiate a compromise with Van Rensselaer on behalf of his tenants. However, the landlord remained obstinate regarding the payment of back rent, and, after discussions quickly deadlocked, the anti-rent insurgents employed a new tactic, the obstruction of distress sales. Dozens if not hundreds of rioters, some armed, would attend a sale and, through sheer intimidation, drive off prospective bidders, thereby forestalling the sale and preventing the loss of tenant property. Before a distress sale in Delaware County, one rioter warned that persons who dared enter bids would be "floored and knocked down so quick that they would not know what hurt them."[24] If scare tactics didn't work, conspiring rioters partook in the bidding on single items and drove prices up until nightfall arrived and sales had to be postponed.[25] In many cases, sales were cancelled beforehand because the property of delinquent tenants had been "stolen" by disguised rioters before confiscation could take place. In due time, the property eventually made its way back to its original owner. This strategy of obstruction was so successful in Van Rensselaer County that the sale of one particular tenant's property was cancelled at least eight times.[26]

Also during this time, following a familiar pattern established by the Sons of Liberty and Maine's White Indians, rioters began to appear in elaborate Indian disguises, this time with bright headpieces, calico pantaloons, and tunics adorned with fur, feathers, horns, or other ornaments. They were also armed with swords, pistols, muskets, knives, and clubs. "Indian" sentinels used tin horns to warn neighbors and mobilize "tribes" whenever agents of the landlords were in their midst. As one "Indian" put it, "we resolved to adopt the same kind of protection that was resorted to by the people of Boston when the tea was thrown overboard into the water."[27] Although contemporary accounts usually referred to these insurgents simply as "Indians," they were also called "Calico Indians," a term used here to avoid confusion with Native Americans or Maine's White Indians. Beyond its functions of disguise and intimidation, the Calico Indian persona had symbolic meaning. Many tenants had based their opposing land claims on the purchase of deeds from the original Native American owners; consequently, as historian Reeve Huston noted, these anti-rent Indians were, in a sense, reclaiming what was historically theirs, while underscoring the fraudulence of the landlords' titles. Huston also noted that Indian activity provided a psychological outlet for insecure tenants, reinforced community moral standards, gave an active voice to the cause, and undermined traditional hierarchical notions of deference and subordination.[28] Amos Adams, the new sheriff of Albany County, who witnessed the "mighty war whoops" and "grotesque dresses" of the Calico Indians, commented afterwards that he "would give fifty dollars if the patroon himself would witness what my eyes have beheld."[29]

In September, Deputy Sheriff Bill Snyder, having set out to deliver writs near Rensselaerville, was accosted by Calico Indians. What followed is a matter of dispute. As Snyder described the episode, he was kidnapped but escaped into the woods and barely averted death as gunshots whistled past him. According to the popular anti-rent ballad "The End of Bill Snyder," he initially challenged his captors but, horrified by their appearance, quickly ran to the woods like a frightened coward:

> The moon was shining silver bright;
> The sheriff came in the dead of night;
> High on a hill sat an Indian true,
> And on his horn, this blast he blew—

> The Indians gathered at the sound,
> Bill cocked his pistol—looked around—
> Their painted faces, by the moon,
> He saw, and heard that same old tune—

Says Bill, "This music's not so sweet
As I have heard—I think my feet
Had better be used;" and he started to run,
But the tin horn still kept sounding on,

He ran and ran, til he reached the wood,
And there, with horror, still he stood;
For he saw a savage, tall and grim,
And he heard a horn, not a rod from him;

And he thought that he heard the sound of a gun,
And he cried in his fright, "Oh! My race is run!
Better had it been, had I never been born,
Than to come within the sound of that tin horn."[30]

Soon, anonymous letters began to appear on the property of agents working for the landlords. One threatened to use "TAR AND FEATHER" and "A DOSE OF PISTLS PILS" and warned that "THE PUBLIC FEELING IS AGAINST YOU."[31] For the next three years, Van Rensselaer made no further attempts to collect rent, and, accordingly, Calico Indian activity assumed a short respite.

IV.   The Anti-Rent Movement Expands

While the Hudson rioting temporarily dissipated, the anti-rent controversy continued to complicate state politics. A new Democratic administration headed by Governor William Bouck swept into office in January 1843, and, a year later, the Assembly's Judiciary Committee issued a scathing report that condemned the anti-rent movement as an attack on the inviolability of contracts, and criticized former Governor Seward for having encouraged the false hopes of expectant tenants. The resistance movement, however, remained undeterred, as anti-rent associations soon appeared not only in Albany County but also in nearby Rensselaer, Columbia, and Delaware counties, as well. These county anti-rent associations were crucial in establishing political credibility. While the Calico Indians represented the paramilitary wing of the movement, the associations coordinated legal strategies, circulated petitions, raised funds, and helped shape public opinion. There was, no doubt, a certain overlap between legitimate membership in the associations and covert participation in Indian activity. In due time, anti-rentism would spread to 11 counties, attracting the support of perhaps 60,000 sympathizers.[32] Meanwhile, insurgents formulated a more sophisticated campaign of resistance, seeking fuller and wider communication of their motives and objectives.

Two individuals were especially crucial in this regard: Dr. Smith A. Boughton, who became the chief Calico Indian leader and the movement's primary spokesperson, and Thomas Ainge Devyr, an Irishman and Chartist exile from England.

Smith A. Boughton, a charismatic and articulate doctor from the village of Alps, came from a family of troublemakers and demonstrated his own rebelliousness during his medical studies at Vermont's Middlebury College. Middlebury was then under denominational control, with required church attendance until Boughton organized such an impressive and reasoned student protest that the school abandoned its compulsion of religious observance. He volunteered to fight in Canada in 1837 during the Patriot's Rebellion and, in addition to practicing medicine, began to lobby in Albany on behalf of the anti-rent cause during the early 1840s.[33] Thomas Ainge Devyr, described as a "globe trotting moral adventurer," had been an active Irish land reformer before moving to England and plotting with Newcastle Chartists to overthrow the British government. Forced to flee in 1840 when their conspiracy was discovered, Devyr ended up in New York, where he was inspired by the Helderberg War and subsequently edited several anti-rent newspapers, including the *National Reformer,* the *Albany Freeholder* and the *Anti-Renter.* Greatly influenced by biblical concepts of land and natural rights theories, Devyr was a tireless propagandist for the anti-rent cause. Unfortunately, his later attempt to merge the movement with the National Reform Association contributed to a bitter division within the anti-rent ranks.[34]

The Calico Indians under Boughton's leadership were further refined, incorporating secret oaths, Chartist-like cell structures, mass costume construction, and an organizational hierarchy complete with Indian titles based on rank. Boughton, for instance, was known in the anti-rent underground as "Big Thunder."[35] The anti-rent Indians were initially divided into three "tribes," each with their own "chief." The Indians from Blenheim Hill were led by Christopher Decker, known as "Black Hawk." Henry Cleveland, known as "Red Jacket," directed the tribe from Middleburgh and John McEntyre, or "Tecumseh," led the Indians from Gilboa.[36] Each Indian's "paleface" identity was known only to the members of his tribe, which constituted a secret society, independent, self-governing, and devoted to the traditions of *charivari.*[37] The Calico Indians often marched in parades and performed other public rituals that not only helped maintain a certain *esprit de corps,* but also were tools by which the insurgents, through their sheer strength and numbers, could intimidate the community. On at least one occasion, more than 500 Indians in Delaware County partook in one such ritual. One particular demonstration was a dance known as the "snake around," in which Indians went through intricate and synchronized maneuvers imitating the movement of a monster snake.[38]

As the saga of Bill Snyder further revealed, the Calico Indians also created an impressive body of songs and ballads that contributed greatly to the anti-rent propaganda campaign. Scores of verses, many of which were written and sung for special occasions, were passed around in handbills, newspapers, letters, and by word of mouth. While "The End of Bill Snyder," written for a 4th of July celebration, was the movement's most popular song, ballads such as "The Landlord's Lament" satirized the patroon's point of view:

The Helderberg boys are playing the dickens!
The night of confusion around me now thickens,
Unless the rent business with some of us quickens,
We'll all have to live without the rents!

I used to get rich through the poor toiling tenants,
And I spent all their earnings in pleasures satanic,
But now I confess I'm in a great panic,
Because I can get no more rent!

I must give up this business I vow it's no use to me,
It's been a continual source of abuse to me;
The friends of equal rights give no peace to me
Until they get clear of the rent.[39]

Songs and ballads not only helped to popularize the anti-rent cause, but they were also sources of Indian solidarity, as newly initiated "braves" were taught their lyrics, and group sing-alongs became yet another element of the underground culture.

In the most complete demographic study of the anti-renters, Reeve Huston noted that those who chose to partake in Indian activities tended to be younger and poorer than their non-violent allies, and that the vast majority were not farmers but landless laborers. He also estimated that eventually the Calico Indians numbered nearly 10,000, most belonging to independent cells organized at the town, county, and regional levels. Huston also described a fairly sophisticated Indian subculture replete with "native" dialects, public gatherings, and tribal rituals. Further, unlike other terrorist organizations covered in this study, the Calico Indians relied greatly on the direct participation of women. Women participated by creating the ornate Indian disguises and providing moral support, but in other areas gender conventions were disregarded. Women took secret oaths, hid fugitives from authorities, wrote petitions, delivered speeches, and committed acts of vandalism against the landlords and their agents. They ran their farms in the absence of their husbands and were also effective sentinels, keeping watch and blowing their renowned tin horns whenever evil forces invaded the neighborhood.[40] The lyrics to one anti-rent song openly courted female participation:

Come join the anti-renters!
Ye dames and maidens fair,
And breathe around us in our path
Affections hallowed air.[41]

More than perhaps anywhere else, the resistance movement in New York was very much a collaborative effort between the sexes.

The anti-rent Indians also escalated their response to landlord provocations by reviving the tradition of tarring and feathering. In late July 1844, Gideon Reynolds, sheriff of Rensselaer County, and George Allen, his deputy sheriff, set out to deliver arrest warrants near Alps, where they were confronted by approximately 600 Calico Indians. Although Reynolds carried no official papers, Allen was not so fortunate. Explaining that their intent was to punish anyone caught bearing official papers on behalf of the landlords, the insurgents blew their tin horns, fired guns into the air, and promptly tarred and feathered the deputy sheriff. In August, Christopher Batterman, sheriff of Albany County, was similarly assaulted, and, adding further abuse, rioters offered a $500 reward to anyone who captured Batterman and tied him to a tree in nearby Maumie Swamp. For the next few months, Batterman wisely avoided the area.[42] In September, Timothy Corbin, one of Stephen Van Rensselaer's trusted aides, was accosted by insurgents near Roxbury, blindfolded, beaten, kicked, and also tarred and feathered.[43] Over the next several months, rioting in the Hudson Valley intensified. In early December, Big Thunder and his Indians accosted Sheriff Henry Miller and destroyed his writs. A week later, a rally was held at Smoky Hollow to stir up the tenants of Livingston Manor and to promote the Columbia County Anti-Rent Association. The featured guest was Big Thunder himself, but, before he could speak, a bullet of unknown origin was fired into the crowd and a young man dropped dead. In his study of the Hudson controversies, David Maldwyn Ellis, prompted by contemporary newspaper accounts, suggested that the young victim had been deliberately targeted by insurgents for refusing to shout "down with the rent."[44] This contention, however, was recently refuted by Charles W. McCurdy, who argued instead that the newspaper accounts were misleading and that the killing was the random result of a stray bullet.[45] What is indisputable is that Dr. Boughton and his aide Mortimer Beldon, or "Little Thunder," were somehow held accountable. They were found undisguised at a roadside tavern, and a subsequent search of their baggage uncovered two loaded pistols, complete Indian disguises, and a sword. They were immediately arrested and charged with manslaughter. The authorities had their men, but it was testament to the air of anxiety created by the Indian insurgency that the subsequent fear of a rescue riot was so pronounced. Widespread panic seemed to engulf Columbia County. Volunteers patrolled the city streets of Hudson, where Boughton and Beldon were held, while town officials hastily devised plans for civil defense. Sentinels were placed at strategic entrances to the city and high atop the steeple of the Presbyterian church. The mayor sent an urgent appeal to the governor for military assistance, and within days more than 300 troops had arrived to help secure the prisoners.[46] Although no attempt to rescue the prisoners was ever made, for a few days, Hudson appeared to be a city under siege, and, even though they never made a move on the town, surely the Calico Indians had to be impressed by the degree of anxiety their tactics had elicited.

The day after the killing at Smoky Hollow, Elijah Smith, a lumberman and up-renter who had purchased a lot from William Van Rensselaer, was transporting timber with his uncle when he was confronted by about 50 Calico Indians near Grafton. After the insurgents demanded that Smith unload his wood, he jumped down from his wagon and rushed at the masked rioters, swinging an axe until he was fatally shot by an unidentified assailant.[47] A distinct message to the broader community of up-renters, Smith's killing seemed to confirm that any type of tenant collusion with the landlords was now considered treasonous to the anti-rent movement and, therefore, subject to severe consequences. Violence against up-renters had been common during the earlier, 18th-century chapter of Hudson rioting, but Calico Indians revived the tactic and now paid increasing attention to the up-rent community and others who would collaborate with the landlords. While the obstruction of rent collection could be perceived as reactionary and defensive, the attacks on up-renters were unquestionably aggressive, proactive attempts to impact an audience beyond the landlords and county lawmen. One tenant, who helped collect rent in Livingstonville, was abducted from a public highway by disguised insurgents, dragged into a nearby gulch, and given a coat of tar and feathers.[48] John Lasher, hired by a landlord agent to haul away fallen timber near Cooper Lake, was overpowered by 20 Indians and also tarred and feathered.[49] Other up-renters throughout the rebellious counties were abducted, threatened in public, abused, shot at, or had their property destroyed. In Delaware County, the homes, barns, and hay bales of some up-renters were put to the torch. In Ancram, two up-renters' houses were pulled down.[50] A correspondent for the *New York Evening Post* suggested that Hudson Valley tenants were now rushing to join the resistance movement because their "life and property are both in danger in case of refusal to respond to the cry of 'Down with the rent.'"[51] In Scholarie County, witnesses reported that disguised Indians were patrolling major roadways and conducting extensive interrogations of all travelers in order to determine their allegiances. Many of these travelers were not allowed to proceed until they shouted "down with the rent."[52] In light of these developments, a resolution that appeared in several Hudson Valley newspapers warned about the "gang of ruthless men in the guise of Indians, instigated and abetted by those known as anti-renters, [who] have for the past year been prowling around in armed gangs, setting at defiance the laws and preventing their execution; threatening, insulting, and assaulting its executors; abusing nonoffending citizens; destroying property; and . . . cold-blooded, deliberate murder."[53] By deliberately victimizing a group wider than the closed circle of Hudson landlords and their agents, the anti-rent insurgents set out to purposely create an environment of fear among the broader community of Hudson tenants, and employed sophisticated propaganda techniques to promote the cause, provoking one newspaper to declare that "a system of terror has been put against all who will not join these organizations."[54]

The government reaction to the twin killings in December was swift. Governor Bouck immediately dispatched state troops to Livingston Manor to round up insurgents; 50 detainees were eventually indicted for riot or conspiracy to riot. The next month, a new Democratic administration took office in New York, and, although Silas Wright, the new governor, offered an early conciliatory tone toward anti-rentism, he was also determined to restore law and order. The *Daily Albany Argus,* an organ serving Wright and his old political allies condemned the anti-rent Indians: "by committing, in the disguise of Indians, brutal and savage outrages upon officers of justice and upon innocent, unoffending individuals, these deluded and wretched beings have at length dipped their hands in blood and perpetrated foul and malicious murders."[55] In February 1845, the state legislature approved new laws forbidding disguises while armed, and granting the governor broad powers to loan arms and troops to county sheriffs unable to cope with riotous activity. If the new governor's actions appeared at times to be somewhat ambivalent, this was with good reason. Most detached observers, as well as many anti-renters themselves, agreed that the violence in New York had become deplorable. Yet, the anti-rent cause continued to attract attention, generating avid supporters throughout New York and across the nation. Reformism had come to define the social agenda of the antebellum era, and large-scale landlordism, one of the last remnants of an aristocratic past, was anathema to the democratizing spirit then animating the country.[56] Many Hudson landlords, sensitive to the changing times, had already begun to transition their lands into freeholds. Consequently, in New York, both Whigs and Democrats sought simultaneously to blame each other for the breakdown of law and order, while courting the influential anti-rent vote, which had begun to flex its political muscle during the 1844 state election.

Despite New York's new laws concerning disguises and a vow to cease "Indian" tactics at a recent anti-rent convention, Calico Indians continued to operate. In February, more than 400 disguised rioters armed with pistols, muskets, and rifles gathered to obstruct a distress sale in Delaware County. After the sale was cancelled, a witness complained that "the anti-renters are insincere in their professions of submissions to the laws and they are determined to persist in their defiance of law and order to the utmost extremity."[57] For the next few months, no distress sales were conducted in Delaware County, as Calico Indians kept the countryside in a state of constant alarm. On March 12, Deputy Sheriff Osman Steele led a posse of about 80 volunteers to Roxbury, where they brawled with nearly 80 Calico Indians before seizing about a dozen prisoners. By the end of March, Steele had conducted additional raids and had rounded up another 20 insurgents, often abusing entire families in the process. Two weeks later, in Scholarie County, Sheriff John Brown and Undersheriff Tobias Bouck, serving writs on behalf of landlord John King, were beaten by Indians under the command of Black Hawk, otherwise known as Christopher Decker.[58] This outburst of Hudson Valley violence, however, did not sit well with increasing numbers of anti-renters. The anti-rent cause had been validated by expanding political support, but its attendant violence could only serve to undermine, not benefit, the movement. The anti-rent movement was becoming less a monolithic movement and more a convergence of different activists seeking the same end through different means. While many anti-renters sought change either through litigation sponsored by their local associations or through the selection of sympathetic officials via the electoral process, the Calico Indians sought to sustain the movement by employing violence to both undermine the landlords and frighten up-renters into compliance.[59]

As if to taunt the anti-rent Indians, Osman Steele's brutal methods remained an irritant, and tensions continued to run high throughout the valley. Finally, on August 7, Steele and several other officials appeared at Dingle Hill to conduct a distress sale of livestock at the farm of Moses Earle, who was $64 in arrears to his landlord. When Steele's party attempted to move Earle's cattle into a clearing, more than 100 Calico Indians surrounded the livestock and obstructed prospective bidders from entering the auction. When one bidder, responding to an Indian inquiry, confessed that he intended to participate in the sale, he was warned, "If you do, you will go home in a wagon, feet foremost."[60] Many times before, this tactic had forced the cancellation of distress sales, but, on this occasion, authorities were determined to press ahead, in open defiance of the Indian presence. What happened next was a source of much controversy and may never be accurately determined. Opinions of the time were dependent on viewpoint and source of information. The *Albany Daily Argus,* which tended to condemn Calico Indian outrages, cited the eyewitness testimony of one of Steele's party, who maintained that the deputy sheriff and a fellow constable, both on horseback, approached the Indians with peaceful intentions.[61] However, the *Albany Freeholder,* an anti-rent mouthpiece, also published eyewitness accounts suggesting, instead, that the lawmen confronted the Indians in a menacing fashion, pointing pistols in their direction.[62] Suddenly, as everyone agreed, several shots rang out, the two horses immediately dropped in their tracks, and Osman Steele fell to the ground, mortally wounded. Three bullets had penetrated his body, and he died several hours later. In his *History of Delaware County* published a decade after Steele's demise, Jay Gould cited eyewitness testimony from a member of Steele's party that suggested that during the standoff, Steele was fired upon deliberately and wounded before discharging his pistol. This testimony described an Indian chief as having shouted orders to "shoot the horses" and to "shoot *him.*"[63] Gould's one-sided account, consistent with the reporting of the *Daily Argus,* was essentially repeated in David Murray's essay that appeared in the 1896 annual report of the American Historical Association, a prestigious publication that would seem to validate this interpretation of events. Murray went so far as to imply that Steele was the target of a murder conspiracy.[64] However, in their 1940 accounts of the Hudson rioting, Henry Christman and John D. Monroe suggested, as did contemporary anti-renters, that on his deathbed Steele confessed to having fired the first shot that triggered the shootout.[65] And both David Maldwyn Ellis and Charles McCurdy have since implied that the rioters, in their attempts to shoot Steele's horse out from under him, mortally wounded the deputy sheriff by accident. Interestingly, both Ellis and McCurdy cited the alleged Indian order to "shoot the horses," but neither mentioned the accompanying order to "shoot *him.*"[66] As with the unfortunate killing the previous December at the Big Thunder rally, contemporary accounts of Dingle Hill's "first shot" were understandably biased, and, in both instances, there is still no way of knowing precisely who among the insurgents fired the fatal shots, let alone what their intentions might have been.

The impact of Steele's death was immediate. Many insurgents fled the valley; some abandoned New York altogether. A huge militia of 300 volunteers helped track down dozens of insurgents in a ruthless three-week dragnet ironically described by one observer as "a reign of terror."[67] On August 27, Governor Silas Wright declared Delaware County to be in a state of insurrection. That fall, nine insurgents pleaded guilty to manslaughter charges, while 68 others had their murder charges reduced and ultimately avoided prison sentences. Despite the lack of any credible evidence against them, Edward O'Connor and John Van Steenburgh were found guilty of Steele's murder and sentenced to death, but Governor Silas Wright eventually commuted their sentences. In a separate trial, Smith Boughton, or Big Thunder, was found guilty, not of manslaughter but of a lesser crime that nonetheless earned him a life sentence. After Silas Wright left office, Governor John Young pardoned Boughton in 1847.

Although a final resolution to the anti-rent controversy was still two decades away, occasional outbreaks of violence would continue to complicate life along the Hudson. During these years, Calico Indian activity would largely disappear, but not without having created a major political, economic, and social impact similar to other "Indian" resistance movements under consideration here. And as with the Sons of Liberty and Maine's White Indians, the anti-rent Indians employed terrorist methods, for, unlike the land rioters in New Jersey, they made a sustained and concerted effort to intimidate a wider target audience through the exploitation of violence. By extending their tactics of intimidation to up-renters and other members of the broader community who sought accommodation with the landlords, the insurgents propagated a message that, beyond sheriffs and landlord agents, any neighbor standing in the way of anti-renter unanimity risked severe consequences. Acts of violence were thus meant not only to obstruct or protect but also to terrorize and manipulate. From a larger perspective, it is evident that the Calico Indians replicated and refined the elements of anti-rent terrorism first employed decades earlier by their 18th-century predecessors, who had introduced elements of *charivari* and had also targeted the up-rent community. Unlike in Vermont, where Green Mountain terrorism drove a community of Yorkers into exile, in the Hudson Valley, Calico Indian tactics did not necessarily create a similar mass exodus of up-renters, who had contractual obligations to consider. But the impact of Calico Indian terrorism was unmistakable, as evidenced by the public consternation, the destruction of property, the repeated cancellation of distress sales, the stout defense of dispossessed or delinquent tenants, and the unfortunate murders of Steele and Smith, which subsequently prompted military intervention, mass indictments, and widely publicized trials. The efficacy of terror along the Hudson, however, was most evident through the difficulty of the landlords to collect rent, which prompted one observer to lament that "an agent dare hardly show his face in the infected district." One landlord agent complained about the futility "to Collect Rents within our Patent so long as disguised men were allowed with impunity to resist."[68] The air of intimidation was so pervasive that, on many leasehold estates, rents went routinely uncollected for months or years at a time.

In addition to targeting both immediate victims and a wider audience through orchestrated acts of violence, Calico Indians employed other tactics associated with terrorism. A specific anti-rent political agenda had been established and articulated through legislative petitions and legal briefs. The Indian subculture was resolute, organized, and had a structural hierarchy led by tribal chiefs. The secret oaths taken by men assuming mock-heroic identities reinforced their status as outsiders, unbound by the ways of the "paleface" world. Moreover, exploits of the Calico Indians were celebrated through songs and ballads that were passed down from generation to generation, adding to a significant body of propaganda largely provided by sympathetic editors such as Thomas Ainge Devyr, as well as anti-rent newspapers such as the *Albany Freeholder* and *Albany Anti-Renter*. In retrospect, the anti-rent insurgents, although mostly ignored and underappreciated by contemporary students of American history, must be considered significant contributors to the legacy of terrorism in America before the 20th century.

Calico Indian terror had helped propagandize the cause, and, in that regard, its work was largely done. By 1846, the anti-rent movement was gaining momentum as the New York legislature adopted a more aggressive pro-tenant agenda, and anti-renters began to network with groups such as the National Reform Association and the Free Soil Party. John Young, the anti-rent Whig candidate for governor who defeated Silas Wright in 1846, pardoned all anti-rent prisoners once he took office. And soon thereafter, the state legislature abolished distress sales and began to tax income from rent collection. For the next few years, anti-rent constituencies were also able to elect empathetic sheriffs and officials, further obstructing the landlords from collecting rent and largely invalidating the need for terrorist activity. Although the courts would continue to uphold the original Dutch and English grants, state legislation would slowly erode the monopolization of land. These developments, along with the endless litigation, adverse public opinion, shifting political allegiances, reformism, the inability to collect rent, and years of violence, would have a cumulative impact upon the landed gentry. Eventually, landlords decided to sell their interests and began negotiations to unload their leases. The Hudson estates, which had long controlled life in eastern New York, would soon become a relic of the past, although the leasehold issue did not die easily. During the late 1850s, a group of speculators led by Colonel Walter Church purchased the land and leases of the Van Rensselaer brothers and once again insisted on collecting rents and ejecting delinquent tenants. By the mid-1860s, Calico Indians had reappeared and violence predictably ensued, culminating in the death of Deputy Sheriff Willard Griggs, who was fatally wounded in 1869 while attempting to dispossess a tenant.[69] This was the last significant Indian action. By then, Church was saddled with tenant lawsuits, debts remained uncollected, and most of the other powerful landlords had sold their interests. He never came close to approximating the fantastic wealth of the great patroons and died virtually bankrupt in 1890. By then, most of the old Hudson Valley leases had been converted into freeholds.

V.   The New York Anti-Rent Wars, in Retrospect

With the exception of a few scattered historical accounts, the anti-rent war was largely overlooked until two books appeared in 1940, John D. Monroe's *History of Delaware County and Border Wars of New York* and Henry Christman's *Tin Horns and Calico*. Of the two, Christman's work was the more thorough and deeply researched; however, he failed to provide any attribution, despite his constant description of dialogue. Nonetheless, his narrative, a sympathetic portrayal of the anti-rent rebellion, is still a valuable source of the various storylines that evolved from the entire anti-rent episode. With the exception of Sung Bok Kim's study of New York's manorial society (1978), this is where matters stood until three significant full-length studies appeared at the turn of the 21st century. All three understandably treated the two eras of the anti-rent rioting as distinctly separate episodes, each focusing solely on either the 18th- or 19th-century iteration. Only Thomas J. Humphrey's *Land and Liberty* dealt exclusively with the 1760s episode, and suggested that rioters helped radicalize the American Revolution and paved the way for farmers to obtain political independence, economic autonomy, and community status. While Humphrey's study might be the most informative source on the Revolutionary Era riots, it is the mid-19th-century "war" that has ultimately attracted the most attention from scholars past and present. Reeve Huston's *Land and Freedom* recently suggested that the second anti-rent movement was a manifestation of the transition from a subsistence-based agricultural society into a capitalist economy, while Charles W. McCurdy's *The Anti-Rent Era in New York Law and Politics 1839–1865* argued that the movement was stymied by both jurisprudential and partisan imperatives. Desperate laborers and farmers in disguise might have propagandized the cause and generated initial awareness, but numerous missed opportunities to resolve the controversy serve as a cautionary tale of what can happen when politicians and lawyers hijack a popular movement.

Regarding the two anti-rent episodes as separate and distinct, given the 60-year interval between them, is certainly understandable, but, upon further reflection concerning the employment of terrorist activity, it is also possible to discern continuity between the two periods. The 18th-century anti-rent terrorists did not tar and feather, but their use of violence to obstruct the collection of rent and the dispossession of tenants is a direct link to their 19th-century successors, who took the resistance movement to a new level of sophistication. Tenant reliance on terrorism, whether isolated or part of a larger campaign, proved the one constant throughout the entire Hudson Valley drama. But the Calico Indians were also more than mere local terrorists operating along the Hudson. They were part of an evolving legacy of American terrorism, a bridge between the resistance groups of the Revolutionary Era to those of the Civil War/Reconstruction Era. At a time when expanding borders, international conflicts, political turmoil, and social upheaval were testing the nation's resolve and leading toward unprecedented civil hostilities, Americans were still sufficiently concerned with the significance of their own lives to terrorize their neighbors.

Notes

1. David Murray, "The Anti-Rent Episode in the State of New York," vol.1, *Annual Report of the American Historical Association* (Washington, DC printing office, 1896), 145.
2. Reeve Huston, *Land and Freedom—Rural Society, Popular Protest, and Party Politics in Antebellum New York* (New York: Oxford University Press, 2000), 5.
3. Thomas J. Humphrey, *Land and Liberty—Hudson Valley Riots in the Age of Revolution* (DeKalb: Northern Illinois Press, 2004), 36.
4. Charles W. McCurdy, *The Anti-Rent Era in New York Law and Politics, 1839–1865* (Chapel Hill: University of North Carolina Press, 2001), 1.
5. Robert Livingston to Lt. Gov. De Lancey, February 12, 1754, DHSNY, vol. 3, 458–459; Affidavit of Sheriff Yates, February 13, 1755, DHSNY, vol. 3, 464–465; Lt. Gov. De Lancey to Gov. Shirley, February 17, 1755, DHSNY, vol. 3, 465–466; Affidavit of John Van Rensselaer, February 22, 1755, DHSNY, vol. 3, 467.
6. Humphrey, *Land and Liberty*, 45.
7. Sung Bok Kim, *Landlord and Tenant in Colonial New York—Manorial Society, 1664–1775* (Chapel Hill: University of North Carolina Press, 1978).
8. Robert Livingston to Lt. Gov. De Lancey, February 12, 1754, DHSNY, vol. 3, 58–59.
9. Robert Livingston to Lt. Gov. De Lancey, March 3, 1755, DHSNY, vol. 3, 469.
10. Testimonies of John Van Rensselaer, April 28, 1755 and John McArthur, April 28, 1755, DHSNY, 471–472.
11. Robert Livingston to Sir Charles Hardy, November 23, 1755, DHSNY, 488.
12. Humphrey, *Land and Liberty*, 106.
13. Proclamation of James De Lancey, DHSNY, 491.
14. Humphrey, *Land and Liberty*, 26–27.
15. Ibid., 52.
16. Irving Mark, "Agrarian Revolt in Colonial New York, 1766," *American Journal of Economics and Society*, vol. 1, no. 2 (January, 1942): 121.
17. Humphrey, *Land and Liberty*, 72.
18. Huston, *Land and Freedom*, 15.
19. Ibid., 29.
20. McCurdy, *The Anti-Rent Era*, 18.
21. Henry Christman, *Tin Horns and Calico* (Cornwallville, NY: Hope Farm Press, 1975), 23.
22. David Maldwyn Ellis, *Landlords and Farmers in the Hudson-Mohawk Region, 1790–1850* (Ithaca: Cornell University Press, 1946) 232–246; McCurdy, *The Anti-Rent Era,* 18–32; Christman, *Tins Horns and Calico*, 16–27; Huston, *Land and Freedom,* 89–94.
23. McCurdy, *The Anti-Rent Era*, 4.

24. "Newspaper Clippings Relating to Anti-Rent Disturbances in New York State With Some Account of the Resulting Trials," a scrapbook on microfiche located at New York State Library, 13, 87.

25. Huston, *Land and Freedom*, 120.

26. Testimony of John O'Brien, March 29, 1742, file 6211, Governor's Papers, Papers of William S. Seward, Green Library, Stanford University.

27. Jay Gould, *History of Delaware County and Border Wars of New York* (Roxbury, NY: Keeny and Gould, 1865), 262; Christman, *Tin Horns and Calico*, 41; Ellis, *Landlords and Farmers*, 248; quote from Huston, *Land and Freedom*, 116.

28. Huston, *Land and Freedom*, 122–124; quote on p. 116.

29. McCurdy, *The Anti-Rent Era*, 71.

30. Christman, *Tin Horns and Calico*, 326.

31. Huston, *Land and Freedom*, 123.

32. Ibid., 3.

33. Christman, *Tin Horns and Calico*, 48.

34. Christman, *Tin Horns and Calico*, 51–59; quote from Huston, *Land and Freedom*, 138.

35. Murray, "The Anti-Rent Episode," 151.

36. McCurdy, *The Anti-Rent Era*, 149.

37. Huston, *Land and Freedom*, 116.

38. Eldrige Honaker Pendleton, *The New York Anti-Rent Controversy, 1820–1860* (PhD dissertation, University of Virginia, 1974), 40.

39. Christman, *Tin Horns and Calico*, 325–326.

40. Huston, *Land and Freedom*, 117, 127.

41. Ibid., 125–127.

42. Christman, *Tin Horns and Calico*, 86, 90.

43. John D. Monroe, *The Anti-Rent War in Delaware County, New York* (Jefferson, NY: 1940), 19.

44. Ellis, *Landlords and Farmers*, 260.

45. McCurdy, *The Anti-Rent Era*, 166.

46. Pendleton, *The New York Anti-Rent Controversy*, 57, 138–139.

47. Murray, "The Anti-Rent Episode," 151.

48. Testimony of John O'Brien, Seward Papers.

49. Christman, *Tin Horns and Calico*, 135; Pendleton, *The New York Anti-Rent Controversy*, 109; Ellis, *Landlords and Farmers*, 262.

50. Pendleton, *The New York Anti-Rent Controversy*, 103–112.

51. Christman, *Tin Horns and Calico*, 90.

52. "Newspaper Clippings," 12; Pendleton, *The New York Anti-Rent Controversy*, 104.

53. "Newspaper Clippings," 7.

54. Ibid., 22.

55. *Daily Albany Argus*, August 8, 1745.

56. Alice Felt Tyler, *Freedom's Ferment* (University of Minnesota, 1944); Ronald C. Walters, *America's Reformers, 1815–1860* (New York: Hill and Wang, 1978).

57. McCurdy, *The Anti-Rent Era*, 178.

58. Ellis, *Landlords and Farmers*, 262; Christman, *Tin Horns and Calico*, 102–104; Murray, "The Anti-Rent Episode," 157.

59. *The Encyclopedia of New York State* (Syracuse: Syracuse University Press, 2005).

60. *Daily Albany Argus*, August 8, 1745.

61. Ibid.

62. *Albany Freeholder*, October 1, 1745.

63. Gould, *History of Delaware County and Border Wars of New York*, 276.

64. Murray, "The Anti-Rent Episode," 160. See footnote 32.

65. Christman, *Tin Horns and Calico*, 180; Monroe, *The Anti-Rent War*, 28.

66. Ellis, *Landlords and Farmers*, 266; McCurdy, *The Anti-Rent Era*, 217.

67. McCurdy, *The Anti-Rent Era*, 218; Christman, *Tin Horns and Calico*, 190.

68. Huston, *Land and Freedom*, 131.

69. Christman, *Tin Horns and Calico*, 302.

8
THE KU KLUX KLAN

I. Background

The American Civil War, fought from 1861 to 1865, is still considered the most cataclysmic event in our nation's history. In that sense, it stands alone with regard to death, destruction, social implications, and political impact. Thus, seldom is it considered within the larger context, as the penultimate event of a 200-year continuum of civil insurrections that began with Maryland's "Plundering Time" of the 1640s. As previous chapters have made clear, civil insurrections were common before and after the American Revolution, although none, of course, save the Revolution itself, came even remotely close to the magnitude of the Civil War. Regardless, the notion of a violent insurrection against governmental authority was hardly foreign to Americans. But beyond the massive military campaigns and the eventual commitment to "total war" by the Union forces, the equally enduring legacy of collective, social violence also continued unabated. Race riots continued to rage in eastern urban settings during the war but were particularly dangerous out west along the Pacific Coast and in mining areas in Wyoming. Frontier violence would plague the New Mexico territory for more than three decades, beginning in the late 1860s. And in New York City, riots protesting conscription in 1863 resulted in more than 100 deaths. Meanwhile, terrorist organizations such as the Ku Klux Klan and the Molly Maguires were about to unleash an unprecedented wave of murder and destruction.

Interestingly, in light of these and subsequent developments, Richard Maxwell Brown argued that the Civil War resulted in a "new era of crime" in which the "tradition of the social bandit declined" in favor of urban gangs, criminal syndicates, and freelance serial murderers.[1] He also noted that the Civil War witnessed the end of the two-man personal duel and the beginning of political assassinations.

Abraham Lincoln, it should be remembered, was the first president to fall from an assassin's bullet. The purposeful taking of another person's life had become less and less personal, as many Americans grew increasingly inured to death and violence. No doubt the 628,000 lives lost during the war would have some impact on the country's frame of mind. Prior to the Civil War, terrorist groups in America rarely set out intentionally to kill and generally took lives only accidentally. During and after the war, terrorists would take lives routinely and without remorse. And since assassination would become a primary terrorist tactic, the Civil War represented not just a "great divide" with regard to the phenomenon of assassination, as Brown maintained, but also with regard to the degree of murderous activity by newly emerging terrorist groups. It should be made clear at this point, however, that assassination would be considered an act of terrorism only if part of a wider, more sophisticated campaign of political violence. Consequently, "one and done" assassins such as John Wilkes Booth and his co-conspirators should be considered murderers but not necessarily terrorists. This "great divide" also represents a transition in terrorist motivation. Earlier grievances focused on deeply personal and local issues: land ownership and contemptible governance. By contrast, post-Civil War terrorists had vastly different and much larger national issues to consider, such as the future of race relations in the aftermath of emancipation and the impact of the newly emerging industrial state, both of which wrought significant and far-reaching changes to society. One of these race-conscious terrorist groups would rise directly from the ashes of the Civil War, as defeated and deflated Confederate soldiers returned to their southern homes and struggled to make meaning of their lost cause and of their uncertain futures.

By the spring of 1866, the young men of central Tennessee were growing especially restless. It had been a year since Robert E. Lee had surrendered his forces at Appomattox, but the Confederate veterans who had returned home to central were still having a difficult time readjusting after four years of bloody civil warfare. Life was certainly safer, but also less exciting. Economic hard times, which limited jobs and opportunities, as well as the lack of social amusements and diversions, contributed greatly to the social inactivity in Pulaski, a small isolated town of 2,000 persons near the border with Alabama. There were, however, broader forces in the South that would begin to coalesce and manifest themselves in very sinister ways in Pulaski and its surrounding environs. The states that had once formed the Confederacy remained impoverished, their infrastructures greatly damaged and their populations decimated by death and injury. The emancipation of slaves necessitated a restructuring of southern society, a severe transformation that southern conservatives would vehemently oppose. Carpetbaggers and scalawags roamed the South, exploiting business and political opportunities. The political rights of the vanquished Confederates remained ambiguous and uncertain. In Tennessee, the administration of governor William G. Brownlow was particularly contentious. Brownlow, originally from Virginia, wasn't a carpetbagger, but his close association with the Republican Party and Unionists in eastern Tennessee made him an enemy to conservatives throughout the state. Adding to white conservative frustrations was the formation of the Union (or Loyal) League, a northern patriotic society that politicized and militarized emancipated blacks. And, as if to subject the prostrate South to further indignity, Congress had just passed the Civil Rights Act of 1866, an attempt to invalidate the Black Codes, a Southern strategy meant to return freedmen to a subordinate status similar to that to which they had been reduced during the dark days of slavery. Southerners, then, certainly had much to contemplate and larger issues to resolve, but for six men in particular escaping the boredom of life in Pulaski was foremost on their minds. They were John C. Lester, James Richard Crowe, John Kennedy, Calvin Jones, Richard Reed, and Frank O. McCord. Sometime during that spring (the exact date is unknown), the six met in the law office of Judge Thomas Jones and began to brainstorm. They had much in common. All were Confederate veterans from respectable Scot-Irish families. Envisioning a fraternity-like society strictly for fun and amusement, the Pulaski Six held a series of secret meetings to shape and develop their creation. What they originally conceived was a far cry from what would eventually evolve beyond their limited control: the most notorious terrorist organization in this nation's history. Then and now, the Ku Klux Klan has been shrouded in mystery and myth, a group both reviled and revered. Accordingly, from the very beginning, perceptions about the Klan were various and subject to bias on any number of levels: personal, political, racial, social, and moral.

The first book-length histories of the Ku Klux Klan, published during and shortly after the Reconstruction Era, shed little light on what became known as the "Invisible Empire" but managed to be extremely critical nonetheless, largely based on the Klan's well-publicized thirst for violence. In 1868, *Terrible Mysteries of the Ku Klux Klan* appeared, under the suspicious name of M. D. Scalpel. Scalpel was, in fact, a pseudonym for Dr. Edward H. Dixon of New York, the long-time publisher of *The Scalpel,* a medical journal. Dixon's account was a scathing condemnation of the Klan, but one based on wild rumors and an overactive imagination. Dixon wrote of blood rituals, skulls, and boiling cauldrons. He aptly described the impact of terrorism on cowering blacks, but partly ascribed their fear to admonitions from the Union League that the Klan would boil and eat freedmen.[2] The next major account of the Klan, which was far more credible, appeared in 1880, with the publication of Albion Tourgée's *The Invisible Empire,* the second part of a Reconstruction trilogy based on Tourgée's 14 years as a carpetbagger. Tourgée, a veteran of the Union Army and a Radical Republican, hailed from Ohio but became a farmer, lawyer, newspaper editor, and Superior Court judge in North Carolina. The trilogy's first part, *A Fool's Errand By One of the Fools,* was published in 1879 and sold more than 200,000 copies. While *A Fool's Errand* was fiction, *The Invisible Empire* was non-fiction, based on testimony from congressional hearings on the Ku Klux Klan held in 1871. Tourgée used the testimony to expose the terrorist methods of the Klan, detailing atrocities and describing terror-stricken communities of freedmen, but he also revealed much about the Klan's modes of operation. Readers learned that Klan disguises were far from uniform: other than simple bed sheets, no two disguises were exactly alike. Many hoods were adorned with wild beards and mustaches, quills, hair, plumes, or horns, and were largely conical with varying heights and ornamentation. Robes came in all colors, with red and white predominating. They, too, were adorned with trimmings and various symbols, such as crosses, hearts, or stars. Horses were often likewise disguised with elaborate capes and robes, not so much for coordinated effect but because hooded riders could be nonetheless identified by their mounts.[3] The same year that Tourgée's *Invisible Empire* appeared, John Patterson Green, born to free blacks in South Carolina but raised in Ohio, authored *Recollections of the Inhabitants, Localities, Superstitions, and Ku Klux Outrages of the Carolinas*. Green's account read more like a travelogue, offering his thoughts on southern people, places, and culture while he traveled from Hudsonville throughout the Carolinas looking for a suitable place to raise his family. He devoted but one chapter to the Klan, but made it clear that the hooded nightriders, "conceived in sin," were guilty of "cowardice, perjury, rapine, and murder."[4] He suggested that the Klan's mysterious name originated from the sound made when cocking and discharging a shotgun and noted that thousands of terror-stricken freedmen were already migrating northward in order to evade virulent racism and spiraling violence. This first wave of Ku Klux Klan books represented an immediate backlash to the violent atrocities throughout the South, and all three authors approached their subject in broad, general terms with well-defined northern sensibilities. They did not, however, provide much in the way of specific details about the inner machinations of the Invisible Empire. These details, however, would soon be exposed by a second and more personalized wave of Ku Klux studies.

Of the original Pulaski Six, only John C. Lester felt compelled to record his personal recollections for posterity's sake, and, in 1884, with D. L. Wilson as a co-author, he published *Ku Klux Klan—Its Origin, Growth and Disbandment,* the first of several "insider" accounts of the Klan. Because Wilson was not a Ku Klux, most of the details came from Lester. Here was the first true glimpse into the Klan, promising to fill in the missing details and "lift the veil of secrecy" surrounding the mysterious order. Lester and Wilson explained that the Klan's appellation originated with the word *kuklos,* which is Greek for circle or band. They were, perhaps, influenced by their familiarity with the college fraternity Kuklos Adelphon. From that came "Ku Klux," which was added to "Clan" in a nod to the founders' Scot-Irish ancestry. A slight change in spelling made the alliteration complete. Lester and Wilson attributed much of the Klan's original popularity to the "weird potency" of its mysterious name, which generated much discussion and speculation among the people of Pulaski. Lester and Wilson described the early brainstorming sessions as well as the Klan's eventual relocation to a meeting den outside of town near a spooky, semi-demolished house surrounded by dead, mangled trees that stood "grim and gaunt" like "spectre sentinels." Elaborate rituals, codes, pass words, and initiation guidelines were quickly established, and, keeping true to their intent of creating fun and amusement, the new secret order, having added new members, began to parade around town in full hooded regalia, creating an instant stir in small-town Pulaski. The authors also described the Klan hierarchy, which established a Grand Cyclops or president, a Grand Magi or vice-president, a Grand Turk or marshal, a Grand Exchequer or treasurer, and two Lictors or guards.

Despite the best efforts of the Pulaski Six, by the end of summer, interest in the Klan began to wane until a rash of new recruits appeared and the founding members were flooded with outside requests to form new chapters in surrounding communities. Thus began the Klan's transformation from a social club to a "body of desperate men who convulsed the country." According to Lester and Wilson, this conversion came about when the expanded Klan, now infiltrated by "rash and imprudent men," soon realized that whenever they appeared in disguise, superstitious freedmen fled in terror. Taking note of this curious phenomenon, Klan nightriders, presenting themselves as ghosts of the Confederate dead, began to harass black communities. Eventually, the Klan began to realize that "the most powerful devices ever constructed for controlling the ignorant and superstitious were in their hands," thus providing Klansmen with a unique opportunity "to contemplate some great and important mission."[5] Accordingly, the Klan would employ terror to manipulate the behavior of freedmen, who, from the perspective of many southern whites, had grown defiant and disrespectful with their newfound freedom and citizenship. These developments troubled Lester and Wilson, who lamented that the Pulaski den had been unfairly maligned because "all disorder done in the country was charged upon the Ku Klux ... under disguises which they had invented and used"; the "result was that the Klan and its objects were wholly misunderstood and misinterpreted."[6] Fortunately, the Klan's Grand Wizard, Nathan Bedford Forrest, understood this prevailing perversion and wisely disbanded the Klan by edict in early 1869, and, according to Lester and Wilson, the story of the Klan ended there. While slightly repentant in tone, Lester and Wilson, as might be expected, defended the Klan, suggesting that its evolving regulator function was a logical response of white conservatives to unsavory carpetbaggers, Union Leaguers, and malfeasant freedmen bent on "wanton destruction for the gratification of revenge."[7]

Lester and Wilson had set out to redeem the hooded order, but their account, while a significant contribution to the Klan literature, did not sit well with many southerners, who felt that the two had been overly apologetic, when repentance had been wholly unwarranted. Consequently, in 1905, Walter L. Fleming, a Reconstruction historian, felt compelled to reissue the important volume but personally contributed a lengthy introduction meant to set the record straight by updating the documentation and "correcting" the misperceptions generated by the original edition. Fleming argued that the Klan had never degenerated into disorder as Lester and Wilson had implied, and that Klan violence had been greatly exaggerated. Whatever violence committed by the Klan was justifiable, he felt, in light of the

terror propagated by the black militias unleashed on the South by the damnable
Union League and Brownlow Republicans, which raised the real possibility of a
black insurrection not unlike that which had occurred in Santo Domingo. Thus,
according to Fleming, the Klan's function was purely defensive, a popular refrain
among its defenders, which had the additional function of suggesting the compete absence of any political motivation. Fleming's edition emphasized the Klan's
organizational convention held in Nashville's famed Maxwell House hotel during
the spring of 1867. As Lester and Wilson had noted, the surprising growth of the
Klan in just one year forced the Pulaski Six to call for a meeting of the many dens
sprouting throughout the South in order to bind the disparate dens together and
to secure unity of purpose and concert of action. Central to the organizational
blueprint was the Klan's *Prescript,* or constitution, which provided the structural
guidelines of the hooded empire. Lester and Wilson had made only vague references to the *Prescript,* but, in his appendix, Fleming reprinted both the original
Prescript published in 1867 and a second, amended version, which had appeared
sometime in 1868. The first *Prescript* described a greatly expanded Klan hierarchy,
befitting an organization that was growing more quickly than anyone could have
imagined. It also established a judicial branch, complete with a Tribunal of Justice
and a Grand Council of Yahoos, and further described various methods of raising revenue. It did not, however, espouse any particular philosophy or contain
a mission statement of any kind. This lack was amended in the second *Prescript,*
which was not significantly different from the first save for the specification of
three major objectives. Klansmen swore to uphold the Constitution of the United
States; to assist in the execution of all constitutional laws; and to "protect the weak,
the innocent, and the defenseless, from the indignities, wrongs, and outrages of the
lawless, the violent, and the brutal."[8] Interestingly, both versions of the *Prescript*
failed to identify the Ku Klux Klan by name anywhere, using asterisks where a
name would normally appear. This allowed readers of the *Prescript* to deny any
"knowable" link to the Klan.

Fleming's views on Reconstruction had been shaped during his doctoral studies at Columbia University, where he was greatly influenced by Professor William
A. Dunning, who, more than any other single person, was responsible for the
prevailing popular perceptions of Reconstruction. Dunning, swayed by the anti-
Reconstruction propaganda of southern Democrats, taught generations of future
historians that Reconstruction had been an unmitigated disaster, due to the vile
influences of the misguided Radical Republicans, who had forced black supremacy upon demoralized southern whites and unleashed a vindictive bacchanal of
conspiracy and corruption directed by armed freedmen, carpetbaggers, scalawags,
and Union Leaguers. Dunning cast the Ku Klux Klan as saviors of the South who
inspired southern whites to obstruct the radical agenda, overthrow Republican
mismanagement of southern states, and restore home rule through the reestab-
lishment of white supremacy. Dunning's viewpoints and those of his academic
legions would come to dominate historical orthodoxy regarding Reconstruction

for the first half of the 20th century. The publication of Thomas Dixon's fictional work *The Clansman* (1905) and the filming of D. W. Griffith's classic film *Birth of a Nation* (1915), based on Dixon's novel, were well-publicized contributions to this "Dunning School" in historiography.[9] This romanticization of the Klan was also responsible for the reemergence of the Invisible Empire during the 1920s, when its powers grew to unprecedented national levels. Consequently, the second wave of Klan literature, accounts meant to redeem the former Confederacy and its hooded nightriders, would parallel Reconstruction in general.

Beginning in 1914, three major contributions to this new wave appeared, all similar in tone and all consistent with the Dunning school of thought. *The Ku Klux Klan or Invisible Empire* (1914) by S.E.F. Rose, *Authentic History: Ku Klux Klan* (1924) by Susan L. Davis and *A Story of the Original Ku Klux Klan* (1934) by Mr. and Mrs. W. B. Romine were also written by persons who used their status as insiders as a means of promoting their credibility. Rose was the granddaughter of Thomas Martin, whose vacant home was used early on by the Pulaski Six as a secret meeting place; Davis was the daughter of a Confederate colonel who organized the first Klan den in Athens, Georgia; and Mr. W. B. Romine was the news editor of the *Pulaski Citizen*. The three accounts argued that black–white relations in the postwar–South had been peaceful and harmonious until the carpetbaggers, Union Leaguers, and Freedmen's Bureau agents began to appear. All portrayed blacks as ignorant, superstitious, gullible, and responsible for initiating the wave of violence engulfing the entire South through their armed militias and thirst for crime. The shortcomings of freedmen they described contributed to the disastrous and corrupt state legislatures that were dominated by black Republicans. Rose maintained that the greatest ambition in life for black men was to marry white women.[10] All denied that any transformation or co-opting of the Klan had taken place. The violent atrocities attributed to the Klan had actually been committed by a "counterfeit" or "spurious" Klan, that is, bands of imitators and wannabes who gave the "true" Klan a nasty and undeserved reputation. The Romines managed to add a curious footnote to an ongoing legend of sorts by pointing out that many men from Pulaski had served in the Mexican War, where they became acquainted with Cukulcan, the Mexican god of light. Since the Klan saw themselves as champions of goodness and light, surely this explained the mystery surrounding the Klan's unusual name, as they would have it, John Lester's firsthand account notwithstanding. Davis might have boasted of direct access to the original Pulaski Six, and some information gleaned from some of her interviews is useful, but, in the end, her chronicle was a disjointed jumble of half-truths, errors, and bizarre digressions. The three accounts further maintained, as did Lester and Wilson, that the Klan officially disbanded after the Grand Wizard's edict in early 1869. This bit of convenient denial would aid their collective attempt to disavow subsequent Klan terrorism.[11]

Not until 1939 did a broad, comprehensive approach to the Ku Klux Klan first appear, Stanley F. Horn's *Invisible Empire*. Although it is tempting to refer to

Horn's study as the first scholarly approach, its lack of footnote documentation is especially troubling for academicians. Horn set his sights on objectivity and denigrated the Klan apologists, yet managed to become one as well, referring to the hooded order as an "effective protective organization of regulators." He, too, downplayed Klan violence, claiming that it was much exaggerated and merely a product of the times, when "life was cheap." He likened the whippings of blacks to the spanking of disobedient children. He further suggested that the Klan was really no different from Italy's Carbonari or America's own Sons of Liberty, arguments not particularly convincing, either then or now. Still, Horn's state-by-state analysis was unique and useful and highlighted the expansive and decentralized nature of the Klan. Also fascinating was Horn's description of the extent to which the Klan permeated southern popular culture, especially in Tennessee. There was a Ku Klux baseball team that played in Nashville; a Ku Klux burlesque show; Ku Klux songs, poetry, and cocktails. Commercialism and name recognition led to the Ku Klux label on paint, pills, tobacco, hats, a circus act, and knives! Unfortunately, Horn also tended to portray blacks as passive victims, while ignoring their own accounts of victimization and defiant attempts to resist their brutalization at the hands of hooded terrorists.[12]

Although not discernable back then, Horn's study would be the last of the Klan's literary redeemers. Writers such as W.E.B. Du Bois had begun to chip away at the Dunning school of Reconstruction as early as the 1930s, and by the 1960s the civil rights movement would begin to influence greatly all perspectives of Reconstruction and African American history. The historiography of Reconstruction and that of the Ku Klux Klan, although separate and distinct, continued to run along parallel, revisionist tracks. Reconstruction historians such as Kenneth Stampp, James McPherson, Joel Williamson, and Eric McKittrick argued that generations of Americans had unfairly maligned the Radical Republicans, who had acted appropriately and realistically. The failures of Reconstruction were squarely attributable instead to the intransigent southern conservatives and former Confederates, who refused to countenance the social revolution that the Civil War and Reconstruction had effected. Revisionists also suggested that the vision of corrupt, southern legislatures dominated by blacks was a complete fabrication and that Reconstruction governments authorized by Congress had performed reasonably well, given the obstructionism of white conservatives. Yes, Reconstruction was not without faults, they averred, but, on the whole, it made positive strides by educating blacks, legislating citizenship, and providing an array of social services via the Freedman's Bureau. By the same token, members of the Ku Klux Klan, once considered saviors of the South, reverted to the brutal, racially charged terrorists they were.

This postwar revisionism was also undoubtedly influenced by the third incarnation of the Klan during the 1950s and 1960s, which was responsible for unspeakable atrocities against civil rights activists, both black and white.[13] William Peirce Randel's *The Ku Klux Klan* (1965) was the first of the revisionist studies to challenge historical orthodoxy surrounding the hooded empire. For too long, Randel maintained, Americans had justified the Klan's systematic terror, which had been inflicted in the name of white supremacy and as a means toward preserving a racist caste system in the South. His account of Klan terrorism was stark but somewhat contradictory, condemning the violence yet referring at times to Klan members as jolly, hooded pranksters and rationalizing that, on occasion, good people do bad things. Randel rightly emphasized the political nature of the Klan, their rabid opposition to the Republican Party, and their outrageous manipulation of voters. He suggested that Nathan Bedford Forrest's official edict to disband the Klan in 1869 had been a ruse, mere "window dressing" for the purpose of providing "invisibility" for the Klan, which carried on its campaign of terror into the early 1870s. Even if Forrest had been sincere (and there is no way of knowing), Randel pointed out, the Klan was much too useful as a tool for white resistance by local dens to obey his edict, sincere or otherwise, and its disbandment at that point in time would have been tantamount to abandoning the principle of white supremacy. The terrorism of the Klan was only beginning in 1869, not coming to an end. Certainly, the indisputable evidence supports this contention.[14] As critics have noted, Randel set the histories of the Reconstruction Klan back on the right track but fell short of displacing Horn as the chief authoritative source on the hooded terrorists, ignoring geographic, economic, class, and cultural issues and treating the South as if it were a homogeneous whole.[15] Interestingly, however, Randel did manage to cover the revival of the Klan during the 1920s and 1960s in his volume, the first major study to span the first three generations of the Invisible Empire.

One year after Randel's study was published, Everette Swinney finished his doctoral dissertation at the University of Texas entitled *Suppressing the Ku Klux Klan: The Enforcement of the Reconstruction Amendments, 1870–1877*. The dissertation won approval in 1966 but remained unpublished until 1987; no editorial changes were made during the 21-year interim. Swinney contended that Klan violence could not be understood apart from the wider phenomenon of mob activity and the southern code of honor, or *code duello*, which propounded the "cult of killing to avenge wounded sensibilities."[16] And the hooded nightriders had historical precedents: the antebellum slave patrols, which were common throughout the South, and the predominance of vigilantes, who established extralegal authority in many frontier areas. Swinney also downplayed the early Klan transformation, arguing instead that the Klan was probably terroristic from its very beginning. Swinney's focus, of course, was not so much on the Klan itself but on the impact of the three Enforcement Acts (1870–1871) approved by Congress, the last of which became popularly known as the Ku Klux Klan Act. The first two Acts were intended to enforce the 15th Amendment, which prohibited the denial of suffrage, by providing federal oversight of elections. The Ku Klux Klan Act imposed fines and prison sentences on anyone found guilty of obstructing another's right to vote. It allowed the use of federal troops to police election sites and to arrest offending Klansmen. Unfortunately, the legality and enforceability of the Acts were called into question, and the Klan began to change its election tactics once southern Democrats regained control of their state governments. As a result, the Enforcement Acts had but mixed success and collapsed by the mid-1870s.

Until the end of the 1960s, Stanley Horn's *Invisible Empire,* for all its many faults, remained the most popular authority on the Klan, an unacceptable condition that was finally rectified with the publication in 1971 of Allen Trelease's *White Terror—The Ku Klux Klan Conspiracy and Southern Reconstruction.* Here at last was the comprehensive, scholarly, and objective study of the Klan that had been lacking since the Pulaski Six had first donned their hoods more than 100 years earlier. For starters, Trelease included more than 100 pages of source notes, as well as an excellent bibliographic essay. The scope of research was impressive, relying on state as well as federal archival material, newspapers, and a wide spectrum of secondary sources. Like Horn, Trelease included a state-by-state, blow-by-blow account of the Klan's transgressions throughout the South once it expanded beyond central Tennessee, but, at the same time, was able to maintain a sense of chronology. Given the expansive and diversified nature of the Klan, this would appear to be the most reasonable approach. Trelease acknowledged the Klan's early nonviolent origins, but maintained that the transformation occurred within two months of its founding when the Klan was "commandeered" by ex-Confederate officers for their own malevolent purposes, probably with the blessings of the Pulaski Six. Trelease also argued that attempts to distinguish between the "true" and "spurious" Klan were meaningless because, given the circumstances, such distinctions were impossible to make. Contriving such distinctions did not legitimize racial violence; further, the informal and local organization of the Klan in most places made it futile to try to differentiate between real and counterfeit members of the Invisible Empire. Certainly, there were other hooded organizations scattered throughout the South, and any thug with a hood could proclaim himself a Ku Klux, but, given that they all employed similar tactics for similar objectives, they collectively constituted a "Ku Klux Klan conspiracy," as Trelease suggested in his subtitle.

Trelease, more than any other researcher, emphasized the Klan's political nature. This is, perhaps, the most misunderstood element of the Ku Klux Klan. After elections in 1867, when black support for the radical agenda of the Republican Party doomed the candidacy of Democratic candidates in Tennessee, the Klan turned its attention increasingly toward those who did not publicly proclaim themselves Democrats, black and white alike. According to Trelease, at that point, the Klan began to operate as a "terrorist arm" of the Democratic Party. Yet, it was imprecise to regard the Democratic Party as a monolithic political movement entirely committed to terrorizing Republicans, as there were certainly those who harbored legitimate concerns over the violent tactics.[17] As one white conservative put it, "I do not say that all Democrats are Ku-Klux, but I do say all the Ku-Klux are Democrats."[18] Regarding Nathan Bedford Forrest and the disbandment issue, Trelease conceded that it is impossible to say what exactly happened or what was intended to happen. He noted that the Grand Wizard's edict never called for the entire dissolution of the Ku Klux Klan as many had long maintained, just a curtailment of activities. Yet many did interpret the edict as one to disband; consequently, although violence would escalate in most areas, by the spring of 1869, the Klan essentially disappeared in places such as Tennessee, Arkansas, Virginia, Louisiana, and northern Alabama.[19]

Given the scope of Trelease's research and his judicious use of sources, *White Terror* is likely to remain the most authoritative and unassailable source on the Reconstruction Ku Klux Klan conspiracy. Since then, other than Wyn Craig Wade's *Fiery Cross* (1989), which spanned all of the Klan's many incarnations and only briefly touched on the Reconstruction Era, most recent Klan studies have focused on its 1920s iteration, including an impressive array of local studies, or the contemporary Klan, which continues to don hoods, burn crosses, and zealously defend white supremacy.[20] In fact, the literature about the Klan is so extensive that a Ku Klux bibliography compiled by Lenwood G. Davis and Janet L. Sims-Wood listed more than 9,700 entries, and this was back in 1984.[21] Recent scholarly studies that focus on the Reconstruction Klan do so from local or more specialized perspectives. Lou Falkner Williams's *The Great South Carolina Ku Klux Klan Trials* (1996), Jerry West's *The Reconstruction Klan in York County* (2002), and J. Michael Martinez's *Carpetbaggers, Calvary, and the Ku Klux Klan* (2007) all examined the notorious Klan in York County, South Carolina, and the subsequent federal trials that managed to bring convictions against several Klansmen.[22] Martinez, in particular, focused extensively on the important contributions of U.S. Army Major Lewis Merrill, who, more than any other person, was responsible for bringing indictments against the York County Klan. Merrill also received extensive treatment in Stephen Budiansky's *The Bloody Shirt—Terror After Appomattox* (2008), whose subtitle suggested that this was a study of Reconstruction terrorism. Budiansky documented instead the intertwined legacies of a handful of players, large and small, whose stories unfolded against the larger backdrop of the racial revolution in the South.[23] Kwando Mbiassi Kinshasa's *Black Resistance to the Ku Klux Klan in the Wake of Civil War* (2006) promised to examine a much-neglected subject and provided some interesting material, but ultimately fell short of providing a comprehensive, scholarly analysis.[24]

In total, the long and contentious historiography of the Ku Klux Klan reveals much not only about the Klansmen as a whole but also about the impact of racial, political, sectional, and moral perspectives upon one's interpretation of the Invisible Empire. Still, despite the many differing accounts stretching over 100 years, a basic outline of the early Klan does emerge. The Pulaski Six intended their fraternal order to be one of fun and amusement, and, early on, the initiation rituals were farcical, and the hooded parades generated much curiosity, but such thrills did not last particularly long. At some point within a couple of months of the group's founding, there were two apparently surprising developments: hooded Klansmen discovered that their night riding intimidated many blacks, and the Klan began a period of rapid growth, eventually extending far beyond the control of Pulaski. This ultimately created a new, more sinister purpose, a need for greater centralized administration, and a transition in leadership that necessitated a major reorganization conference in Room 10 of Nashville's Maxwell House during the spring of 1867. Soon thereafter, Nathan Bedford Forrest assumed control as Grand Wizard, and the *Prescript* became the Klan's constitution. Even then, no one could have foreseen that the Ku Klux Klan would, through various manifestations, persist into the 21st century, certainly not the Pulaski Six, who witnessed the evolution of their whimsical social diversion into a band of notorious terrorists.

II.   The Early Growth of the Klan

Following the Nashville conference, the Ku Klux Klan embarked on an ambitious organizing campaign that bound together various dens scattered throughout central Tennessee. Acts of violence were, for the most part, racially motivated and sporadic, with seemingly no political connections. From mid-1867 through the first half of 1868, the Klan continued to experience a period of phenomenal growth, expanding beyond Tennessee into the far corners of the South. Although the very first accounts of the Ku Klux Klan failed to provide any demographic information regarding its rank-and-file membership, there seemed to exist a generally held notion that members were primarily drawn from the more respectable elements of southern society, which was partly true and partly an attempt to establish credibility. The widely recognized participation of ex-Confederate officers such as Nathan Bedford Forrest certainly helped establish this impression. Albion Tourgée acknowledged only that the "best citizens" constituted the Klan's membership, while Susan L. Davis implied through brief biographical sketches that the Klan was mostly composed of men of status and substance.[25] In fact, the Klan drew its legions of predominantly young men from every rank and class of white society. Women participated in Klan activities only on extremely rare occasions; otherwise, their support was generally limited to the sewing of costumes. Blacks were occasionally identified among Klansmen during night raids, but in most cases they were victims of coercion. Yet, there apparently were rare instances where blacks rode with the Klan for other, inexplicable reasons. More specific demographic detail is probably impossible, given the secretive and fluid nature of the Klan's membership, which made it equally difficult to estimate the number of Klansmen who swore allegiance to the Invisible Empire. Forrest famously boasted that Tennessee was home to 40,000 Klansmen and that the Klan's total membership exceeded 550,000, but these numbers were never confirmed. Allen Trelease noted that, in general, the Ku Klux Klan was more apt to appear in certain regions than in others. The Klan was least likely to appear in overwhelmingly white counties like those of the Appalachian highlands and in counties where blacks outnumbered whites by three to one. Thus, the Klan was least in evidence where white conservatives either already possessed a clear majority or were hopelessly outnumbered. The Klan tended to be strongest in areas where the two races and two political parties were nearly equal, or where there was a white minority large enough to intimidate freedmen.[26] Ultimately, the states that experienced the greatest number of Klan outrages over a sustained period of time were North and South Carolina, Alabama, and Mississippi. Other states such as Tennessee, Arkansas, Texas, and Louisiana experienced equally horrific outbreaks of terrorism, but the violence there had begun to wane by 1869.

Because of the decentralization and diversity of Klan dens, organizational and operational details differed markedly from place to place. While some dens maintained organizational links to the Pulaski order, many did not. Dens varied in size from fewer than a dozen to nearly a hundred members and often operated in each other's territory in order to shield local Klansmen from complicity in heinous crimes. The Klan's *Prescript,* inspired by the Pulaski Six's original bylaws, had described a detailed organizational structure and a clearly defined chain of command, and, although Klan dens tended to vary in their strict adherence to the *Prescript,* even the most undisciplined dens had a hierarchy, however informal it might have been. Some dens maintained odd titles, as the *Prescript* had suggested, and conducted regular elections, while others simply appointed a captain and two lieutenants.[27] Some voted as a group on operational details, but many deferred blindly to their leaders. Attacks could be spontaneous or premeditated and did not always involve the participation or approval of den leaders. The extent and intensity of Klan motives were, of course, also based primarily on local conditions, but Klansmen everywhere would consistently identify certain grievances in common to justify the "regulator" functions they had assumed.

High on the Klan's enemy list was the federal government, Congress in particular. By invalidating the southern state governments that Andrew Johnson had quickly ushered back into the Union, the Radical Republicans made it clear that they would control the future of Reconstruction. The passage of the 13th, 14th, and 15th Amendments, the Civil Rights Act of 1866, the Reconstruction Act of 1867, and the three Enforcement Acts further offended Klan sensibilities as southerners saw their long-established way of life rapidly disintegrate. But other than the federal troops deployed throughout the South, which the Klan would wisely avoid provoking, the federal government was seemingly beyond the reach of the hooded terrorists, distant and unassailable. An exception, however, was the Freedman's Bureau, the first federal welfare agency, which was designed to provide an array of social services for newly freed blacks. First formed in March 1865, the bureau sent its many legions into the South to build schools, churches, hospitals, charities, and the self-esteem of freedmen making the difficult transition from bondage to emancipation. As noted earlier, recent historians of Reconstruction have emphasized the bureau's positive contributions while acknowledging its many shortcomings. The Klan, however, had a much different spin, maintaining that bureau agents provoked trouble by agitating blacks, filling them with false hopes, building schools and churches for brainwashing purposes, and securing black support for the Republican Party, all the while engaged in corruptive use of federal monies. Many of the black schools and churches, built in conjunction with northern charitable and missionary societies, were burned to the ground by the Klan, who also terrorized teachers and preachers, demanding that they abandon the South immediately. In Mississippi's Monroe County alone, 26 black schools were forcibly closed in 1871 and Klansman whipped the county super-intendent.[28] A congressional report by Democrats described bureau agents as "fanatics without character or responsibility" and accused the bureau of uproot-ing southern society and creating a situation wherein "the former master became the slave, and the former slave became the master, the elector, the law-maker, and the ostensible ruler."[29] Even more calamitous for Klansmen, Freedman's Bureau agents were allegedly organizing black militias and encouraging them to defend themselves at all costs.

Also accused of arming and militarizing blacks was the northern-based Union (or Loyal) League, which expanded into the South during Reconstruction. A patriotic society replete with its own secret oaths and rituals, the League, essen-tially a branch of the Republican Party, primarily drew its members from white and black Unionists. On the one hand, the League engaged in legitimate political and social activities by sponsoring parades, picnics and rallies, despite the seething resentment of Democrats. On the other hand, the League also engaged in activities that, while not illegal, were bound to provoke the Klan. Urging blacks to defend themselves against hooded nightriders, the League helped train and arm black militias, who drilled and carried out military maneuvers in public while dressed in colorful, decorated uniforms. The militias were a significant and collective act of black defiance, but they also fed the southern paranoia regarding black insur-rections and confirmed the worst fears of white conservatives. It certainly didn't help matters when, on occasion, some black militias, testing the bounds of their new-found freedom, engaged in outrages and disturbances of their own. Although the most common complaint against these black troops was petty larceny, the southern Democratic press routinely magnified these acts into the first salvos of a black insurrection. During his testimony before a congressional hearing in 1871, Nathan Bedford Forrest claimed that the Ku Klux Klan originated in Tennessee for self-protection, a direct response to the formation of the Union League mili-tias. According to the former Grand Wizard, the League had encouraged blacks to become "insolent," prompting freedmen to "ravish" southern ladies. Worse yet, as far as Forrest was concerned, Republican state governments, exploiting their pardoning powers, quickly released these black rapists back into society without trial or punishment.[30] In fact, much to the consternation of Forrest and the Klan hierarchy, the largest of the black militias was the state militia of Tennessee, which was virtually all black because whites, scornful of the Republican administration of Governor William Brownlow, refused to volunteer for service.

Aside from citing the Freedman's Bureau and the Union League, the Klan and its sympathizers would identify other reasons to justify its existence, blaming carpetbaggers, corrupt politicians, inferior magistrates, lax pardoning powers by the state, and political disabilities placed on ex-Confederates for the many problems confronted by southern conservatives. In his study of southern railroads during Reconstruction, Scott Reynolds Nelson offered another possible motive for some of the Klan violence. Analyzing the establishment of a railroad corridor between Richmond and Atlanta, Reynolds argued that the Ku Klux Klan evolved in certain areas along the corridor in order to sabotage the proposed railway, which conservatives viewed as a symbol of corporate corruption and an institution that offered empowerment to black employees.[31] Most of the early explanations and attempted justifications of Klan activities were later dismissed by a Congressional Joint Select Committee, which conducted a Klan investigation in 1871. The committee's report argued that, stripped of the many misleading pretexts for violence, the Klan existed for three primary reasons: to oppose the Republican Party, to oppose the Reconstruction amendments, and to maintain white supremacy in the South.[32] For all practical purposes, these three motives were interwoven into one overriding objective: to preserve the antebellum racial hierarchy in the postwar South, with its attendant white hegemony over a now emancipated, yet dependent population of black vassals. Hence, most targets of Klan violence were those who directly obstructed the Klan's agenda: Republican voters, black or white, as well as party officials, scalawags deemed disloyal to the South, and agents of the Freedman's Bureau or Union League. In some places, the Klan also assumed the role of the "morality police," punishing miscreants for immoral behavior, but these instances were the exception, not the norm. Without question, of course, the Klan's primary and most visible targets were blacks.

Seemingly, blacks were the targets of the Klan for no reason other than their being black, but, while Klansmen had no logical explanation for victimizing this group, they always seemed to have a rationale, however petty. Testimony taken by the Joint Select Committee disclosed a number of reasons why blacks found themselves at the wrong end of a Ku Klux whip or noose. Victims were blamed for large crimes such as murder, rape, robbery, and arson, but were also likely to be charged and punished for petty "crimes" as well: stealing corn, quitting jobs, owning land, abandoning families, giving political speeches, voting Republican, suing white persons, sleeping with white women, or just acting plain "uppity." Some victims were targeted as a form of economic coercion: successful blacks were punished for accumulating too much wealth. Small tradesmen and farmers had their jobs threatened, labor contracts violated, and crops illegally confiscated. In other specific instances, men were whipped for refusing to supply whiskey, for failing to maintain a firewood supply, for allowing children to cry endlessly at night, and for arguing over a watermelon. In one incident, the Klan assaulted an interracial married couple, explaining that the mulatto wife was being beaten for marrying a man too black and the black husband was being whipped for marrying a woman too white. One black preacher, Elias Hill, was severely beaten for his social and political activism, despite being an elderly dwarf suffering from paralysis.[33] It is the juxtaposition of petty offenses committed by their victims with unspeakable retributive atrocities committed by the Klan which set the Invisible Empire apart from any other terrorist group in American history.

By the fall of 1868, the Ku Klux Klan had established dens in all states of the former Confederacy, including Kentucky, which had remained loyal. In some states, such as Virginia and Florida, violence was minimal, but, as the November elections approached, several states experienced an unprecedented wave of violent activity. During the spring, Republicans, backed by the black vote, had won several elections, and southern Democrats vowed that things would be different in the fall. During the months preceding November and during the election itself, the Klan began a wholesale campaign of intimidation, threats, outrages, and murder in order to manipulate the vote. Hooded nightriders terrorized black communities, warning them to stay away from the polls. Crowds of armed thugs surrounded polling places, intimidating voters and creating a volatile environment. Black and white Republicans who did attempt to vote were routinely beaten with brickbats and pistols and driven into hiding. Republican ballots were destroyed or confiscated. Many blacks voted the Democratic ticket under direct threats to their lives. In several areas, dozens of blacks were jailed on trumped up charges just before election day, and were suddenly released after the polls had closed. State testimony regarding election fraud in Louisiana revealed that during 1868 alone, leading up to the November elections, there were 297 persons killed in the parishes adjacent New Orleans and a total of 784 statewide.[34] Forty were killed or wounded in New Orleans.[35] In Georgia during the same time period, there were 336 incidents of murder or intent to kill.[36] According to reports submitted to the governor's office, more than 200 murders were committed in Arkansas during the three months preceding the November elections.[37] The Joint Select Committee also read and published testimony declaring that, during a six-month period in 1868, there averaged in Tennessee a Ku Klux Klan murder every 24 hours.[38]

Evidence of the Klan's effectiveness in manipulating the November elections was equally stunning. In this regard, events in Louisiana were both representative and instructive. It was reported that more than 12,000 voters had been prevented from casting their ballots in St. Bernard Parish. In one precinct, the Democratic presidential candidate Horatio Seymour outpolled Ulysses S. Grant, the Republican nominee, 728 votes to zero. The total vote in New Orleans was nearly 24,000 for Seymour, but only 276 for Grant. Seven combined parishes had cast more than 4,700 Republican votes during the spring elections; in November, however, Grant received a combined zero votes from the same seven parishes. In another eight parishes, Republicans received 5,520 votes during the spring, but only 10 in November. In one district, the Democratic candidate for Congress outpolled his Republican opponent 10,884 votes to 107.[39] In Jasper County, Georgia, where there were 960 registered black voters, Grant received only 10 votes. In Columbia County, Georgia, Seymour outpolled Grant 1,120 to 1. One witness in Louisiana testified about the election: "It was utterly impossible to distribute Republican tickets among the voters of the parish without the danger of being mobbed and killed. The threats and outrages of these 'Klans' of the Democratic Party against the Republicans produced such terror and alarm amongst the freedmen and other Republican voters, that it was impossible to induce but a very few of them to go to the polls."[40] In Arkansas, the chair of the Lafayette County voters' registration board fled for his life, reporting to Governor Powell Clayton, "There was an organization formed of from one to two hundred men, for the avowed object of killing Union men, of both colors, who would not join democratic clubs and vote their ticket. Some ten to fifteen colored men were shot down for this cause, and I had reliable information that if I attempted to register [voters] I would be assassinated."[41] Similar irregularities were so commonplace in 1868 that the results of several congressional elections were eventually overturned, and Democratic candidates in South Carolina and Louisiana who thought they had won office in November were eventually displaced by Republicans beginning in early 1869.

As stories of Ku Klux outrages began to circulate widely, the Invisible Empire found itself increasingly under severe criticism, and its hierarchy struggled to maintain control over its more violent elements, which continued to remain active after the fall elections. Because of this and other reasons, on January 25, 1869, Grand Wizard Nathan Bedford Forrest issued his infamous edict that, as noted earlier, either dissolved the Klan or merely curtailed its activities, depending on one's viewpoint. And while some dens faithfully disbanded, others beyond Tennessee carried on, either oblivious to Forrest's orders or dismissive of them. In late February, Tennessee Governor William Brownlow did the unthinkable by declaring martial law in nine counties, following the lead of Arkansas, which had declared martial law the previous fall. Also in February, Congress passed the 15th Amendment, which prohibited the denial of suffrage, a direct response to the fraudulent elections of 1868. In early March, the Arkansas legislature passed an anti–Ku Klux law that levied stiff penalties on those who conspired with the Klan or engaged in violence while roaming the countryside in disguise. Tennessee had already passed a similar law. The cumulative impact of these developments resulted in the disappearance of the Ku Klux Klan in areas such as Tennessee, Texas, Louisiana, and Arkansas by early 1869. However, in other locales, the Klan grew increasingly violent, creating a concerted system of terror, shocking in its wanton disregard for human life.

III. Hooded Terrorism

The violence perpetrated by the Ku Klux Klan was commonly described by contemporaries as a "reign of terror." The southern tradition of slave patrols, vigilantism, the *code duello*, and an unyielding determination to preserve a way of life precious to them led to a combustible environment in which Klansmen would commit horrific atrocities against their perceived enemies, black and white alike. But just as the Klan's justification for terror varied from place to place, so too did the acts of terror, which ranged from psychological intimidation to premeditated murder. Perhaps the most common form of Klan victimization was coercion, usually a specific demand followed by a threat. White schoolteachers, for example, were regularly visited by hooded nightriders demanding that they desist from teaching blacks or face punishment, usually a severe whipping. Disguises were meant not solely to shield identity but to add an element of mystery to this intimidation, hence the wild and elaborate ornamentation. Convincing "gullible" blacks that Klansmen were Confederate ghosts similarly contributed to this type of psychological manipulation, though it is questionable how gullible blacks might have really been, given that stories of their cowering fear before the living dead were largely the figments of white imagination. Reliance on disguises was, however, subject to local preferences. Some Klansmen never bothered to hide their identities, and some paid very little attention if they did: one witness described local Klansmen as "some of the worst disguised persons you ever saw."[42]

Warnings weren't always delivered in person; just as earlier terrorist groups in American history had done, the Klan made effective use of coffin notices. These letters, usually strategically placed or delivered to the homes of Klan targets, consisted of ominous threats to life and limb, often written in poetic, literary styles and were frequently accompanied by crude pictures of hostile symbols such as coffins, daggers, and skulls and crossbones. This particular coffin notice was found in Florida:

KKK
No man e'er felt the halter draw
With good opinion of the law
KKK
Twice the secret report was heard
When again you hear his voice
Your doom is sealed
Dead Men tell no tales   KKK
Dead! Dead! Under the roses   KKK
Our motto is, death to radicals—beware! KKK[43]

Students enrolled at the University of Alabama in Tuscaloosa once found coffin notices hanging from daggers stuck onto the doors of university buildings ordering the young scholars to leave the state institution or face punishment. Many students immediately complied and left.[44] Other Klan victims had actual coffins placed at their doorsteps with threatening letters inside.[45] Stephen Davis, a white Democrat turned Republican from Demopolis, Alabama, might have been the first American ever subjected to a form of chemical terrorism when he found a coffin notice that warned, "caution, the contents of this is poison." The letter, poisoned or not, had its desired, manipulative effect: Davis armed himself constantly and recruited four to 12 people to come to his home every night as a means of protection against an attack.[46] Some notices were extremely blunt. For example, one delivered to Edward Johnson, a Florida state senator, demanded that he resign or face assassination.[47]

Forms of physical violence included beating, raping, mutilating, and the most common form of brutality, whipping. But a whip wasn't just a whip. As Kwando Mbiassi Kinshasha described it, the whip had become an emblem of white empowerment, "both a tool for punishment and a symbol of institutional coercion and repression."[48] Leather whips inflicted the most pain, but if one of these was not available, any tree switch did the job, especially one from a black gum tree. Branches from this type of tree had sharp edges that broke skin, and being whipped with one was especially agonizing. It is extremely difficult, if not impossible, to assess accurately the total number of men and women whipped by the Ku Klux Klan, though many local estimates were offered as testimony before various bodies. In South Carolina alone, estimates suggested that at least 600 persons had been whipped in York County and 500 in Limestone County. Lisa Cardyn recently estimated that in total, at least 23,000 persons received whippings at the hands of Klan members.[49]

Many of the Klan outrages were sexual in nature. Perhaps this should come as no surprise, given that some of the Klan initiation rituals were sexualized and occasionally homoerotic.[50] Klan victims were routinely stripped of their clothes before being whipped and sodomized. Women had their pubic hair set afire. Men were forced to kiss the private parts of other men. Gang rapes were common; as historian Wyn Craig Wade maintained, "the desire for group intercourse was sometimes sufficient reason for a den to go out on a raid."[51] Men and women of both races were forced into sexually evocative positions or coerced into sex acts for the sheer amusement of their captors. Genital torture and mutilation were commonplace. Men were turned face down and had sticks or lit cigars shoved into their posteriors. In North Carolina, one woman was vaginally penetrated with a knife. Another had her labia pierced by Klansmen who then slipped a lock through the open wounds and threw away the key. A freedwoman in Georgia, who was married to a former Union soldier, had her genitalia whipped and was penetrated with a pistol held by a Klansman who threatened to pull the trigger. He raped her instead.[52] One black man from Wilkinson County, Georgia, was given a choice by his hooded captors: perform self-castration or die at their hands immediately. He chose to "alter" himself. Another victim in Georgia reportedly had his penis nailed to a wooden block sunk into the ground. The block, which held a sharp knife, was then set on fire, giving the poor victim but two choices: burn to death attached to the block or castrate himself in order to escape the fire. He, too, chose to live.[53]

In a study of sexualized racism and gendered violence during Reconstruction published in 2000, Lisa Cardyn suggested several reasons for these types of outrages. She explained, "sexual terror was in actuality among its most starkly defining features, designedly effected to compromise the stability, resolve, and selfhood of the newly freed slaves."[54] It also fulfilled the voyeuristic and sadistic needs of Klansmen, she added, while simultaneously "reviving the privileges of white masculinity." Lou Falkner Williams agreed with this latter explanation, arguing that because the sexual exploitation of black women had become institutional-ized under slavery, sexual violence "served to reaffirm the community value of white male authority." Williams further maintained that sexualized violence was "layered with social and political meaning directed primarily against the assertion of black male political power rather than against women per se . . . the outrages against black women were part and parcel of the white males' efforts to render the black men powerless."[55] Noting that Klansmen often encouraged witnesses to participate in sexual attacks, Cardyn further argued that these acts of "collective accomplishment" were not just sadistic but narcissistic, as well. Aside from this psychological dependency, in the end, there were larger forces involved, Cardyn observed: the "ongoing struggle to define the political and social contours of the post-war South, a struggle in which sexuality quickly emerged as a principle site of contestation." Cardyn summarized her arguments thus: "The terror perpetrated against freed people and sympathetic whites did much to determine victims' con-ceptions of their place in the world, their viability, and their worth. It undermined financial stability, limited residential and employment options, influenced the bal-ance of power and the division of labor within families, and impinged upon child development. More insidiously, the sexual terrorism of those years inevitably cir-cumscribed victims' sense of what was possible, of what they could dream about and strive for, and what was beyond their grasp."[56]

What made Klansmen's sexualized terror even more perverse and hypocriti-cal was their self-perceived obligation to act as moral watchdogs. Klansmen were known to punish blacks and whites for engaging in "offensive" sexual behav-ior: miscegenation, incest, prostitution, adultery, and cohabitation. Even in such cases, as Martha Hodes suggested in a 1993 study of the sexualization of Recon-struction politics, Klan punishments had political overtones: as long as they were known supporters of the Democratic Party, white men were left undisturbed, despite their sexual involvement with black women.[57]

Mutilations ranged from ear cropping to the most horrid outrages imaginable. One witness described the corpse of a Klan victim: "the calves of his legs were split up and his thighs were split open and cut across and his knee looked like they tried to take the cap off the knee and his hands and arms were cut and split up too."[58] One survivor of the Klan's wrath described his treatment: "They laid me on the ground and held me there with my face to the ground; they cut my arms, legs, and back with their knives; across the other way they cut deep gashes crosswise; they split open my feet with their knives and cut deep gashes in my thighs and calves of my legs, first up and down, and then across. After they had done beating me, they told me to stand up, but I could not, from weakness caused by the loss of blood from the cuts they gave me in the back, legs, and arms; then two of the men held me up, and some of them knocked me down by hitting me on the head with their pistols."[59] In Mississippi, the Klan killed a freedman, slashed open his front body from the throat to the groin, disemboweled the corpse, and threw the body into a nearby creek. In Georgia, a black preacher was whipped and mutilated so severely in the stomach area that his entrails protruded out of his body.[60] Throat slitting was not only common but also symbolic: it was a legacy of pro-Confederate vigilantes who had committed a number of atrocities during the Civil War.[61]

The Ku Klux Klan was commonly associated with lynching, but, according to the Joint Select Committee testimony, when it came to the taking of lives, the double-barreled shotgun was the Klan's preferred weapon of choice, although pistols were probably more widespread. In addition to blacks and white radicals, murder victims included more than 60 state senators, judges, legislators, sheriffs, constables, mayors, county commissioners, and other various officeholders.[62] As with quantifying Ku Klux whippings, estimating the total number of lives taken by the Invisible Empire is fraught with problems. Aside from the "authentic" versus "spurious" Klan issue, spontaneous race riots claimed a number of lives in addition to those ended by the more deliberately planned terrorist operations typical of the Klan. As George Rable noted in his study of Reconstruction violence, aside from the systematic terrorism associated with the Klan and other supremacist groups, there were innumerable random murders in the postwar South due to the breakdown of order and to racial friction caused by emancipation.[63] Without attempting to distinguish solely Klan-related killings, which is probably unrealistic anyway, Stephen Budiansky recently asserted that during Reconstruction, terrorists murdered more than 3,000 freedmen. He offered, however, no references or documentation to back his contention.[64] Citing a 1977 study by Edward Magdol, Kwando Mbiassi Kinshasa recently estimated that the number of Klan murders exceeded 20,000. Again, neither offered any supporting primary evidence.[65] Local estimates provide the most reliable numbers of Klan-type murders but left only hints of the larger picture. The outrages cited above surrounding the 1868 fall elections, for example, were horrendous but probably not typical over a three- or four-year period. Major Lewis Merrill's investigation of the York County, South Carolina, Klan in 1871 documented 17 murders and more than 600 whippings prior to his arrival.[66] Testimony before the Joint Select Committee in 1871 offered evidence of Klan operations in six Alabama counties between 1868 and 1871: at least 27 victims killed and 330 whipped or otherwise "maltreated."[67]

A few infamous but representative episodes of Klan violence provide additional insight into the larger picture of the Klan's thirst for blood. In Georgia, hooded nightriders fired gunshots into the home of Perry Jeffers, a black man with a wife and five sons, one of whom was infirm. Instead of cowering in fear, the Jeffers family fired back, killing one raider and wounding several others. Several nights later, the Klan returned and, as Jeffers and four of his sons watched from behind some trees, lynched his wife and shot his crippled son 11 times. Mrs. Jeffers miraculously survived, but local authorities had to put Jeffers and his four remaining sons in jail to protect them from a reprisal raid that the Klansmen were surely planning. The local sheriff eventually ushered Jeffers and sons onto a train to help make good their escape to Augusta. Unfortunately, when the train reached

Dearing, a crowd of Klansmen boarded the railcar, absconded with the Jeffers family, hauled them out into the woods, and, with the exception of one son who managed to escape, shot them all to death and dumped the bodies into a well.[68] Also in Georgia, Dr. D. W. Darden, a white Republican, was jailed for shooting and killing the reputed leader of a local Klan den but was busted out of jail by hooded terrorists, stripped naked, shot 30 times, and then his riddled corpse was fully reclothed.[69] In York County, South Carolina, the Klan set out one night to confiscate arms from suspected black militiamen. The Klansmen came away with more than 20 firearms, but none of the militiamen received further punishment because none were to be found—all of them had fled ahead of time. All, that is, except one: Jim Williams, the leader of the black militia, hid under the floorboards of his home. The Klan discovered his hiding place, dragged him outside, and, in full view of his family, lynched him from a nearby tree and hung a sign around his neck that read "Capt. Jim Williams on his big muster."[70]

Aside from the knife, firearm, and noose, testimony about the Klan suggested other means of murder. Some victims were said to have been poisoned, and there were many instances of death from arson. In Mississippi, nightriders burst into the home of a freedman, shot him to death, and then set his house on fire, with his two children trapped inside.[71] In Georgia, a suspected black rapist was bound to a stake and burned alive.[72] As is plainly evident, the breadth and scope of Ku Klux violence was both overwhelming and incomprehensible. Even the most hardened souls, witness to innumerable wartime atrocities, had difficulty grasping the shocking violence unleashed by the hooded terrorists. The net impact of this virulent terrorism was unmistakable, producing a psychological reaction that extended far beyond the Klan's immediate victims. Thousands of blacks slept in the woods rather than risk encounters with nightriders. Untold numbers fled the South, seeking shelter, physically as well as politically, out west or up north. White Republican officials and schoolteachers heeded Klan warnings of violent retribution and simply abandoned the South. Thousands of Republican voters shied away from the polls purely out of fear. A frightened woman from South Carolina, cognizant of Klan outrages, lamented, "I never lie down to sleep with the sense of safety which I could feel, if my husband's principles were democratic."[73] Even white conservatives who opposed the use of violence were cowed into silence lest the Klan turn on them. As one witness in Louisiana testified, the Invisible Empire, through its orchestrated campaign of violent outrage, had created not the perfect storm, but "the perfect terror."[74]

IV.   Resistance to the Klan

The audacity with which the Ku Klux Klan committed outrages in many areas betrayed a sense of impunity, created in large part by the sympathy and complicity of local officials. As did earlier terrorist groups in America, Klan dens occasionally held mock trials in a symbolic form of extralegal authority, which, in many cases, supplemented other forms of unsanctioned political control. Their self-ascribed regulator role and their punishment of miscreants who violated local mores was consistent with this particular function. The Klan, however, had so deeply penetrated local institutions that, in some communities, it in essence operated as a *legal* authority as well. In Arkansas, a state senator warned Governor Powell Clayton that, in Little Rock, "the Sheriff's militia is entirely controlled by the Ku Klux Klan . . . without an active armed militia and martial law, there cannot be even an attempt made to administer justice."[75] When Major Lewis Merrill began his crackdown on the York County Klan, he was obstructed by the Grand Jury, which included several Klansmen and the local telegraph operator, a Klansman who leaked all of Merrill's confidential messages.[76] Another equally notorious example of the Klan's long, clandestine reach involved a railroad shipment of 2,000 muskets and 40,000 rounds of ammunition purchased for the Florida state militia by Governor Harrison Reed. Although the arms were guarded by a detachment of federal soldiers, because every engineer, conductor, brakeman, and telegraph operator between Jacksonville and Tallahassee was a Klansman, by the time the train had reached its destination, all of the arms had disappeared. Undetected, other Klansmen had boarded the train and, with inside help, managed to throw all of the arms overboard, where they were later destroyed or confiscated by other conspirators.[77] Reporting on conditions in Louisiana, General O. O. Howard, director of the Freedman's Bureau, declared, "In some sections . . . outrage and crimes of every character have been perpetrated with impunity. In these sections the character of the local magistracy is not as high as could be desired, and many of them have connived at the escape of offenders, while some have even participated in the outrages."[78] A newspaper reporter from Cincinnati investigating the Klan ominously concluded, "Were all the Ku Klux arrested and brought to trial, among them would be found sheriffs, magistrates, jurors, and legislators, and it may be clerks and judges. In some counties it would be found that the Ku Klux and their friends comprise more than half of the influential and voting population."[79]

Aside from this widespread collusion between Klansmen and local authorities, many other communities with honest officials were simply paralyzed by fear, rendering local government powerless to protect the lives of its citizens. A report from Tennessee submitted to the Joint Select Committee warned, "A reign of terror exists which is so absolute in its nature that the best of citizens are unable or unwilling to give free expression to their opinions. The terror inspired by the secret organization known as the Ku Klux Klan is so great, that the officers of the law are powerless to execute its provisions, to discharge their duties, or to bring the guilty perpetrators of these outrages to the punishment they deserve. No one dares to inform upon them, or to take any measures to bring them to punishment because no one can tell but that he may be the next victim of their hostility or animosity."[80] A Freedman's Bureau agent in Tennessee reporting from Nashville conceded to his superiors that "civil authorities take no action in the matter of arrest to punish the murderers . . . loyal men say they dare not act for fear of assassination."[81] Everywhere, the story seemed to be the same. General Alfred H. Terry, reporting on outrages in Georgia, wrote, "There can be no doubt of the existence of numerous insurrectionary organizations known as the 'Ku Klux Klans,' who, shielded by their disguises, by the secrecy of their movements, and by the terror which they inspire, perpetrate crime with impunity. There is great reason to believe that in some cases local magistrates are in sympathy with the members of these organizations. In many places they are overawed by them and dare not attempt to punish them."[82] General O. O. Howard reported that, in Arkansas, "the administration of justice by the civil authorities has been deplorable. Lawless violence and ruffianism have prevailed to an alarming extent."[83] In South Carolina, a congressional investigation conceded that "terror and intimidation run supreme . . . very nearly in a state of rebellion against the U.S. Government."[84]

Also complicit in the influence of the Ku Klux Klan was the southern Democratic press. In many communities, newspapers were the primary means of announcing that Klan dens had been formed, and they additionally provided ways for Klansmen to communicate with one another. Many newspapers were unabashedly pro-Klan, suppressing or distorting the facts about Klan outrages, either by denying that such acts had actually taken place or by suggesting that the hooded nightriders harassing blacks were actually other blacks seeking personal vendettas and framing innocent Klansmen in the process. In Spartanburg, South Carolina, the Ku Klux Klan coerced, under the threat of death, more than 45 Republican voters to renounce their party allegiance by announcing their newly established Democratic proclivities in the *Spartan,* the local Democratic newspaper.[85] The *Nashville Gazette,* the *Pulaski Citizen,* the *Tuscaloosa Independent Monitor,* the *Raleigh Sentinel,* and the *Richmond Enquirer & Examiner* are just a few examples of newspapers that would sympathize with this bit of editorial hyperbole which appeared in the *Daily Columbia Phoenix* in 1870: "No one can fail to be struck . . . with the many vague, incoherent and ludicrous accounts given by these poor, colored people, many of whom were so ignorant as not to know their own names, of the herculean size, hideous proportions, and diabolical features of what they called the Ku Klux. After having thoroughly investigated the mater, I am of the opinion that the ghosts, hobgoblins, jack-o-lanterns and Ku Klux . . . are but allotropic conditions of the witches of New England, whose larvae, having long remained dormant until imported hither in the carpet-bags of some pious political priests, germinated in the too credulous minds of their poor proselytes, and loomed into luxuriance in the fertile fields of their own imagination."[86] Race baiting was a specialty; the *Nashville Gazette* once remarked that "niggers are disappearing . . . with a rapidity that gives color to the canibalisitc [sic] threats of the shrouded Brethren. Run, nigger, run, or the Kuklux will catch." An article in the *Richmond Dispatch* read, "The Ku-Klux Klan are kalled upon to kastigate or kill kullered kusses who may approve the konstitution being koncocted by the contemptible karpet-baggers at the kapital. Each Klan is kommanded by a karniverous kurnel, who kollects his komrades with kare and kaution commensurate with the magnitude of the kause."[87] Three short-lived southern newspapers even incorporated Ku Klux into their titles: the *Ku Klux Kaleidoscope* of Goldsboro, North Carolina, the *Ultra Ku Klux* of Jefferson, Texas, and the *Daily Kuklux Vedette of Houston*.[88] These Klannish newspapers and their respective editors were but a part of the larger attempt by the Democratic press to demonize anything that smacked of radical politics, and were largely responsible for creating the anti-Republican perspectives that dominated Reconstruction histories for more than half a century. Republican newspapers would counterattack, and, though they did their best to report faithfully Klan outrages and the pressing need for government intervention, they were badly outnumbered and labored in the midst of hostile political territory.

Counterattacks by the minority press constituted but one aspect of the many individual and institutional responses to the Klan, which, at times, became obscured by the Klan's hostile, unrelenting vendetta against all perceived enemies. However, blacks adapted to their circumstances and adopted survival strategies that ranged from the benign to the most extreme. Most commonly, thousands slept at night in the woods rather than in their homes, for fear of nightriders. This could last from a few days to several weeks at a time. Many homes were equipped with loose floorboards to provide hiding places, but, as in the sad case of Jim Williams, this was not always effective. As John Patterson Green had noted early on, tens of thousands of blacks migrated northward for many reasons, including escape from racial persecution.[89] In just a few years, they would begin to move westward as well. Some blacks decided to repatriate to Africa with the help of the American Colonization Society. Elias Hill, the paralyzed black preacher beaten by the South Carolina Klan, eventually led about 60 families from Clay Hill to Monrovia in late 1871.[90] In total, John Hope Franklin estimated that less than 15,000 black refugees emigrated to Africa during the 19th century.[91] Estimating how many of them fled, like Hill and company, to escape Ku Klux Klan terror would constitute mere guesswork.

What particularly upset the Ku Klux Klan and other southern conservatives were the efforts of blacks to arm themselves in self-defense, hence the constant Klan raids to confiscate arms from black families. Early Klan apologists had written of entire black communities cowering in fear before the hooded nightriders; yet, resistance and defiance were commonplace as blacks everywhere bravely defended themselves, their homes, and their families. Testimonies taken by the Joint Select Committee are filled with examples of defiant blacks who, at some-times great personal sacrifice, fought back against the Klan on their own terms. Perry Jeffers and his six sons decided to shoot it out with the Klansmen and took a life before succumbing to the vast force of the Klan. Essie Harris of North Carolina once engaged in a 90-minute shootout with more than 50 assailants.[92] The courage exhibited by isolated individuals and families to stand up to the hooded terrorists is remarkable in hindsight, testimony to the unbreakable human spirit possessed by those who either knew no fear or would not let fear manipulate their lives. Black men were not alone in their defiance. At least one white woman, Anna Davis, refused to capitulate to terrorists. A schoolmarm from the north, Davis taught black school children in Tupelo, Mississippi, and, despite receiving coffin notices and other threats from the local Klan, refused to leave or stop teaching. On several occasions, alone and armed only with a pistol, she bravely managed to prevent nightriders from crashing through her front door.[93] In his study of black resistance to the Klan, Kwando Mbiassi Kinshasa noted that individual responses to hooded terrorism included the torching of dwellings, barns, gin houses, and crops, as well as the slaughtering of livestock and destruction of farm equipment.[94]

Aside from individual resistance, blacks often relied on their armed militias that drilled regularly and could muster in a moment's notice. Many of these militias were involved in rescue riots, freeing fellow blacks from false imprisonment. In Georgia, when terrorists threatened the life of Reverend Henry Turner, 150 armed blacks quickly rallied to his defense. One thousand armed men once assembled within 15 minutes to protect Florida state senator Robert Meachem from assassination. During the infamous 1868 election in New Orleans, P.B.S. Pinchback, a black state senator, warned Klansmen, "the next outrage of the kind which [white Democrats] commit will be the signal for the dawn of retribution, of which they have not yet dreamed—a signal that will cause ten thousand torches to be applied to this city."[95] The city wasn't set on fire, but, as established earlier, the cycle of violence that enveloped New Orleans was unprecedented. Also in 1868, about 20 to 30 armed blacks ambushed a Ku Klux Klan meeting in Columbia, Tennessee, killing one and wounding several others before retreating behind the lines of federal soldiers.[96] Blacks and Republicans consistently argued that the black militias were a necessary defense against Klan outrages, but conservatives saw them as mere provocation. One newspaper correspondent expressed the conservative viewpoint when he wrote, "The fact is inevitable that bloodshed will follow. Reconstructed governments are bad enough with negro legislatures, negro magistrates, negro police, and negro commissioners of education and other matters; but when armed negroes appear as military forces to keep white men in order . . . the spirit . . . must revolt."[97] In his groundbreaking work on Reconstruction in South Carolina, Joel Williamson contended that the black militias were effective in forging black pride and further inspired unorganized blacks to become more assertive in defense of their lives and property.[98] The organized black militias represented problem enough for white conservatives, but there were other opposing forces in some scattered places in the South. Violent outlaw gangs roamed the countryside, plaguing radicals and conservatives alike. The Cullen Baker Gang, which operated around the Texas–Arkansas border, notoriously targeted blacks and Republicans, and in Alabama the Mossbacks, which consisted of white Unionists, conducted a guerrilla war against the Klan. But perhaps the most infamous of these gangs was the Lowrie Gang, whose members resided in "Scuffletown," a rough and tumble community near the Lumbee River in North Carolina. Described as a band of "cutthroats and assassins," this gang, which mostly consisted of mulattos and Cherokee mixed-bloods, was led by Henry Berry Lowrie and originated when Confederates murdered members of his family in 1865. Moving in and around the swamps in Robeson County, the Lowrie Gang carried out a guerrilla campaign against the Klan and other Democrats. A robbery of over $22,000 in 1872 was said to be the gang's last operation, and members mysteriously disappeared shortly thereafter, although in 1937 a great-nephew of Lowrie claimed that the gang leader was still alive at the age of 92.[99] Hence, whether acting alone or in groups, blacks refused to respond passively to racial outrages. In a study of 33 major Reconstruction race riots, Melinda Meek Hennessey discovered that in 73% of them, blacks responded defiantly and "fought back at least initially, and usually until they were overwhelmed by superior numbers and firepower."[100]

Institutions sympathetic to blacks also developed survival strategies to help combat Klan terrorism. As Kinshasa noted, the Union League developed a carefully designed response to the Klan that included the following elements: engagement of civil institutions; investigation of Ku Klux Klan outrages, accountability of local law enforcement authorities, supervision of local officeholders, inclusion of League members in local governance to challenge the discretion of conservative sheriffs and magistrates, and the quick apprehension of suspected criminals.[101] Subsequently, the Union League helped draw up hundreds of indictments against suspected Klansmen. While some of these agenda items may have constituted nothing more than wishful thinking, the Union League, as well as others frustrated in their attempts to stamp out Klan terrorism, certainly understood that only the active engagement of civil authorities, both at the state and federal levels, could muster the resources necessary to combat the Klan. Several state governments did, in fact, take legislative action against Klan terrorism, but seldom did these largely symbolic efforts result in convictions of any kind. In addition to Tennessee and Arkansas, which had earlier passed legislation designed to curtail Klan violence, by early 1871, North Carolina, Alabama, Mississippi, Texas, and Kentucky approved similar laws, which forbade the committing of crimes while in disguise. Alabama approved two additional laws, one of which exempted from prosecution anyone who killed a disguised person committing a criminal act and the other of which permitted Klan victims to recover financial damages from Klansmen in court. In Texas, where state authorities acted as aggressively as anywhere, more than 4,500 suspects were arrested for violating new anti-Klan legislation. Mississippi approved a special fund to finance covert operations against the Invisible Empire.[102] Unfortunately, in most cases, lack of resolve at the state level, compounded by obstruction at the local level, rendered most anti-Ku Klux laws meaningless.

In addition to Tennessee and Arkansas, which had earlier declared martial law, North and South Carolina also initiated militia laws to take on the Klan. In North Carolina, the Shoffner Act of 1870 gave Republican Governor William Holden vast powers to proclaim a state of insurrection and to employ the militia

For the next two years, McParlan gleaned all he could about the inner workings of both the AOH and the Molly Maguires. To protect his cover story, he spent brief periods working the mines but usually found excuses to avoid the exhausting work. By 1875, Lawler had been replaced as bodymaster by Frank McAndrew, who soon after departed for Luzerne County in search of work. This fortuitous turn of events left McParlan as the ranking officer of the Shenandoah AOH, placing him near the top of the Molly Maguire hierarchy. From this lofty vantage point, McParlan would observe and assist in the planning of several Molly murders, establishing the basis of later claims that he was, above all else, an agent provocateur. Two years later, when he made his surprising appearance in court to testify about the Molly Maguires, his riveting testimony made him the state's star witness and provided most of what we now know about the infamous Mollies.

While McParlan was earning the confidence of his newfound acquaintances, tensions were building in the coal region. The Depression of 1873 had prompted a reduction of wages, and, by the fall of 1874, a labor strike was imminent. Moreover, in Mahanoy City, a community divided along ethnic lines between the Irish and English, street fighting between rival gangs added to the tense environment. On the night of October 30, a fire broke out in the center of Mahanoy City. Immediately, two volunteer fire companies, one Irish and the other predominantly Welsh, rushed to the scene. In previous similar situations, the dousing of fires was usually followed by all-out brawls between competing fire companies. In this particular instance, the fire was relatively minor, but the ensuing melee would lead to the reemergence of the Molly Maguires, thereby initiating a new phase of violence. When the brawl broke out, shots were fired, and several bystanders were wounded. Attempting to restore order, George Major, the city's chief burgess, stepped out onto the street, drew his pistol, and shot a dog to death. Someone from the crowd, later identified as John McCann, then fired a shot that hit Major, who fired off two more shots before falling, mortally wounded. One of Major's bullets allegedly struck the head of Daniel Dougherty, who was quickly arrested under the mistaken presumption that Major had targeted him in retaliation for the fatal gunshot. As fate would have it, Major was also the foreman of the Welsh fire company, while Dougherty was a member of the AOH, compounding the ethnic tensions and leading to accusations that the Molly Maguires were behind the killing. Dougherty went to trial the following spring but was dramatically acquitted after the bullet, still lodged in his head, was removed by a surgeon and subsequent testimony demonstrated that it could not have come from George Major's pistol. James McParlan was among the select Mollies who knew of Dougherty's innocence but let him stand trial anyway, confident that he would be exonerated. Meanwhile, John McCann, the likely triggerman, managed to flee the coal region, leaving the murder of George Major unresolved.[62]

Seven weeks after Major's death, Frederick Hesser, a watchman for the Hickory Swamp Colliery near Shamokin, was killed while on duty. Although the reason for his death was obscure then and remains so to this day, two Mollies,

Peter McManus and John O'Neil, later stood trial for the murder and were sentenced to death. McManus, bodymaster of the Coal Run AOH, would hang in 1879, but O'Neil had his sentence commuted to life imprisonment because of his alleged feeble-mindedness. By mid-1875, ethnic gang warfare and disturbances associated with the disastrous "Long Strike," now nearing its fifth month, had precipitated an epidemic of violence. On March 17, in Mahanoy City, William "Bully Bill" Thomas, a Welshman, shot Thomas McAneeny in the leg during a fight. On March 29, Aaron King, a Coal and Iron Policeman, was shot in the head at the Pink Ash Colliery during a riot. On May 22, having survived the surgery which extracted a bullet from his head, Daniel Dougherty was shot at again, this time by two men, including "Bully Bill" Thomas. Evidently, after Dougherty's acquittal in the murder of George Major, the Welsh "Modocs" had sworn revenge. Thomas escaped this time unscathed, but now became a marked man. Also targeted for retribution were two brothers of George Major, Jesse and William Major, who had helped plot the attempt on Dougherty's life. Meanwhile, the local Catholic Church, long divided over the Molly Maguires, began to turn against them. Father Henry O'Reilly of the BVM Church in Shenandoah, an outspoken critic, railed against the Mollies from the pulpit and exposed them by reading a list of Molly Maguire names before his startled congregation. Among the names he read was James McKenna, James McParlan's alias. So successful was McParlan's infiltration of the Molly Maguire underground, even outsiders had come to think of him as a legitimate Molly. On June 27, "Bully Bill" Thomas was attacked by three Mollies but survived two pistol wounds. McParlan participated in the plotting of this attack but made no attempt to warn Thomas. According to one account, the conspirators had nearly voted to beat Thomas rather than kill him, but McParlan cast the deciding vote for assassination.[63] The planned attack on the surviving Major brothers, who had since left Mahanoy City, never took place.

By July, the Long Strike had ended and Franklin Gowen's destruction of the WBA was complete. Miners who were not already blacklisted, grudgingly returned to the mines for significantly reduced wages. Consequently, the violence in the coal region continued unabated. On July 6, Benjamin Yost, a policeman, was shot and killed in Tamaqua during his night watch. The murder of Yost was a particularly brazen affair; he was shot only a few doors from his home while he and another officer were extinguishing street lamps. Court testimony later provided by McParlan and James Kerrigan, a Molly turned informer, would lead to five convictions and subsequent executions for this killing. Apparently, the murder of Yost was an act of revenge. Sometime earlier, Yost had beaten and arrested Thomas Duffy, a member of the Tamaqua AOH. Duffy arranged for Yost's killing by contracting neighboring lodges, which provided the assassins.[64]

On August 14, a day dubbed "Bloody Saturday," the summer violence reached a murderous peak. In Girardville, following a day of gang disturbances, Thomas Gwyther, the justice of the peace, was fatally shot by William Love. Love, who fled and was never apprehended, killed Gwyther to prevent a friend's arrest. Over near

Shenandoah at a place called Glover's Grove, a Welsh fire company was holding a picnic when Gomer James was shot and killed while he tended bar. A lone assassin then disappeared into the crowd. Two years earlier, James had been acquitted of killing Edward Gosgrove, a member of the AOH, and had been a Molly Maguire target ever since. Thomas Hurley, James' alleged assailant, also fled prosecution, but seven Mollies were later convicted for conspiring to reward Hurley for the James murder.[65] Meanwhile, in Mahanoy City, Bully Bill Thomas was involved in yet another shootout, this time with an Irishman named James Dugan. When an innocent bystander was struck and killed by a stray bullet, Thomas was arrested. Charges were dropped after Bully Bill, despite his long criminal background, agreed to cooperate with the Coal and Iron Police in its investigation of the Molly Maguires.

Less than two weeks later, on September 1, Thomas Sanger, a foreman at Heaton's Colliery at Raven Run, and William Uren, his friend, were murdered while on their way to work. Both were English, immigrants from Cornwall, but the motives for the killings were never established. Sanger was allegedly the recipient of several coffin notices before his death.[66] Two days later, John P. Jones, a Welsh superintendent at the Lehigh and Wilkes-Barre mine in Lansford, was also murdered on his way to work. Jones, according to subsequent court testimony, was killed for having earlier blacklisted Hugh McGehan. McGehan, eager for revenge, had secured outside assassins from Tamaqua to deal with Jones by taking part in the murder of Benjamin Yost two months earlier. In reciprocation, the Tamaqua AOH provided the three gunmen who shot and killed Jones. As he was in the plot to kill Bully Bill Thomas, James McParlan was deeply involved in the planning of the three September murders. His testimony would ultimately help convict the Sanger–Uren–Jones murderers, but court testimony would also reveal that, although McParlan knew of the three murder plots well in advance, he again failed to provide any warnings to his superiors. When pressed later in court on the matter, McParlan would argue that circumstances prevented him from doing so. While that argument, weak as it may be, could be made in the Sanger–Uren murders, it certainly does not hold up regarding the plot to take the life of John P. Jones. As many have pointed out, McParlan had plenty of opportunities to prevent Jones's death but chose to remain silent.[67] Whatever one thinks about McParlan's infiltration of the Molly Maguire underground, it is apparent that, in an effort to secure incriminating evidence, McParlan was willing to stand aside and let murder plots play themselves out to their bloody ends.

Not long after John P. Jones was shot and killed, a posse came upon three suspicious men on the outskirts of town. Two of them, Edward Kelly and Michael J. Doyle, both of Mt. Laffee, were carrying AOH badges. The third was the notorious troublemaker and Tamaqua bodymaster James Kerrigan. These were the three killers recruited from Tamaqua to avenge McGehan. The Jones murder is generally considered the last of the Molly Maguire killings, and the capture of Kerrigan and his two accomplices ultimately set in motion a series of confessions, including one from Kerrigan himself, who would turn state's evidence and testify against his fellow conspirators during the infamous Molly Maguire trials that would begin the following January. His testimony, combined with that of McParlan, would provide the bulk of the evidence that would send several Mollies to the gallows, including Kelly and Doyle.

The violence in the coal country, unfortunately, did not diminish after these trials. On September 8, Patrick Dugan assaulted Bully Bill Thomas and was arrested, but subsequently jumped bail. On October 9, a large number of men fired on the Shenandoah home of Muff Lawlor, McParlan's first significant acquaintance in Pottsville two and a half years earlier. That same day in Shenandoah, an Irishman named Richard Finnen was shot and killed in a saloon; James Johns, a Welshman, was also shot and had his throat slashed. The violence and gunfire continued throughout what newspapers called the "night of terror."[68] Finally, on the evening of December 10, an event unfolded that is generally considered to be the most shocking atrocity of the whole Molly Maguire saga. A mob of disguised men broke into the home of Margaret O'Donnell in Wiggans Patch and captured Charles O'Donnell, her son and a suspect in the Sanger–Uren murders. The mob dragged him outside the house, put 15 bullets into his head, ten bullets into his torso, and then set his body on fire. The mob also sought out the McAllister brothers, James and Charles, also suspects in the twin murders. Both managed to escape, but when Charles McAllister's wife, Ellen, appeared in her nightshirt, the mob riddled her with bullets. Ellen McAllister was Charles O'Donnell's sister, as well as the sister of John Kehoe's wife, Mary Ann O'Donnell Kehoe. Ellen was also pregnant. The Wiggans Patch Massacre, as it became known, was most likely an act of vengeance by a committee of vigilantes, although different theories circulated at the time. Some argued that the attack was the result of an intra-ethnic rivalry between Irish gangs. Others suggested that John Kehoe, the alleged "King" of the Molly Maguires, directed the attack in order to silence Charles O'Donnell, who had expressed anxieties over the Sanger–Uren murders.[69] The rumors implicating Kehoe were probably an attempt to undermine his standing within the community, for it is highly unlikely that he would've ordered an attack that ultimately resulted in the murder of his wife's brother and sister. Most telling, however, was a vigilante-style note found near O'Donnell's body which read: "You are the murderers of Uren and Sanger."[70]

What cannot be denied is that the hostile environment that had long plagued the coal country seemed to necessitate unusual and extralegal forms of law enforcement, hence the growth of a vigilante movement. Certainly Franklin Gowen and Allan Pinkerton saw it this way. Conventional police forces had failed miserably to curb the violence. In retrospect, these developments should have come as no surprise. For some time, the *Miners' Journal* and the *Shenandoah Herald* had called for the formation of local vigilance committees to fight the Mollies on their own terms. As the *Herald* editor Thomas Foster put it, "a remedy to strike terror into the hearts of such cowardly assassins is what is needed and must be had."[71]

His call did not go unheeded, for several vigilance groups had already formed with the help of Pinkerton agents, many of whom had been integrated into the Coal and Iron Police. Moreover, the Pinkerton Agency provided the identities of known Molly Maguires directly to vigilance committees in Schuylkill County. One document, addressed to "The Vigilance Committee of the Anthracite Coal region," contained a list of known Mollies, the crimes for which they were allegedly responsible, and their home addresses. Much of this information, of course, had come from McParlan. On the list was the Wiggans Patch home of Charles O'Donnell, one of the accused assailants of Thomas Sanger and William Uren.[72]

In hindsight, there doesn't seem to be much doubt that vigilantes were responsible for the Wiggans Patch Massacre, that vengeance for Sanger and Uren was their primary motive, and that the Pinkertons provided the crucial incriminating information. What remains unclear is whether or not Pinkerton agents were part of the murderous mob. In his own semi-fictional account of the Molly Maguire episode, Allan Pinkerton refused to admit any complicity in Wiggans Patch, but openly admitted his view that the murders were simply an example of "fighting fire with fire."[73] No one ever stood trial for the Wiggans Patch Massacre, although Margaret O'Donnell had managed to pull the mask off one of the assailants, whom she immediately identified as her butcher, Frank Wenrich. Wenrich was a lieutenant in the newly formed Stillman Guards, a division of the state militia assigned to protect the coal region.[74] Wenrich was arrested but soon released when Mrs. O'Donnell, on the advice of son-in-law John Kehoe, refused to cooperate in the prosecution of Wenrich. Evidently, Kehoe planned to exact his own kind of justice, rather than place his faith in the judicial system. Given the longstanding hostilities in the coal region, one might expect the locals to be quite inured to incidents such as Wiggans Patch, but the double murder struck a sensitive chord. The vile treatment of Charles O'Donnell's body was distasteful enough, but the murder of an unarmed and pregnant woman crossed a line that even the Molly Maguires dared not touch. Even James McParlan, on hearing of the murders, sent a letter of resignation to Pinkerton headquarters. His complicity in the murder of Ellen McAllister sickened him, and he feared that the Molly Maguires, who had consciously avoided victimizing women, would now reply in kind.[75]

In the end, McParlan remained on the job at least for a while, and Kehoe would be arrested before exacting his revenge. In the aftermath of the John P. Jones murder and the subsequent capture of James Kerrigan and his two accomplices, events began to unfold rather quickly. In February 1876, two months after killing Jones, Kerrigan turned against the Molly Maguires, a change of allegiance that led to a series of arrests. Meanwhile, the attack at Wiggans Patch provided further evidence of what many Mollies had begun to suspect: that an informer was in their midst. In early March, James McParlan disappeared from the coal country soon after deflecting accusations that he was the offending informant. It was an expedient departure, for John Kehoe and others were convinced that McParlan was, indeed, the betrayer. Abandoning the Molly Maguire underground and leaving his wild Irishman persona behind, McParlan would surprisingly resurface in May as an agent for the Pinkerton National Detective Agency. By then, the long judicial process known as the Molly Maguire Trials had begun, and the man known to the miners as James McKenna would be the prosecution's star witness. The violent conspiracy of Irish coal miners, be they known as sleepers, buckshots, or Molly Maguires, was about to unravel.

VI. The Molly Maguire Trials

Despite the long legacy of coal country violence—the murders, riots, assaults, gang rivalries, and incidents of industrial sabotage—what continues to fascinate many about the Molly Maguire saga are the trials, which resulted in 20 executions and a number of other convictions. Perhaps this should come as no surprise. Despite the stunning success of the prosecutors, most of the murders attributed to the Molly Maguires remain clouded. The lack of incriminating forensic evidence back then contributes to the uncertainty today. But the court testimony survives as a matter of public record, thus allowing historians and Molly Maguire enthusiasts great insight not only into the court proceedings but also into the public consciousness as well, for these trials would become both a spectacle and a sham.

The trials began in January 1876, although several Mollies were acquitted during earlier trials for the murders of Alexander Rea and Morgan Powell. While the proceedings are known collectively as the Molly Maguire Trials, there were 22 separate trials, the last held in August 1878. One would have needed a scorecard to keep track of the major participants, which included five different presiding judges, nine prosecuting attorneys, 16 defense attorneys, and 32 defendants. Nineteen of the trials were held in either Pottsville or Mauch Chunk (now Jim Thorpe). By any stretch of the judicial imagination, the trials would appear to be a dubious proceeding at best, and an organized lynch mob at worst. The list of legal irregularities was endless. The state of Pennsylvania surrendered most of its jurisdictional authority to private interests. Most of the prosecuting attorneys worked for the railroads and coal companies, including the ever-resolute Franklin Gowen, who personally prosecuted the murderers of Benjamin Yost, Thomas Sanger, and William Uren. Some of the presiding judges had either personal or political connections to the corporate heads of the local coal and railroad companies. The bulk of the incriminating evidence was provided by informants of suspicious character or an alleged agent provocateur. Forensic evidence was non-existent. Railroad and mine company employees served as witnesses and jurors. Irish Catholics were excluded from the juries, many of which were packed with German immigrants with limited English. In Pottsville and Mauch Chunk, agents of the Coal and Iron Police guarded the courthouse and prison. As Harold Aurand famously put it, "The Molly Maguire investigation and trials marked one of the most astounding surrenders of sovereignty in American history. A private corporation initiated the investigation through a private detective agency, a private police force arrested the supposed offenders, and coal company attorneys prosecuted—the state provided only the courtroom and hangman."[76] Media coverage also rendered the trials as public spectacle. The *Miners' Journal,* the *Shenandoah Herald,* the *New York Evening Post,* and competing publishers of pulp fiction all vied for the public's attention and spending money by providing sensationalized accounts of the trials. The audaciousness of the original murders, the emotionalism engendered by the testimony, and public demands for justice all contributed to a feeding frenzy that only guilty verdicts and lynchings would seemingly satisfy.

The first of the trials was held to establish the complicity of Michael Doyle in the murder of John P. Jones. Doyle was one of the three Tamaqua assassins, along with James Kerrigan and Edward Kelly, who were apprehended shortly after the attack on Jones. This trial, which led to the first conviction of a Molly Maguire, would establish a pattern that all of the subsequent trials would largely follow. The prosecuting district attorney, E. W. Siewers, was assisted by a team of corporate lawyers, including Francis W. Hughes, an attorney with the Philadelphia and Reading; retired Civil War general Charles Albright, an attorney with the Lehigh and Wilkes-Barre Coal Company; and Allen Craig, an attorney with the Lehigh Valley Railroad. Doyle was defended by local attorneys Edward Mulhearn, an inexperienced trial lawyer, and Daniel Kalbfus, who was institutionalized four years later for mental illness. The presiding judge was Samuel Dreher, a man known as "the hanging judge" for his propensity to pronounce death sentences. Dreher also happened to be a close personal friend of Asa Packer, the president of the Lehigh Valley Railroad. During Doyle's trial, Kerrigan, who was awaiting trial for the same charges, decided to confess and turn state's evidence. In February, to the surprise of virtually no one, a guilty verdict was delivered and Doyle was sentenced to death. Doyle's fate did not bode well for Edward Kelly, who was tried in March and received a similar sentence in April.

And so it went, trial after trial, conviction after conviction. The prosecution would portray the Molly Maguires as a vast criminal conspiracy, incorporating the AOH and dominating political affairs from local to state levels. James McParlan created a stir when he appeared in Pottsville during the May trial of four Mollies charged with the murder of Benjamin Yost. Despite his earlier agreement that he was under no obligation to appear in court, McParlan well understood the impact his direct testimony would have. This was also the first trial in which Franklin Gowen took an active role in the prosecution. Adding to the circus-like atmosphere, ex-general Charles Albright, assisting the prosecution, appeared in court in full military regalia. McParlan's testimony, which extended through several trials, combined with that of several Mollies who testified for the prosecution, provided unique insight into the inner workings of the AOH and the Molly Maguires. Franklin Gowen had long considered the two entities as one, and McParlan's testimony corroborated that view. In reality, the link between the AOH and the Mollies was overstated, but their overlapping membership in the coal region was particularly incriminating. Just as damaging was the manner in which the organizational structure of the AOH lodges provided the foundation of the Molly Maguire hierarchy. The AOH lodges and taverns provided meeting places where the Mollies often employed secret language codes and hand signals imported from Ireland. AOH bodymasters, secretaries, and other officials served similar leadership roles with the Mollies. As the trial testimony made clear, the Mollies had a well-defined organizational chain of command that mirrored very closely the inner structure of the AOH.

Other surprises were in store during the next two years. In early 1877, John Kehoe was convicted and sentenced to death for the murder of F. W. Langdon 15 years prior, despite sworn statements from his two co-defendants that he was innocent. When James Kerrigan testified for the prosecution regarding the murders of Benjamin Yost and John P. Jones, his testimony was rebutted by his wife, Fanny, who denounced him from the witness stand as a "dirty little rat" and fingered him as the triggerman in the killing of Jones.[77] The prosecution brought to court more than 120 witnesses in all, and in the defense's cross-examination there were other revelations. Robert Breslin testified in the Yost murder case and then admitted on the stand that he did so because of a promise from the Lehigh and Wilkes-Barre Company that he would be rewarded with a mine-boss position.[78] Other witnesses were offered inducements by the prosecution. McParlan's testimony suggested that he might have saved lives had he quickly informed his Pinkerton contacts of impending assassination plots he helped plan. Nonetheless, despite attempts by the defense to portray McParlan as an agent provocateur and to taint prosecution witnesses as corruptible, during the next four years, 20 Mollies were convicted for murder and sentenced to death. Eight other Mollies, also tried for murder, were acquitted. Twenty-five Mollies and their associates received prison sentences ranging from life to one year for various offenses, including two women convicted of perjury. Because of their testimony for the prosecution, James Kerrigan, the notorious Manus Cull, and a number of other Mollies were either pardoned or never tried for their alleged crimes. James McDonnell turned against Martin Bergin in the trial for the murder of Patrick Burns, but was executed nonetheless for the murder of George Smith. Of the 20 condemned men, only three—Michael Doyle, Edward Kelly, and Alexander Campbell—were directly tied to the crime for which they were charged and executed, the shooting of John P. Jones. James Roarity, who had supplied the pistol that killed Benjamin Yost but wasn't present at the scene of the crime, was among those executed. Thomas Duffy and James Carroll were convicted for the murder of Yost based entirely on the hearsay testimony of James Kerrigan, who richly deserved his nickname, "the squealer." Peter McManus was convicted for the murder of Frederick Hesser based solely on the testimony of Dennis Canning, a Locust Gap bodymaster charged and later pardoned for conspiracy to assault Bully Bill Thomas. Twelve suspects were never apprehended and were designated as fugitives by the Pinkerton Agency. Of the 16 "Molly Maguire murders" committed between 1862 and

1875, convictions were returned in 12 of them. Only the murders of David Muir, Henry Dunne, William Littlehales, and Thomas Gwyther remained unresolved.

The trials proved such a travesty of justice that Anthony Bimba, a Molly revisionist, was convinced that collaboration between the prosecution and various media outlets had created "an atmosphere of terror around the trials and the men who were being tried." The Coal and Iron Police forces were further guilty, he charged, of threatening harm to witnesses who did not testify convincingly on the prosecution's behalf, and the trials as a whole had spread "terror over anthracite Pennsylvania."[79] Others, though not as expressive as Bimba, were also extremely critical of the whole judicial process. Wayne Broehl, Jr., described the trials as "blood lust running rampant."[80] H. T. Crown argued that the only real conspiracy in the coal region was that conceived by Franklin Gowen, Allan Pinkerton, James McParlan, and all of their various accomplices, their ultimate objective being to seize economic power and "usurp and trample upon the liberties of the people."[81] Charles McCarthy, in his pro-Molly treatment, saw the trials as part of Gowen's "immoral lust for power." Gowen was a "disciple of the devil," he added, and, for securing death penalties under false pretenses, a "miserable assassin."[82]

If the exaggerations emanating from the trial participants, journalists, historians, and Molly Maguire enthusiasts are to be believed, it is a challenge to discern exactly who the terrorists were and who was terrorizing whom. Strip away the inflammatory rhetoric, and what remains is still a sordid tale of intrigue, conspiracy, and murder, all leading to a climax of vengeance, perversely administered under the guise of justice. Were the Molly Maguires guilty of industrial sabotage and murder? Most likely, yes. Did the Mollies constitute a broad and murderous conspiracy extending throughout the coal region? Yes and no. The Molly Maguires never constituted the vast economic and political force that Franklin Gowen, Benjamin Bannan, and others had maintained, but their AOH connections certainly helped constitute a network of criminal reciprocity. Were the Mollies who were eventually hanged guilty of their alleged crimes? In the case of the Jones murderers, probably; in John Kehoe's case, probably not. In most cases, we can never know for sure. By today's standards, most of the testimony was simply too prejudicial to be admitted into evidence. This does not, of course, mean that the Mollies did NOT commit said crimes, only that the evidence against them could not pass judicial muster today. But there is also the undeniable outcome that in the aftermath of the trials, executions, and prison sentences, the Molly Maguires were never heard from again in any significant manner. As a tightly knit group of Irish coal miners seeking their own brand of justice, the Molly Maguires certainly did exist. And it appears equally undeniable that their violent tactics struck terror into certain individuals and corporations. The farcical nature of their trials notwithstanding, the Mollies had become quintessential American terrorists. Their violent methods were driven by specific political, economic, and social rationales; they operated within a bureaucratic and hierarchical structure; and the psychological impact of their terrorist acts extended far beyond the pain suffered by those more directly victimized. In the end, their methods were so outrageous, so beyond the scope of normal law enforcement, that only an equally unconscionable application of justice could bring them down.

VII. Epilogue

Just as the 22 trials are often thought of as one, so it is with the Molly Maguire executions. This is, no doubt, a result of "Black Thursday," or "the Day of the Rope," when ten Mollies were executed in Schuylkill and Carbon counties. However, the execution of the remaining ten Mollies actually occurred on eight different occasions stretched over a two-year period. The "Black Thursday" executions on June 21, 1877, were merely the first. James Boyle, James Carroll, Thomas Duffy, Hugh McGehan, and James Roarity were executed in Pottsville for the murder of Benjamin Yost, and Thomas Munley was hanged for the killings of Thomas Sanger and William Uren. In Mauch Chunk, Alexander Campbell, John Donahue, Michael Doyle, and Edward Kelly were executed for their parts in the murders of Morgan Powell and John P. Jones. The last of the Molly Maguire hangings, on October 9, 1879, was that of Peter McManus for the murder of Frederick Hesser. In the interim, nine others were executed, either in Pottsville, Mauch Chunk, Sunbury, or Bloomsburg.[83] One of them was Alexander Campbell, who, according to legend, placed his dusty hand against his cell wall and vowed that his handprint would endure forever as a sign of his innocence. If contemporary accounts are to be believed, the handprint survives, despite many attempts to have it removed.[84]

The "Black Thursday" hangings were extensively covered by the press, particularly the *Miners' Journal,* which published a lengthy description of the executions, as well as detailed historical accounts of each of the crimes and criminals involved. Thousands of spectators poured into Pottsville and Mauch Chunk hoping to attend the executions. Unfortunately for most, the demand for seats was so great that only several hundred tickets were granted for entry into the prisons to witness the day of reckoning. Many of the seats were reserved for journalists, who were consequently offered generous sums of money to part with their tickets. Contributing to the circus-like environment, newspapers reported that the Molly Maguires were planning a desperate, last-minute assault on the two prisons to liberate their fellow terrorists. The governor of Pennsylvania subsequently dispatched state troops and other auxiliary forces to Mauch Chunk and Pottsville to augment the Coal and Iron Police already on the scene. The sensationalized newspaper reporting, the military occupation of the two towns, and the thousands of men and women who attended the executions, either inside or outside the prison walls all contributed to what Kevin Kenny called a "macabre theatrical spectacle."[85]

The 20 condemned Mollies were buried in graveyards scattered throughout the eastern Pennsylvania coal region. But while these fates were collectively sealed, the lives of the other major participants in the Molly Maguire story would end in a variety of ways. James McParlan would capitalize on his celebrity status and climb the ranks of the Pinkerton Agency, ending up in Denver, Colorado, as a superintendent. The sordid details of his infiltration of the Molly Maguire underground would resurface in 1907, when he was called on to testify in the trial of William "Big Bill" Haywood for the murder of Frank Steunenberg. During the last years of his life, convinced the Mollies would attempt revenge, he lived in a house patrolled by attack dogs and surrounded by high walls. Paranoid to the end, McParlan died in 1919. Due to economic setbacks, Franklin Gowen struggled to maintain his leadership of the Philadelphia and Reading and eventually returned to private practice as an attorney in 1886. Three years later while visiting Washington, D.C., he bought a gun and put a bullet through his head. Not surprisingly, rumors and newspaper reports suggested that the Molly Maguires had finally taken revenge. James Kerrigan, the infamous informer, never stood trial and later reconciled with his wife, Fanny, despite her damaging testimony against him. He changed his name and together the two moved to Richmond, Virginia. He died in 1898 and was buried in an unmarked grave. William "Bully Bill" Thomas continued his wild ways, drinking, brawling, and spending significant periods of time behind bars. By the time he died in 1916, evidently due to natural causes, he had survived 17 bullets and two knife wounds. Benjamin Bannan, editor of the *Miners' Journal,* died in 1875, and, although he didn't live to see the Molly Maguires hang, he had as much to do with their demise as anyone. Because of that influence, the *Journal* continued its crusade against the Mollies long after his death.

Today, the Molly Maguire legend lives on in Pennsylvania's coal region. Visitors travel the "Molly Maguire Tour," which takes them to various significant sites associated with the Molly saga, including the O'Donnell home, scene of the Wiggans Patch Massacre, and John Kehoe's Hibernian House in Girardville, still owned by his descendants. In 1979, the state of Pennsylvania granted a posthumous pardon to the "King" of the Molly Maguires. During the 1990s, mock retrials were held for Kehoe and Alexander Campbell, acquitting both defendants. Visitors to the Historical Society of Schuylkill County can still see snippets of the ropes used to hang John Kehoe and his fellow Mollies. But perhaps the most popular site of all is the supposed handprint of Alexander Campbell, high on the wall in the old jail in what was once Mauch Chunk. The mysterious handprint should have disappeared long ago, but, more than 135 years on, both it and many elements of the Molly Maguire legend endure, somewhere between myth and reality.

Notes

1. Kevin Kenny, *Making Sense of the Molly Maguires* (New York: Oxford University Press, 1998), 5.
2. Allan Pinkerton, *The Mollie Maguires and the Detectives* (New York: Carlton and Co., 1877), ix. Reprinted in 1973 by Dover Publications, New York.
3. F. P. Dewees, *The Molly Maguires* (New York: Burt Franklin, 1877), iv.

4. Edward Winslow Martin, *The History of the Great Riots and of the Molly Maguires* (Philadelphia: National Publishing Co., 1877); *History of Schuylkill County, Pa.* (New York: Munsell and Co., 1881), 106.

5. E. H. Heywood, *The Great Strike: Its Relations to Labor, Property, and Government* (Princeton, MA: Co-Operative Publishing Co., 1878), 15.

6. Anthony Bimba, *The Molly Maguires* (New York: International Publishers, 1950), 133.

7. J. Walter Coleman, *The Molly Maguire Riots* (Richmond: Garrett and Massie, 1936), 75.

8. Wayne G. Broehl, Jr., *The Molly Maguires* (Cambridge: President and Fellows of Harvard College, 1964). Reprinted in 1983 by Chelsea House Publishers, New York.

9. Charles A. McCarthy, *The Great Molly Maguire Hoax* (Wyoming, PA: Cro Woods, 1969); Sidney Lens, *The Labor Wars—From the Molly Maguires to the Sitdowns* (Garden City, NY: Doubleday & Co., 1973).

10. Harold W. Aurand, *From the Molly Maguires to the United Mine Workers* (Philadelphia: Temple University Press, 1971).

11. Mark Carnes, ed., *Past Imperfect: History According to the Movies* (New York: Henry Holt and Company, 1996), 143.

12. Kenny, *Making Sense*, 7.

13. Regarding Molly Maguire monographs, see Patrick Campbell, *A Molly Maguire Story* (Lawrenceville, NJ: Princeton University Press, 1992); H. T. Crown and Mark T. Major, *A Guide to the Molly Maguires* (Frackville, PA: Broad Mountain Publishing Company, 2003; H. T. Crown, *A Molly Maguire on Trial . . . The Thomas Munley Story* (Frackville, PA: Broad Mountain Publishing Company, 2002).

14. *Miners' Journal*, June 22, 1877.

15. *Philadelphia Ledger*, June 21, 1877.

16. Samuel T. Wiley, *Biographical and Portrait Cyclopedia of Schuylkill County* (originally published in 1893 by Rush, West & Co.; reprinted in 1993 by Windmill Publications, Mt. Vernon, IN), 131.

17. *Catholic Standard*, October 17, 1874.

18. Michael Beames, *Peasants and Power—The Whiteboy Movements and Their Control in Pre-Famine Ireland* (New York: St. Martin's Press, 1983), 27–29.

19. Kenny, *Making Sense*, 19; for more on Irish roots, see James McParlan report to Pinkerton Detective Agency, October 10, 1873, Accession 1520, Box 979, HML.

20. Beames, *Peasants and Power*, 80.

21. Kenny, *Making Sense*, 8.

22. Lens, *Labor Wars*, 12; Broehl, *The Molly Maguires*, 25; MJ, June 22, 1877.

23. W. E. H. Lecky, *History of Ireland in the Eighteenth Century*, Volume I (London: Longmans, Green & Co., 1902), 360.

24. Kenny, *Making Sense*, 22; James Donnelly, Jr., "The Whiteboy Movement, 1761–1765," *Irish Historical Studies*, 21 (March, 1978): 20–54.

25. Bernard A. Weisberger, *Many People, One Nation* (Boston: Houghton Mifflin, 1987), 118.

26. MJ, October 3, 1857.

27. Crown and Major, *A Guide*, 157.

28. Bimba, *The Molly Maguires*, 39–40.

29. Crown and Major, *A Guide*, 190.

30. Allan Pinkerton to Franklin Gowen, February 7, 1874, file on Molly Maguires-Pinkerton Report, Box 27, HSP; Kenny, *Making Sense*, 70.

31. MJ, March 30, 1867; for another estimation of murders, see Owen Hunt Papers, 1935–1975, Box 52-B, HSP.

32. Dewees, *The Molly Maguires,* 50: Crown and Major, *A Guide,* 151; Kenny, *Making Sense,* 97.
33. Dewees, *The Molly Maguires,* 54–57.
34. Statement of Manus Cull, August 22, 1876, F2, Accession 1520, Box 1001, HML; MJ, March 23, 1867.
35. MJ, Otober 3, 1857.
36. *The Molly Maguires and Their Victims* (Pottsville, PA: The Miners' Journal Print, 1876), introduction.
37. Martin, *History of the Great Riots,* 467.
38. Kenny, *Making Sense,* 163.
39. Ibid., 38.
40. Broehl, *The Molly Maguires,* 158.
41. Kenny, *Making Sense,* 80, epilogue.
42. Crown and Major, *A Guide,* 216.
43. Kenny, *Making Sense,* 143, 146.
44. Crown and Major, *A Guide,* appendix.
45. Kenneth T. Jackson, review of Kenny, *Making Sense,* for History Book Club (January, 1998).
46. Dewees, *The Molly Maguires,* appendix.
47. Report by James McParlan to Pinkerton Agency, April 13, 1875, F2, Accession 1520, Box 1001, HML.
48. Kenny, *Making Sense,* 175.
49. Dewees, *The Molly Maguires,* appendix.
50. *History of Schuylkill County, Pa.,* 104.
51. *Shenandoah Herald,* October 2, 1875; reprinted in Kenny, *Making Sense,* 201.
52. MJ, March 23, 1867.
53. MJ, June 22, 1877.
54. Wiley, *Biographical and Portrait,* 131.
55. Dewees, *The Molly Maguires,* 355; for more evidence of Molly Maguire terror, see Allan Pinkerton to Franklin Gowen, April 20, 1874, file on Molly Maguires-Pinkerton Report, Box 27, HSP.
56. Franklin Gowen's life was also said to be in danger; see Henry Pleasants to Franklin Gowen, March 29, 1875, Accession 1520, Box 979, HML.
57. A. Monroe Aurand, *Historical Account of the Mollie Maguires* (Lancaster, PA: The Aurand Press, undated), 8.
58. Dewees, *The Molly Maguires,* 32–33.
59. Pinkerton, *The Mollie Maguires,* 15.
60. Ibid., 16–17.
61. Ibid; for Pinkerton's problems in finding a reliable agent, see Allan Pinkerton to Franklin Gowen, March 27, 1874, file on Molly Maguires-Pinkerton Report, Box 27, HSP.
62. Broehl, *The Molly Maguires,* 181; Dewees, *The Molly Maguires,* 127–128; Kenny, *Making Sense,* 165–166; Bimba, *The Molly Maguires,* 84.
63. Crown and Major, *A Guide,* 211.
64. Crown and Major, *A Guide,* 155; Broehl, *The Molly Maguires,* 218–219, 222–227; Dewees, *The Molly Maguires,* 152–164; Kenny, *Making Sense,* 194–197.
65. Allan Pinkerton to Franklin Gowen, September 22, 1880, F2, Accession 1520, Box 1001, HML; Dewees, *The Molly Maguires,* 164–174; Kenny, *Making Sense,* 191–192; Broehl, *The Molly Maguires,* 228–231.

66. Allan Pinkerton to Franklin Gowen, August 28, 1875, F2, Accession 1520, Box 1001, HML; Kenny, *Making Sense,* 198.
67. Broehl, *The Molly Maguires,* 236; Kenny, *Making Sense,* 199–200.
68. Kenny, *Making Sense,* 193.
69. Crown and Major, *A Guide,* 86.
70. Broehl, *The Molly Maguires,* 261.
71. *Shenandoah Herald,* September 4, 1875.
72. Broehl, *The Molly Maguires,* 258–266; Kenny, *Making Sense,* 206–7; Bimba, *The Molly Maguires,* 70.
73. Pinkerton, *The Mollie Maguires,* 457.
74. Crown and Major, *A Guide,* 87.
75. Broehl, *The Molly Maguires,* 264.
76. Harold Aurand, *From the Molly Maguires,* 57.
77. *Pottsville Evening Chronicle,* May 17, 1876; quoted in Kenny, *Making Sense,* 230.
78. Bimba, *The Molly Maguires,* 96–97.
79. Ibid., 85.
80. Broehl, *The Molly Maguires,* 339.
81. Crown, *A Molly Maguire on Trial,* 161.
82. McCarthy, *The Great Molly Maguire Hoax,* 151.
83. MJ, June 22, 1867; Crown and Major, *A Guide,* 226–227.
84. Crown and Major, *A Guide,* 96.
85. Kenny, *Making Sense,* 246.

EPILOGUE

As the historical evidence suggests, groups of Americans, for a variety of reasons, began to employ terrorism much earlier than previously suggested by historians and other social scientists. Four of the case studies presented here began during the years immediately preceding the American Revolution, and a fifth occurred during the Revolution's aftermath. They, together with the Molly Maguires and Ku Klux Klan, represented a pre-modern wave of terrorist groups, a collective body of political violence that would ultimately provide a prelude to modern-day terrorists and their non-discriminate weapons of mass destruction. A closer examination of these seven groups reveals much about violent resistance in pre-20th-century America and the people who constituted the darker side of political discourse, those who would employ the methods of terror in order to attain their objectives. We can deduce, for example, that the very first American terrorists of the 18th century were greatly impacted by an Anglo American political culture that legitimized dissent and popular uprisings. This mindset helped create a political climate that witnessed innumerable civil insurrections and instances of rioting that would eventually enable the growth of terrorism. Motivated by Enlightenment thinking and subsequent notions of natural law, polity, and social relationships, these original terrorists viewed their actions as advancing, rather than retarding, the causes of freedom and democracy.

All seven groups had seemingly reached the point of desperation before relying on terror. The Regulators, Green Mountain Boys, Sons of Liberty, and White Indians had long sought relief through legitimate legal channels, only to be denied time and time again. Anti-rent insurgents in New York tried for decades to convince their patroons to negotiate an end to abusive leasehold titles and the monopolization of land. The Klansmen were a desperate element of a larger southern population that had lost a cataclysmic war and was losing, in their minds, an equally calamitous peace. The Mollies found themselves in a losing struggle against the exploitation of corporate power. These groups viewed terrorism as a means of establishing justice and order during times of political upheaval fomented by persons perceived as sinister tormentors, be they landlords, government office-holders, corporate officials, industrial bosses, or armed freedmen. Their objectives were political in nature: securing and confirming land titles, battling corrupt governmental authority, protecting the rights of the dispossessed, or maintaining white supremacy. Their terrorist tactics were meant to provoke reactionary responses among target audiences extending far beyond the immediate victims of their violent acts. The North Carolina Regulators had hoped to intimidate corrupt local officials and other farmers from the Piedmont. The Green Mountain Boys and both the White and Calico Indians targeted land agents, surveyors, government officials, and other tenants in their midst who supported the land claims of opposing forces. The Sons of Liberty harassed both native-born citizens and Englishmen who supported royal policies meant to generate tax revenue and deny Americans their just rights. The Molly Maguires terrorized corporate officials and mine superintendents, while the Ku Klux Klan set out to victimize freedmen, Republicans, moral miscreants, collaborators, and intruders from the North.

The violent provocations instigated by these groups were usually the result of purposeful, systematic, and hierarchical decision making. Some associations were more formalized, as with the early Klan and the Molly Maguires, but most, as with the Regulators and Sons of Liberty, were more fluid. All relied on violence to persons or property as a means of propagandizing their political causes, although such violence did not become consistently lethal until after the mid-19th century. And although their acts of terror were direct responses to local grievances, they also represented reactions to larger prevailing social and political conditions: the growth of the early frontier and attendant issues related to land ownership, the evolution of republican ideology and the legitimization of dissent, the broad impact of the industrial revolution, and the machinations of post-war Reconstruction. All seven also represented protracted movements, varying in duration from the three years of the Regulator campaign to more than ten years, as in the cases of the White Indians (1792–1809), the Sons of Liberty (1765–1775), and the Molly Maguires (1862–1876). The New York anti-rent insurgency was a unique case, split into two resistance movements separated by 75 years, with the latter campaign lasting nearly three decades. In some instances, these violent campaigns borrowed heavily from resistance strategies that first evolved in England and Ireland. The Sons of Liberty and the Molly Maguires, in particular, were ever mindful of their connections to Old World traditions of popular dissent and violence which they adapted to conditions in America.

Despite the commonalities among these early American terrorists, the methods used to counteract them were varied, both in their style and their degree of success. Significantly, military intervention alone was not always able to eradicate terrorism. Two of the groups, the White Indians and the Molly Maguires, were successfully eliminated through vigorous legal prosecution. A combination of military

occupation, legislative initiative, and legal action helped curb Ku Klux Klan terrorism in isolated pockets of the South, but it was the cumulative impact of many
broader social and political forces that ultimately contributed to diminishing Klan
violence. Rigorous prosecution and military intervention helped forestall New
York's anti-rent insurgency from time to time, but Calico Indian resistance did
not cease until after 100 years of painstaking land reform and public sympathy
had slowly worked in their favor. Two groups were never collectively prosecuted
nor punished for their crimes and provocations: the Green Mountain Boys and
the Sons of Liberty. Both were ultimately subsumed by the American Revolution,
which, in the end, seemingly validated their antebellum revolts and culminated in
political consequences that far exceeded their original objectives—statehood for
Vermont and independence for the colonies. Significantly, only the North Carolina Regulators were eliminated through a strict military campaign, falling as they
did before Governor William Tryon's militia at the Great Alamance Creek in 1771.
Even then, one could reasonably wonder whether a military resolution would
have proven effective had the Regulators chosen instead to sustain their terroristic
campaign as opposed to an open and decisive battle between opposing armies.
Interestingly, at least three of the original seven terrorist groups provoked draconian responses from authorities that were considered terroristic in their own right.
William Tryon's brutal methods following the Alamance showdown, the response
to the killing of Deputy Sheriff Osman Steele and the vigilante attack at Wiggans
Patch were all instances of retributive terror that were equally outside the bounds
of law and social decency. As the United States currently ponders the use of torture
in its war on terror, it is worth considering that the use of "irregular" tactics to
combat an "irregular" campaign of terror has its historical precedents.

As suggested earlier, there is also a marked distinction between the pre– and
post–Civil War terrorist groups, most notably, the use of deadly force by the Molly
Maguires and Ku Klux Klan. With one exception—the murder of Paul Chadwick—
the Regulators, Green Mountain Boys, Sons of Liberty, and White Indians avoided
the taking of lives, and this can be largely attributed to the notions of restraint,
democracy, and personal freedoms openly associated with their resistance movements, as evidenced by their often skillful attempts at propaganda, both written and
symbolic. Even the two deaths attributed to the Calico Indians were likely the product of extremely contentious circumstances rather than of premeditated murder. But
by the late 19th century, Americans, perhaps partially inured to death by two major
wars against foreign powers, a catastrophic civil war, and an ugly series of wars against
native Americans, fell victim to shocking murder sprees committed by the Molly
Maguires and the Ku Klux Klan. Only through death and wanton destruction could
terrorists now generate the fear and notoriety upon which terrorism feeds.

The long-term legacy of these first American terrorist groups, aside from their
records of violence to persons and property, is decidedly mixed. The Regulators
and Molly Maguires were clear losers, having failed to attain anything of lasting
significance in either North Carolina's Piedmont or Pennsylvania's coal country.

The Green Mountain Boys and Sons of Liberty, largely because of their subsequent association with the American Revolution, managed to attain some measure of long-term success. Vermont eventually became the nation's 14th state, and the New Hampshire Grants controversy was eventually resolved, much to the satisfaction of the original Wentworth grantees. The Sons of Liberty helped void the Stamp Act, helped enforce non-importation, and helped nullify the Tea Act, only to witness a war culminating in what had been unthinkable during the early days of the resistance: complete separation from the mother country. The effectiveness of White Indian, Calico Indian, and Ku Klux Klan terrorism, however, is less clear. The murder trial following the 1809 Malta War certainly put an end to White Indian resistance and the Great Proprietors continued to hold title to the finest lands in mid-Maine, but terrorism helped induce passage of the Betterment Act, which led to peaceful compromise between proprietors and squatters. The New York anti-rent insurgency generated unprecedented publicity surrounding the controversial monopolization of land and the need for reform, but it took nearly a century to effect any meaningful change along the Hudson River. The Klan's nightriders provoked federal legislation, a congressional investigation, and a series of trials that together contributed to their temporary demise, yet successful prosecutions and harsh sentences were rare and hooded terrorists still managed to undermine the Republican Party, manipulate state and local elections, subvert Radical Reconstruction, and help preserve white supremacy and racial discrimination in the South. In the end, however mixed the legacy of early terrorism in America may be, it is difficult to deny that terrorism, on occasion and under specific conditions, did meet with some degree of success. The experiences of the seven groups profiled here would seem to indicate that terrorism was most effective when local issues became connected with popular ideology and broader resistance movements. The Green Mountain Boys, Sons of Liberty, and White Indians were able to couch many of their aspirations and actions within the newly emerging republican ideology associated with the American Revolution, while the Klan was able to exploit notions of white supremacy and southern antagonism toward the federal government. Anti-rentism, unfairly or not, became closely identified with the free-soil movement and other reform agendas. Conversely, the Regulators operated apart from the independence movement and the Molly Maguires failed to articulate a viewpoint capable of generating popular support, and these shortcomings contributed to their respective failures.

Based on this historical account, it is abundantly clear that terrorism has much deeper roots in our nation's past than previously understood. By combining and exploiting the tactics of violence and psychological manipulation, America's first terrorists not only challenged the perceived injustices of their immediate tormentors, but also, in so doing, defined the parameters of popular resistance in America before the 20th century. And as the nation continues to confront terrorism both at home and abroad, social scientists would do well to examine more closely this dark and fairly obscure legacy.

NOTES ON SOURCES

A note on the sources: during the investigation of primary source materials, the author discovered many documents cited by other authors in secondary works discussed in this narrative. This is an inevitable element of the research process. For the most part, the original documents are referenced in the chapter endnotes, but, at times, both primary and secondary sources are cited as well.

Abbreviations

BEP	*Boston Evening Post*
BG	*Boston Gazette*
BLY	Beinecke Library, Yale University, New Haven, Connecticut
BN	*Boston Newsletter*
CRNC	William L. Saunders, ed. *The Colonial Records of North Carolina* 10 Volumes (Raleigh, 1886–90)
DHSNY	E. B. O'Callaghan, M.D., *The Documentary History of the State of New York* (Albany: Charles Van Benthuysen, 1851)
HLH	Houghton Library, Harvard University, Cambridge, Massachusetts
HMD	*House Miscellaneous Documents,* U.S. House of Representatives
HML	Hagley Museum and Library, Wilmington, Delaware
HSP	Historical Society of Pennsylvania, Philadelphia, Pennsylvania
JSC	*Testimony Taken By The Joint Select Committee Appointed To Inquire In To The Condition Of Affairs In The Late Insurrectionary States* (Washington, DC: Government Printing office, 1872)
KKK	*Report Of The Joint Select Committee To Inquire Into The Condition Of Affairs In The Late Insurrectionary States* (Washington, DC: Made to Two Houses of Congress, 1872)
MA	Massachusetts State Archives, Boston, Massachusetts
MHS	Massachusetts Historical Society, Boston, Massachusetts
MJ	*Miners' Journal*

MNHS   Maine Historical Society, Portland, Maine
NA   National Archives, Washington, DC
NYHS   New York Historical Society, New York, New York
NYPL   New York Public Library, Manuscripts Division, New York, New York
PEM   Peabody Essex Museum, Salem, Massachusetts
RNCD   William S. Powell, James K. Hunta, and Thomas J. Farnham, eds., *The Regulators of North Carolina: A Documentary History, 1759–1776* (Raleigh: State Department of Archives and History, 1971)
UVB   University of Vermont, Burlington, Vermont
VA   Vermont State Archives, Montpelier, Vermont

INDEX